W9-BZK-692

Past and Present Publications

Family and Inheritance

Past and Present Publications

Past and Present Publications will comprise books similar in character to the articles in the journal *Past and Present*. Whether the volumes in the series are collections of essays – some previously published, others new studies – or monographs, they will encompass a wide variety of scholarly and original works primarily concerned with social, economic and cultural changes, a. ' their causes and consequences. They will appeal to both specialists and non-specialists and will endeavour to communicate the results of historical and allied research in readable and lively form. This new series continues and expands in its aims the volumes previously published elsewhere.

The first volumes to be published in the series by Cambridge University Press are:

Family and Inheritance: Rural Society in Western Europe 1200–1800, edited by Jack Goody, Joan Thirsk and E. P. Thompson
French Society and the Revolution, edited by Douglas Johnson
Peasants, Knights and Heretics: Studies in Medieval English Social History, edited by R. H. Hilton

Volumes previously published with Routledge & Kegan Paul are:

Crisis in Europe 1560–1660, edited by Trevor Aston
Studies in Ancient Society, edited by M. I. Finley
The Intellectual Revolution of the Seventeenth Century, edited by Charles Webster

Family and Inheritance

Rural Society in Western Europe, 1200-1800

Edited by
JACK GOODY
JOAN THIRSK
E. P. THOMPSON

CAMBRIDGE UNIVERSITY PRESS

Cambridge
London · New York · Melbourne

Published by the Syndies of the Cambridge University Press
The Pitt Building, Trumpington Street, Cambridge CB2 1RP
Bentley House, 200 Euston Road, London NW1 2DB
32 East 57th Street, New York, NY 10022, USA
296 Beaconsfield Parade, Middle Park, Melbourne 3206, Australia

First published 1976

Printed in Great Britain by
Western Printing Services Ltd, Bristol

Library of Congress Cataloguing in Publication Data

Main entry under title:

Family and inheritance.

(Past and present publications)

Includes index.

CONTENTS: Goody, J. Inheritance, property and women: some
comparative considerations. – Ladurie, E. L. Family structures
and inheritance customs in sixteenth-century France. – Berkner,
L. K. Inheritance, land tenure and peasant family structure: a
German regional comparison. [etc.]

1. Land tenure – Europe
– History – Congresses.   2.   Inheritance and succession –
Europe – History – Congresses.   3.   Peasantry – Europe –
History – Congresses.   4.   Family – Europe – History –
Congresses.   I.   Goody, John Rankine.   II.   Thirsk, Joan.
III.   Thompson, Edward Palmer, 1924–

HD584.F33   333.3'234'094   76–10402

ISBN 0 521 21246 4

Contents

v

Introduction

JACK GOODY

TO MANY READERS THE IDEA OF EXAMINING SYSTEMS OF INHERITANCE
will smack of dull legal records, of outdated practices such as gavelkind and tanistry, of custumals and codes formalized by hair-
splitting lawyers. Such a picture is not altogether incorrect. Yet
transmission *mortis causa* is not only the means by which the reproduction of the social system is carried out (in so far as that
system is linked to property, including the ownership of the means
by which man obtains his livelihood); it is also the way in which
interpersonal relationships are structured. I mean by this that
since inheritance normally takes place between close kin and
affines, the emotional tone and reciprocal rights characterizing such
critical relationships are often influenced by the possibility of
pooling or dividing the farm or by the anticipation of future gains;
the plots of many plays and novels make the point in a more
dramatic way than is available to the historian and the social
scientist. Consequently a different quality of relationships, varying
family structures, and alternative social arrangements (e.g. greater
or lesser migration, age of marriage, rates of illegitimacy) will be
linked to differing modes of transmission, whether transmission is
primarily lateral or lineal, whether agnatic or uterine, whether to
females as well as males, whether equal or unequal. All these and
other factors will be related, in complex, subtle and sometimes
contradictory ways to the social and cultural patterns, to the institutions and *mentalités*, to the formal and informal structures of
the people who practise (or are forced to practise) particular ways
of passing down rights over material objects.

The inheritance system of any society (and it clearly may be
more or less 'systematic') is the way by which property is transmitted between the living and the dead, and especially between
generations. It is part of the wider process whereby property relations are reproduced over time (and sometimes changed in so
doing), a process that I speak of as devolution. That is to say,
devolution describes the inclusive transactions that take place between the holder of rights in property and those who have continuing interests in such rights. To put the matter in a less guarded
way, whether the transfer of property between father and son, or

1

father and daughter, takes place on the attainment of adulthood, upon the marriage of the heir or upon the death of the holder is not, from our standpoint, of critical importance as far as it concerns the reproduction of the social system (or the continuity of particular social relationships over time). These transactions should be seen as a whole over time; whether a son or daughter receives a 'portion' by dowry or by inheritance is, from the standpoint of equity, of little importance; the fact is that the child of either sex shares in the parental wealth.

From another angle the timing is of critical importance. An endowment at marriage is more likely to be of movables than of land itself. While the unity of the agricultural holding may be preserved, both in the case of farms (as the chapter by Howell on the English Midlands clearly shows) and of aristocratic estates (as we see from Cooper's examination of the situation in England, Spain, Italy and France), this unity is often achieved at the expense of burdening the productive unit with heavy debts. Out of the future proceeds of the farm the heir is obliged to service the mortgage entered into on behalf of his 'non-inheriting' siblings. Indeed, despite the norm of primogeniture, younger sons and even daughters sometimes received land. It is the solution to the problem of allocating resources to the siblings who 'inherit' as well as those who do not (either because they leave the farm or else because they remain as unmarried co-parceners) that forms the basis of Yver's analysis of French custumals, so interestingly generalized in the chapter by Le Roy Ladurie. It indicates some of the many ways in which differences in the timing and finality of a distribution of 'familial' property is linked with a particular type of socio-economic system. Thus the seigneurial system of open fields in the champion country is distinct from the less dependent tenures of the woodland country, with its scattered farms and enclosed farmlands, the former tending towards the inheritance of the farm by one heir, the latter towards division. This is a theme which is taken up again in Berkner's chapter comparing inheritance system, land tenure (in its widest sense) and the structure of the household over time in two German parishes in the seventeenth century, an essay that makes full use of the model of the developmental cycle of domestic groups developed by Fortes[1] in order to illuminate a long-standing historical con-

[1] M. Fortes, 'Time and Social Structure: an Ashanti Case Study', *Social*

troversy on the distribution and incidence of the 'stem-family' and its relationship with the dominant mode of transmitting 'family' property.[2]

The linking of patterns of inheritance with patterns of domestic organization is a matter not simply of numbers and formations but of attitudes and emotions. The manner of splitting property is a manner of splitting people; it creates (or in some cases reflects) a particular constellation of ties and cleavages between husband and wife, parents and children, sibling and sibling, as well as between wider kin. Cooper has drawn attention to the possible connection in Italy between lateral inheritance, the *fratelanza* (Fr. *frèreche*) and the relationship between brothers and cousins. He might equally have quoted the observations of Francis Bacon on the Italian family:

> The Italians make little difference between children and nephews and near kinsfolk; but so they be of the lump, they care not though they pass not through their own body (*Essays*, 'Of Parents and Children').

The mode of tenure and system of inheritance are linked not only to household structure but also to a whole constellation of 'demographic' variables, factors which affect growth of population and preferences for male or female children. The ways in which these links occur are many and complex. Suffice to say that where marriage for men is delayed through the Irish type of retirement system, there will tend to be either more spinsters or more widows (and hence more orphans) in the particular community. But late marriage also implies a certain degree of sexual abstinence on the part of males, a subject that has recently been examined in a particularly interesting way by Flandrin.[3] This topic is one that has not been explored in the present volume but certainly merits the attention in other parts of Europe that has already been given to the subject by French scholars.

The question of population growth may be more directly affected

Structure, ed. M. Fortes (Oxford: Clarendon Press, 1949), reprinted in *Time and Social Structure and Other Essays* (London: Athlone Press, 1970).

[2] See, for example, P. Laslett and R. Wall (eds), *Household and Family in Past Time* (Cambridge University Press, 1972).

[3] *Les Amours paysannes* (*XVIᵉ–XIXᵉ siècle*) (Paris, Gallimard–Julliard, 1975); 'Contraception, mariage et relations amoureuses', *Annales E.S.C.*, 1969, pp. 1374–7; 'Mariage tardif et vie sexuelle', *Annales E.S.C.*, 1972, pp. 351–78.

by the type of inheritance. Hallam claims that partible inheritance in Lincolnshire, in an area which lay outside the normal Midland pattern of open field agriculture and impartible transmission, meant denser populations; the question of partibility 'largely determined the structure and mobility of the population',[4] a suggestion that is supported by Habakkuk.[5]

A further aspect of the interaction between inheritance and population, touched upon in this volume in Cooper's paper, arises in connection with the strategies that an individual adopts in the absence of an heir, or an heir of the preferred sex. This absence may be circumvented by 'lineage type' rules, i.e. by the passage of property to collaterals. Even so, if the old are to benefit, then they need a presumed heir before their death rather than afterwards; help with the farm may involve a transfer of residence. Alternatively the heirless couple can hire labour, though this seems an improbable solution among the poorer groups; or they can rejoin dispersed kin (e.g. a married daughter), selling their own plot; or they can live out their lives as widows or widowers on the family land, given some help (as the reports of French charivaris indicate) by the other villagers; or finally they can 'adopt' an heir from another family.

The relationship between 'practice' and 'mentality', raised by Flandrin (1975) in matters of sex, is the subject of Sabean's chapter, which calls for more systematic research into the whole area. For this we need to examine not only the material on national law and local custumals prepared by legal historians, but also adequate examples of 'trouble cases', to use the phrase of Llewellyn and Hoebel, in order to ascertain the nature of local norms, rules or customs, as well as the conflicts to which these give rise in operation. Indeed the development of national laws and written custumals introduced further possibilities of conflict, not just between one idea and the next, between the principles of equity (division) and unity (impartibility), between the operation of norm and practice, but by bringing about 'the conflict of laws' on various levels of jurisdiction. The complexity, conflict and resolution of the processes of transmission is neatly illustrated in

[4] H. E. Hallam, 'Some thirteenth century censuses', *Econ. Hist. Rev.*, x (1958), p. 341.
[5] H. J. Habakkuk, 'Family structure and economic change in nineteenth-century Europe', *Jnl of Economic History*, xiv (1955), pp. 1–12.

Douglass's recent study of a Basque village. He notes there are three main sources of law for inheritance. Firstly, the Spanish Civil Code, which dictates that all legitimate offspring share equally in the estate. Secondly, the local laws or *fueros* which take precedence over the national code and guarantee 'the donor couple's right to name a single heir to the *baserria*', without specifying which one, nor mentioning any compensation to the other children. But the third element, local custom, 'resolves both of these issues. In Murelaga there is a preference for male primogeniture; the remaining siblings of the heir are compensated with dowries.'[6] Very similar types of resolution are reported by Cooper in the transmission of aristocratic estates as well as by Spufford for smaller holdings in Cambridgeshire and by Howell for the English Midlands. The resolution often differed of course as between large landowner and small proprietor, the former tending towards primogeniture, the latter towards partibility. It also differed over time. But as Thirsk's chapter indicates, the continuing ideological debate clearly recognized the injustice of preferring one member of a sibling group all of whom were in other respects equally deserving. The specific reasons for such preference differed for large and for small holdings, but there is some evidence that similar tensions to those exhibited by the upper classes in the literary debate also manifested themselves in the oral discourse of the peasantry. Indeed the nature of the conflicting pulls for any 'estate manager' is clearly brought out in a recent study of the southern Tyrol by Cole and Wolf.

He would like to see every daughter well married and every son with land enough to support a family. Then too, he would like to see the holding that he has maintained against the world for a lifetime remain essentially intact to provide a material basis for perpetuation of the family line. However, the meagre resources at his disposal are, more often than not, insufficient to fulfill both these goals. He must balance his desires to perpetuate his name against the future of his children.[7]

This whole question of the resolution of conflict raises the question of whether the differences in custom that emerge from

---

[6] W. Douglass, *Death in Murelaga* (Seattle: University of Washington Press, 1968), p. 98.

[7] J. W. Cole and E. R. Wolf, *The Hidden Frontier: Ecology and Ethnicity in an Alpine Valley* (New York: Academic Press, 1974), p. 176.

documentary sources do in fact reflect differences in practice; if all eventuate in similar resolutions, then we need discuss only the quirks of innumerable lawyers and the irrelevance of praxis to theory. Such a view has something to be said in its favour; from a wider perspective, the transmission of property in Europe displays many common features (in contrast to much of the rest of the world). Moreover the differences that do exist are not as absolute as terms like primogeniture and impartibility suggest. If they are not so absolute, neither are they necessarily so permanent, an observation that constitutes one of the themes of my own contribution. Nevertheless, the constellation of relationships in Europe certainly differs significantly from those in other parts of the world, with important effects on the structure of roles and the quality of intercourse; the contrast with Africa comes out particularly clearly in the interaction between men and women, whether as husband and wife, parent and child, brother and sister, indeed over the total range of cross-sex relations. Moreover, even the smaller differences that do exist within Europe, though they may be less pronounced and less permanent than they sometimes appear, have important links with the socio-economic system on the one hand and with the network of nuclear relations on the other. I would see all the contributions to this book as providing evidence of this association.

One other point to come out of the essays on English villages is the significance of the custom whereby the senior generation handed over the control of farms to their sons (and sometimes sons-in-law or 'adopted' sons) during their lifetime, in return for their bed and board. Both in Cambridgeshire and the Midlands this custom, that I have elsewhere referred to by the Czech name of *výměnek*, had an important bearing upon the transmission of property and the handing over of domestic authority. For example, those who had handed over their rights in their lifetime did not need to make a will; they became 'sojourners', as Spufford points out. Contrary to expectations that it is the rich who make wills, she finds that it was the small man who tended to do so, those with less property, who had not handed over control in their lives and who still had children to provide for. By retirement the parental couple had already handed over their property by pre-mortem transfer, frequently creating a kind of 'stem-household', with effective control in the hands of the junior generation. But whether any contemporary listing specifies a joint or extended household may depend upon the physical form of the farmstead, the nature of the cooking arrangements or the categories of a particular recorder.

In speaking of the transmission to heirs both before and after death, we do well to pay heed to Thompson's reminder that property is not an undifferentiated concept. Rights relating to material objects constitute a 'bundle' (to use Maine's phrase) that can vary over time, vary with the object of rights, with the technology used in the productive enterprise, and with the hierarchy of class or strata that dominates the social system. More concretely, land differs from movables in the kind of rights (i.e. property) that can be established over it; these rights again differ depending upon whether the productive system utilizes hunting and gathering (as in parts of eighteenth-century Berkshire and in the fen country around Willingham), or whether the farm is cultivated by hoe, plough (*araire* or *charrue*) or by tractor; and the more complex the productive system, the more likely one is to find the bundle of rights split up in accordance with the hierarchy of status, class or government. The way in which the balance is distributed at any one time is described by terms such as share-cropping, tenancy and ownership, though clearly different views of the nature of an individual's specific rights may be held by the 'tenant' and the 'owner', and the resolution of this particular difference may sometimes lie outside the realm (or even the shadow) of the courts of law, depending rather upon the subtleties of local reciprocities, the vaguer rights *in personam* rather than the more precisely defined rights *in rem*. Both tenancy and ownership are themselves a variable bundle of rights and duties, whose transmission concerns both parties; and even the offspring of a share-cropper may inherit some limited right of continued service or a yet more shadowy right to work the land in the district in which he was born. Of course, at the end of the continuum are the landless peasants, the rural proletariat, the permanent 'younger sons', whose numbers varied from region to region, but who came to dominate many parts of rural Europe after the agricultural changes of the eighteenth century. The studies in this book do not deal with transmission among this important element in the population of the countryside, an element that had little to pass on but their need to work for others. And while some of the studies refer to those who exercise rights to the common resources of forest and stream to provide a livelihood (and where again continuity of claim is of some considerable importance), they say nothing about transmission in a pastoral economy. In parts of Scandinavia, at least in the period before 1800, cattle-raising rather than land formed the cornerstone of the rural economy; as movable inheritance, this basic productive resource was transferred more easily to daughters than land,[8] as indeed is the case with Lapp reindeer herders in the same country, where men without an adequate labour force used sons-in-law to help, a system that inevitably involves the distribution of livestock to women as well as men.[9]

We need then constantly to remind ourselves of the differing quantum of rights, and especially rights in the basic resources of livelihood, that are indicated by terms such as property and ownership. The limiting case of 'absolute' ownership is rarely if ever found; rights in land are usually distributed in a complex hierarchy that represents the political/legal/economic system of the society. When we get beyond hoe farming into more advanced agriculture, a wider variety of man–land relationships are found that range from the absence of any continuing use right (as with landless labourers), to limited 'garden' rights, to more extensive crop-sharing, to peasantries involved in a wide-ranging variety of relations with landlords, to peasant proprietors and large land-owners. The range is wide. But each property relationship is preserved by a particular mode of inheritance or devolution that serves to reproduce this central aspect of rural society.

The theme of this volume is in line with the work of Bloch and Homans, as well as with that of the great sociolegal historians of an earlier period, of Vinogradoff and of Pollock and Maitland. These writers too made use of comparative material to throw light on the European experience, in the spirit of Kiernan's wide-ranging essay on 'Property in History'. But apart from the light thrown on European society by placing it in contrast with Africa or India, we are now able to draw upon an increasing number of works that deal with the problem of devolution in contemporary European villages. While Bloch called upon his own experiences in the French

[8] For this comment, I am indebted to O. Löfgren of the Institute of European Ethnology, University of Lund.

[9] See R. N. Pehrson, 'The bilateral network of social relations in Könkämä Lapp district', *International Jnl of American Linguistics*, 23 (1957), part 2.

countryside, Homans drew upon the work of Arensberg and Kimball on County Clare. Since that day much new work on inheritance practices has appeared in English, among the best of which is Barnes on northern Norway, Friedl and Campbell on Greece, Pehrson on the Lapps, Davis on southern Italy, Loizos on Cyprus and most recently Cole and Wolf on the Tyrol.[10] It is in the combination of insights from historical and contemporary studies that the future surely lies.

[10] C. M. Arensberg and S. T. Kimball, *Family and Community in Ireland* (Cambridge, Mass.: Harvard University Press, 1940); J. A. Barnes, 'Land rights and kinship in two Bremnes hamlets', *Jnl of the Royal Anthropological Institute*, 87 (1957), pp. 31–56; E. Friedl, *Vasilika: A Village in Modern Greece* (New York: Holt, Rinehart and Winston, 1962); J. K. Campbell, *Honour, Family and Patronage* (Oxford: Clarendon Press, 1964); J. Davis, *Land and Family in Pisticci* (London: Athlone Press, 1973); P. Loizos, *The Greek Gift* (Oxford: Blackwell, 1975).

1. Inheritance, property and women: some comparative considerations

JACK GOODY

If one looks in a broad comparative way at systems of agricultural production, one of the significant features of European societies, as indeed of the major states of Asia, is the fact that the property from some kind of conjugal estate devolves on both men and women, either by inheritance or by some form of pre-mortem endowment. From the standpoint of social organization, the implications are extensive and can best be brought out in drawing a contrast with other agricultural societies, such as those in Africa. One implication is that even when a certain type of property (such as land) is restricted to males, women are nevertheless seen as the residual heirs in preference to more distant males. This diverging system of devolution is in stark contrast to most of traditional Africa where, if a man did not have a male heir, then a search would be made among the male children of his brothers (or of his sisters in a matrilineal society). Virtually everywhere the rule existed that property descended from males to males and from females to females. In Europe, however, women became heiresses to land even when they were not entitled to inherit immovable property in the first instance. Roughly 20 per cent of all families would have daughters and no sons; the former would therefore be heiresses who could attract men to them as marriage partners and perhaps to live with them in uxorilocal residence, giving rise to the institution of in-marrying sons-in-law (e.g. the *primak* of rural Russia).

Where women receive land, the basic means of production, either as a dowry or as part of their inheritance (that is, even when they have brothers), the social implications are greater because its ownership is drastically reorganized at every generation. Land changes hands between the sexes at every marriage or death, and large quantities of land may come under the direct or indirect control of women. It has been estimated that almost half the agricultural land in Sparta was held by women by the fourth century B.C. In England of the early eighteenth century, the importance of the 'female presence' is brought out in Thompson's chapter in this volume.

10

property makes the woman

One aspect of such a system was that women varied in their attractiveness as marriage-partners according to their endowment, encouraging a tendency to make matches between individuals of similar wealth and status. And in-marriage, as Bloch maintained, is a prerequisite (or anyhow a concomitant) of 'class'. In a sense women were more valuable as wives than they were as daughters, since in the latter capacity they had to share in the estate. Indeed female infanticide was not altogether unknown in dowry systems, if one includes within that term the differential treatment of males and females leading to the earlier death of girls.[1] Since both spouses often brought property into marriage, there was usually some kind of continuing right in the conjugal estate assigned to the surviving partner, whether in terms of the widow's free bench (a variant of the dower) or the husband's courtesy.[2] In other words the junior generation did not acquire complete rights to the property until both parents were dead.

The attachment of property to women was important not only in the making of a match; it was just as relevant for a woman whose marriage had ended either by widowhood or by divorce. For if such a woman was young and had control of property (either by dowry or dower), she could increase her attractiveness as a marriage partner.[3] While women suffered many disabilities,

---

[1] For evidence of this in Europe, see E. R. Coleman's work on infanticide in Saint-Germain-des-Prés, 'L'Infanticide dans le Haut Moyen Age', *Annales E.S.C.*, xxix (1974), 315–35. Coulton recounts the effect of female infanticide upon the life of St Liudger. 'About 750 A.D., there lived a noble in Frisia whose wife, after many years of marriage, had produced only girls; and Frisian law permitted the extinction of female children, so long as the deed was done before the new-born infant had tasted of earthly food. When Liafburga, mother of St Liudger, was born, her pagan grandmother sent a henchman to seize her before her mother could give her suck, but the child clung to the bucket in which she was going to be drowned and a woman ran and took the child, hastily gave it some food, and she was spared, though she had to be hidden as long as her grandmother lived.' G. G. Coulton, *Medieval Village* (Cambridge, 1925), p. 279.

[2] Of changes in English inheritance between the thirteenth and sixteenth centuries, Faith writes that, 'widow's rights seem to have been by far the most durable and firmly established of all inheritance customs'. R. J. Faith, 'Peasant Families and Inheritance Customs in Medieval England', *Agric. Hist. Rev.*, xiv (1966), p. 91.

[3] Faith suggests that one motive for (and hence presumably affecting the rate) marriage with widows was stronger where they were full rather than conditional heirs of the conjugal estate; Titow sees the rate of widow marriage as varying with the availability of land. Faith, *op. cit.*, p. 91, citing J. Z. Titow, 'Some Differences between Manors and their Effects on

the role of merry widow (and later of the gay divorcée) was nevertheless distinctive of certain groups of European societies, as Chaucer's Wyf of Bath reminds us. Marriage chances varied significantly with wealth. Moreover, the greater the difference in the marriage age of males and females, the more property will fall under the control (albeit temporary) of the surviving spouse, i.e. the widow.

The emphasis on the conjugal estate and the making of a match was closely linked to the emphasis on monogamous institutions. Under these conditions, to acquire a second spouse is to diminish the interest of the first. Concubines of course were another matter because this form of union rarely involved property. But even the marriage of a widow who had borne children could damage the interests of the conjugal estate that was established by her previous marriage. Hence the complexities that centred around the 'second bed', *le deuxième lit*; the fate of a marriageable widow was of critical concern to the children of her late husband and became an important theme in European charivaris. Elsewhere, the hostility towards the remarriage of widows took more definite forms, as in the virtual prohibition of such marriages in high-caste Hindu society. Here again property considerations were closely linked with the whole ideology of one body and one flesh, and of the indissolubility of particular unions; indeed the greater the property interest, the more profound the effects of dissolving a particular estate.

The position of women with regard to the transmission of property is then associated with a specific structure of roles. But it is also related to the nature of kin groups and to the mode of transmitting office. I do not want to discuss in any detail that complex and (to many) boring subject, beloved by anthropologists, the organization of kin groups. But any system of so-called clans and lineages that allows women to take substantial property, landed or otherwise, into marriage, must be a very different system from that we find in Africa. For it means that only through in-marriage can one prevent the alienation of the property of the kin to another group.

With regard to succession, many situations in European history

the Condition of the Peasant in the Thirteenth Century', *Agric. Hist. Rev.*, x (1962).

turn on the possibility of women succeeding to office, both to the paramountcy (monarchy) and at subsidiary levels. The question of female succession to office is linked to the inheritance of land, and that in turn to the transmission of immovables; both possibilities are potentially available as options because of the fact that women share in male (or rather conjugal) property. The entitlement to valuables is easily generalized to land or to office.

In Africa the situation is very different. Offices, like property, pass between members of the same sex rather than between men and women (whether as kin or spouses). The result is a great separation between the sexes, a separation that is evident in ordinary social intercourse as well as in the management of the family estate. Even in matrilineal systems women do not succeed to political offices assigned to men; on the other hand, there are other offices to which they alone are entitled. This separation of the sexes has sometimes been of value to women in the process of development since it has kept the profits of marketing in their own hands, a factor that has been significant in the achievements of women traders in many parts of Africa.[4] For the idea of shares in a conjugal estate, especially when one partner is more powerful than the other, has some disadvantages as well as the obvious advantages.

These then are some of the broad features that distinguish European systems, and which, mesmerized by the intricacies and varieties of local custom, we may tend to overlook. These local differences, between primogeniture and ultimogeniture, between partibility and indivisibility, equality and preference, dowry and inheritance, have all to be viewed in the light of these general similarities; while some variations may be responses to different conditions, others may be alternative solutions for similar circumstances. In this paper the particular variation I want to discuss relates to the nature of the conjugal estate and its relationship to inheritance, especially as these affect the claims of women.

European modes of transmission of property have been discussed in relation to such factors as size of household,[5] urban migration,[6]

    [4] E. Boserup, *Woman's Role in Economic Development* (London, 1970).
    [5] F. Le Play, *L'Organisation de la famille* (Paris, 1871).
    [6] H. J. Habakkuk, 'Family Structure and Economic Change in Nineteeth-Century Europe', *Jnl of Economic History*, xiv (1955), pp. 1–12.

the market in land, capital accumulation[7] and related variables. The whole subject has recently been extended by the work of Le Roy Ladurie, Berkner and Sabean (and on the English scene by Thirsk, Faith and others).[8] The first two of these authors have commented upon the work of Jean Yver entitled *Egalité entre héritiers et exclusion des enfants dotés*,[9] which looks at the relation between inheritance and endowment (a term that includes transmission of the conjugal estate to both sons and daughters, an association that tends to be obscured in English usage).

In making a further comment upon themes already well aired, I shall try to add a comparative perspective in order to bring out some of the particularities of the European situation and to relate these, *inter alia*, to the position of women in the social reproduction of property as well as to the more general theme of which children are 'preferred'. To do this I have to define a few terms that are needed for analytic purposes.

Inheritance is the transmission of (rights in) material property at death (*mortis causa*). It is everywhere dominated by kinship and conjugality; property is usually redistributed among the 'relatives' cooperating in a unit of consumption and, in non-industrial economies (and sectors of economies), of production. Indeed in these latter societies, inheritance involves the transmission of rights in the means of production (though the allodial rights may ultimately be vested in a landlord), a process critical to the reproduction of the social system itself.

In non-literate societies, inheritance 'rules' operate with varying degrees of flexibility; in some cases a kind of oral testament may

7 J. Hajnal, 'European Marriage Patterns in Perspective', in D. V. Glass and D. E. C. Eversley (eds). *Population in History* (London, 1965), pp. 101–46.

8 E. Le Roy Ladurie, 'Système de la coutume: structures familiales et coutumes d'héritage en France au XVIᵉ siècle', *Annales E.S.C.*, xxvii (1972), pp. 825–46, a translation of which appears as Chapter 2 in the present volume; L. K. Berkner, 'The Stem Family and the Developmental Cycle of the Peasant Household: an Eighteenth-Century Austrian Example', *Amer. Hist. Rev.*, lxxvii (1972), pp. 398–418; 'Rural Family Organisation in Europe: a Problem in Comparative History', *Peasant Studies Newsletter*, i (1972), pp. 145–56 and Chapter 3 of the present volume; D. Sabean, 'Famille et tenure paysanne: aux origines de la guerre des paysans en Allemagne (1525)', *Annales E.S.C.*, xxvii (1972), pp. 903–22 and Chapter 4 of the present volume; J. Thirsk, 'The Common Fields', *Past and Present*, xxix (Dec. 1964), pp. 3–25; 'The Family', *ibid.*, no. 27 (Apr. 1964); 'Younger Sons in the Seventeenth Century', *History*, liv (1969), pp. 358–77; Faith, *op. cit.*

9 J. Yver, *Egalité entre héritiers et exclusion des enfants dotés* (Paris, 1966).

allow a limited measure of freedom in the disposition of a man's earthly goods. But in essence the concept of a binding testament is the result of literacy. Initially a will is a written deviation from oral custom. An outward and visible sign of wealth and a check upon the 'wrongful' disposition of property, it enshrines the wishes of the individual holder as against the demands of the potential heirs. It is in effect the written version of the 'dying words', the permanent expression of the deathbed wish.[10] As such it became an instrument for the alienation of property not only to 'irregular' heirs (mistresses rather than wives) but also to organizations such as the church. All of the thirty-nine Anglo-Saxon wills edited by Whitelock include bequests to the church, and twenty-four to the lord.[11] In the accumulation and maintenance of property by the ecclesiastical and secular authorities, the will played a fundamental part.

From one standpoint there is little difference if property is passed down at death, at the point when the son is ready to take over the farm, or on the occasion of a marriage. Both inheritance and dowry, heritage and donation, are part of the more general process of devolution. From another standpoint, however, timing is critical. When I speak of dowry as 'devolution', I mean of course to bring it into close association with 'inheritance' by males, who in French are also said to be *dotés* when they are paid (off) on leaving home.[12] If dowry and inheritance are closely related, then so are marriage contracts and testaments. The relationship between these is brought out very clearly in Yver's discussion of French customs with regard to the inclusion or exclusion of *les enfants dotés* from the inheritance, a custom which varied in different parts of France.[13] The *enfants dotés* are essentially married children who have been established (*établi*) or provided for (*pourvu*). They have been provided for because, in many

[10] F. Pollock and F. W. Maitland, *The History of the English Law*, 2nd edn (Cambridge, 1898), ch. 6.

[11] L. Lancaster, 'Kinship in Anglo-Saxon Society', *Brit. Jnl of Sociology*, ix (1958), pp. 230–50, 359–77. See also D. M. Stenton, *The English Woman in History* (London, 1957), where she points to the more favourable position of women in Anglo-Saxon as compared with post-Conquest society.

[12] Yver, *op. cit.* Just as French ethnography has been and still is confused by the use of the term '*dot*' for bridewealth and dowry, so English ethnography is led astray by the failure to link '*dot*' (dowry) with inheritance by males and females.

[13] For brief description, see: E. Le Roy Ladurie, *op. cit.*, and L. K. Berkner, 'Rural Family Organisation . . .'.

places, marriage required the allocation of property to the bride and groom in order to make a match, for the property provided for one partner in the marriage had a definite relationship to that brought in by the other.[14] Whether or not these arrangements took place by written contract (as in parts of Occitania)[15] is beside the point. Some definite allocation had to be made in order to clinch the deal. 'André, père de Jacques de Douay, "li avait promis en son mariage dis livres de parisis de rente, et deus cenz livres de parisis en deniers contans . . .".'[16] In England the same custom obtained: Latimer noted of his father that 'he maryed my sisters with five pound . . . a piece', his farm being worth three or four pounds a year.[17]

In England, the dowry could involve the father in building a house for his daughter and her husband at their marriage, as witness the case from Belper, Derbyshire, in 1312 where the son-in-law complained about non-receipt.[18] In southern Italy today, the provision of the house is often the job of the bride's father, though there a woman's dowry may also include land.[19]

In the champion country of England daughters rarely got land as dowry. On the other hand, they did get land from their husbands as dower;[20] this was the future endowment given to the bride at

[14] On the concept of the match, see: C. M. Arensberg, The Irish Countryman (New York, 1937); K. H. Connell, 'Marriage in Ireland after the Famine: the Diffusion of the Match', Jnl Stat. Soc. Ireland, xix (1955–6), pp. 82–94; J. R. Goody, 'Strategies of Heirship', Comparative Studies in Society and History, xv (1973), pp. 3–16. For medieval England, see G. C. Homans, English Villagers of the Thirteenth Century (Cambridge, Mass., 1941), pp. 154, 162. Since marriage was not only a question of finding the right person, or category of person, but also of making a proper bargain, it was necessary to have a go-between, that is a 'mean' person, to make a proposal to the girl's father. 'Bargaining went before marriage in all the old peasant communities of Europe'; Homans, op. cit., p. 160. The go-between is one of the recurrent roles in the major Eurasian societies. I discuss this and other such roles in my Production and Reproduction (Cambridge, 1976).

[15] A. Collomp, 'Famille nucléaire et famille élargie', Annales E.S.C., xxvii (1972), pp. 969–76.

[16] Yver, op. cit., pp. 17, 19.

[17] G. G. Coulton, Medieval Panorama (Cambridge, 1938), p. 88. For many instances of dowry transactions, see Homans, op. cit.

[18] Homans, op. cit., p. 140.

[19] J. Davis, Land and Family in Pisticci (London, 1973) p. 160 refers to the rule that 'daughters should get houses, sons and daughters should get land'. The same applies to rural Cyprus.

[20] A York manual prescribes: 'Then if land is given to her in dower, let her fall at the man's feet' (Homans, op. cit., p. 171).

the church door, which she would use for support after her husband's death – 'with all my worldly goods I thee endow'. In addition the groom made an immediate gift to the bride, which might include gold or silver. The amount of the dower was announced in the wedding service; indeed the wedding was critical both to the widow's entitlement to the dower and to a child's claim to inheritance; the plighting of troth, though recognized as marriage, was insufficient.[21] The dower was either specified at the wedding or implicit in local custom, varying from one third to one half (known as 'free bench'). Variable too was the length of time a woman held her life-interest, that is, as long as she 'remained a widow' (chaste and unmarried) or else until death. In certain parts of France (principally in the South), this allocation was all that a departing son or daughter was given. The dowry (*dot*) was his or her portion; the endowed child was excluded from subsequent inheritance.[22] This 'inegalitarian system' helped to preserve 'l'indivisibilité familiale et patriarcale de la tenure paysanne, sous la haute autorité du seigneur'.[23] For here, as in the Paris region, impartibility was encouraged by the interests of the overlords. It was associated with the liberty of favouring one above the other, with testamentary transmission, and with the passage of the land to the co-resident son.

In other areas, also around Paris, the endowed child could opt to take the divided property back into the familial pool, which would then be redivided according to the principles of equal division (though of course equality may not be maintained as between different items; a son who had set up in town might well prefer money to land, leaving the agricultural holding intact, though possibly in debt). The principle obtained that no person could receive both gifts *inter vivos* and heritage at death;[24] dowry and inheritance were alternative not cumulative.

The third area, Normandy and the West, differed radically from the other two in that an individual was obliged to bring back any

[21] See the involved history of mantel-children, who were legitimized by the subsequent marriage of their parents.
[22] For the English equivalent, significantly a feature of champion country, see Homans, *op. cit.*, p. 141: 'a daughter who, with a portion from her father's goods and chattels, had either married or left the manor was excluded from inheriting . . .'.
[23] Le Roy Ladurie, *op. cit.*, p. 841.
[24] 'Aumonnier et parchonnier nuls ne peult estre'; 'légataire ou héritier'.

property he had received before the death of the holder, so that it could all be redistributed on an egalitarian basis.

In Normandy the links between marriage contract and inheritance were particularly clear.[25] An unmarried girl might be excluded from the inheritance on the grounds that she was destined for marriage and 'est en droit de reclamer à son frère un mari'; alternatively she would be allotted some of the patrimony at a later stage.[26] In all these cases the woman's share consisted of movable property. Indeed, Yver sees the exclusion of endowed daughters from land as an indispensable means of keeping the patrimony in the 'lineage'. But while the oldest Frankish law prohibited a woman from succeeding to ancestral lands, this was not true of Anglo-Saxon England; of the thirty-nine wills listed by Whitelock, ten were made by women and all included land.[27]

Of course, even in France it was not only the male children who could take over the farm. In eighteenth-century Provence, ten per cent of marriage contracts relate to a daughter bringing her husband under the same roof as her parents,[28] no doubt when there were no male heirs. In fact a somewhat higher percentage of uxorilocal marriages could be expected if brotherless daughters inherited – 20 per cent according to our suggested calculations[29] – although this figure relates to families without sons at the time of the father's death.

Marriage contracts, then, may provide for an outgoing son or daughter, or an incoming bride or son-in-law; in both cases they provide for the devolution of property, and the character of such contracts is connected both with the arrangements for a particular marriage and with the pension rights of the parents. To these considerations I return. First I want to stress that the endowments on departure are part of the more general process of family fission, the input–output of the domestic unit, which determines the size of specific households at specific times.

[25] For England, see Homans, *op. cit.*, and Faith, *op. cit.;* the court rolls show 'how closely inheritance was linked with marriage': Faith, *op. cit.*, p. 87.

[26] Yver, *op. cit.*, p. 38.

[27] Lancaster, *op. cit.*, p. 362. Faith refers to cases of sisters inheriting land in preference to brothers in thirteenth-century England: *op. cit.*, p. 88.

[28] Collomp, *op. cit.*

[29] G. A. Harrison and J. R. Goody, 'The Probability of Family Distributions', *Comparative Studies in Society and History*, xv (1973), pp. 16–20.

The first input comes from within, with the birth of children. Here the critical question is the role of the new generation. Supposing that all farm families attempt to secure their own continuity (either because of sentiment or because of the absence of alternative employment), children (male and female) could serve in some 80 per cent of the cases. The heir may simply stay on the farm and take over when the parents become infirm (or die) or when he himself marries (or comes of age). In this case we have a farm family of the stem variety. If the two families from adjacent generations live under the same roof, we may speak of a stem houseful; if they also eat out of one pot, a stem household. In current situations in south-western France, each of these possibilities can occur within the same community. I take my example from a contemporary *commune* in the Lot. At farm *A*, the farmer has built two houses on his property, one for his son and his family, one for his daughter and her family. In farm *B*, a farmer and his wife have handed over control of the property to their son and his family; all live in the same house for part of the year and in adjacent houses for the rest. In farm *C*, the farmer, his son and family all live in one house, the son having taken over effective control.[30] In yet another case, the widowed owner took his meals with his (unrelated) tenant, formerly his *métayer*, on his weekly visits from the town.

The difference in household type and inheritance system may appear great if we think in typological terms. In one case we have nuclear families; in another, stem families. In one case, the property passes by inheritance at death; in another, there was a handing over *inter vivos* (by donation or by sale) of the kind described by Arensberg for Ireland in the 1930s, by Homans for thirteenth-century England and by Collomp for Provence in the 1730s. As far as eating out of a joint pot is concerned, the problem may be simply one of the size of the house, since it is unlikely (though not impossible) that people will have a joint household unless they share the same roof.

Associated with the problem of the take-over of the farm is the timing of 'family fission'. Demographic factors apart, the critical

---

[30] Berkner, 'Rural Family Organisation . . .', p. 147, makes the same point about variation at the local level. This being the case one should perhaps put less emphasis on the negative implications of household size or the number of conjugal units in a dwelling.

feature in determining the size of the household in monogamous societies is the point where the residential group splits. Given that daughters generally leave at marriage unless they have no siblings, what about the sons? Among the Gegs of Albania, they remain together in their father's house even after his death;[31] among the LoDagaba of West Africa sons stay until they themselves have children old enough to help them on the farm.[32] Late fission means large households. Equally, early fission means small households. If sons and daughters leave the parental house at an earlier stage in the developmental cycle, then households will be smaller. If one son stays (as in some versions of the 'stem household'), then the average household size will be somewhat larger. If all sons stay, larger still, especially if they can also marry.

Very often the point of family fission is determined by marriage, for sons as well as for daughters. Sometimes they leave before marriage as when children go out on extended fostering,[33] as servants[34] or for apprenticeship.[35] But marriage is usually the critical point at which both men and women leave and are endowed.

Whether the property they receive at this time includes the basic means of production, land, is important in the cases of both sexes. When we speak of equal or of impartible inheritance, these terms refer to land rather than goods (chattels). Some of the factors related to partible and impartible systems have been discussed by Homans, Habakkuk, and Sabean.[36] When both land and goods are given to women as an endowment, then the results are striking not only because of the subdivision itself, but also because of the continual recombining of portions in new conjugal estates. The consequences of a landed dowry are several; one at least is to stress in-marriage or alternatively the sale or exchange of

---

[31] I. Whittaker, 'Tribal Structure and National Politics in Albania, 1910–1915', in I. M. Lewis (ed.), *History and Social Anthropology* (London, 1968).

[32] J. R. Goody, 'The Fission of Domestic Groups among the LoDagaba', in J. R. Goody (ed.), *The Developmental Cycle of Domestic Groups* (Cambridge, 1958).

[33] E. N. Goody, 'Fostering in Gonja: Deprivation or Advantage?', in P. Mayer (ed.), *Socialisation: the Anthropological Approach* (London, 1968).

[34] Berkner, 'The Stem Family . . .'.

[35] A. Macfarlane, *The Family Life of Ralph Josselin* (Cambridge, 1970).

[36] Homans, *op. cit.*; Habakkuk, *op. cit.*; Sabean, *op. cit.*

scattered plots;[37] such a scattering is especially likely to occur when the rules, such as those of the Catholic churches, prohibit close marriage (though pardon was always possible at a price). It is a marked feature of these religious regulations, which were promulgated with such force in Europe, that they prohibited the kinds of unions of first cousins that earlier societies in the area permitted and even encouraged; one thinks specifically of Roman law, but the same would hold of earlier Greece and later Rome. But despite these later prohibitions, such marriages often took place.

The process of family fission needs further specification. It may refer to the dwelling group, the consuming group or the productive group, the splitting of each of which may involve the transmission of property rights between heirs or potential heirs, that is, devolution. On the other hand, such transmission may occur at death without any division; this type of universal succession (to use Maine's phrase) is characteristic of some Indian forms of the joint family.

Looking at the process of transmission (inheritance, endowment, etc.), two of the most significant variables (apart from direction, with which I am not here concerned)[38] are timing and inclusiveness. Timing may involve either the actual transmission of control or else a promise to pay;[39] both may be subject to qualifications, since pre-mortem transmission (to those who leave or stay) may be subject to recall at death (in Yver's 'lineage' systems of the West of France,[40] and to some extent in the system of optional recall, or rather optional re-entry, that obtained in the Ile de France) while the promise to pay (as in Collomp's description of the Midi) can be revoked in the event of non-support, though here non-support referred to failure by the parents to support the married children.

[37] For Greece, see E. Friedl, *Vasilika: A Village in Modern Greece* (New York, 1962); for Ceylon, see N. Yalman, *Under the Bo Tree* (Los Angeles and Berkeley, 1967).

[38] For a discussion of direction, see my *Death, Property and the Ancestors* (Stanford, Calif., 1962); and 'Marriage Prestations, Inheritance and Descent in Pre-Industrial Societies', *Jnl Comp. Family Stud.*, i (1970), pp. 37–54.

[39] Homans remarks that English law 'expected a real change in management to accompany the grant of the land': *op. cit.*, p. 154.

[40] 'Lineage' is used in the medieval way, very different from current anthropological use.

Collomp's analysis, like that of Daumard and Furet,[41] is based upon marriage contracts. Of 183 such contracts from a mountainous village in Haute Provence in the early eighteenth century, 53 per cent refer to 'nuclear families' (that is, housefuls or dwelling-groups) and 47 per cent to 'enlarged families'. The difference between the two turns on whether the new couple will live communally with the senior generation, co-residence being given a contractual basis presumably to limit conflict and to define the future conjugal estate of the newlyweds. These contracts relate to:

1. lodging, food, maintenance,
2. the conditions of separation (*insupport*).[42]

The contract stipulates the dowry (*dot*) of the wife and a *donation de biens* to the husband; where a communal household is envisaged (and in some other cases as well), the donor retains control of the property allocated and promises the newly married a part, or even the whole of the subsequent inheritance, at the same time agreeing to support the son, his wife and their children.

Such a contract is the complement to the Czech *výměnek* whereby the son takes over the farm at the same time as promising to maintain the parents in their old age. In thirteenth-century England, too, the son and heir often took over the estate at the time of marriage and entered upon similar obligations.[43] The Provençal arrangement, however, is likely to permit earlier unions than in those cases where marriage involves the retirement of the father. Both are related to the existence of 'stem housefuls', though these will be more frequent in the first type of situation (that is, each houseful will last longer).

The alternative arrangement, which insists on conjugal households, is connected with the automatic separation of children at marriage (or even before, by service), producing housefuls by automatic fission when each new couple is established (*établi* as well as *doté* in the terms used by Yver and the repositories of customary law).

An English example of the Provençal kind of arrangement is

---

[41] A. Daumard and F. Furet, *Structures et relations sociales à Paris au milieu du XVIIIᵉ siècle* (Cahiers des Annales, xviii, Paris, 1961).

[42] Such clauses were absent in contracts from Languedoc and Provence dating from the later Middle Ages.

[43] Homans, *op. cit.*, p. 152; Faith, *op. cit.*, p. 88.

implied in the account of the Chancery petition of c. 1475 which shows an action brought by Thomas Alexander, Gentleman, against the executors of John Jeny 'for breach of agreement to provide complainant with meat, drink, and lodging if he married Agnes, daughter of the said deceased'.[44] Here we appear to have a case of an in-marrying son-in-law being promised support at the time of marriage. Presumably the same understanding was reached when a son brought his wife into the house.[45]

Clearly larger households are obtained by delaying the point of family fission. Smaller households (or at least housefuls) are obtained by advancing that point up to the limiting condition, where no more than one married couple remains under one roof. The size of household related to the timing of family fission (i.e. the developmental cycle) and this in turn to the devolution of property.

What is the relationship of the form of household to the exclusion of endowed children? The dispersion of children tends to involve a preliminary division of the property, to daughters as dowry, to sons as an endowment. The exclusion of such children from a further share in the inheritance, which is characteristic of the 'community' system, was a factor that inhibited break-up.[46] Contrast the 'egalitarian' custom of Normandy, under which children left knowing they could always claim an equal share at the death of their parents. Moreover, the community system is associated with a tighter form of conjugal estate established at marriage. The husband and wife enter into an explicit community of property, and the children are then allocated shares in that conjugal estate according to various criteria. If on the other hand the property brought into marriage by man and wife remains associated with their own kin groups (as in the 'lineage' system),

---

[44] Coulton, *op. cit.* (1938), p. 314. Some indication of the frequency with which pre-mortem transfers occurred is given in the figures for Hindolveston, Norfolk, 1309–29: death and inheritance, 74; transfer during holder's lifetime (esp. to children), 136; poverty (bad harvests), 100; private convenience (including marriage settlements), 443. As Rodney Hilton reminds me, the difference between French and English landowners, after the Conquest, lay in the fact that in England all villein holdings lapsed into the lord's possession at the death of the tenant and that the only official way to transfer land *inter vivos* was to surrender it to the lord to the use of A, i.e. to be reissued to A. However, custom usually determined who was to be the heir.

[45] 'The records of the Percies and the Pastons show how it was quite common for young married couples to live, often for many years, in the house of one of their parents': Coulton, *ibid.*, writing of the upper classes.

[46] Berkner, 'Rural Family Organisation . . .'.

then these estates will be separately distributed to the children at the death of the individual spouses.

Associated with the 'exclusion of the endowed children', a system that insisted upon the continuing presence on the estate of all those who were going to inherit, was another aspect of the 'community of wealth', namely the emphasis given to 'the majesty of the conjugal bed';[47] in other words, stress was laid upon the division of property by maternal origin, a mode of division that is never found in 'egalitarian' Normandy, where every male child had his share, irrespective of maternal filiation or of residence. Around Paris, however, the emphasis fell upon conjugality rather than individual filiation. In the words of Le Roy Ladurie, the Norman system which in some respects is closer to the English pattern (at least before the adoption of primogeniture) was favourable to childhood but not to love.[48] However maternal filiation was relevant in lateral transmission since goods were abandoned to the lord before being transferred between half-bloods, an aspect of English law that Pollock and Maitland saw as encouraged by the lords themselves.

Laws of inheritance supported by church and state often upheld the interests of landlords in controlling (as with impartibility) and obtaining property (as with escheats). The refusal to admit half-bloods to the inheritance was 'eminently favourable to the king; it gave him escheats'.[49] Equally the church had an interest in the dead man's third in the devising of his chattels, and in the transfer of title of his bookland that would alienate property from his 'avaricious' kinsfolk, as the clergy automatically called them.[50]

In Wallonia the establishment of a community of property involved a *ravestissement* in the case of death, the attribution of all the property to the surviving spouse, providing there was a child of the marriage who had been heard to cry,[51] the same cry as was required by the English custom of courtesy by which the husband acquired a similar right in his dead wife's property as long as he lived. With this communality is associated 'division by beds' rather than by heads (*per capita*) and (in some parts) with the custom of ultimogeniture that assigned the house to the youngest son

47 Le Roy Ladurie, *op. cit.*, p. 831; Yver, *op. cit.*, p. 272.
48 Le Roy Ladurie, *op. cit.*, p. 838.
49 Pollock and Maitland, *op. cit.*, ii, p. 305.
50 *Ibid.*, p. 319.
51 Le Roy Ladurie, *op. cit.*, p. 844.

(*maineté*). I would add that such systems of preference are wrongly seen as *necessarily* unequal. To take a monetary payment at the age of twenty provides the opportunity of making (or indeed losing) one's fortune, if the wider society presents opportunities for expansion, either in the rural or in the urban spheres; one needs an open frontier. But at least one is free, not bound to look after ageing parents, which is the lot of the stay-at-home. In any case with a low rate of population growth, only a small percentage of children would normally be unable to marry on to another farm or to acquire a property where the direct line had become extinguished. However, with an increasing population, partibility did tend to keep men on the land[52] as well as leading to a more active land market.[53]

Owing to differential longevity and marriage ages, the husband will usually be the first to die. In the 'community' system the widow controlled part at least of the property under a jointure. In the 'lineage' system, the separate property of husband and wife returns to their own kin (*paterna paternis, materna maternis*) if the individual in question has no direct heir; here too we find parentelic reckoning and inheritance by representation, both of which involve the search for distant kin.[54] The delay in the final distribution of property (for no-one knows what he has until the last bell) would appear to inhibit marriage settlements as well as the early retirement of the senior generation, since any advantage an individual wishes to a successor can be nullified at his death. Such a system inevitably emphasizes post-mortem rather than pre-mortem transmission. So it may well lead (as Berkner suggests) to a high rate of celibacy, late marriage and (less certainly) a low incidence of stem households.[55] The community system, on the other hand, allows for earlier marriage, earlier transfer and more stem households. The main variables here are two, the conjugal estate and family fission. What is involved is partly the relative control of the conjugal estate by husband and wife (a difficult

---

[52] Faith, *op. cit.*, p. 84; H. E. Hallam, 'Some Thirteenth Century Censuses', *Econ. Hist. Rev.*, x (1958), pp. 340–61.
[53] According to Homans' impression, the traffic in land in the thirteenth century was more active in the areas where partibility obtained, viz. Kent and East Anglia (*op. cit.*, p. 204). The same conclusion is drawn by Habakkuk for nineteenth-century Europe (*op. cit.*).
[54] Le Roy Ladurie, *op. cit.*, p. 838.
[55] Berkner, 'Rural Family Organisation . . .', p. 151.

matter to define precisely), which affects the point of family fission, and partly too the timing of the transfer between generations.

Essentially similar practices to those we find in France appear in rural England. The exclusion of endowed children, those who had received their 'portions', is exactly what is described in the acts of the Synod of Exeter (1287) on which Homans has perceptively commented.[56] Examples of the exclusion of endowed children appear in the well-known case of the manors of Bray and Cookham, anyhow for daughters. For if all but one are married ('with his chattels') then, 'she at the hearth shall retain the whole tenement'.[57] Here the right of the 'hearth-heir', the *astrier*, the possessor, is all important, in contrast to the areas of strict 'equality'.[58] While Pollock and Maitland may be right in thinking that in Europe strict ultimogeniture, like strict primogeniture, is hardly ever found 'save where some lord has been able to dictate a rule of inheritance to dependent peasants',[59] there are other 'equitable' reasons for favouring one son above another.[60]

Unigeniture should be viewed as an instance of impartibility where, for whatever reason, the division of the land is considered undesirable. Often the pressure comes from the top, both for primogeniture in the case of feudal (military) tenures,[61] or for

[56] Homans, *op. cit.*, p. 135.

[57] Pollock and Maitland, *op. cit.*, ii, p. 281.

[58] It is in this context that seisin, possession, becomes nine-tenths of the law. See Homans, *op. cit.*, for a comment on the same case. See Faith, *op. cit.*, for the distribution of 'Borough English'.

[59] Pollock and Maitland, *op. cit.*, ii, p. 282. 'Primogeniture, the system most favourable to seigneurial interests, developed, probably under seigneurial pressure, where lordship was strong and when demesne farming became important': Faith, *op. cit.*, p. 85.

[60] Imbued with an abstract, post-Revolutionary Gallic egalitarianism, Yver and Le Roy Ladurie tend to overlook the reasons in equity for 'advantaging' one child as against another. One example of the actor's preference for inequality is given in Douglass's study of a Basque village. 'In the actor's view it is reprehensible on both moral and economic grounds to dismember a *baserria* (farmstead) either through land sales or divisive inheritance practices (for example, naming two or more heirs to the patrimony in a given generation).' The result is that the household 'normally' consists of an active man, wife and children, 'and the parents and/or unmarried siblings of the spouse who is residing in his (or her) natal household, and sometimes a male or female agricultural hand or servant' (W. A. Douglass, *Death in Murelaga: Funerary Ritual in a Spanish Basque Village* (Seattle, 1969), pp. 6 and 7.

[61] Pollock and Maitland, *op. cit.*

unigeniture in parts of Germany,[62] when impartibility was desired; as Berkner and Mendels observe: 'in general, the areas of impartibility in western Europe were those with strong manorial control over land tenure and settlement rights'.[63]

Schemes of unigeniture, then, tend to be linked to feudal tenures, where they are favoured partly for military reasons and partly for generalized control. 'The peasant', runs a German proverb, 'has only one child.'[64] Elsewhere the interests of landlords take the more general form of an insistence on impartibility.[65] Nevertheless, such pressure from above is not inconsistent with a recognition from below that impartibility and unigeniture may in certain circumstances, be 'necessary', though as Sabean has clearly pointed out, this tendency is unlikely to assuage the 'excluded' in times of rising population and diminishing opportunities. For 'preferential' unigeniture (the *préciput* of French custom) can also be seen as part of a parental strategy (and one accepted or at least acknowledged by the junior generation) that offers an advantage to the heir remaining in the house in return for his assistance in running the farm and his support in their old age.

Of course, the 'exclusion' of the other siblings is rarely if ever total, only exclusion from the land; the other children have to be paid off in a manner that may insist upon equality in value as distinct from equality of object. One could indeed argue that there was always a tension between equality from below (e.g. socage, *roture*) and inequality from above (e.g. manor, *noblesse*). While this opposition did exist, it presents too simplified a view. As we have pointed out, smaller tenants are often forced to be more conscious of strategies of heirship than larger ones.[66] In any case the opposition falls between generations as well as between classes. The senior generation, the holders, are single (or rather a conjugal pair), the offspring often many. On general grounds the parents wish to preserve intact what they have put together, whereas the solidarity of siblings stresses equality and, if necessary, division.

[62] Sabean, *op. cit.*
[63] L. K. Berkner and F. F. Mendels, *Inheritance Systems, Family Structure, and Demographic Patterns in Western Europe (1700–1900)* (mimeo, 1973), p. 6.
[64] Pollock and Maitland, *op. cit.*, ii, p. 283.
[65] E.g. in Poland: see W. Kula, 'La famille paysanne en Pologne', *Annales E.S.C.*, xxvii (1972), p. 955.
[66] J. R. Goody, *op. cit.* (1973), p. 17.

Again, the three-field system of the champion country may, as Homans insists, favour a single heir. However, another factor intervenes, one that the old stress, but whose justice is often recognized by the young as well. This factor is the 'pension right'.

Looking at the situation from the standpoint of the controlling generation, there are two contradictory pulls at work in dowry systems. On the one hand, to get a spouse of the right standing for one's offspring there has to be (at least as a promise) a specific settlement from the estate. Moreover, to retain the new couple on the estate and to give them the right motivation for work, one may have to hand over control. On the other hand, this process of pre-mortem transmission weakens the control of the senior generation over their very livelihood.

The resolutions of these contrary pulls are various. In eighteenth-century Provence the parents agreed upon a future settlement at the time of their children's marriage, promising to support them out of the family fund which was to be handed over at a later date.[67] In twentieth-century County Clare, the property was handed over at the wedding, the senior generation then going into retirement.[68] As we have noted, the former allows for earlier marriage, possibly later retirement, but also a higher percentage of 'stem households'. And it involves a different set of authority relations and potential conflicts than the system of marriage-cum-transfer. Moreover, the later marriage of men, as Flandrin[69] has argued, may have important consequences for attitudes towards sex as well as for the role of adolescents.

The time of transmission clearly affects the authority of the senior generation. To take a very different society, Sieroshevski reported seeing among the Yakut, 'a weak old man of seventy beat his forty-year-old son, who was not only well-off but independent.' The author explained that the old man still had an important amount of property at his disposal and 'ruled the family by the fear that he could deprive any recalcitrant one of a share in the inheritance'.[70] Late transmission retains generational control; early transmission weakens it.

[67] Collomp, *op. cit.* The same system obtained in parts of twelfth-century Italy.

[68] Arensberg, *op. cit.*

[69] J.-L. Flandrin, 'Mariage tardif et vie sexuelle: Discussions et hypothèses de recherche', *Annales E.S.C.,* xxvii (1972), pp. 351–78.

[70] L. W. Simmons, *The Role of the Aged in Primitive Societies* (New Haven, Conn., 1945), p. 58.

The evidence for pre-mortem transmission in Europe is widespread (though not of course universal). Sometimes the parents are given a separate room (the west room, the end room), sometimes a separate house (the dower house, the cottage). In the first instance a stem family will usually be detectable from census material, in the second place, probably not. Yet both might occur in the same community or in the same region.

Settlements of this kind were common in the court rolls of the thirteenth and fourteenth centuries from all parts of England, though they were not always spelt out in great detail.[71] The arrangement might allow for residence in the same 'messuage' (or central plot in the village, toft) or in a dependant cottage in the same courtyard, which might be occupied by kin or labourers. A single dependant was more likely to have a room at the end of the house. 'In the commonest form of these settlements, a father or mother handed his or her holding over to one of the children, bargaining at the same time for sustenance in old age.'[72] Some arrangements could also involve a kind of 'adoption' of adults.

In his account of medieval England, Coulton gives examples of both the provision of a separate room and of a separate house.[73] On taking over a cottage from his mother in 1281, Thomas Bird of Romsley undertook to maintain her 'fully and honourable so long as she shall live'. The food which he pledges himself to give her is plentiful; she is to have 'five carts-loads of sea-coal' (for here we are on the edge of the Black Country); and he is to build a 'competent dwelling for her to inhabit, containing 30 feet in length within the walls, and 14 feet in breadth, with corner posts and three new and competent doors and two windows'.[74] These proprietors were of above average wealth; but cottages could be built and even moved with relative ease, so that the decay and renewal of houses and villages were not all that uncommon; in medieval society there were many cases of men moving their houses to the hill tops for the sake of safety.

Such separation, not at marriage but at the death of one of the spouses, is implied in the dower right of English common law. To assign a widow's dower was the duty of the heir or guardian, and had to be performed within forty days of the husband's death.

[71] Homans, *op. cit.*, p. 145. [72] *Ibid.*, p. 146.
[73] See *ibid.* for evidence of similar arrangements.
[74] G. G. Coulton, *Medieval Village* (Cambridge, 1925), p. 99.

During these forty days the widow could, by the right of quarantine (German: *Dreissigste*, the widow's month), reside in the principal house and be maintained at the cost of the yet undivided property. 'A fair third of the land was to be assigned to her, and she was entitled to a "dower house" but not to the capital messuage, though if her husband held but a town house she had a right to one-third, or by custom one half, of it, as representing her "free bench",'[75] the free bench being the widow's right to stay (German: *Beisitz*). Note that here is a suggestion of a possible difference in the pattern of residence depending upon its location in a scattered or nucleated settlement; in the former it is possible to separate, in the latter one has to co-reside. If so, the implication runs somewhat contrary to the suggestion of Collomp that terrace (town) houses are not easily extended and hence cannot accommodate more than two conjugal units.[76]

The right of dower became linked to the endowment of the wife by the husband at the church door at the time of marriage. Normally this *dos rationabilis* or 'common law dower' consisted of the right to one third of the husband's lands,[77] under certain conditions, a situation resembling that of Normandy, where again there was no community of property. As in Normandy, the husband acquired a similar right if a child had been born; this was known as a *veufeté* in Normandy and courtesy in England, though in the latter case it endured even though he married again. Although Pollock and Maitland speak of 'a latent idea of a community . . . which cannot easily be suppressed',[78] and although the husband becomes effectively the wife's guardian at her marriage, married women could play a significant part in legal transactions to do with land in the twelfth and thirteenth centuries.[79]

The varieties of conjugal estate in Europe are many and complex; Pollock and Maitland remark that in Würtemberg alone the number could be reduced to sixteen if one neglected minor differences. But in England under socage tenure (the free tenure of ordinary law) the widow had a third or a half, while at the villein level there seems to have been an effective community of property in England since the surviving spouse was entitled to half or even

[75] Pollock and Maitland, *op. cit.*, ii, p. 422.
[76] Collomp, *op. cit.*, p. 974.
[77] The *tercia* of medieval Italy.
[78] Pollock and Maitland, *op. cit.*, ii, p. 407.
[79] *Ibid.*, p. 411.

more of the other's land. This certainly existed in the Kentish custom of gavelkind, where it was associated with precisely the kind of equal sharing that characterized Normandy;[80] husband and wife enjoyed free bench of half the lands, and could also become guardian over the rest. In manorial extents 'it is common to find a widow as the tenant of a complete villein tenement',[81] especially where lords are insisting upon impartibility. However, the association of community and equality (total equality) runs against the 'lineage' system of Normandy. Saxon laws favoured equal division — of real and personal property (between both sons and daughters, according to some authorities), and socage lands seem to have been subjected to the same kind of division, as persisted until much later under the Kentish gavelkind. The Norman conquest introduced no change in this respect, since Normandy was committed to the equal division of socage lands among the sons[82] and this practice was confirmed in England by a law of William I. The — right of primogeniture first gained a footing by the introduction of military tenures, and gradually descended to socage lands.

Marriage agreements, involving immediate transfer, provide for co-residence as well as for separate dwelling; they provide for sons-in-law as well as sons. Coulton gives another example of a handing-over when describing peasant clothing. 'Hugh Coverer, marrying Emma Lord and taking over her father Richard's land', undertakes to 'keep the said Richard in board as well as he (Hugh) keeps himself and will give him every year one garment and one pair of shirts and one pair of hose and shoes.'[83] These contracts were mostly verbal; as Coulton remarks, 'these folks, again, are pretty certainly above the average, or their covenant would not have come down to us'.[84]

Writing of Provence, Collomp makes the general point that not simply are richer families the ones to leave written settlements but they are also the most likely to have extended households (a point often made for Chinese and Indian families).[85] He concludes that

[80] T. Robinson, *The Common Law of Kent*, ed. J. D. Norwood (Ashford, Kent, 1858).
[81] Pollock and Maitland, *op. cit.*, ii, p. 427.
[82] Robinson, *op. cit.*; Pollock and Maitland, *op. cit.*, ii, p. 309.
[83] Coulton, *op. cit.* (1925), pp. 101–2.
[84] *Ibid.*, p. 102.
[85] See also Berkner, 'Rural Family Organisation . . .'. Homans makes the same point by relating marriage chances to land holding.

the 'bourgeois' of the village 'living in high style as active merchants kept their sons under their roofs after marriage'.[86] How was this organized? In more than three-quarters of the cases the parents promise to feed, lodge and maintain their children in their house. The latter work for the profit of the community, for the common fund, but it is the father (or sometimes the widowed mother) who heads the household and holds the purse-strings. The son (sometimes the son-in-law) remains in a condition of complete economic dependence on the parents. The son does not control any property of his own (the dowry of his wife has been handed over to the father and will only be given to him 'in the event of non-support') nor yet any of the profit. In order to attach the son (and of course to get a proper bride) and, in a way, to guarantee his future, the father always gives him a 'donation of goods' in the marriage contract, but he nevertheless reserves the usufruct for himself.[87]

One of the clauses dealing with fission may include the reservation of a room in the house for the parents. In only five out of eighty-six cases was the control of the joint household handed over to the son, in which case the senior generation (often a widowed mother) reserves the right to live in the house, sometimes receives a sum of money, and always gets an annual pension (usually in the form of wheat).

The question of maintenance of the old is dealt with very specifically in Scandinavian law, which resembled that of Normandy in its emphasis on equality. Whereas in Germany one finds the exclusion of the Parisian region, among the Vikings (the ancestors of the Normans) equality prevails. Equality of rights meant equality of obligations. When a man divided his property among his children, the law permitted him to make a circuit, known as *flaetfoering*, spending the number of days with each heir in exact proportion to the quantity of goods he had received.[88]

But larger households in Europe do not take the form of the stem variety alone. Sometimes married brothers remain together on the farm, as Giono's account of the Dominici household vividly reminds us.[89] People may continue to reside together if they stand

[86] Collomp, *op. cit.*, p. 973.
[87] *Ibid.*
[88] Yver, *op. cit.*, p. 287.
[89] J. Giono, *The Dominici Affair*, trans. P. de Mendelssohn (London, 1956).

to lose their inheritance by leaving, if (in Yver's terms) there is 'exclusion des enfants dotés', male as well as female. A particularly vivid example comes from Franche-Comté. According to the local custom:

> If serfs wish to be and to remain capable of inheriting from each other, they are bound to live together under the same roof, at the same fireside, and at the same table. And if this 'community' be dissolved, if they separate from any motive whatsoever, they may never come together again . . . without the lord's consent.

The inhabitants petitioned the States General at the time of the French Revolution, claiming that 'each house seems to be a mere prison, in which captives are obliged to shut themselves up together, under pain of losing their share in the few roods of ground which they have so often watered with the sweat of their brow'. When the sons marry and their wives are not sympathetic, it becomes the interest of each pair to wear out the other's patience, since the departure of one will increase the heritage of those who stay.[90] This is the kind of situation one would expect where the landed property is shared by all, yet where departure means exclusion; only co-resident members inherited, the rest taking their endowment with them.

These differences in inheritance system are a marked feature of European peasantry. Some have attempted to explain their distribution by reference to earlier migration, of the Norsemen in Yver's case, of the North German tribes in the case of Homans.[91] While inertia is undoubtedly a factor, it is easy to exaggerate the persistence of 'custom' when so much is at stake. More important has been the attempt to link transmission with forms of socio-economic organization of the village.

Homans saw joint families as being encouraged by the 'Celtic' system of dispersed settlement that marked the woodlands, while stem families were to be found in the open-field settlements of the champion country of the Midlands. Like Marc Bloch, he saw these settlement patterns as linked to different types of agricultural exploitation. Translating his terms into those of Yver, egalitarian Normandy is a region of *bocages* (hedged enclosures), while open fields dominated the champion country around Paris, the country of preference and of *seigneurs*. The correlations are perhaps too

---

90 Coulton, *op. cit.* (1925), p. 476.
91 Homans, *op. cit.*, p. 120.

sweepingly drawn, for types of devolution have no one-to-one association with technological systems nor with modes of production. Nevertheless, the links are often clear enough, as Mendels has shown in his study of agricultural change in Flanders. The heavy soils of the Polder area required large ploughs and large holdings; the sandy light soils of the interior were well-suited to labour-intensive agriculture on small family farms.[92]

In addition to the 'ethnic' and the 'economic' explanations, we must consider another fact. There is no one-to-one correlation partly because the pulls between transmission and retention, between forms of conjugal estate, are so constant and so balanced, that a number of situations may trigger a swing from one form to another. For example, while preference and impartibility may reflect the interest of the landlord, they can also express the ideas of the family about viability and justice.

We can take as an example the case of unigeniture. As Homans has pointed out, there was a certain amount of movement between primogeniture and ultimogeniture (or Borough French and Borough English) in different parts of England, a fact appearing to contradict his suggestion that the actors did not think about their 'customs'. He quotes the case of the men of Brookham, Surrey, who in 1339 petitioned their lord (the Abbey of Chertsey) to change from inheritance by younger to elder son; despite the antiquity of the former, it was to the grave hurt and detriment of the whole homage and of their holding.[93] Elsewhere the opposite change was made, and each change carried with it certain implications for the community in question.

Since inheritance was so often tied to marriage, it seems likely that primogeniture delayed the event at least for the eldest son, while ultimogeniture made it more possible for him at the expense of quitting home; those best able to look after themselves left home first.[94] The other side of the coin is that ultimogeniture might well lead to an heir succeeding while he was under age, and hence to all the problems of 'regency' or guardianship. If the regent was the widow by the custom of the locality (as in Bucksleep, where she held all her late husband's tenement until her youngest

92 Berkner and Mendels, *op. cit.*, p. 15.
93 Homans, *op. cit.*, p. 126.
94 Gross figures for age at marriage may conceal important differences between siblings.

son reached the age of fifteen), both were protected; if it was a brother or elder son of the dead man, the problems were more acute.

The possibility of change from partibility to impartibility was also present, sometimes even in the actors' view of the situation. The 'disgavelling' of lands in Kent (4 Edward I) recognized that if a plurality of sons press the claim to their own shares, none of them may have land that will 'suffice for his subsistence',[95] which is the substance of Le Play's comment on the application of the egalitarian Napoleonic code to the Auvergne and the Nivernais.[96]

In looking at the variations within Europe, we need also to think of the broad similarities within which these variations occur. These similarities are brought out more clearly when we contrast Europe (and for some purposes the major societies of Asia) with the agricultural societies in Africa, where some writers have also claimed to have found peasantry and feudalism.[97] When we make this contrast we find that the relations of family to land differ significantly, especially the arrangements over marital property and the role that these allocate to women in their interaction with men and things. I see these differences as closely related to the modes of agricultural production, 'intensive' in the one case (involving plough or irrigation), 'extensive' in the other (involving swidden and the hoe). But whatever the reasons, these differences have consequences for the position of women, the structure of social roles, the behaviour of kin and the strategies of family organization.[98] It is against this broad background that we have to look at the variations in the customs of Western Europe. For example, the differences in the nature of the conjugal estate and in the timing

[95] A frequent formula for inheritance was 'as two sons and one heir': i.e. property was held 'in common', each individual having equal rights in a joint concern rather than rights of partition (i.e. 'share and share alike'), though I think the dissolution of the corporation must always be envisaged. It can never be as truly 'perpetual' but always has a developmental aspect to it, as Maine realized in India despite the stress on the jointness of the domestic corporation.

[96] Homans, *op. cit.*, p. 113.

[97] See J. R. Goody, *Technology, Tradition and the State in Africa* (London, 1971).

[98] I have elaborated this argument, here given scant treatment, in a number of papers published since 1969 in *Sociology, Comparative Studies in Society and History*, and elsewhere. The results of this work will appear in *Production and Reproduction* (Cambridge University Press, 1976).

of family fission are certainly important in their consequences and need examining more closely, especially in their influence on behaviour between kith and kin. So too the causal factors behind these variables need further investigation. But we need to recall the contradictions (or countervailing factors) that exist in the type of situation encountered in Europe and that emerge in the more advanced agricultural systems of Asia. For example, the contradictory pulls towards the equal treatment of offspring on the one hand and towards the preservation of the estate on the other are present in a whole range of such societies, in Ceylon as well as Tibet (a country that displays some surprising similarities with pre-industrial Europe). So the factors involved in shifting the emphasis from one to the other may be large in number and sometimes slight in nature, if only because individuals and groups must have been constantly aware of the customs of their neighbours, and hence led to assess their comparative costs and gains.

2. Family structures and inheritance customs in sixteenth-century France*

EMMANUEL LE ROY LADURIE

As one starts to create an anthropological history of France[1] and found a discipline that would be at one of the pioneering fringes of a new kind of history, one realizes that it is unfortunately not possible (at least for the period from 1450 to 1700) to make use of those 'elementary structures of kinship' that twenty years ago set out a universal basis for the ethnography of the primitive world: in spite of a clear endogamous pattern at village level, even peasant rules of marriage and kinship in classical France are too open and unsystematic, too 'anomic' – even the computer finds it is simply wasting its Fortran on them – for one to be able to look for criteria for regional differentiation comparable to those suggested by Claude Lévi-Strauss for simple societies. But still, a rigorous study of the rules of inheritance relating to the devolution of property, as they are enunciated in the provincial custumals, supplies one of the grids that allow us to distinguish between different cultural zones; such a study leads from the examination of particular phenomena to the defining of techniques of transformation that make it possible to pass logically from zone to zone and from period to period. This highly-detailed and meticulous research on the ethnography of customary law also allows the historian to discern certain fundamental divergences or lines of demarcation in the foundations of family life, according to the different parts of France under consideration. The first in the field was Jean Yver: in a densely written book, together with a series of articles, he has put forward in demanding prose a suggestion for a suitable geography of our ancient customs, taking up the torch, more than

---

* Translated by Olive Classe. This chapter has appeared in French as 'Système de la coutume: structures familiales et coutumes d'héritage en France au XVIe siècle', *Annales E.S.C.*, xxvii (1972), pp. 825–46.
[1] Drawing largely on military archives, I have attempted in several articles to suggest various approaches to the establishment of a historical anthropology of the French people. These articles may be found in *Studi Storici*, x (1969), and in my *Le Territoire de l'historien* (Paris, 1973).

a century on, from Henri Klimrath, whose excellent work has been overtaken by later scholarship.[2]

I propose to give a good broad outline of Yver's analysis and I shall try as far as possible to incorporate the down-to-earth preoccupations of a historian of the peasant world. First I must point out that Yver has drawn into systematic shape the bits and pieces of data amassed by a number of pioneers in the subject, among whom we should note Bourdot de Richebourg,[3] whose enormous compilation, the *Coutumier général* (General Custumal), published in 1724, assembled for the first time under one title the hitherto scattered texts brought out in separate volumes by sixteenth-century jurists. Mention has also to be made of Klimrath, who in the 1830s drew up a map that for long remained the only one of its kind, showing the zones where the different customary laws were practised.

The regional custumals, mostly written down at the end of the fifteenth century and during the sixteenth century, are of interest to both medievalist and modernist: they provide us with a vivid image, at the same time traditional and new, of the kingdom as it was when it was being rebuilt and reshaped after the Hundred Years War. For the Renaissance jurists, who performed the task of local compilers, brought together elements of customary law originating in several temporal strata; some of these elements represent an archaic layer of rural property law in the form in which it was still functioning (with differing degrees of vigour) at the end of the Middle Ages. When put alongside these, other elements reveal the evolution of this law towards the more modern, even urban forms imposed upon it by people's practice and lawyers' theories during the sixteenth century or even earlier. When he is confronted with these sometimes heterogeneous strata, the ethnographer-historian is obliged to select some suitable criteria whose presence, absence or diverse forms are linked to a whole

[2] Jean Yver, *Essai de géographie coutumière* (Paris, 1966). Also, by the same author, 'Les caractères originaux du groupe de coutumes de l'Ouest de la France', *Revue historique de droit français et étranger*, 1952, pp. 18–79; and 'Les deux groupes de coutumes du Nord', *Revue du Nord*, xxv (1953), and xxvi (1954); Henri Klimrath, 'Etudes sur les coutumes', in his *Travaux sur l'histoire du droit français* (Paris–Strasbourg, 1843), published posthumously in two volumes, with a map in volume ii showing the distribution of customary law in France.

[3] Charles Bourdot de Richebourg, *Nouveau Coutumier général* (Paris, 1724).

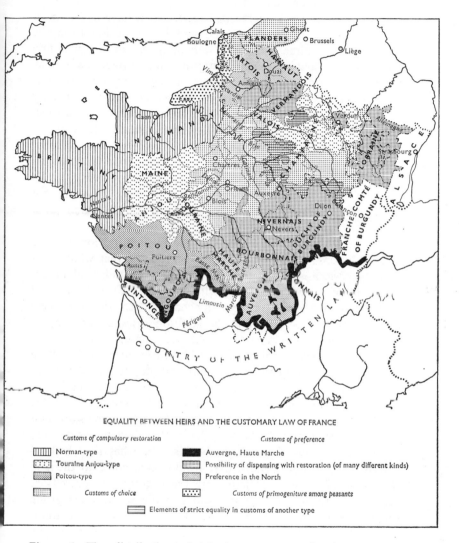

Figure 1. The distribution of inheritance customs in sixteenth-century France (after Jean Yver, *Essai de géographie coutumière*, by permission Editions Sirey)

family of cultural features which give to each zone of customary law its own particular character.

√   The contradictory but interrelated criteria that have in fact been selected are: equality among heirs, and the exclusion from the inheritance of children previously advantaged. On a rough first analysis, we find that over the country as a whole three main areas of differentiation appear in the system of customary law. To simplify things we may call these the Paris–Orléans zone; Normandy and Armorica; and the Midi to which are added, as we shall see, sizeable portions of the North, some of them, notably the Walloon areas, very northerly indeed. The principle on which this regional differentiation is based has been very well described by Yver, so I shall simply quote him on this matter, explaining points in his text, from time to time, for the benefit of those who are not familiar with the historiography of customs. This Norman jurist writes that:

> Quite early, French customs had turned in the direction of three main solutions, A, B and C. One possibility is that which provides *préciput* among the children [*préciput* – a unilateral advantage granted to one child, allowing him to take a determined part of a heritable whole before any sharing out with his brothers and sisters]: preference A is the solution we shall find in the southern and Walloon spheres. At the opposite extreme, we have the customs of complete equality B, in all cases imposing on the children who had been advantaged [before the inheritance of the father and mother's estate took place] the restoration of any such advantages and gifts they had received. These the children were not allowed to retain even if they gave up their claim on the estate; at the very least, they had to restore any difference in value there might be between what they had received and the equal share that would have come to them in the event of intestacy. These were the customs of compulsory restoration, to which category belonged the whole large group of customs of the west of France. Between these two extreme solutions, A and B, the customs of the Parisian type (C) decided, as always, in favour of more finely graded systems.[4]

---

4 The passage I quote here is from Yver, 'Les deux groupes de coutumes du Nord', p. 11. With regard to the different solutions described in this passage, I should like to mention the excellent comparison suggested to me by Pierre Bourdieu: the purpose of inheritance customs is nearly always (but

He goes on to explain that in the first of these solutions (C1), widely attested in the Middle Ages, the child who had received a portion from the father and mother, bestowed by them during their lifetime, was *ipso facto* excluded from future inheritance; another, more flexible, Parisian system (C2), which came into use after the one just mentioned (at the end of the Middle Ages and in the sixteenth century), provides that the advantaged heir may 'opt'; he has the choice between holding on to his advantage and giving up his claim on the estate, and coming back into the division and 'restoring' to the common stock the advantage in question. The Parisian customs now become ones of simple equality and of option. These distinctions between three great systems of customary laws are not simply theoretical. In practice, they lead to emphasis, according to region, sometimes on one familial role, sometimes on another. For example, we shall see that in the old Capetian lands the father and mother could exercise a right of *mainbournie* (power of guardianship), though it is true that this right tended to be modified progressively in the direction of an increasing egalitarianism. In Normandy, it would be more proper, objectively, to speak of a law favouring the sons as a group; and finally the Provençal-speaking Midi sets up at the centre of the decision-making process the formidable figure, so dear to Roman jurists, of the father supreme over all.

The intermediate solutions

In the oldest juridical stratum (which is mentioned in the thirteenth century, but destined to survive, officially at least, until 1510) of the law of the Paris–Orléans region, of the world of the 'centrist' solutions (C1 and C2), it is the power of the parents, the father and mother, that prevails. Associated with this is a concern for preserving the tenement intact.[5] 'What the father and mother do cannot be changed' ('*quanquez fait père et mère est estable*'). Such

not quite – see the anomalous case of Brittany) to avoid excessive fragmentation of the patrimony, just as in chess the aim common to all categories of players is to checkmate the opponent's king. But as some players like to open with a Queen's gambit, while others prefer different tactics, so the customs of the various provinces select for themselves very different solutions and methods in order to arrive at the generally identical goal of preventing an undue fragmentation of the family land.

[5] Similarly in England: see G. Homans, *English Villagers of the Thirteenth Century* (Cambridge, Mass., 1941; repr. 1970).

at any rate was the original concept of the custumals, solid evidence
for which exists from the Gothic era; afterwards it persists in some
places but decays in others. In the rude law of ordinary villages
(which, perhaps because of the drift of peasants away from the
land, became also the law of the Capetian towns), this stability,
this immutability of parental dispositions acquired a precise meaning: for on the strength of such a disposition the parental couple
would give a plough, a cow, cash, or, very rarely, a plot of land,
to a son or, more often, a daughter who was leaving home to marry
elsewhere, and to live or found a family away from the one in
which he or she had grown up. As regards the inheritance that
would take place later, on the death of the parents, the child who
had been 'set up' in this way was obliged by customary law to
give up his claim.[6] Leaving the family nest to marry and settle
in another meant, simultaneously, dowry and disinheritance. On
the other hand, the child or children, sons or daughters, who had
strong roots reaching into the soil of their own people, into their
holding, however poor and humble, and who stayed in their natal
home to carry on, under the command of the old folk, caring for
the family farm – these could expect, when the time came, to inherit their parents' plot of land. In such cases it did not matter
much whether this heir (presumptive by virtue of his living with
the parents) was male or female, elder or younger, one or several.
Though it was hard on offspring who left home to set themselves
up elsewhere, the custom of the old Capetian provostries was kind
and indulgent to children who remained 'at the hearth' in order
to help their parents in their old age. In this respect, the provisions
of customary law were unencumbered by prejudice, whether about
primogeniture, male succession, or (in this case) keeping the family
property intact. They allowed a younger son, or a daughter, to
inherit; and they ensured that there would be equal shares or
'simple equality' (in other words, no advantaging of one child as
against another) whenever several children or heirs who had not
exercised their right to establish themselves elsewhere and to
receive a marriage portion, claimed a share in an estate. This

---

[6] 'In Paris this practice of excluding children who had been set up in
homes of their own had to be reconciled with a principle of equality
between children concerned in the inheritance; from this would emerge the
well-known system of option and restoration': Yver, 'Les deux groupes de
coutumes du Nord', p. 211.

accounts for the paradox in these very ancient Paris–Orléans customs, which seem to blow hot and cold at the same time: they support the cause of the stability of marriages and of the endowment of children and therefore always leave the possibility of favouritism in the interests, or to the disadvantage, of the child who has been set up, married or portioned; and on the other hand, they stipulate simple equality as between the children who have remained at home. The exclusion of those who have been advantaged is obviously intended to reconcile somehow or other these two incompatible provisions. In spite of the ever-present possibility of these contradictions, we see that the property of a villein (for example in the Orléanais system) generally remained entire except for the removal of a few minute fragments previously subtracted by the parents to provide portions for those of their children who had left to make their home under another roof.

The actual characteristics of this system of devolution call for a few general remarks. First of all, it is clear that the aim, or at any rate the effect, of these customs of the Ile-de-France or Orléanais is to limit the number of inheriting offspring so as to prevent excessive fragmentation of land-holdings. Though it is far from always being achieved, this 'aim' is at any rate objectively enshrined (if not consciously pursued) in these old laws, and with remarkable consistency. The oldest texts emphasize the rural character of the phenomenon of disinheritance of previously advantaged children: they present it bluntly as typical of 'villeinage'.

This characteristically peasant effort to direct the devolution of property towards the conservation of a holding large enough to support a family fitted in well, moreover, with the conditions of contemporary demography. We know that among those earlier populations that have recently been quantified,[7] the average number of children per family to escape infant and juvenile mortality and arrive finally at marriageable age was, taken over all, very little more than two: or statistically, according to the biological probabilities, a brother and a sister. This being the case, the system of inheritance I have just described was more or less consciously programmed to reproduce as far as possible, from one generation to the next, those peasant farming and land-tenure structures that

[7] P. Goubert, *Beauvais et le Beauvaisis au XVIIᵉ siècle* (Paris, 1960).

were considered to be the best within the static framework of a seigneurial economy. One of the two surviving children (generally the boy), living with the father and mother, served his apprenticeship as a farmer in this familial community; he was destined, when the time came, to take possession of the property. As for the other child, the daughter in many cases (the exclusion of advantaged children, in practice and even sometimes according to the letter of the law, was often synonymous with the exclusion of advantaged *daughters*), 'they found her a husband, and that was that'; she left home with a dowry of varying meagreness and no 'expectations', to make a place for herself if possible in another family group whose structure she too helped to 'reproduce'. Naturally, real situations often departed from this simple scheme. But even in the very many anomalous cases, the system was flexible; it allowed for portions to be given to several children leaving home to settle elsewhere; if there was no son, it permitted a son-in-law to be installed under the parental roof; lastly – but this was an undesirable solution, though a frequent one (as is shown from before 1500 by the fragmentation of small-holdings) – lastly, the old Paris–Orléans law resigned itself more than once to sharing out the tenement between several offspring,[8] on condition that these latter (in theory, at least) had previously agreed to collaborate with their parents, if the need arose, in a disciplined system of co-residence. And so these structures, that were so convenient for the farmers, seem to have been spread, at the end of the Middle Ages and sometimes well beyond, over a very large territory far outside the Paris–Orléans zone. They are found in fact sporadically in the region of Lille and even that of Amiens;[9] also, in the east as well as in the south-east of the northern part of France; in Germany; in Poland even; and finally in Switzerland. A study of the Germanic data gives the French researcher the chance to make a Dumézil-style comparison and to ponder on the origins of the system: beyond the Rhine, the exclusion of the advantaged child, followed by the sharing of the inheritance among the children who remained at home, is not just a legal phenomenon. It remains closely linked with habits of thought, with folklore, and even with mythology! In fact, in some peasant families in Germany, the household furniture was not shared out on the father's death.

[8] This is the system of 'simple equality'.
[9] Yver, *Essai de géographie coutumière*, chs 1 and 2.

Keeping it together helped to preserve the continuity of the family, and this was made possible by a trick, a fictitious three-way collective division, so to speak: one part going to the children living at home; the second to the wife, also living at home; and the third to . . . the soul of the dead father! Similarly, in the French-speaking parts of Switzerland, in the cantons closest to tradition, custom favoured the children termed *intronqués*: those who lived at home in the familial community were destined one day to have a share in the inheritance, whereas the children who were *détronqués*, who had thought fit to get married and go and live elsewhere – they received a marriage portion and were then disinherited.[10]

These habits are also attested much farther south: in some farming as well as urban areas in the Provençal-speaking part of France, the study of various customs and especially of actual wills shows that the exclusion of the portioned child and the sharing out of the inheritance only among those children who had remained at home was widely practised until the fifteenth century; and this notwithstanding the popularity of the extended family in the south. Finally, these same habits, either indigenous or imported by the colonists, are found in the Jerusalem of the Crusaders, as well as in the ancient customary law of Armenia.[11]

Let us confine our attention to western Europe, or even simply to the regions of France: the wide diffusion of the institutions of inheritance just described tempts one to accept the hypothesis that derives these customs from a very distant past, from a Ligurian, Celtic or Germanic stratum. But, Yver asks, is it really necessary to 'go back to these remotest ethnic origins? Before we get back as far as the Menapii, or even the Ligurians, couldn't we economize our efforts and stop at some intermediate stage?'[12]

And indeed, without dismissing these paleo-ethnographic speculations, it would seem that one should be content with more modest assertions: let us simply say, with Yver, that the exclusion of endowed children and the privilege accorded in the inheritance to children who remained in the home fulfil particularly well, whatever the ethnic origins may be, the requirements of a very demanding agricultural and seigneurial society. A powerful seigneury signifies (according to the period concerned) a cellular tissue of *manses* (small tenant farms), or, later, the constraining bonds of

[10] *Ibid.*, p. 277.   [11] *Ibid.*
[12] Yver, 'Les deux groupes de coutumes du Nord', p. 30.

villeinage. But these constraints produce a structure; they engender a law of inheritance which, in order to fit in with the demands of the seigneur, must be founded on exclusion. Suppose we have, for example, a seigneur of the medieval and classical type, still wielding exorbitant power: how could he tolerate, so far as he has influence in the matter, that the holdings of peasants, over which he exercises a superior right, should be broken up into tiny bits for the benefit of endowed heirs who have gone off to settle elsewhere, when 'elsewhere' might very well be outside the usually restricted area over which the power of his manor extends? From the point of view of the overlord, excluding the migrant villein from the right to inherit is the ideal solution. As for the tenants themselves, their view of the problem is very unlikely to differ much from that of their noble master. After all, for a very long time they have been in only very precarious possession of their piece of land, holding subject to mortmain 'a tenement that was barely hereditary'.[13] For them, the notion of inheritance was merely the *de facto* continuity of a certain family on a certain piece of land. Under these circumstances, the requirement that the presumptive heirs should have been living at home, together with the exclusion of previously advantaged children, was a wise precaution, a sort of taking possession in advance, like that which made the fortune of the Capetians. It guaranteed that on the death of the head of the family, the farm or tenement would be transmitted as a matter of course to the children who were on the spot, without the unpleasant risk that the overlord might claim back the land on the grounds of some 'seigneurial right of withdrawal'. So, if we accept Yver's suggestions, at the end of the Middle Ages, the Paris–Orléans custom represented the tough superstructure, still alive to varying degrees, of a formerly very powerful seigneurial world.

We may note another sign of an earlier system: the customs based on exclusion and co-residential inheritance that characterize the former Capetian domain (and also, at the end of the Middle Ages, some regions of southern France) are linked with different types of extended families; and in fact, in the Paris–Orléans group the exclusion of previously advantaged offspring casts into outer darkness 'the children who by establishing themselves elsewhere have become separated from the familial home, the parental couple

[13] *Ibid.*, p. 34.

and the little domestic group (single, and sometimes married, grown-up children) that lives together with this couple'.[14]

As for the southern part of the Massif Central, the exclusion of endowed children derives expressly from the desire for cohesion manifested by the most classic type of extended family: where two (or more) households of parents and children, or of brothers and sisters with their spouses, live sharing hearth and board under the same roof and, to ensure continuity, keep the main part of the inheritance for the descendants living at home.

As we are dealing with familial institutions that go into serious decline in the thirteenth century (in the north)[15] or in the sixteenth century (in the Midi),[16] it is understandable that the customs of exclusion in their turn come under revisionist attack at the time of the Renaissance.

Yet there still remains, and will remain as an extremely durable feature, the most stable and perhaps the most touching element of the Paris–Orléans structures: their insistence on the special status of the joint decision of father and mother, and on the desirability of a 'simple and trustful' collaboration between parents and children within the rural milieu. In this respect, the practices of the old Capetian lands will form a clear contrast to the paternalism of the south, as well as to the fierce patriarchalism of Norman law, so harsh towards women and towards the wishes of the dead father. The privileged position of the spouses and the great consideration given to maternal prerogatives surely provide some of our most reliable data about familial archetypes, and even about the emotional sensibility of people living on the land in the Paris Basin at the time the customs were taking shape.

As well as being favourable to the parental couple, Paris–Orléans custom (as one would expect) places a high premium on the majesty of the marriage bed. Take the case of a man married several times, with children by several of his wives. His property at death will be divided into shares whose number corresponds not to the total number of children, but to the number of wives in the conjugal career of the departed. Here we have 'division according to marriages', widespread over an area stretching from

[14] *Ibid.*, p. 38. I leave aside the problem of living-in servants, who by definition have no share in the inheritance.

[15] R. Fossier, *La Terre et les hommes en Picardie* (Louvain, 1968).

[16] J. Hilaire, *Le Régime des biens entre époux dans la région de Montpellier* (Montpellier, 1957).

the Orléanais to the Beauvaisis; this practice is quite unknown, however, in egalitarian Normandy, where equal shares are allotted to each male child, irrespective of which wife he was born to, or of whether he lives at home.[17]

Nevertheless, though they appear to remain faithful to the archetypes I have just described, the customs of the Paris–Orléans region develop from the time of the Renaissance. The changes have been on the way for a long time: already from the thirteenth to the fifteenth centuries the custumals of Paris or Amiens allowed for various improvements in the hitherto quite harsh lot of the child who left home. If, for example, the parents had a special 'revision' clause inserted into the marriage contract of their daughter or their son, the endowed child could, in spite of having left the parental roof to make his or her home elsewhere, come back after the death of the parents and claim a share in the estate. In all other cases, if this *rappel exprès* (specific revision) had not been provided for, the endowed offspring found themselves well and truly disinherited . . . This revision clause was of capital importance in the urban milieu, where, because of its ingenious flexibility, it ensured for a long time the survival of the old custom of exclusion, which, thanks to the *rappel* (revision clause), was now able to adapt itself to the most diverse situations, since it was possible to declare at any moment that it no longer applied. In rural areas, on the other hand, such a system of revision was not always easy to operate; for it was certainly rare, at least in the north of France, for peasants to treat themselves to a written contract when they got married. (It is true that their number will grow, but this comes later, with the increased volume of notaries' activities at the end of the Middle Ages, or even later still.) And without a contract, no revision clause is feasible in customary law.

This then was the old structure: exclusion, with the possibility of a revision available to varying degrees. However, new usages were instituted or simply confirmed around Paris in 1510 (they had been in existence for a long time in the Beauvaisis of Philippe de Rémi, sire de Beaumanoir). These new usages can be summed up in two words: option and restoration. It is true that to all appearances there is no great change. The previously advantaged child is still, in principle, excluded from the inheritance. In fact, if one may

[17] Yver, *Essai de géographie coutumière*, p. 273 and *passim*.

make an overworked comparison, just as in chess the moving of one piece can sometimes alter the whole balance of the game, so the insertion of a new rule makes a marked change in the spirit of customary law. From the second decade of the sixteenth century onwards, a child who has left the parental community in order to marry and make a home elsewhere, and has been endowed by the father and mother, need not be excluded from inheriting from the older generation contrary to all principles previously laid down. It is enough for this child to 'restore' to the common stock of the family fund 'what he received on marriage'.[18] After having relinquished this, he is admitted to the equal division of the common fund, together with his brothers and sisters, without any discrimination. So, after a long process of birth, traced by Yver from the thirteenth to the sixteenth century, the new system has taken shape, as the result of a simple bending of the old rules. These latter are completed by the availability of a choice between the status of *aumônier* (donee), *légataire* (legatee) or *donataire* (donee) on the one hand; and that of *héritier* (heir), *parchonnier* (co-parcener), or even *communiste* (joint-owner) on the other.[19] Whereas formerly the child at marriage (or non-marriage) headed irrevocably along one or other of these paths, he or she was now able – not, it is true, to go along both of them simultaneously – but to branch off at a later stage towards the one or the other well after marriage, and at the time the inheritance of the parents' property becomes due. That is the meaning of the famous rule '*aumônier et parchonnier nul ne peut être*' (no one may be both legatee and co-parcener), signifying that, at the decisive moment when the question of inheritance is being settled, one must opt. *Either* to stick to the rights acquired through a gift, a legacy or a dowry (or portion) received earlier during the life and from the hand of the deceased. *Or* to come back into the pool, and, in order to do so, to make restoration: to make restoration of this earlier advantage, paying it back into the common fund, thereby regaining the full right to participate as *parsonnier* (co-parcener) or member of the familiar community entitled to a whole share, in the division and devolution of the property originating in this community and passing rightfully to the heirs. So, in this new system, option and restoration are two sides of the same coin.

[18] Formulation of 1510, *ibid.*, pp. 21–2.
[19] *Ibid.*, pp. 43, 66.

These rejuvenated structures produce a law that is more flexible, more permissive, and much less concerned than formerly with preserving the integrity of the tenement. In their way, they are an expression of the relaxation of seigneurial constraint that had come about much earlier; in fact, by the sixteenth century, the seigneurial system, though it makes a very handsome ruin, is no longer powerful enough to resist the fragmenting of peasant landholdings for the benefit of heirs living elsewhere. In a more general way, this final form taken by inheritance custom reflects and completes the passing of the extended family. Since, for a long time, small nuclear family groups had predominated among the peasants of northern France, it was natural that these should be in a position to inherit without difficulty, and not be disinherited for the benefit of a wider community that now seemed more and more like a backward-looking myth. So the evolution of the superstructure of custom reflects the lessons that have belatedly been learned from the seigneurial or familial infrastructure.

Does this evolution also mirror the temporary consequences of the more relaxed demographic conditions at the end of the Middle Ages? It is permissible to ask this precise question, which has already been considered by historians of English customs within the frontiers of their own studies.[20] Since demographic pressure had eased for a time, it appears that on both sides of the Channel there was less insistence than in the past – in the fifteenth century for example – on the previously sacrosanct imperatives decreeing the conservation of the patrimony. For what was the point of restraining people in that way, when in any case there was plenty of room, plenty of land, for everyone? At least, so it was thought for a while, and that could help to account for the laxer tendencies of the 1510 compilations.

However, reaching beyond ephemeral conditions of population, these custumals express the continuous growth of egalitarianism at a more general level; spreading progressively through the rural world this current of egalitarianism will, as we know, finally submerge all the hierarchies of ordered society. But already in 1510 the next texts, which of course reflect the way people live, definitely have levelling effects: for children who practise option and restoration are back on an equal footing with their co-heirs when the

---

[20] Rosamond Faith, 'Peasant Families and Inheritance Customs in Medieval England', *Agricultural History Review*, xiv (1966).

parental property comes to be shared out. But it is true, and Yver has emphasized this strongly, that this egalitarianism is not complete. If the generously advantaged descendant, the favourite child in this case, finds it more profitable to keep his pre-inheritance portion, all he has to do is keep it when the inheritance falls due, and not come back into the division.[21] In this instance such an attitude is the result of a calculation – or miscalculation perhaps – according to which it seems better to keep the status of *aumônier* or legatee rather than acquire the lesser benefits that would be conferred by the title of heir or *parsonnier* (co-parcener).

Socially, the old Paris–Orléans custom had gone up in the world, from the obscure levels of small farms and of villeinage up to the more exalted practices of the magistrates' courts. On the other hand, the new custom that was made official in 1510 is a law that goes downwards through the social layers, as a conclusive reference proves.[22] It goes down from the legal, clerical and bourgeois élite and from urban modes of life (which favour egalitarianism and give every child his chance) down to the rural populace; as the peasants are influenced in their turn, they finally give up the fossilized habits long preserved in the old type of exclusion.

Geographically, and in spite of innumerable variants and the mutations that occurred in boundary areas, the improved system of option–restoration with its characteristics of flexibility, relative egalitarianism, and lighter seigneurial and familial restraints, is shown to extend between 1505 and 1570, the classic period for the compilation of custumals, over considerable areas. These cover a large part of the open-field country in the centre of the Paris Basin, in a zone stretching from the Beauvaisis in the north to the Orléanais and the Blois country in the south, and from Champagne in the east to the Grand Perche in the west. At the same period, enclaves of option–restoration and tempered egalitarianism are also found further north and north-west. These are tiny in Lorraine, but very sizeable in the coastal parts of Flanders, where in the classical period of the Middle Ages they take over from a system of complete equality which seems to have flourished earlier in the Flemish-speaking regions.[23]

---

[21] Yver, *Essai de géographie coutumière*, p. 253; 'Les deux groupes de coutumes du Nord', pp. 9 and 30.
[22] Yver, *Essai de géographie coutumière*, p. 253.
[23] Yver, 'Les deux groupes de coutumes du Nord'.

The west: the egalitarian and lineal extreme

In spite of the egalitarian tendencies just noted, the Paris–Orléans custom of option–restoration (formerly the system of excluding endowed children) still gave considerable weight to paternal or parental wishes, which might involve an advantage for one of the offspring; the fulfilment of these wishes might be uncertain, because the exercise of option could intervene, but they retained some influence even after the death of the person who had expressed them. On the other hand, once we cross the border into the *bocages* (hedged enclosures) and the provinces of the west (Normandy, Anjou), the western customs proclaim fiercely and frequently that the father's death is total and final: *après moi le partage* (the share-out), moans this father, whose wishes can be thus revoked. The most ancient Norman custom runs: 'Though the father has divided out his property among his children during his lifetime and each of them has long held his share in peace, yet these shares shall not be tenable after his death.'[24] In other words, the gifts, the portions, the setting up of children on marriage, occurring during the father's lifetime and with his consent, are not permanent. They are not 'firm and stable'. Necessarily insecure and subject to obligatory restoration, in no case do they deprive the child concerned of his rights as an heir to the patrimony. The father's wishes are valid only as long as he lives; when he dies, they too expire.

This type of system tends to lead straight to equality: for if parental preferences are nullified there cannot be either a favourite or an outcast among the offspring. As we have seen, egalitarianism was reached by the Paris–Orléans customs only after centuries of evolution and by means of tortuous contrivances like the *rappel* (revision clause), then option–restoration, but this aim exists right from the start in the very ancient custumal of Normandy,[25] and is strongly confirmed in that province by the new formulation of customs drawn up in 1583. This gives the children an automatic share in the estate; and in many cases, it gives them equal shares, an arrangement that leads to individualistic behaviour.

Let us take the automatic share first: the right of a child or descendant to a certain portion of an estate or of a consolidated

[24] Yver, 'Les caractères originaux du groupe de coutumes de l'Ouest de la France', *loc. cit.*; and *Essai de géographie coutumière*, ch. 2.
[25] *Ibid.*

dowry does not derive from the wishes of the spouses or of the father, as is the case respectively in the Paris region and the south. It arises simply from the place occupied in the family tree by the child in question. Having been born gives you the right to inherit, irrespective of the goodwill or ill-will of your parents. Of course, this automatic right does not always rule out injustice in allocating different shares in the estate. In Normandy, where, as we have seen, male rights are supreme, daughters are not allowed to inherit, only sons. The daughters have to find themselves a husband (it is their brother's duty to help them, if need be): and they rest content with a pittance as their share in the estate[26] (but in the other western provinces, which also practise automatic lineal inheritance but in a very strictly egalitarian spirit, non-noble daughters are admitted to the succession on an equal footing with their brothers).

On the other hand, to come back to Normandy, some parts of the province, luckily the exceptions, take inequity to the limit within the system of the automatic share: this is the case in the district of Caux, where there obtains, even among the commonalty, an English-style right of primogeniture that constitutes *ipso facto* an enormous disadvantage for younger sons.

But let us beware of failing to see the wood for the trees. In Normandy itself (except for the Caux district) popular law knows no right of primogeniture as a 'general custom'; it has equality between male heirs quite unequivocally as its first provision. How desirable this would look to the young men of the Midi, of Wallonia, or even of the old Capetian lands, who are often disinherited by their parents in so cavalier a fashion!

This spirit of complete equality comes fully into play when, leaving Normandy but still staying within the broad region of western customs, we enter the Breton and Angevin domain. There too the customs, often drawn up in the sixteenth century, forcefully proclaim an egalitarianism which is not merely superficial, but intrinsic, and which this time concerns all offspring, boys *and* girls. For example, the texts of Touraine and Anjou whether they were drawn up in the thirteenth century or at the Renaissance, are explicit on this.[27] The customs of Maine are no less firm: they lead inevitably to egalitarianism among the common people, which is in direct opposition, all along a class barrier, to the nobility's

26 Yver, 'Les caractères . . . de l'Ouest de la France', p. 32.
27 Yver, *Essai de géographie coutumière*, p. 113.

right of primogeniture. 'For the custom is that no person who is not noble may make the condition of any of his heirs presumptive worse or better for one than for another.'

We hear the same tune in Brittany. The common people, unlike the nobles, may not advantage any of their heirs. 'The children of burgesses or other people of low condition must be as great the one as the other, as well in goods as in inheritance.'[28] And in the revolts of 1590 and 1675 the Breton peasants will make it their business to show that for them egalitarian claims are not just a legalistic formula or an empty phrase. On the other hand, the gentlemen of Armorica, and other persons 'possessing blood', as the expression went, enjoyed, as a privilege, the power to favour one or other of their heirs, for example by making use of the *préciput*[29] (preferential legacy).

Hostile to this inequality practised by the nobles, egalitarianism among the lower orders appears again, still in the west, as far as Poitou. There, in spite of the influence of *préciput*, coming from the south and the statute-law regions, there reigns the maxim forbidding the parents to 'make one of their heirs better than another'.[30]

These levelling tendencies so strongly rooted in western France are not, however, confined to one geographical area: they are to be found a long way from this region, even to the east of the eastern boundaries of the Paris–Orléans zone practising option–restoration – in Champagne and in Brie. There we find a curiously isolated enclave of *complete* equality which President de Thou, trying to spread the Parisian ideas of *simple* equality and option, will attempt in vain to subdue. 'No more to one than to another' – that will be the reply given to him in 1556, as with one voice, by the jurists of Champagne and of Brie.[31]

Opposed as they were to inequality between heirs, these different customs tend objectively to devalue parental or paternal roles in favour of the group of 'rightful inheritors', whether these be sons (in Normandy) or sons and daughters (in the other western provinces). In a world where, statistically speaking, adults died before reaching a very advanced age, this attitude must work out on average in favour of very young heirs, who could be adolescents or even small children. Let us say, to follow a line that is nowadays

28 *Ibid.*, p. 122.
30 *Ibid.*, p. 127.
29 *Ibid.*, p. 123, note.
31 *Ibid.*, pp. 145–6.

fashionable in research, that these western customs implied a certain idea about childhood and in the end a very positive appreciation of it. Which is more than can be said, for example, about the law in the south.

Whatever the value of such an incursion into the domain of psychological history, strict equality, as practised in the western provinces, entails a 'restoration' after the death of the father that is no longer optional, as was the case in the Paris region, but obligatory. This system of 'forced restoration', *voulist ou non*, willy-nilly, is especially strict in Normandy. There, in accordance with the rule that after the father's death cancels the arrangements he made for his children during his lifetime, the heirs are obliged to restore to the common stock of property subject to division by inheritance, all the liberalities, gifts, portions and advantages granted to them by the deceased before his death. In such a system, there is no chance of obtaining, or at any rate of keeping, the special status of *enfant chéri* (favourite child).

The customs of Maine and Anjou seem a little more flexible in this respect than that of Normandy: but on the whole it really comes to very much the same thing: for after his father's death the Angevin heir who was advantaged during his lifetime, has to restore not the whole of this advantage but the surplus: that is to say, the amount by which his endowment exceeds the share that would normally fall to him under a system of complete equality. 'And if it should so happen that a son had received too great a share and did not wish to come back into the division of the estate of the father and mother, and the others should say to him "You have had too great a share", then his share would be examined by a council of wise men: and if he had had too much, he must make just return to them . . .'[32] This rule about restoring the surplus can go a long way: in its crudest local variants, it extends to movables and acquisitions, with a single exception covering gifts made to children and young people when they went to school, were fitted out for the wars, or got married. Interpreted in this way egalitarianism goes so far that disadvantaged children may always come back when the estate is being settled and claim the excess unfairly held by more 'favoured' brothers or sisters, even if these disadvantaged children are madmen, spendthrifts, or loose women.[33]

[32] *Ibid.*, pp. 111–12.   [33] *Ibid.*, p. 111.

Yver has made an excellent job of extracting the philosophy underlying these systems of the west of France. In the main, they do not accord a privileged position to the parental couple, nor to the consolidation of the agricultural tenement, both of which, in the earlier Paris system, benefited from the exclusion of the advantaged child. The western systems are not concerned about the danger of fragmentation; they scorn the double unit consisting of the spouses and the estate. Fundamentally, they favour the long, ramified continuity of the lineage: in other words, throughout the generations, the unbroken succession of descendants, down which property flows, is harmoniously shared according to the main stems, the branches and the furthest forks, twigs and stalks of the line. In Norman and Angevin customs, the property seems to descend like sap flowing downwards, according to some mysterious force, to nourish the lower limbs and offshoots of a tall tree. The final aim is to grant to each child, and beyond him to the progeny he will engender, a fair and equal share of the original property, issued from the common stock of the *gens*. For their part, the Capetian customs are concerned with the stability of the family household; before all else, they strengthen the union of the Christian couple, who virtuously are one flesh, share all their worldly goods. and endeavour to order the life of their offspring so as best to ensure what they consider the perpetuation of the family property, which must be protected as far as possible against dispersal through fragmentation. The customs of the west, on the contrary (and also other customs observed in places outside the west – in Brie, Champagne, and early Flanders), choose to give preference to the ancient claims of lineage. Faithful to the formula *paterna paternis, materna maternis* (the father's property to the father's kind, the mother's property to the mother's kind), they attach only slight importance to the act of marriage which they seem to regard as an ephemeral union of two perishable creatures, each issued from a different line whose own value lies in its permanence. Therefore these western customs give first priority to the strict circulation of inheritances along the genealogical method. They are archaic, and appear sometimes to originate (in the case of the Normans) in the distant Scandinavian and even pre-Christian past of the ethnic group. And yet, paradoxically, they are vehicles of modernity. For most of them manage to rise at the first attempt, even in the oldest formulations, to that ideal of complete egalitarianism and even of

fierce individualistic insistence on shares that Paris–Orléans jurisprudence will attain late in the day, and then only hesitantly, in-
completely, and by doing violence to its own structure.

From this follows a whole series of 'special characteristics'
typical of western customs, the first of these being the dominance
of *per capita* division, and the absence of shares arising out of a
conjugal union alone. There is nothing surprising in this. The
marriage bed is a piece of furniture, an ephemeral link between
one lineage and another, and as such is not highly valued by the
customs of Normandy, which are concerned with the branches,
forks, and furthermost buds of a family tree, but not with the
passing alliances it may contract, through marriage, with some
other line. On the other hand, the people of the west unanimously
practise representation *ad infinitum*; logically, this was absent from
the Paris–Orléans customs, in so far at least as they excluded, at
their most archaic period, the previously advantaged child. And
indeed, why, if I have disinherited my daughter after providing
her with a dowry, would I allow the son of this now deceased
daughter to exercise his rights in my estate, and be represented
in the division of my property? On the contrary, in 1510, when
the force of the Parisian clause on the exclusion of the advantaged child is weakened, the lawyers drawing up the new
text, acting perfectly in accordance with their own logic, will
hasten to introduce into their formulae representation in the direct
line.[34]

Now in all the regions of western France the first customs, and
after them the later formulations, proclaim the representative
system from the very outset and without hesitation. This is quite
natural: for in this way these customs favour consanguinity and
encourage the most distant buds and twigs, right at the end of a
descending family line, to be represented in the inheritance; and
finally, if one of the branches becomes sterile and dies, thus ceasing
for ever to produce scions, these western customs have no hesitation
in making the property of this branch revert to the nearest fork,
in ascent, backwards in time; that is, back to a member of an
earlier generation, the better to make that property descend again
freely along the natural slope of the lineage, towards the still fertile
branches, issued from the collateral line, which also goes back to

[34] *Ibid.*, pp. 21 and 266.

the same fork.[35] Thus in the province of the west the rule that *'propres ne remontent'* (property shall not ascend) is foiled. But this rule is favoured by the Paris–Orléans customs:[36] this was natural, since, in order to favour parental dispositions, they would quite shamelessly cut off the upstream and downstream currents of the lineage when they thought fit. Let us say that the parent-oriented structure is typical of the customs of the west; whereas the community— and couple—oriented models are characteristic of the great Capetian open-field area and its scattering of worthy towns.

From the same cause, in the western part of the kingdom the rule of *paterna paternis, materna maternis* is also strictly applied.[37] Everything proceeds as we have remarked, as if marriage merely created a fragile link between the two branches, each stemming from a different lineage, a link moreover that was without consequences, if it remained without issue: the customs of the west smile on children, but not on love. The most extreme among them, notably those of Brittany and Normandy, reduce this rule to the absurd: in the absence of offspring of a union, rather than give the property coming from the paternal line to non-lineal outsiders on the distaff side, they prefer to hand it over to the local lord, or even (what a catastrophe for a dead Norman, born law-dodger that he was!) choose rather to abandon it to the tax-collector! As a jurist coolly writes, as late as the eighteenth century, in a humour-less text in which he comments on these habits that come straight from the barbarism in lineal inheritance: 'the paternal and maternal kin are not co-heirs. They have nothing in common, and the local seigneur would succeed, rather than a paternal relative to a maternal one.'[38]

One could continue almost indefinitely, instancing the consequences of this somewhat caricature preoccupation of the Normans with safeguarding the lineage. Actually, though they seem strange to us, they are entirely logical. Still, it will be better

---

[35] Yver, 'Les caractères originaux du groupe de coutumes de l'Ouest de la France', citing R. Besnier, *La coutume de Normandie* (Paris, 1935).

[36] Yver, *ibid.*, p. 38; and also, for some interesting problems concerning the boundaries between customs, *ibid.*, p. 61 note 2.

[37] 'The father's property to the father's kin, the mother's property to the mother's kin.'

[38] Yver, 'Les caractères originaux du groupe de coutumes de l'Ouest de la France', citing H. Basnage, *Oeuvres*, 4th edn, 2 vols (Rouen, 1788).

to go on and touch briefly, within the limited framework of the present study, on the problems of causes. And Yver, fascinated though he is by the description of structures, does not evade the difficult question of origins. How came there to be, in the ancient lands of the west, this formidable block of customs tending variously towards lineal, egalitarian, partible, and finally (only an apparent paradox) individualistic systems of inheritance? Yver's suggested explanation takes us back to the eleventh century and even further; it moves, with delicate caution, in the direction of three types of causality, namely: one, the political configuration of the region and the nature of its boundaries; two, its social and seigneurial (or rather non-seigneurial) history; and finally, in the last analysis, the possible influence of the ethnic background.

Let us deal with the political history first. However unlikely this may seem as a way of elucidating the origins of custumals, it is certain that this history did play a part – for example, in the crystallization of Norman customs. For that crystallization occurs over an area corresponding almost exactly to the boundaries of the old duchy. And this 'almost exactly' is itself significant for the purposes of our demonstration: for it is by means of his study of the 'anomalies' found in marginal districts (and in particular the case of the curious enclave constituted on the eastern edge of the province by a group of twenty-four parishes that had kept the Beauvais law) that R. Genestal has been able to date the crystallization of Norman law to the reign of William the Bastard.[39] On a wider view, it may seem that on several occasions it is the whole of the western *bocage* or woodland country that stands out from the rest; in the times of the dukes of Normandy, in the case of the northern part; and under the Plantagenets, in the south. Does this isolationism go back, as Yver suggests on one of the very rare occasions when he allows himself to hypothesize freely, to the creation of the *Tractus armoricanus* at the end of the Roman Empire?

However that may be, and without our having to 'regress' so far, it is certain that political demarcations had something to do with the existence of that sharply drawn line, at the level of customary law, which separates the *bocages* and other regions of the west from those that formed the 'Capetian' heart of France.

---

[39] Referred to by Yver, *ibid.*, p. 5, note 2.

However, the study of origins cannot stop at these assertions which, if taken literally, are rather too reminiscent of the dear old history of events. Yver is a legal historian, but also an enthusiast of social history, and he does not separate the genesis of his groups of customs from the general background conditions nor even from the precise level of society, where they find the environment most suitable to their development. Unlike the customs of Paris–Orléans perhaps, Norman law was not born under the abject conditions of villeinage; it is more the creation of a superior stratum of free yeomen,[40] not yet won over, with the exception of the Caux district, to the snobbery of primogeniture (which is to become widespread in England); but since they are sure of their right, and not much in danger of encroachment by the seigneur on their rural holding, the chief desire of these men is to hand down equitably, to each of their descendants, his uncontested due. The miraculous existence of an already efficient political and judicial constitution, and of a more open social structure, where the peasant population, freed from serfdom,[41] was not sunk in seigneurial dependence so deeply as elsewhere, allowed, if we accept Yver's ingenious description, the rapid diffusion or 'percolation' of this law of lineage and free men right down through society, from the superior groups who were present at its birth to the lower classes who accepted it in the heyday of the dukedom of Normandy.

Lastly, the author whose path we are following does not avoid dealing with the difficult material concerning the remotest origins of customs; and indeed these origins supply explanatory data which, though by no means exhaustive, are essential. The case of Norman custom has all the conditions most helpful in this pilgrimage to the sources, which are not always present in other regions. If we use a Dumézil-style approach, a rapid survey of the old Scandinavian laws allows us to observe some important facts. In the homelands of the Vikings, we are a long way from the habits beloved of the Germanic customs in the proper sense of the term; as we have seen, these propounded, in the Parisian fashion, first the exclusion of advantaged children, then option–restoration. But the laws of Magnus Hakonarson in Norway, the Jonsbok of Iceland in 1281, the customs of Scania, and of Sjaelland in Denmark, offer the historian of comparative law rules very similar,

---

[40] Yver, *Essai de géographie coutumière*, pp. 109 and 120.
[41] Yver, 'Les deux groupes de coutumes du Nord', p. 4.

right down to the smallest details, to the oldest law of the Normans (and so, probably, of the Vikings): strict equalization of shares in an inheritance, scrupulously measured out, and vouched for by twelve sworn co-jurors, obligatory restoration, and so on. So the Nordic contribution to the shaping of at least a part of the customs of north-west France is not necessarily negligible. Structural description does lead in this case, as in Dumézil, to the explanation of origins.

The ' préciput' and 'household' extreme

Compared with the hybrid solutions of Paris–Orléans law, stuck halfway between freedom to advantage an heir on the one hand and complete equality on the other, the customs of Normandy and, even more, those of western France in general, represent the lineage-favouring polarization towards complete egalitarianism, infused widely into an old peasant and non-noble culture. At the other extreme, we have the Provençal-speaking south and the whole group of regions practising *préciput*[42] – some of them situated far to the north. These offer us an example of the opposite tendency, highly favourable to the freedom to advantage one heir above another. The Normans killed off the father. But the Romans, whose law will have such a strong influence on the peoples of southern France, believed on the contrary that the father's wishes survive in this world even when he himself has passed on to a better one.

At the end of the Middle Ages and up until the sixteenth century these patriarchial and paternalist ideas, directly implanted into the Midi by the renaissance of Roman law, had easily taken root in the plains and hills of the south, on the old substratum (predating this renaissance) formed by a local customary law that was tacit and imperfectly known: about this 'old substratum' and this *taisible* (tacit) law, we know only, from a few scattered texts[43] and

[42] The *préciput* systems, in the terminology of legal historians and in particular of Jean Yver, are those that allow a father to confer a permanent advantage, by gift or by will, on one or other of his children or heirs: Yver, *Essai de géographie coutumière*, pp. 155 and 158.

[43] Cf. the earliest of the customs of Montpellier (thirteenth century) which contain both the old customary disposition of exclusion of endowed children and even at that date the typically Roman right of the father to prefer as he wishes one or other of his children: Yver, *ibid.*, pp. 25 and 156.

especially from the practice of rural notaries,[44] that it was markedly non-egalitarian, and that, just like the most archaic customs of the Paris–Orléans zone, it encouraged the exclusion of advantaged children. In this case, the aim was always to preserve the familial and patriarchal indivisibility of the peasant tenement, under the high authority of the local seigneur, though this to be sure was pretty decrepit.

Thus the tendencies towards freedom to favour an heir, which is so dear to renascent Roman law, will germinate in southern France on a substratum and soil that are already fertile. At the Renaissance, the modern Languedoc paterfamilias, encouraged by the jurisprudence of the local courts, will be able to go back to being more Roman than Christian (with the easy manner born of old habit, as well as the clear conscience conferred by juridical modernity). Whereas in the southern zones the mother, whose presence is so strongly felt in Orléanais or Parisian custom, fades more than ever into the background, amid trivial household tasks. On the wide keyboard which, with its diversity of methods, allowed tenements to be protected against excessive fragmentation, the north used to play the theme of the exclusion of portioned children, or else, in the special case of the Caux district and the Boulogne area, that of a stern commoners' primogeniture; the Normans, though they were so strict about equal shares, practised automatic disinheritance of daughters in favour of male heirs. But now the southern paterfamilias fights against fragmentation by using the right to advantage,[45] *préciput*, donation *inter vivos*, and the testamentary absolutism of statute law, all of which were aimed at securing a larger share for one of the children, not necessarily the eldest. So this favoured descendant will succeed to virtually the whole of the family land or plot (often after a period of co-residence during his parents' lifetime). Whereas the other children must be satisfied with portions of varying degrees of meagreness, with crumbs distributed in the will, or with a *légitime* or legal share

---

[44] Hilaire, *op. cit.*; L. de Charrin, *Les Testaments dans la région de Montpellier* (Montpellier, 1961), especially the conclusion.

[45] Among the main customs of the Midi influenced by Roman law (Montpellier, Bordeaux, Bayonne, Agen) and cited by Yver in this connection, we need refer here only to the ancient custom of Agen: 'the father may prefer any child he wishes, *as* he wishes' (quoted by Yver, *Essai de géographie coutumière*, p. 157, note 305). For rural practice, cf. Hilaire, *op. cit.*

that is merely a custom-prescribed hand-out of a few sous.[46] At this point, these underprivileged offspring run the risk of falling into the proletariat, if they are of the people; or into the church, if they come from the middle or upper classes.[47]

The 'anti-paternal' west, egalitarian as it was, and in favour of automatic succession, did not trust wills.[48] The Midi, on the contrary, uses them as an instrument for spreading inequality, perpetuating the father's arbitrary power, and preserving the family property intact.

And so the characteristic devices that had been included in the Paris–Orléans customs at the end of the Middle Ages and in the sixteenth century in order to encourage a tardy, even a tempered egalitarianism, fall to the ground, or rather, don't exist, in the Midi. Southern jurisprudence contains no option, readily gives dispensation from restoration,[49] and could not care less about the dilemma of 'legatee or heir' that is so agonizing in the Paris–Orléans region.

Now another remarkable fact: even north of the traditional dividing line running from Saintonge to Bresse and separating the southern regions of statute law from the northern regions of custom, the rights concerning *préciput* (preferential legacies), which are entirely hostile to egalitarianism, have influenced very large areas. This shows clearly at the great period of custom-compilation (the sixteenth century), and there are many indications that we are concerned here with a situation dating from earlier times. Thus the group of 'central' provinces, forming, according to how one looks at it, the northern limits of the Provençal-speaking south, or the southern limits of the northern dialects, represents a disputed battleground, where influences coming from the Midi, favouring *préciput* or against egalitarianism, fight it out, often victoriously, with the egalitarianism of the north; whether it be a matter, in Poitou, of the 'absolute egalitarianism' of the west, or, in Burgundy and Berry, of the 'tempered egalitarianism' of the new-style Paris–Orléans group, which sporadically practised the system of option–restoration from the end of the Middle Ages. Thus, in the different

---

[46] De Charrin, *op. cit.*

[47] H. Forster, *The Nobility of Toulouse in the 18th Century* (Baltimore, 1960).

[48] Yver, *Essai de géographie coutumière*, p. 156.

[49] Texts of the *parlements* of Toulouse and Bordeaux, dated respectively 1584 and 1587 (Yver, *Essai de géographie coutumière*, p. 158).

sectors of this 'central' region (Auvergne–Marche, Poitou–
Angoumois–Saintonge, Berry–Bourbonnais–Nivernais, Burgundy),
we find, in competition with the customs having a precipitate of
egalitarianism, juridical and cultural features that have a very
strong 'whiff of the south'. Let me mention rapidly, referring you
for the details to Yver's subtle analyses: donations *inter vivos*,[50]
enjoyed through the use of *préciput*, with no question of 'restoration' later; dispensation from restoration; donations by *préciput*
of the whole estate except for the ear-marked *légitime* (legal share
falling necessarily to the heirs); and the pluralist enjoyment of the
dual status of legatee and heir. In certain cases at the end of the
Middle Ages, for example in Berry,[51] custom made use of option
and was relatively egalitarian; but during the Renaissance it comes
down on the side of the southern habit of *préciput*, which favours
the 'liberty' of the father. Hence the name given to the processes
of this kind: 'liberalization' – somewhat misleading to the un-
initiated. In fact, in this respect we are witnessing a real 'southern-
izing' of the Centre provinces, right in the midst of the sixteenth
century. In some regions (as in Auvergne) phenomena of this type
may be explained by the common culture of southern France,
which makes quite natural the spread of the statute law now
typical of this dominant southern ethos. Due account must also
be taken of the prestige attaching to a learned law, which is exactly
what Roman law is: it is clear that the Renaissance would have
been especially favourable to its spread. But, fundamentally, is not
the continuance or the triumph, as the case may be, of an anti-
egalitarian law, opposed to fragmentation, favouring the father's
authority, also linked, in central and southern France, to the still
very recently persisting familial, even *taisible* (tacit) communities?;
at any rate, the spirit behind them is very different from that found
in the egalitarian, individualist, land-fragmenting (and lineage-
vaunting) phratries that are rampant in Normandy. This fact seems
clear enough in the Nivernais country, where analyses of the jurist
Guy Coquille, who writes in the middle of the sixteenth century,
bear witness both to the firm implantation of these familial com-

50 Cf. for example, in Auvergne: Yver, *Essai de géographie coutumière*,
p. 160. On donation *inter vivos*, seen as belonging to statute law, as opposed
to the customary law of the north, cf. Molière, *Le Malade imaginaire*,
act I, scene 7 and *passim*.
51 Yver, *Essai de géographie coutumière*, p. 166.

munities[52] and to the unrivalled prestige of the right of *préciput*. This is even more the case (or rather, to be more precise, the case is even more clearly and perfectly demonstrated) in the regions covering the north-east, and especially the extreme north, of the *langue d'oïl* speaking part of France. But in the north, I hasten to point out, our demonstration deals with structures some of which 'survive' in the sixteenth century, if one may use the expression, only as fossils.

In fact, far distant from the Mediterranean zones from whence Roman law launched its successive conquests, there exists a '*préciput*-group' of the north-east and the north; it involves to varying degrees Lorraine, the Verdun area, and the Vermandois; and especially Wallonia and Picardy, which it is instructive to compare systematically with neighbouring Flanders, where the customs are different.

The *préciput*-practising zone of Wallonia–Picardy extends roughly from Amiens to Liège.[53] In the sixteenth century, at the time the customs were being recorded, the following practices are widespread: 'liberalism' of the father and the mother (in other words, the freedom to advantage an heir); absence of or dispensation from restoration, notably for donations *inter vivos*; the simultaneous enjoyment of the status of legatee and heir (*aumônier* and *parchonnier*, in local parlance); the granting of a *préciput* or 'advance share'; the general maxim 'to the one more, to the other less'; and 'the power of the father, mother, and ascendants to confer on marriage settlements the character of a *préciput*'.[54] Nowhere is this 'liberalism' (in the worst sense of the word!) carried further than in the depths of the rural and traditional zone of the *bailliage* of Orchies and Douai, where the texts proclaim both complete dispensation from restoration, and the simultaneous enjoyment of the roles of heir and legatee.

Walloon liberalism, anti-egalitarian and pro-*préciput*, is all the more suggestive and striking because it forms a violent contrast, along a frontier roughly corresponding to the linguistic boundary,

---

[52] Texts and conclusive analyses in G. Thuillier, *Aspects de l'économie nivernaise au XIX* siècle* (Paris, 1966), pp. 32–45.
[53] This zone includes the Amiens region, Artois, Cambrésis, Hainault, French Flanders and the Walloon country.
[54] Yver, *Essai de géographie coutumière*, pp. 201–21; and 'Les deux groupes de coutumes du Nord', pp. 17–213.

with the Flemish custumals, of which there are several hundred: these, unlike the others just mentioned, lay down a system of simple equality that makes use of option, and forbids 'making one child a favourite', a *chier enffant* or *lief kindr*. In certain extreme cases (which may be typical of the most ancient stratum of Flemish-language custumals), one even finds, in Flanders, localized enclaves of complete equality, practising compulsory restoration, and reminding one of the Norman structures.

In fact, the comparison between Wallonia and Flanders can be taken a very long way: *préciput* and freedom to advantage an heir, which are characteristic of the French-speakers of the extreme north, form part of a general architecture of customs and even of families that contrasts point by point with its Flemish-language opposite numbers. If Picard–Walloon gives first place to the easy conveyance, large shares in the estate, and massive donations made possible by the right to advantage (whereas the Flemish laws, on the contrary, try to ensure an equal and just share in the inheritance right down to the furthermost ramifications and sprouts of the family tree), it does so in order to encourage (in Wallonia) the household community, functioning first for the benefit of the spouses, and then for that of the children who consent to remain part of it; and it does so (still in Wallonia) at the expense of scattered members of the lineage, of collateral branches and '*détronqué*' children; whereas in Flanders scattered members of the line are the primary consideration. In the same spirit, non-noble Wallonia lays down (but Flanders rejects) *ravestissement* (the award of the *whole* joint patrimony, if one of the couple dies, to the surviving spouse); this *ravestissement* becomes possible as soon as the couple have proved definitely that they are one flesh, by producing a baby, even if it is the only one, even if it dies young; so long as it has had time, even though it be only a moment, to '*braire et crier*', to 'howl and bawl'! Contradicting as it does in this way the rule *paterna paternis*, and contesting the principle that the patrimony should go to the lineage on the two separate sides, in order the better to ensure the fusion of the spouses' property into one 'household' fund, the Picard–Walloon area cannot do otherwise than practise quite naturally 'division according to marriages'; and not, of course, as happens in so many Flemish cantons, indiscriminate *per capita* division 'between the children of all the marriages, without distinction'. With the same intention of giving preference to the conjugal community, Wallonia (once again unlike Flanders) also adopts a system of devolution, which means, in practice, that real estate coming from the father and the mother goes to the children of the first marriage.[55] Lastly, as a similar consequence of an immutable logic, we find here again in Wallonia–Picardy the classic measures of exclusion so dear to all the customs which (like the earliest Paris–Orléans structures) prize above all, even at the expense of members of the lineage, the perpetuation of the household community and the keeping intact of its land, which must if possible survive as a unit even after the death of the parents. Picards and Walloons, therefore, practise to differing degrees discrimination against endowed children; they allot an inferior situation to daughters; and they exclude bastard children whereas Flanders, which is decidedly lineal, and utterly faithful to the rule of *materna maternis* as embodying the sovereign rights conferred through the act of giving birth, Flanders proudly proclaims that 'een moder maakt geen bastaard' – ('no one is a bastard through his mother').[56] In the French-speaking regions of the extreme north, one sometimes finds also the law of *maineté* (the awarding of the *mez* or family house in its entirety to the youngest child, that is to the one who in all statistical probability will live in longest and latest co-residence with his parents). On all these points, most Flemish customs are once more in radical opposition to their Walloon and Picard counterparts.

In the case of the latter, the crucial test remains the absence of representation. We are in the presence here of a real primitive feature in Walloon customs, since, as Yver writes, 'a custom that pays such scant regard to equality between children had no reason to be any more particular, if one of them should predecease the others, about seeing that his share should go instead to his children'.[57]

But Flanders, on the contrary (most anxious, like Normandy, to pass on 'to each his due') practises conscientiously, and almost perversely, representation *ad infinitum*, 'even to the hundredth degree and beyond', as the 1545 Custumal of Antwerp declares in all seriousness.[58] One of the inevitable consequences of this

[55] *Ibid.*, pp. 13 and 209.
[56] *Ibid.*, pp. 16–36 and note 3.
[57] *Ibid.*, pp. 21, 217.
[58] *Ibid.*, pp. 8, 28.

divergence of attitudes is the absence in Picardy–Wallonia of the curious institution of the *fente*, or 'split' (absent also from the old Paris–Orléans customs). For in cases where descendants die without issue, and collateral kinsmen inherit, the Picards and Walloons give the movables and acquisitions belonging to the patrimony of the deceased descendant to the nearest relative. But Flemish custom goes the other way, and, faithful to the distinction between one lineage and another, and to representation *ad infinitum*, it literally splits this heir-less patrimony down the middle like a log, and shares it out half and half between the members of the father's and the mother's lines; and even divides it into quarters or eighths, between members of the lines of the four grandparents and eight great-grandparents!

This polarization of Wallonia, in the direction of a household- or even *manse*-oriented jurisprudence, unfavourable to lineage, probably reflects the existence of a distinct political territory and a well-defined cultural zone, these differences also being strongly emphasized by the linguistic individuation; should we read into it the clear effect of social structure? In this hypothesis, cautiously advanced by Yver on the basis of a suggestive text,[59] the pro-family-community law of the Walloons would be initially that of a population of dependant peasants, or *meisenedien*, who have to take careful account of the precarious, barely hereditary nature of the holding of their tenement or their *manse;* and who therefore attach prime importance to what constitutes their only protection: the unity of the couple and the continuity of the land-tenure. While Flemish law, just like Norman customs, would represent, inside the framework of another ethnic group and a different culture, the habits of a stratum of free men, accustomed to more liberty of action; men able to put into practice for the individual members of their own lineage the egalitarian formula 'to each man according to his right', precisely because they are not imprisoned by the iron constraint of the seigneurial system.

But of course the main thing is not this hypothesis, which, its author himself admits, is only exploratory. What is important is that thanks to Yver we now have a grid that fits over the apparent chaos of French customs, whose diversity puts one in mind of a kind of Disneyland, and introduces into it a Cartesian logic and rigour. Around the two opposite poles, that of genealogical *con-*

[59] Yver, 'Les deux groupes de coutumes du Nord'.

sanguinity and that of *alliance* through marriage, antinomic solutions take shape at both extremes of the curve of possibilities; thus egalitarianism and lineage-favouring egoism contrast with the right to advantage heirs for the benefit of community and household. From this point of view, Normandy and Flanders are seen to be, each in its own fashion, at the antipodes of Wallonia or the south of France. In between, we have been able to discern hybrid or centrist constructions, in a continual state of imbalance and movement (as in the Paris–Orléans region). Isolated features – some important, others mere freaks – such as *ad infinitum* representation, or the *fente* (or 'split'), have fallen into their logical place in this or that regional configuration. Last but not least, this grid I have been speaking of can be used to account not only for actual custumals, but for the whole body of possible customs in the territory under consideration.

The highly deductive nature of the model we are offered by no means implies that on this occasion Clio is breaking off relations with empirical reality as it existed in the past. When he pulls the geographical study of customs out of the rut of purely factual description and guides it, quite logically, towards comparative methods, Yver is coming back ultimately to the best-tried paths of historical comprehension. For when he studies a series of northern regions that because of their ethnic background and their bias in favour of lineage, practise egalitarianism from an early date (Normandy, Flanders) or that are trying to achieve it by means of a tempered but vigorous evolution (the Paris–Orléans region), he is confirming the discoveries that historians made long ago about the earliest rural revolts, that were also inspired by the quest for equality; whether in the case of the rebellion of Norman peasants described by Wace, that of the Flemings, studied by Henri Pirenne, or that of the fourteenth-century peasants in the Ile-de-France and the Beauvaisis (the *Jacquerie*). Formidable egalitarian traditions, then, often but not everywhere go into action among the common people in the northern half of France. They are of interest to the historians of development, who observe in them the early advent of modernity in the north of France; and they should also be highly interesting to specialists in the French Revolution, concerned with the eternal problem of its origins. Finally, what emerges from Jean Yver's extraordinarily minute and meticulous researches (provided of course that they are brought down from their limpid firmament and constantly supplemented, strengthened or corrected by researches in the field, using notarial registers and legal documents) – what emerges is a new approach to the history of the family. The extended families of the Massif Central and the Nivernais, the marriage-alliance household communities of the old Ile-de-France or Picardy–Wallonia, the Flemish and Norman lineage-observing groups which paradoxically give rise to individualism and egoism – all these are not merely discernible (with some difficulty) at the level of private life and collective manifestations. In the sixteenth century and even well before that, they have left, in the custumals, an indelible mark.

3. Inheritance, land tenure and peasant family structure: a German regional comparison*

LUTZ K. BERKNER

Our conception of peasant family structure is very much based on the relationship between property rights and residence. Property rights are determined by land tenure and transmitted through inheritance. When the land is not divided and the property rights are inherited by a single heir, we usually speak of *impartible* inheritance, and this is often associated with a residential pattern of 'stem family' households formed by the co-residence of the parents and one married child. When the land is divided and the property rights are inherited by all or several children, we usually speak of *partible* inheritance, which is associated with a residential pattern of separate 'nuclear family' households formed as each child marries and establishes a new household on his portion of land.[1] The purpose of this essay is to demonstrate this relationship by comparing peasant households in two regions of Germany which had different inheritance systems at the end of the seventeenth century.

It is not easy to define an inheritance system because inheritance may refer to the laws, the customs, or the actual practices, and the three need not correspond. Inheritance laws require that the family property be distributed in certain proportions, ranging from

* The research for this paper was made possible by a grant from the Ford and Rockefeller Foundations' Program in Support of Social Science and Legal Research in Population Policy. I want to thank Franklin F. Mendels, John W. Shaffer, Carol Srole, Nancy Fitch, Joel Singer, Fedwa Douglas, Richard Quintino, Evelyn Nagai and Joanne Ratkovitch for their help on various aspects of this project.

[1] There is also the third possibility of partible inheritance and co-residence of the married brothers to form joint family households. These are old themes with many variations in terminology and emphasis recently restated in the cross-cultural study by Walter Goldschmidt and E. J. Kunkel, 'The Structure of the Peasant Family', *American Anthropologist*, lxxiii (1971), pp. 1058–76. The classic historical study of inheritance and family structure is George Homans, *English Villagers of the Thirteenth Century* (Cambridge, Mass., 1941) and there is an excellent anthropological discussion of the older historical literature in Jack Goody, *Death, Property and the Ancestors* (London, 1962), pp. 273–327.

equal portions for all the children to favouring a single heir. But they rarely determine the form of the settlement, which depends on the land tenure, the peasant customs, or economic conditions. If the farms are held on short term leases or by personal serfs with insecure rights of succession, the land may not even be part of the inheritance. When the land is held under a secure form of impartible tenure, it must be passed intact to a single heir and the other children will be compensated in some other way, no matter how equal their inheritance rights are. But if the land tenure does not restrict the division of the land, then peasant customs and other conditions play an important role in determining the practices.[2]

By 'customs' we mean the peasants' traditional rules of behaviour. These are often based on older common law, and they may come into conflict with statutory laws imposed from outside. One of the best documented cases is the maintenance of impartible customs in the Pyrenees against the equal inheritance provisions of the French Civil Code.[3] Although we usually think of customs as being the traditional practices, Cole and Wolf have shown in their recent study of two villages in the Tyrol that inheritance customs may also become an 'ideology' which is not carried out in practice.[4] The peasants might say that the holdings ought to be divided among their children, they may actually give each of them the right to certain parts of the land, but in fact the management of the farm is transferred to only one child who either rents from or eventually buys out the other heirs. The farm is divided in principle, but it is kept intact as an economic unit by agreement among the heirs.

[2] L. K. Berkner and F. F. Mendels, 'Inheritance Systems, Family Structure, and Demographic Patterns in Western Europe (1700–1900)', in Charles Tilley (ed.), *Historical Studies of Changing Fertility* (Princeton, 1976) examines these conditions in more detail. H. J. Habakkuk, 'Family Structure and Economic Change in Nineteenth-Century Europe', *Journal of Economic History*, xv (1955), pp. 1–12 includes a good short survey of inheritance laws. For the special problems of serfs see Andrejs Plakans, 'Seigneurial Authority and Peasant Family Life: The Baltic Area in the Eighteenth Century', *Journal of Interdisciplinary History*, v (1975), pp. 629–54.

[3] Pierre Bourdieu, 'Célibat et condition paysanne', *Etudes rurales*, v–vi (1962), pp. 32–135 and 'Les stratégies matrimoniales dans le système de reproduction', *Annales E.S.C.*, xxvii (1972), pp. 1105–27. The excellent work on the legal history of the Pyrenees is brought together in Jacques Poumarède, *Les successions dans le sud-ouest de la France au moyen âge* (Paris, 1972).

[4] John W. Cole and Eric R. Wolf, *The Hidden Frontier: Ecology and Ethnicity in an Alpine Valley* (New York, 1974), pp. 175–205.

We would always like to know what the actual practices are, but this requires a detailed study of family contracts and land records, which is difficult enough to do for a few villages, let alone a whole region. The first regional surveys of inheritance practices in Germany were prepared in the late nineteenth century, based on questionnaires answered by local officials. They established a general division between the partible practices in the southwest, and the impartible practices in the north and east. The line on the map (p. 75) roughly indicates this division, but it should not be taken literally, and there were many regional pockets of mixed practices which are not indicated. Although we cannot assume that these practices necessarily existed earlier in any particular region, historical evidence suggests that the same general division can be traced back at least to the seventeenth century.[5]

The historian cannot ask the peasants what their customs are, and there are no surveys before the nineteenth century, so the historical evidence for regional inheritance systems is usually indirect, based on land tenure, the common law of inheritance, and the changes in the number and size of holdings. If the land is held under a form of impartible tenure, the inheritance law favours a single heir, and if the number of holdings do not substantially increase in number or decrease in size, one can be fairly sure that the peasants were not dividing the land in practice. On the other hand, if the land tenure does not restrict division and the inheritance laws sanction equal division, one cannot assume more than *potentially* partible practices.[6]

Partible inheritance always leaves open a wide range of strategies

[5] The survey was published by Max Sering (ed.), *Die Vererbung des ländlichen Grundbesitzes im Königreich Preussen*, 4 vols (Berlin, 1899–1910) and each regional study includes historical material which varies greatly in quality and scope. Bartel Huppertz, *Räume und Schichten bäuerlicher Kulturformen in Deutschland* (Bonn, 1939) used this and other historical studies to try to show regional cultural continuity and prepared a series of very interesting maps, which are more readily available in Gottfried Pfeifer, 'The Quality of Peasant Living in Central Europe', in William L. Thomas (ed.), *Man's Role in Changing the Face of the Earth* (Chicago, 1956), pp. 240–77, where the inheritance map is reproduced on p. 257. The question of historical continuity and change is discussed by Alan Mayhew, *Rural Settlement and Farming in Germany* (New York, 1973), pp. 130–5 and Eric Wolf, 'The Inheritance of Land among Bavarian and Tyrolese Peasants', *Anthropologica*, xii (1970), pp. 99–114.

[6] Eric Wolf, *Peasants* (Englewood Cliffs, N.J., 1966), p. 74 suggests the term but uses it in a different context.

for each individual family, depending on their personal, economic and demographic situation.[7] If there is no surviving heir, or only one heir, the question of division never arises. In one northern French village in the nineteenth century with partible inheritance, demographic accidents of mortality or planned fertility can explain the difference between those farms which were kept intact and those which were fragmented.[8] Similarly, family pressure, socialization, or personal choice may lead some potential heirs to accept cash or other settlements rather than claiming their inheritance in land. This will depend on such things as the economic feasibility of dividing the farm, the financial ability to raise the cash settlements, and the accessibility of non-agricultural employment. Partible inheritance systems are basically flexible, and division can almost always be avoided in such a way that the laws are not actually broken and the peasant customs are accommodated.[9]

The territories of Calenberg and Göttingen lie in the southern part of a rather loosely defined cultural area of north-western Germany known as Lower Saxony.[10] The two territories provide an interesting comparison, for they were quite similar except that in Calenberg the peasant holdings were impartible, and in Göttingen they generally were not. There is an excellent printed source which allows us to study the peasant households in one year, a detailed tax list prepared in 1689.[11]

[7] The important idea of treating inheritance as part of a family strategy rather than a fixed practice is discussed by Jack Goody, 'Strategies of Heirship', *Comparative Studies in Society and History*, xv (1973), pp. 3–20 and Bourdieu, 'Stratégies matrimoniales', who points out that in the Pyrenees division of the land is considered a family disaster (p. 1112). It seems to me that the best way to think of partible inheritance is any legal and value system which includes division of the land as a viable option in the family strategy.

[8] Marie-Claude Pingaud, 'Terres et familles dans un village du Châtillonnais', *Etudes rurales*, xlii (1971), pp. 52–104.

[9] For the many variations within France, the classic country of partible inheritance in the nineteenth century, see Alexandre de Brandt, *Droit et coutumes des populations rurales de la France en matière successorale* (Paris, 1901).

[10] The shaded part of the map includes all the territories which make up the contemporary *Land* of Lower Saxony. Other cultural and historical boundaries are described by Wilhelm Pessler, *Niedersächsische Volkskunde* (Hanover, 1922), pp. 7–21.

[11] *Die Kopfsteuerbeschreibung der Fürstentümer Calenberg–Göttingen und Grubenhagen von 1689*, ed. Max Burchard and Herbert Mundhenke, 13 vols (Hanover, then Hildesheim, 1940–1972).

Figure 1. Inheritance customs in Lower Saxony, eighteenth and nineteenth centuries

> *Note* The cross-hatched areas show the position of Calenberg and Göttingen within the general region of Lower Saxony (stippled area) and within the expanded political boundaries of the electorate of Hanover later in the eighteenth century (solid line). The broken line roughly indicates the division between partible inheritance (on the western side) and impartible (eastern side) at the end of the nineteenth century. At that time only about half of the Göttingen area was partible (for sources see note 5).

In the seventeenth century the two territories were a small political unit of no particular significance. But the duke who ruled them became an Elector in 1692, and his successor became King George I of England, who acquired a number of additional territories to form the Electorate of Hanover, one of the larger German states in the eighteenth century.[12]

Calenberg and Göttingen were physically separated, but the major cities in each, Hanover and Göttingen, are little more than fifty miles apart. Except for the area immediately around the city of Hanover, which is marshy to the north and a flat plain to the south, the geographical features are quite similar, consisting of rolling hills with patches of forest. Both regions have open fields and concentrated village settlements, and most of the arable land is suitable for growing grains. In the seventeenth century linen-weaving was apparently widespread among the smallholders, but the economy was predominantly agricultural, based on the output of a grain-producing landed peasantry.[13]

The administrative and manorial organization of the two territories was also basically the same. The income of the manorial landlords consisted almost entirely of tithes, dues and fixed rents, and they were prohibited by the state from evicting peasants. Superimposed on the fragmented and dispersed manors was a much more important administrative district, the *Amt*. This was usually run by an appointed state official who served as a kind of overlord, holding judicial and administrative authority over all the peasants in the district, and in addition was the manorial landlord of many of them. He also ran a large estate farm in the district, which consisted of ducal domain lands leased to him, and worked them with labour services imposed on the peasants through his rights as judicial overlord. But these estates dominated neither the economy nor the peasant society as they did in Prussia. There were relatively

---

[12] There is a short political history in G. W. Sante and A. G. Ploetz-Verlag (eds), *Geschichte der Deutschen Länder: 'Territorien-Ploetz'* (Würzburg, 1964), i, pp. 362–71; an excellent political and social history of northwestern Germany is now available in English: G. Benecke, *Society and Politics in Germany, 1500–1750* (London, 1974).

[13] The basic monographs on the peasant economy of southern Lower Saxony in the early modern period are Diedrich Saalfeld, *Bauernwirtschaft und Gutsbetrieb in der vorindustriellen Zeit* (Stuttgart, 1960) and Walter Achilles, *Vermögensverhältnisse braunschweigischer Bauernhöfe im 17. und 18. Jahrhundert* (Stuttgart, 1965) which focus on Braunschweig, which lies between these territories. Gustav von Gülich, *Über Verhältnisse der Bauern im Fürstenthume Calenberg* (Hanover, 1831) and Grafen von Borries, 'Die Bauerhöfe', in *Festschrift zur Säcularfeier der Königlichen Landwirtschafts-Gesellschaft zu Celle; Beiträge zur Kenntniss der landwirtschaftlichen Verhältnisse im Königreiche Hannover*, 3 vols (Hanover, 1864–5), i, pp. 248–280 are still important overviews.

few of them, they were usually run by state officials rather than local noble landlords, and although they used peasant labour services, the bulk of the income came from tithes, dues and services paid in money rather than from the agricultural production of the estate farm.[14]

In Calenberg most of the peasants held their land under *Meier-recht*, a secure form of hereditary tenure with fixed dues. Although it was hereditary, the land was held by a written, periodically renewable, contract from the landlord, who had the legal right to approve every transfer effected through a marriage contract, inheritance settlement, or sale, and could deny any provisions that threatened to reduce his income. This was specifically aimed at preventing the peasants from dividing their holdings or burdening them with debts paid out as marriage portions.[15]

It was also the policy of the state to maintain the economic viability of the peasant holding, both by prohibiting the lords from evicting their peasants and by passing laws which treated the peasant holdings as legally impartible units. Large impartible farms provided the most effective base for taxation and were required to render the largest number of days of labour services on the estate farms. Combining the functions of state administrator, judicial overlord, manorial landlord, and estate agent, the officials in charge of the districts were in a strong position to see that the laws were enforced.[16]

The impartible holdings in Calenberg were transmitted to a single heir, who inherited all of the property except the 'allod'

[14] Werner Wittich, *Die Grundherrschaft in Nordwestdeutschland* (Leipzig, 1896), pp. 1–16, 141–58, 171–84, 194–219.

[15] *Ibid.*, 19–37. Wittich's book is the classic study of rural institutions in early modern Lower Saxony which shows how impartible land tenure, inheritance, and state policy were integrated into a system everywhere except the south and the northern marshes. More recent local studies have of course found many exceptions to his arguments in particular regions, although most of the debate concerns the origins of *Meierrecht*. (See Friedrich Lütge, *Geschichte der deutschen Agrarverfassung vom frühen Mittelalter bis zum 19. Jahrhundert* (Stuttgart, 1963), p. 76.) One of the few serious local studies of land holding in the territories under consideration is Horst-Rüdiger Marten, *Die Entwicklung der Kulturlandschaft im alten Amt Aerzen des Landkreises Hameln-Pyrmont* (Göttinger Geographische Abhandlungen, liii, Göttingen, 1969).

[16] Wittich, *Grundherrschaft*, pp. 81–2, 169–71, 374–5, 387–9. State policy is also discussed by Dietmar Storch, *Die Landstände des Fürstentums Calenberg-Göttingen, 1680–1714* (Quellen und Darstellungen zur Geschichte Niedersachsens, lxxxi, Hildesheim, 1972), pp. 240–51.

which was what the peasants owned outright and consisted of the farm buildings, equipment, animals, produce, personal property, and any parcels of freehold land. The debts were subtracted from the assessed value of the allod, and what remained was divided among all of the children. The heir kept the house and equipment and was responsible for paying the other children their shares as marriage portions. This was a highly inequitable settlement. The non-heirs in Calenberg received only a small fraction of the total property of their parents and were to stay in the household only until the age of fourteen, when they could be asked to leave. If they remained as servants, their inheritance portions could not be claimed until they left home.[17]

The legal transfer of the farm to the heir was often made during the lifetime of the parents, who then went into retirement, in an arrangement called *Leibzucht*. The retirement contract usually stipulated that the heir would provide a defined amount of food, shelter and clothing for the retired parents, and it guaranteed them the produce or income from certain parts of the farm. Widows were put in an unusually strong position under this system. A woman's dowry was merged into the impartible estate, and she became the sole heir to the entire farm, whether or not she had any surviving children, for as long as the heir was under the age of majority. If she had young children, she could remarry and her second husband became the so-called *Interimswirt*; they could run the farm together until the heir was about twenty-five, when they were both assured of retirement provisions. All of these arrangements contributed to keeping the farms as economically viable, and therefore tax-and-dues-paying, units with no more than one active and one retired couple to support, and to minimizing the claims of the non-heirs which might disperse the productive resources.[18]

[17] Wittich, *Grundherrschaft*, pp. 44–58; Achilles, *Vermögensverhältnisse*, pp. 70–4. The only loose aspect of the inheritance system concerns the freehold parcels which were not legally part of the holding. These rotating (*walzende*) lands could be sold separately or divided among heirs. Achilles' excellent study of the marriage contracts in Braunschweig finds that they were usually kept as part of the holding in the inheritance settlement. Marten, *Kulturlandschaft Aerzen*, pp. 58–60, 83–9, 98, 127 shows changes in the size and number of holdings through sales, land clearance, and reclamations but not through inheritance.

[18] Wittich, *Grundherrschaft*, pp. 37–44, 72–82. The inheritance system is also described in F. Grossmann, 'Provinz Hannover', in M. Sering (ed.), *Vererbung*, ii, 16–29 and Borries, 'Bauerhöfe'.

TABLE 1 *Peasant social structure 1689*

Peasant status	Mean holding-size (ha)		Number of households				Total amount of land (ha)			
	Calenberg	Göttingen	Calenberg	%	Göttingen	%	Calenberg	%	Göttingen	%
Brinksitzer	0.5	1.0	262	26	182	20	129	3	186	6
Köter	1.7	2.3	347	34	553	61	604	15	1,246	37
Grossköter	3.5	6.2	109	11	92	10	366	9	564	17
Halbmeier	7.7	14.0	75	7	76	8	532	13	1,063	32
Vollmeier	12.0	25.5	227	22	11	1	2,457	60	281	8
Total peasants	4.3	3.7	1,020	100	914	100	4,088	100	3,340	100
Others[a]			49		164					
Not indicated			4		78					

[a] Primarily *Häuslinge* (renters or lodgers) and *Leibzüchter* (retired persons) when listed separately, clergymen, schoolteachers, and village herders; a few millers and artisans if peasant status was not also indicated.

Impartible inheritance in Calenberg is reflected by the considerable proportion of large holders in the village social structure in 1689 (Table 1). At the top of the peasant hierarchy was the *Vollmeier*, the full-holding peasant. With an average of twelve hectares, he often employed two or more servants and owed labour services one day a week with a full team of horses. Those with less than a full holding were called 'half' or 'three-quarter' *Meier*, held an average of eight hectares, and performed labour services every other week. In Calenberg these large holders comprised almost one-third of the peasant households and held three-quarters of the land. From the lords' point of view, the essential thing that distinguished the *Köter* was that they owed only hand labour services, that is, service without a team of horses. Socially they constituted the smallholders who lived within the village and shared rights to the commons, but the amount of land which they held varied considerably, ranging from little more than a house and garden to four or five hectares in the open fields. The average *Köter* had about two hectares, and those with more than that were usually designated as *Grossköter*.[19]

At the bottom were the *Brinksitzer*, those who lived on the brink, which was an area of common land just outside the legal limits of the village proper. These cottagers held little or no land, had no common rights, and were dependent on day-labour or artisanal activities. Although most of them were not landed peasants, they did own their own houses which could be inherited. This was not the case for *Häuslinge*, who rented their living space.[20] Most of these were listed as lodgers living with peasant families in nearly one-fifth of the households.

If impartible inheritance was actually practised in Calenberg, then the number of holdings should not have increased over time, and their size should not have decreased. The change in the number of holdings between 1664 and 1766 in the sample villages in five of the districts is shown in Table 2, which indicates an overall increase of only 18 per cent in one hundred years. The two districts with the higher rates were located in a forested area where there was extensive clearing and reclamation of land.[21] The change in

19 Wittich, *Grundherrschaft*, pp. 84–101, 111–15. The considerable variations in holding size are discussed by Marten, *Kulturlandschaft Aerzen*, pp. 81–9, 104–7.
20 Wittich, *Grundherrschaft*, pp. 102–10.
21 Marten, *Kulturlandschaft Aerzen*, pp. 90–110.

holding size is more difficult to determine, because usually only the peasants' status is indicated, and the categories are not consistent from one list to another. But the general pattern is clear: in most villages the number of larger and middle-size holders (*Meier* and *Grossköter*) remains nearly the same, and any increase consists of cottagers and smallholders (*Köter*, *Kleinköter*, and *Brinksitzer*).

TABLE 2 *Number of holdings 1664–1766*

District	No. of villages	No. of holdings			Increase 1664–1766	
		1664	1689	1766		
		Calenberg (impartible)				
Neustadt	4	84	87	90	+6	7%
Lauenau	5	168	169	172	+4	3%
Ohsen	4	147	152	164	+17	12%
Lachem	5	144	156	187	+43	30%
Polle	4	155	183	210	+55	35%
Total	22	698	747	823	+125	18%
		Göttingen (partible)				
Adelebsen*	4	121	122	171	+50	41%
Jühnde*	2	56	84	103	+47	84%
Nienover*	2	55	78	94	+39	71%
Imbsen*	3	48	56	75	+27	56%
Hardenberg	4	139	135	224	+85	61%
Münden	5	136	179	290	+154	113%
Total	20	555	654	957	+402	72%

* Impartible practices in the nineteenth century.
Sources: For 1664: *Niedersächsisches Staatsarchiv, Hannover*, Cal. Br. 19 XL L Nr. 1;
For 1689: *Kopfsteuerbeschreibung 1689*;
For 1766: *Niedersächsisches Staatsarchiv, Hannover*, Dep. 7 C730–2; Hann. 74 Münden C1342; Hann. 74 Uslar CA XI 2 Nr. 4.

In the territory of Göttingen the peasant house and lands did not usually constitute a legal impartible holding. The reason for this is a bit complicated and is based on the distinction between the types of land tenure under which the individual parcels of a farm were held, and the legal status of the farm as a whole. In both regions the individual parcels of land could fall under three basic types of tenure: (1) *Meierland*, which was 'owned' by the lord but held under secure hereditary rights by the peasants and fell under all manorial restrictions and control; (2) *Erbzinsland* (something like copyhold), on which only minimal manorial dues were paid and which could be more freely disposed of by the peasants; (3) *Eigenland* (freehold), which the peasants owned outright, free of manorial control. At the beginning of the seventeenth century most of the land in Calenberg was manorial *Meierland*; most of the land in Göttingen was under the two freer forms of tenure. During the course of the seventeenth century, a number of laws were passed at the request of the lords, prohibiting the division of the holding without the consent of the manor. In Calenberg, where most of the land fell under the strictest manorial controls, this could be enforced initially and was applied to holdings of every size, linking the house and the parcels of land associated with it in a legally defined impartible unit; in Göttingen this did not happen.[22]

In 1689 the majority of the peasants in Göttingen were designated as *Köter*, who were usually smallholders. But this really referred to the fact that their house was owned as a *Kothaus* and they therefore owed only hand labour services. Their farms could consist of land held under any combination of tenure forms. Those parcels held as *Meierland* could not be divided, but they were not legally attached to any particular house and could be sold as a unit. Those parcels held under the freer forms of tenure could not only be detached from the house, but could also be divided into smaller fragments.[23]

The major exception to this were the *Meier* in Göttingen. They were also the largest holders, and in fact their farms were twice as large on the average as in Calenberg, but there were very few of them. Furthermore, in Göttingen the *Meier* did not have secure hereditary tenure, holding both the house and land on short-term

---

[22] Wittich, *Grundherrschaft*, pp. 19–28, 62–72, 387–9. Why the lords and the state should not have been able to enforce impartibility has not really been explained very well for Göttingen, and there were undoubtedly strong local differences. For the adjoining territory of Grubenhagen, where conditions were very similar, there is an excellent study by Franke, 'Über die Theilbarkeit des bäuerlichen Grundbesitzes im Fürstenthum Grubenhagen', *Magazin für hannoversches Recht*, vii (1857), pp. 24–48.

[23] Wittich, *Grundherrschaft*, pp. 67–72, 91–3, 97–100.

leases and paying variable rents. These holdings were impartible, but were not transmitted through inheritance.[24]

For the majority of the peasants in Göttingen the conditions of land tenure allowed partibility, and the common law of inheritance in this region provided for equal division among all of the children.[25] Did they actually divide their land in practice? That could only be determined through a systematic study of contracts and land records for individual villages, but the indirect evidence certainly suggests that many of them did. The clearest case of partibility is found in the district of Münden in the south-western corner of the territory, where the custom seems to have been particularly ingrained. In 1713 an annoyed district official described the situation this way:

> Parents owning smallholdings which owe labour services give their children parts of their houses, sheds and lands as marriage portions, who then try to make homes out of them but do not inform the district officials or get the marriage contracts confirmed as they are required to do by law; furthermore, when the parents die, the children divide the inherited buildings, meadows and lands without permission, split the holding, make two homes out of one or even live in the sheds, and likewise divide the payments which they owe for labour services among themselves, which causes great confusion in the registry.[26]

A land survey in the 1830s indicated that 95 per cent of the land in the district of Münden and around the city of Göttingen was legally partible; in the rest of the districts the legally partible land varied from 40 to 80 per cent.[27] According to the survey of inheritance practices in the late nineteenth century, partibility was predominant in Münden, varied from village to village around the city of Göttingen, and the rest of the districts had impartible practices.[28] In a preliminary and very unsystematic look at the seventeenth-century contracts, both practices are found nearly everywhere.[29] Nor is there a consistent relationship between the

[24] *Ibid.*, pp. 21, 35, 44, 91, 389.
[25] *Ibid.*, pp. 63, 66, 70; Grossmann, 'Hannover', pp. 144–6.
[26] Niedersächsisches Staatsarchiv Hannover (hereafter NSSA), Hann. 74 Münden E 954.
[27] Borries, 'Bauerhöfe', p. 259.
[28] Grossmann, 'Hannover', pp. 147–64.
[29] The contracts in NSSA series Hann. 72 are very incomplete for the seventeenth century.

nineteenth-century inheritance practices and the increase in the number of holdings between 1664 and 1766, as is shown in Table 2, where some of the districts are listed from least partible to most partible according to this survey. However, the overall increase in holdings of 72 per cent is four times as great as in Calenberg. Since the majority of the peasants were only designated as *Köter*, and this group grew everywhere, it appears that many of the holdings were being divided.

So in Calenberg we find impartible land tenure, single inheritance, the predominance of large holders, and a very slow increase in holdings; in Göttingen we find partible land tenure, a customary law of equal inheritance, the predominance of smallholders, and a much more rapid increase in new holdings. The difference is not as absolute as to present a perfectly clear-cut typological distinction, but we can certainly speak of an impartible inheritance system in Calenberg, and at least a potentially partible inheritance system in Göttingen.

When impartible inheritance corresponds to a residential pattern of the married heir living with his parents, we often refer to a 'stem family'. As with most social categories, there is no agreement on exactly how to define this. The stem family has sometimes been defined in terms of impartible inheritance, sometimes in terms of co-residence, and is usually described in terms of both.[30] The term 'nuclear family' raises just as many problems. It means a married couple and their children, but it can be used to refer to them as part of an extended family network or as a separate residential unit. These definitional issues cannot be resolved here and will probably never be resolved at all.[31] In any case, residence is

[30] Frédéric Le Play, *L'Organisation de la Famille* (Paris, 1871), pp. 10, 28–9 focused on the residential pattern but always closely associated it with inheritance; Homans, *English Villagers*, p. 119 defines the stem family only in terms of impartible inheritance, although he describes it as co-residence (pp. 144–59). William J. Goode, *The Family* (Englewood Cliffs, N.J., 1964), p. 45 defines it as single inheritance; Goldschmidt and Kunkel, 'Peasant Family', p. 1062 define it as co-residence; both discuss it in terms of households. For other definitions and a generally sceptical approach see Peter Laslett, 'Introduction', in Peter Laslett and Richard Wall (eds), *Household and Family in Past Time* (Cambridge, 1972), pp. 16–23.

[31] For a survey of the definitional thicket see G. Castillo, A. Weisblat, and F. Villareal, 'The Concepts of Nuclear and Extended Family: An Exploration of Empirical Referents', *International Journal of Comparative Sociology*, ix (1968), pp. 1–40. Laslett, 'Introduction', pp. 23–8 argues that the criterion

an important aspect of any study of family organization and provides at least one way of distinguishing stem family households from nuclear family households.[32]

The basic historical sources for establishing residential patterns are nominative listings of inhabitants, preferably censuses. However, before the nineteenth century such lists were rarely drawn up just to count the population. Usually they were prepared for other purposes, such as taxation or military recruitment, which might affect both who was included and how the households were recorded.[33] For Calenberg and Göttingen there are head-tax lists prepared in 1689 which appear to be almost as detailed and complete as a nominative census.[34] The lists vary somewhat in their format but they usually include the names, ages, and status of all the members of the immediate family and their relationship to the head of the household, as well as any relatives, lodgers or servants living with him. They appear to be divided into residential groups, although it is not clear whether they are living in the same house or on the same property. The majority of the village lists for Calenberg are very complete; the ones for Göttingen often do not include the name of the wife and very rarely indicate the ages of the head couple, although they do record the ages of their children. The data presented below are based on a sample of about two thousand households in seventy-five villages drawn from administrative districts grouped by geographical region within the two territories.

By classifying and counting the various household groups which appear in the 1689 lists, we can determine the frequency with which certain categories are found in the two territories. But this only tells us about the household composition at one point in time, that is, who happens to be living together on a particular date. In order to transform this into information about the organization of

should be residence, but in the narrowest sense of living under the same roof. For a criticism of his definitions see L. K. Berkner, 'The Use and Misuse of Census Data for the Historical Analysis of Family Structure', *Journal of Interdisciplinary History*, v (1975), pp. 721–38.

[32] William J. Parish and Mosche Schwartz, 'Household Complexity in Nineteenth Century France', *American Sociological Review*, xxxvii (1972), pp. 154–73 discuss the entire question and use aggregate data to show the regional distribution of stem-family households.

[33] The problems of using such lists are discussed in Berkner, 'Use and Misuse'.

[34] *Die Kopfsteuerbeschreibung*, ed. Burchard and Mundhenke.

the family, which involves roles and relationships that change over the life cycles of the individual family members, the categories must be analysed to take into account the developmental cycle of the household.[35]

The distinctive residential pattern of the stem family is a household composed of two couples, the parents and one married child. But the stem family does not consist of just this particular household form, which is only one of a series of phases through which the stem family household goes. In principle, these phases should follow this sequence: (1) parents with unmarried children (nuclear phase); (2) the married heir as the head of the household living with the retired parents and perhaps some unmarried brothers and sisters; (3) the married heir with a widowed parent and/or unmarried siblings; (4) the married heir with only his wife and children. The timing and sequence of these phases is very sensitive to a large number of factors, of which the most obvious is demographic. The longer the retired parents live, the more likely that they will be found in the household. On the other hand, some couples will have no surviving child to become the heir; some heirs will not reach marriage age until both parents have died; and some heirs will have no surviving brothers and sisters. So the stem family may include a large variety of forms of household composition at any given point in time. In addition to the head couple there may be any of the following: retired parents and unmarried children, retired parents alone, a widowed parent with

---

[35] Jack Goody (ed.), *The Developmental Cycle in Domestic Groups* (Cambridge, 1958) presented this important concept, further applied to property rights in Robert F. Gray and P. H. Gulliver (eds), *The Family Estate in Africa* (London, 1964), and re-emphasized by the translation of A. V. Chayanov, *The Theory of Peasant Economy*, ed. D. Thorner, B. Kerblay, and R. E. F. Smith (Homewood, Ill., 1966). In the last few years it has become one of the central ideas in the study of the peasant family: E. A. Hammel, 'The Zadruga as Process', in Laslett and Wall (eds), *Household and Family*, pp. 335–74; Jack Goody, 'The Evolution of the Family', in *ibid.*, pp. 103–24; John W. Cole, 'Social Process in the Italian Alps', *American Anthropologist*, lxxv (1973), pp. 765–86; Hironobu Kitaoji, 'The Structure of the Japanese Family', in *ibid.*, lxxiii (1971), pp. 1036–57; Orvar Lofgren, 'Family and Household among Scandinavian Peasants: An Exploratory Essay', *Ethnologia Scandinavica* (1974), pp. 17–52; Plakans, 'Peasant Family Life'. The best discussion of all is the long delayed paper by E. A. Hammel, 'Household Structure in Fourteenth-Century Macedonia', to be published in a collection provisionally entitled *Mediterranean Family Structure*, ed. John K. Campbell.

children, a widowed parent alone, or just unmarried brothers and sisters alone.[36] Table 3 shows the distribution of the household forms found in the 1689 tax lists for the villages in Calenberg and Göttingen, and there is a clear difference. In Calenberg with impartible inheritance, 28 per cent of the peasant households appear as possible stem

TABLE 3 *Peasant household composition*

	Calenberg (impartible)	Göttingen (partible)
Nuclear family	%	%
Head couple without relatives	65 (660)	90 (819)
Stem family forms		
Retired parents with or without children	8 (73)	1 (11)
Widowed parent and child(ren)	4 (37)	<1 (2)
Widowed father	3 (28)	1 (10)
Widowed mother	6 (61)	2 (21)
Unmarried siblings	6 (62)	1 (7)
Married child	2 (22)	1 (7)
Other extended forms		
Co-resident married siblings	1 (18)	<1 (3)
Co-resident unmarried siblings	1 (12)	<1 (3)
Other relatives (uncle, nephew, grandchild)	1 (13)	<1 (2)
Non-family forms		
Single individuals	3 (26)	2 (20)
Unrelated couples	1 (10)	1 (9)
Summary		
Nuclear	65 (660)	90 (819)
Stem forms	28 (281)	6 (58)
Other extended	4 (43)	1 (8)
Non-family	4 (36)	3 (29)
Total households	100 (1020)	100 (914)

[36] L. K. Berkner, 'The Stem Family and the Developmental Cycle of the Household: An Eighteenth-Century Austrian Example', *American Historical Review*, lxxvi (1972), pp. 398–418 used the same approach. Horace Miner, *St. Denis: A French Canadian Parish* (Chicago, 1939), ch. 4 demonstrated this family cycle long ago. For an excellent discussion of the interpretation of household categories see Robert Wheaton, 'Family and Kinship in Western Europe: The Problem of the Joint Family', *Journal of Inter-disciplinary History*, v (1975), pp. 601–28.

family forms; in Göttingen with partible inheritance, it is only 6 per cent. In both regions additional variations appear as a small proportion of other extended family forms – married brothers, unmarried siblings living alone, households with nieces, nephews and grandchildren. Although the most common household form consists only of a couple and children without any other relatives, in Calenberg the distribution of these 'nuclear' households follows a consistent pattern inverse to the 'stem' family households, according to measures of age and wealth, while in Göttingen they do not.

TABLE 4   *The stem-family cycle in Calenberg*

	Mean ages of head-family members[a]			
Household composition	Male head	Female head	Oldest child	N
Retired parents with or without children	33	28	4	49
Widowed parent and child(ren)	35	29	4	25
Widowed parent (father or mother)	37	33	8	66
Unmarried siblings	39	34	8	35
No relatives (nuclear family)	46	41	13	343
Married child	60	56	13	12

[a] Households with land only.

In Calenberg the household forms which could be part of the stem family developmental cycle stand out. About half of these are in the distinctive stem family phase of two co-resident couples – those households with a retired couple, a widowed parent with a child, or a married child who is not listed as the head. But the presence of a widowed father, mother, or just some unmarried brothers or sisters could also be phases of some other kind of family structure. The fact that these fit a consistent developmental pattern is shown in Table 4 where the mean age of the male and female household heads and that of their oldest child is calculated for each household form. When we find a retired parental couple, the mean age of the male household head is thirty-three; when one of the parents has died but the survivor is still living with an unmarried child, the head is thirty-five; when there is only a widowed mother or father present, the head is thirty-seven; when both parents are dead and only unmarried brothers and sisters are found, the head is thirty-nine; when there are no parents or unmarried siblings, the head is forty-six. This is exactly the kind of pattern one would expect to find in the stem family, reflecting the changes brought about by death of the parents and the movement of the siblings out of the household as they reach adulthood.

This is not to say that every family in Calenberg went through all of these phases, for there are other factors which will also influence the household composition. 'Impartible inheritance' does not specify *which* child will become the heir, or *when* that child may marry and take over the farm. Peasant customs may favour the eldest (primogeniture), the youngest (ultimogeniture), or leave the choice open.[37] If the eldest is favoured, he will reach marriage age while the parents are still relatively young, and the transfer of the holding will probably take place during their lifetime. If the youngest is favoured, there is a high probability that one or both of the parents will have died before the heir marries. If no child is favoured, the one who happens to be at home and is ready to marry when the father either decides to retire or dies will probably become the heir.[38] These practices are especially difficult to determine and vary not only from village to village, but also according to the wealth of the peasants. If the farm is large, the parents will be able to make a comfortable retirement arrangement and may choose to transfer the farm relatively early. This appears to have been common in Calenberg, and in the eighteenth century a law was passed to prohibit retirement before the age of sixty.[39] But if the farm is small, the parents will put off retirement or may not be able to retire at all because the holding could not support two married couples. Then the inheritance transfer would take place only after the death of the father, and the probability of finding a co-resident couple will be small.

The analysis of a single household list does not allow us to untangle all of these factors, but two patterns are clear in the

[37] Homans, *English Villagers*, pp. 123–8; Goody, *Death*, pp. 325–7.

[38] William A. Douglass, 'Rural Exodus in Two Spanish Basque Villages: A Cultural Explanation', *American Anthropologist*, lxxiii (1971), pp. 1100–14 shows the consequences of either designating an heir early or leaving the choice open and shows why the favoured heirs do not necessarily take over the farm. Cole and Wolf, *Hidden Frontier*, pp. 182–7 beautifully illustrate the interplay between the age of the father and the age of the apparent heir in determining which child actually gets the farm.

[39] Wittich, *Grundherrschaft*, p. 43. In Calenberg the choice of the heir was left to the parents (p. 47).

TABLE 5   *Household composition by age of oldest child*

Age of the oldest child	Calenberg				Göttingen			
	Nuclear	Stem	Other	N	Nuclear	Stem	Other	N
	%	%	%		%	%	%	
0–3 years	44	49	7	(195)	82	16	2	(175)
4–6 years	59	38	4	(80)	90	8	2	(89)
7–9 years	69	29	3	(115)	97	4	0	(115)
10–14 years	80	15	5	(215)	97	3	1	(202)
Over 14	87	9	4	(297)	97	3	0	(272)

Calenberg family structure: the frequency of households in the stem family phase increases with the wealth of the peasants, and decreases with the number of years that the head of the household has been married. In Table 5 the age of the oldest child of the head couple is used as a measure of the family life cycle. When the couple does not yet have any children or the oldest child is three or less, 49 per cent are living with relatives in one of the stem family household forms. This proportion drops about 10 per cent

TABLE 6   *Household composition by status and holding size*

Other	Calenberg				Göttingen			
	Nuclear	Stem	Other	N	Nuclear	Stem	Other	N
	Peasant status							
	%	%	%		%	%	%	
Brinksitzer	81	15	4	(231)	93	6	1	(173)
Köter	73	21	5	(320)	94	5	1	(531)
Grossköter	64	35	1	(98)	84	14	2	(88)
Halbmeier	54	38	7	(68)	99	0	1	(75)
Vollmeier	67	28	5	(205)	100	0	0	(11)
	Holding size							
	%	%	%		%	%	%	
No land	83	12	5	(179)	95	3	1	(152)
0–1 ha	71	26	3	(185)	93	7	1	(107)
1–5 ha	72	25	4	(261)	93	7	1	(439)
5–8 ha	59	32	9	(99)	92	8	0	(86)
8+ ha	64	31	6	(144)	95	2	3	(92)

for every three-year increase in the age of the oldest child. When the oldest child is over fourteen, roughly the mid-point of the family cycle, only 9 per cent of the households are still in a stem family phase.

In Table 6 the influence of the peasants' status and holding size can be seen to work in the opposite direction. The cottagers and smallholders are much less likely to live in stem family households than the more substantial peasants, but the *Vollmeier*, who are usually the largest holders in a village, fall below what one would expect. This may be due to local variations in holding sizes (in some districts the *Vollmeier* had much larger holdings than in others) or it could reflect differences in the choice of heirs or the timing of the transfers. The appearance of stem family households is more regular when we look at holding sizes than at nominal status: about one-tenth for those with no land, one-quarter for those with less than 5 hectares, and one-third for those with more than 5 hectares.

Finally, in Table 7 the effects of the family life cycle are combined with measures of peasant status and holding size to see what proportion of the households are in the stem family phase when there is the highest probability that the parents will still be alive or some of the unmarried brothers and sisters will still be at home. The pattern is still the same: the cottagers and those with no land are least likely to live in stem family households, while about half of the higher status groups and the largest holders are living with their parents or unmarried brothers and sisters. So even under the conditions of maximum probability, for the most substantial peasants in the early phase of the life cycle, the proportion of households with a stem family household composition does not go much higher than 50 per cent. This does not mean that the other half do not have a stem family organization; these 'nuclear' households could be the result of any combination of factors: the early death of the parents, no surviving heirs, the choice of a younger child as heir, or a delayed retirement.

In Göttingen we find almost no evidence of a stem family organization in the household lists of 1689. The highest concentration of stem family households with relatives is again when the head family is very young, but it is only 16 per cent. The size of the holding does not seem to make a difference except at the extremes – both those with no land and those with the largest

TABLE 7   *Proportion of stem-family households*

| | Age of oldest child | | | |
| | Calenberg | | Göttingen | |
	Under 10	10 and over	Under 10	10 and over
Peasant status				
	%	%	%	%
Brinksitzer	21 (117)[a]	9 (111)	11 (88)	1 (80)
Köter	35 (146)	10 (169)	9 (267)	3 (249)
Grossköter	54 (54)	12 (41)	24 (37)	6 (50)
Halbmeier	55 (31)	25 (36)	0 (30)	0 (43)
Vollmeier	47 (87)	13 (110)	0 (7)	0 (2)
Holding size				
	%	%	%	%
No land	16 (97)	7 (81)	6 (86)	0 (58)
0–1 ha	42 (83)	13 (100)	11 (54)	2 (48)
1–5 ha	41 (117)	11 (142)	11 (209)	4 (217)
5–8 ha	51 (51)	13 (47)	14 (37)	4 (49)
8+ ha	52 (160)	16 (83)	5 (38)	0 (50)

[a] Total households in this category.

holdings very rarely live with any relatives. One reason is that in Göttingen the largest holders, the *Meier*, did not have hereditary rights to their land. They were leaseholders who could not set up retirement contracts because they had no claim to the land. Not a single *Meier* household in the Göttingen region was supporting a retired parent. The only group that stands out are the *Grossköter*, who were the most substantial peasants with secure hereditary tenure, and almost one-quarter of these with young children lived in stem family households. The smallholders (*Köter*) who predominated in the villages of this region, and were probably smallholders because they practised partible inheritance, rarely lived in stem family households even in the early stages of the family cycle. In Göttingen only 9 per cent of the *Köter* with children under ten have a stem family household composition, compared to 35 per cent in Calenberg, where this group could not divide their holdings.

We have quickly reached the limits of what a household list can tell us about family structure. The evidence from the lists indicates that nuclear family households predominate in Göttingen, and this is consistent with the land tenure which allowed partibility and the inheritance laws which sanctioned it. But it also appears that not all the peasants were actually dividing their holdings – so why are there so few stem-family households? One possibility is the choice of younger children as heirs, although there is no written evidence that this was the custom. In the adjoining territory of Grubenhagen, which had very similar land-tenure conditions and partible inheritance, in some villages there was also a custom of ultimogeniture in the sense that the youngest child received the parental house as his or her portion.[40] If the Göttingen peasants who did not divide their land also favoured the youngest child, this would explain why there are so few households with co-resident couples.

Another reason for the small number of stem family households reported in Göttingen may have to do with a simple difference in architecture between the two regions. In Calenberg the peasant houses are usually constructed in the 'old Saxon' type, which is a large, 'longhouse' with the living quarters, sheds and stalls located around a central court, all of which are covered by one enormous roof. In Göttingen many houses are of the 'middle German' type, where the sheds and stalls are separate from the farmhouse, and one often finds additional outbuildings, some of which are specifically designated as 'retirement houses' in eighteenth-century registers.[41] We cannot assume that the seventeenth-century officials who drew up the tax lists had any consistent notion of what constituted a household. In Calenberg where the retired parents usually lived under the same roof in these huge 'longhouses', they were listed as part of the household, even if they were taxed separately for any land which they continued to farm. But in Göttingen, where the retired parents might live in a separate outbuilding, they were more likely to be listed as a separate household. In fact retirement houses also appear in some Calenberg districts.[42] In the 1689 lists

[40] *Ibid.*, p. 64; Franke, 'Theilbarkeit', pp. 38–9. J. Davis, *Land and Family in Pisticci* (London, 1973) studies a southern Italian village with partible inheritance where the youngest daughter gets the parental home (p. 44).

[41] Pessler, *Niedersächsische Volkskunde*, pp. 80–92 shows the distribution of housing forms and W. Boman, *Bäuerliches Hauswesen und Tagwerk in alten Niedersachsen* (Weimar, 1941) illustrates their construction. The eighteenth-century fire-insurance registers listing individual buildings are in NSSA series Hann. 330.

[42] Marten, *Kulturlandschaft Aerzen*, p. 99 and plate 14.

there were twenty-five retired persons listed separately in the Calenberg villages, and fifty in Göttingen, which would raise the proportion of stem-family households, but would not make any substantial difference.

This raises another problem in the comparison of the two regions. In the villages of both territories there was a large group of individuals and families called *Häuslinge*, who were either lodgers in peasant houses, rented a cottage or outbuilding, or lived in a community-owned house like the schoolmaster, the pastor and the village herders. These make up the bulk of those classified as 'others' in Table 1, and have been excluded from the analysis because they had no land to transfer through inheritance. In Calenberg this group is quite small because most lodgers are listed with peasant households, and the officials did not bother to list schoolmasters and pastors, who were not taxed. In Göttingen this group is so large that it looks as if there is a major difference in the social structure, but actually it is only a difference in recording and in the housing pattern. For some reason the officials in Göttingen almost always listed the village schoolmaster, pastor, and herders, and the lodgers were more often listed separately, probably because they lived in outbuildings rather than in the farmhouse itself. There is always the possibility that what appear to be differences in household composition only reflect differences in the way the lists were drawn up. Nor can we be sure that the pattern found in any particular year will be maintained under changing economic or demographic conditions. This is especially true in a region of partible inheritance like Göttingen, where a wide range of family strategies was possible.

Another household enumeration exists for the two territories in 1766, and this lists the number of relatives in each household by sex and whether they were over or under fourteen, but it does not indicate their relationship to the head.[43] In Calenberg 23 per cent of the households included some combination of two or more relatives, and another 20 per cent included only one relative over fourteen, which suggests a much stronger stem-family household pattern than in 1689. However, in the Göttingen villages, 20 per cent of the households in 1766 also included one relative over fourteen, and another 12 per cent included two or more. The household composition continued to be more complex in the impartible

43 NSSA, Dep. 7 C 730-2.

region, but there is less of a difference between them. At this point in my research it is not possible to say whether the dramatic increase of what may be stem-family households in Göttingen was due to a change in recording, a shift to impartible inheritance practices, or a difference in the choice of heirs. These questions will have to be answered by studying individual families in particular localities, so that it is possible to describe in detail how variations in inheritance practices are directly related to residential patterns and household organization.

The purpose of this study was to demonstrate on a regional level that there is a relationship between impartible inheritance and stem-family households, partible inheritance and nuclear-family households. In Calenberg the secure, impartible land tenure, single inheritance, retirement provisions, large holdings and unified housing-forms are all indicators of peasant stem-family households, and the typical stem-family residential pattern is found in the 1689 tax lists among the landed peasantry in the first half of the family life cycle. Since these conditions were common to most of northern Lower Saxony, it would not be surprising if the stem family represents the typical peasant household of the region. In Göttingen the less restricted land tenure, the common law of equal inheritance, smaller holdings, and less unified farm buildings suggest conditions for separate nuclear family households, which indeed appear as the predominant residential pattern in the 1689 tax lists among all the peasants, even in the first half of the family cycle. Where these conditions coincide – and they appear together quite often in the regions of Germany with partible inheritance in the nineteenth century[44] – one may expect to find a nuclear-family residential pattern, but it is also likely to undergo many rearrangements in response to changing economic and demographic conditions. The basic question is whether or not the peasant family has a wide range of viable options in regard to inheritance and residence: partible inheritance and nuclear family households are more likely to be found together when the options are open, impartible inheritance and stem family households are more likely to be found together when many options are closed.

[44] See the maps in Huppertz, *Räume und Schichten* and Pfeifer, 'Quality of Peasant Living'. The regional relationship of inheritance, holding size, and land tenure is also discussed in Wilhelm Abel, 'Schichten und Zonen europäischer Agrarverfassung', *Zeitschrift für Agrargeschichte und Agrarsoziologie*, iii (1955), pp. 1–19.

4. Aspects of kinship behaviour and property in rural Western Europe before 1800

DAVID SABEAN

In this chapter I would like to raise a few problems associated with the structure of kinship relations and the holding of property in Western Europe, primarily in the period from the late Middle Ages to the eighteenth century. To some degree the chapter is aimed at investigating the rather widely held assumption that pre-industrial rural Europe was a society with many stranded kinship relations where interaction among kin formed the primary focus of an individual's life.[1] A second aspect of the argument will involve a rather loose discussion of some of the variables relating property to systems of kin relations. It must be kept in mind throughout that while there are often ties that bind kin together for certain purposes there are often significant conflicts that drive them apart. It is one of the tasks of the social historian to analyse the basis for such conflicts in so far as they occur systematically.

At present it is difficult to offer a thorough synthesis on property and kinship since much of the material is scattered and does not lend itself to systematic treatment. From the available literature on the peasantry it is certain that there has been a wide variety of possible kinship arrangements. In some places kinship relationships outside the nuclear family are unimportant and as one generation succeeds another the members of the sibling group raised in a household cease to have any dealings at all with each other.[2] Sometimes relations inside the nuclear family are tenuous at best.[3] In other situations kin relations are important, and with patient investigation the historian can begin to understand the principles on which they are or can be built. Until now most of the historical spade-work for such an analysis has been lacking, yet it is here

---

[1] Peter Laslett (ed.), *The World We Have Lost* (New York, 1966), pp. 78–9.

[2] Sigrid Khera, 'An Austrian Peasant Village Under Rural Industrialization', *Behavior Science Notes*, vii (1972), pp. 29–36.

[3] Gerard Bouchard, *Le village immobile: Sennely-en-Sologne au XVIII siècle* (Paris, 1972).

96

that some of the most rewarding research can be done (a case in point is the work of Segalen).[4] What strikes one immediately is that the variation in family and kinship structure over space and over time is often intimately linked to the way resources, particularly land, are held and passed from generation to generation.

At the moment there are several ways in which one can approach the question of kinship behaviour by asking a series of very simple questions: what ties generations together or causes conflict between them? What ties are found among siblings? What variations can one find in the way families regulate their behaviour? In providing answers the most immediately exploitable historical material deals with ritual co-parenthood (godparents), marriage strategy, care of the aged, child-rearing, and disputes among kin.

To start at the bottom of the scale in analysing the way property affects kinship, there are two suggestive cases where the people involved have very little property at all and what they have is mostly in the form of movable wealth. In such situations the important distinctions of status one associates with a peasant society are hardly existent. The households vary only in their demographic make-up and the range of variation is very small. Here the father does not have the function of passing his status along to his children. In those societies where there is a gradation of wealth and property-ownership the farm labourers and other poor people of a village can attach themselves to people of a higher social class through ties of fictive kinship. However, when a large mass of poor develops and the disjunction between them and the wealthy is great, such kinship ties break down.[5] Emmanuel Todd has examined a society of rural day-labourers in eighteenth-century northern France in terms of the choices they make in finding godparents for their children.[6] He can find no system at all. To begin with the people do not use grandparents or siblings, a practice that was widespread in much of Europe at the time. Apparently they do not choose people who could be associated with a system of patronage nor are there reinforced ties of the type that would be found if a series of factions developed. Godparents are simply chosen on a

[4] Martine Segalen, *Nuptialité et alliance: le choix du conjoint dans une commune de l'Eure* (Paris, 1972).

[5] Abbé Berthet, 'Un reactif social: le parrainage du XVI siècle à la revolution', *Annales E.S.C.*, i (1946), pp. 43–50.

[6] Paper presented by Emmanuel Todd to the seminar of the Cambridge Group for the History of Population and Social Structure, 1973.

casual basis. A good deal should be made of this apparently
negative example, for it is clear to anyone who has worked with
family reconstitution in villages where there is a peasant landholding class that godparents are chosen on anything but a casual
basis. Where there is no property there is no basis for emphasizing
ties of kinship that already exist, that is in reinforcing ties of blood
or affinity as social ties, nor for creating new ties that are expected
to be of long duration.

Another recent study that is instructive here deals with the
family in a village in Sologne where the peasants have very little,
if any, land.[7] In this case of extreme poverty the ties within the
nuclear family themselves become very weak. Children were raised
in a slovenly manner with apparently little positive sentiment from
their parents. In any event the children normally left the household
at the age of seven or eight to become servants, shepherds, or
apprentices elsewhere. Parents did little to arrange good marriages
for their children, and marriages themselves seldom lasted longer
than twelve years because of high mortality rates. Remarriage
often took place in haste with the disparity in age between the two
new spouses averaging over ten years. Widows often married the
former apprentices of their husbands; widowers, their wives' former
servants. The author of the study finds few three-generational
families and only one example of a widow living with her son,
she having to pay for her keep. When parents were forced in their
old age to beg, they were generally afraid to do so from their own
children. Family quarrels were standard, siblings often fought over
their meagre inheritances, and there are examples of children
beating their aged parents.

The upshot of these two examples is that, in the absence of
property there is little tendency to develop extended kin ties. It
introduces a note of caution about speaking of a single European
family structure, for the variation from place to place and from
class to class is significant. A good example of a society which
forms the opposite pole comes from Austria in the 1950s.[8] Here
there was significant peasant property which descended from father
to son by primogeniture. Those who received no land found few
options available to them. As a result the sibling group raised in
a single household faced radical differentiation in economic and

[7] Bouchard, *op. cit.*, pp. 230ff.
[8] Khera, *op. cit.*

social status when the members reached maturity. One son got the farm and presumably one daughter married into a situation similar to the one in which she had been brought up. The rest received movable property not commensurate with what the eldest received and not enough to buy into a farm. From one family then came a single peasant proprietor with the rest of the children declining in status often to that of a day-labourer. This fact drove the sibling group apart; brothers did not play cards with each other in the inn, and the labourers did not sit with their peasant brothers at the *Stammtisch*. Siblings tended to avoid each other and apart from a formal bow at the church door on Sunday morning seldom if ever met or exchanged words. In this case the siblings were driven apart while in the two former examples there was nothing to hold them together. The situation in Austria is, of course, only one possible response to primogeniture, and a radically disproportionate system of land holding. However, such a situation must often have characterized areas of unigeniture in Western Europe.[9]

To some extent there is a natural isolation of the household in European peasant society, as indeed in peasant societies in Eurasia as a whole. Goody in particular has stressed the social differentiation that comes with plough culture.[10] In Western European peasant society there is always a careful gradation of status within the village. Agriculture is carried on by the labour of a single household or at least the organization of labour and the holding of land as well as consumption is based on the household. Each household has its own status configuration based on the amount of land that it controls, its size and demographic structure, and its 'moral reputation'. Since the nature of the peasant economy detaches each household from all of the others, the household becomes the primary unit of the society; taxation and military conscription were levied by household; crimes directed against the house were considered more serious than crimes against the individual.[11] In

[9] David Sabean, 'Famille et tenure paysanne: aux origines de la guerre des paysans en Allemagne (1525)', *Annales E.S.C.*, xxvii (1972), pp. 903–22.

[10] Jack Goody, 'Marriage Prestations, Inheritance and Descent in Pre-Industrial Societies', *Jnl of Comparative Family Studies*, i (1970), pp. 37–54; 'Inheritance, Property and Marriage in Africa and Eurasia', *Sociology*, iii (1969), pp. 55–76; 'Class and Marriage in Africa and Eurasia', *Amer. Jnl of Sociology*, xxvi (1971).

[11] K. S. Kramer, *Volksleben im Fürstentum Ansbach und seinen Nachbargebieten (1500–1800)* (Würzburg, 1961), pp. 191–237.

analysing the nature of the wider kinship network the primary focus should be on the ties that connected certain households, or the way individuals were connected to this or that household.

There are a number of ways in which links can be made between individuals and households. Simple exchange relationships involving work, honour, or political allegiance can follow kin lines. Kinship ties can be reinforced by certain kinds of marriage arrangements. With the birth of a child, an opportunity is afforded for creating fictive kin relationships by selecting certain people to be godparents. One concrete example of the attachment to certain specific kin comes from the medieval epic literature.[12] In most of the German epics the crucial kinship link is between sister's son and mother's brother. Bell has gone through all of the epics in an exhaustive fashion to show this as the dominant theme of family relationships and argues that it demonstrates the survival of matriliny. In most of the epics the father hardly appears except to give the son proper genealogical status. Apart from this the son expects to find help, advice, and room for the play of his ambition from his maternal uncle. Parzifal, for example, finds the grail in the keeping of one of his mother's brothers while another reveals its secret.

I would suggest that the explanation for the dyad, mother's brother/sister's son, which is a crucial one for more than a small class of medieval knights, is the result of property relationships.[13] Within a military caste disputes among sons and between fathers and sons were apt to be too disruptive. Those sons without expectation of an inheritance (in the epics they are always looking for heiresses) were forced to leave home. In looking for aid, the closest consanguineal relation with sufficient property to offer a place would be the maternal uncle, since the father's brother would have been excluded from succession by the father. The mother's brother gets a loyal set of retainers with whom there are no conflicts over succession, while the nephews find their needs taken care of and their status as warriors maintained. Although this example involves the effects of primogeniture on a specific set of kin relations within

---

[12] C. H. Bell, 'The Sister's Son in the Medieval German Epic. A Study in the Survival of Matriliny', *University of California Publications in Modern Philology*, x (1920), pp. 67–182.

[13] G. Duby, 'In Northwestern France: the "Youth" in Twelfth Century Aristocratic Society', in F. L. Cheyette (ed.), *Lordship and Community in Medieval Europe* (New York, 1968), pp. 198–209.

the aristocratic class, I suspect that a similar weighting in favour of the uncle/nephew dyad was characteristic of many areas of peasant Europe where unigeniture prevailed.

Marriage, as a way of forming alliance between households, has been the subject of a recent study of a Normandy village since the eighteenth century where weavers and peasant proprietors form the two main groups of the society.[14] The former contract more consanguineal marriages, but for reasons that have nothing to do with the desire to reinforce a specific kin tie. Weavers seek out mates among weavers because of the nature of the artisan economy in which husband and wife form a team. Since the group among which selection can be made is small, marriage with blood-kin cannot be avoided. Peasant proprietors on the other hand quite systematically reinforce through marriage ties that already exist. Families which seek out partners in another village will often in the next generation send one back. One example is given where this alternate exchange was practised in one family for six generations. Often if a child marries into a certain village or family a sibling will follow. There are in addition many examples of reinforcement of kin ties by new marriages in successive generations. The whole system implies the circulation of goods and their control within a loosely knit extended kin group.

There is still a good deal of work left for the historian to do with this kind of material. In particular we have no analysis of the kind of uses to which kinship can be put. A combination of family reconstitution and village study modelled after the anthropological approach would expose a whole range of new material. In Germany, for example, the wealth of material at the village level is enormous. Parish registers going back to the middle of the sixteenth century allow for family reconstitution, the study of marriage alliances and fictive kin-relations. Post-mortem inventories give detail of every strip of land and every item of movable property down to individual pieces of cutlery. In these documents the web of debt relationships can be studied. Peasants seldom kept money around but rather loaned whatever they happened to have to someone who had need for cash. At death there might be as many as twenty small debts and loans outstanding. From this material the historian can reconstruct a complex set of social and economic ties. Village court and council records and church consistory

[14] Segalen, *op. cit.*

records reveal groups of people working together or in conflict. Many villages have complete records of land holding with details about sales and sub-leasing. From all of this material one can reconstruct the web of primary relations) – who marries whom or who is chosen as godparent – as well as study the uses to which such relationships are put.

The nature of fictive kinship needs to be thoroughly investigated, for it too is intimately intertwined with property relationships. One concrete case comes from the Württemberg village of Neckarhausen. In the sixteenth century the population rose rapidly, as it did everywhere in Europe. The result was to put pressure on the fairly substantial peasant holdings tending to fractionalization. In general the breaking up of farms did not keep pace with the rise in population, so that at the end of the century a large group of day-labourers had emerged, and some farms had divided into two or three pieces, with many farms relatively unaffected by the fissioning process. In this situation, which lasted well into the first decade of the Thirty Years War, the selection of godparents reflected the pyramid of economic and social relationships. People at the top of the pyramid stood as godparents to anyone below them, while those lower in the social order did not reciprocate. In this system the village was tied in with the local administrative town as many well-to-do people appeared in the village as godparents. The system, which was destroyed by the Thirty Years War, was one of overlapping social relations of a patron/client type. During the early 1630s the population was decimated. With the quartering of troops, plague, foraging and army recruitment, the dislocation caused by the war left the remaining population, which was reduced to two-fifths of its previous level, in a difficult state. At the end of the war there were no grain stores, no seed, no domestic animals (with a consequent lack of fertilizer); many fields had been left uncultivated; the inventories reveal that many people had no movables worth speaking about. In this situation peasants took on only very small plots, and in the next generation land was available for those who needed it. A process of fission set in as the population slowly recovered from the effects of the war, so that by the end of the seventeenth century partible inheritance was firmly established, and Württemberg became a society of small peasant proprietors. In this situation the peasants no longer chose godparents from outside the range of near kin.

In particular, ties with the local town were ruptured. It is too early in the study to give a definitive analysis of the structure of fictive kinship in the village in the eighteenth century, but it would appear that peoples most often chose their siblings, emphasizing ties based on closely-knit kin groups.

Something needs to be said at this point about the ways in which households regulate their holding of property and the passing of property to the next generation. In this context establishing a new household is itself a fundamental aspect of the process. In passing wealth to the next generation the parents ensure continuity of social arrangements and provide for themselves in their old age. Passing wealth on to the next generation must always be seen in the light of setting up new households or the establishing of new conjugal funds. In this regard there is tremendous variation across Europe, and it is here that one must focus in order to understand how the form of property arrangements affects the very stuff of domestic arrangements and the ties between households. Until now the only means of getting at this problem has been through studies by legal historians on inheritance or family property law. It would be useful to examine some of this literature in order to begin to abstract some of the principles of family structure.

There are three basic ways that the literature focuses on the problem. The oldest sees the basic dichotomy of family systems as the result of two fundamental modes of inheritance; unigeniture (eldest, youngest, or single elected son) or partible inheritance.[15] On the partible side of the continuum the extreme case divides all wealth, movable and immovable, among all of the heirs, male and female. There are systems of partible inheritance that exclude daughters from inheriting land. On the unigeniture side, the extreme case would be one son getting everything, although to my knowledge this never happens. The most frequent practice is to pass all of the land to one son and it is also possible to give him a lion's share of the movable wealth as well. In many cases one son is simply favoured, receiving two-thirds, for example, of the land. In general historians have dealt with this continuum as a dichotomy and studied the results for mobility, household structure and

---

[15] M. F. Le Play, *La réforme sociale en France*, 3 vols, 5th edn (Tours, 1874); H. J. Habakkuk, 'La disparition du paysan anglais', *Annales, E.S.C.*, xx (1965), pp. 649–63; 'Family Structure and Economic Change in Nineteenth Century Europe', *Jnl Econ. Hist.*, xv (1955), pp. 1–12.

economic development. In any future history of the family, post-mortem inheritance systems would be better handled as a continuum, since each permutation introduces important variations.

A second way in which systems have been dichotomized is that of the popular and very stimulating work of the French scholar, Yver.[16] Yver's discussion comes from a highly abstract legal framework and is concerned fundamentally with the different ways pre-mortem inheritance is structured in France. The opposite poles of the system are 'forced recall', largely associated with the West, and the *préciput* (advantaging one or more children), associated with the East. In between these two is the compromise form of 'option'. Under the *préciputaire* system the parents can endow a child in such a fashion as to give him the lion's share of the patrimony, and is similar in effect to the testamentary system of the South. The opposite system in its pure form involves strict equality among the heirs; any endowment must be returned upon the parents' death, the latter being unable definitively to advantage any child. In the compromise system of the Paris–Orléans region the child who is endowed can choose to return to the inheritance or not, but cannot be at the same time both heir and the subject of an endowment. Yver's whole schema is constructed on an analysis of the law pertaining to the child who has left the household while the parents are still living and in doing so has received a portion. So far not a great deal has been done to assess the causes of the two systems or their effects. Yver himself argues that forced recall is associated with extreme egalitarianism and is fundamentally a system involving feudal classes, while the system of option is an urban institution. Le Roy Ladurie has considered the effects of the various systems on morcellization of peasant land, the isolation of the *ménage*, and the development of a strong lineage concept. In any event, to assess the implications of pre-mortem inheritance the historian will have to treat the phenomena once again along a continuum and get down to a less abstract level than that of provincial law codes. The variations in the timing of dowry payments, their size and nature will have important implications for family relationships.

---

[16] J. Yver, *Égalite entre héritiers et exclusion des enfants dotés* (Paris, 1966); E. Le Roy Ladurie, 'Système de la coutume: structures familiales et coutume d'heritage en France au XVIe siècle', *Annales E.S.C.*, xxvii (1972), pp. 825–46.

There is a third moment in the process of family property devolution – the setting up of a new household with a conjugal fund.[17] Here too there is a basic dichotomy with various forms in between: the conjugal community or the lack of it. In the system of universal conjugal community, each spouse brings a portion to the marriage totally integrating the two to form a single property. Upon the death of one the property devolves upon the survivor, movable and immovable property alike. In some community systems only the movable property (and sometimes what is acquired during the marriage) are merged, each spouse keeping his own personal property (*propres, Eigentum*). In any event, community property implies a break with the collateral heirs of each spouse, sometimes at the birth of the first child, whether or not it survives. The opposite system simply means that neither spouse ever inherits from the other, for what each spouse brings to the marriage remains his own personal property however it is administered during the lifetime of the marriage. The property will be inherited either by the children issued from the marriage or, if there are no children, by the collateral heirs of each partner. There are various subsidiary rights, such as a jointure, that can be set up for the lifetime of either spouse. In some cases the survivor receives the right to use the deceased spouse's property for his lifetime if an heir has been produced. In this system, the property interests of the collateral heirs remain strongly involved in any couple's existence.

In trying to analyse the nature of the family and the effects of different forms of property holding, we must avoid treating the family as a static unit. For example, on broad abstract grounds Yver's analysis may provide a general schema for legal historians, but for the social historian its use is limited because it pinpoints only one moment in the cycle that the family goes through. The family by its very nature has a time-dimension. It begins with the personal union of a couple which in peasant Europe entails a property arrangement. With the birth of children the family takes on new responsibilities and functions, and property arrangements are adjusted accordingly, so that in some systems the wife's right to a jointure is contingent upon the birth of the first child. As the children grow up, the process of fission of the old household begins

---

[17] J. L. Gay, *Les effets pécuniaires au mariage en Nivernais du XIV au XVIIIe siècle* (Paris, 1953); R. D. Hess, *Familie und Erbrecht im Württembergischen Landrecht von 1555* (Stuttgart, 1968).

with dowries, portions and gifts of various sorts. Finally, with the death of one or both spouses, the fund is definitively partitioned for the heirs. In trying to understand the nature of the family it would be misleading to focus on any one of these moments, either the setting up of the conjugal fund, or the arrangements made for transmitting wealth before or after the decease of the senior generation.

In tracing-out these dichotomies it is immediately apparent that they do not correlate with each other in any simple way. For example, the universal conjugal community exists with both partible and impartible inheritance after the sixteenth century in the Paris–Orléans region and Bavaria respectively.[18] In Württemberg partible inheritance goes with community or movables and acquisitions (partial community); in Nivernais after the sixteenth century impartible inheritance is found with partial community. The complete lack of conjugal community goes with partible inheritance in Normandy and impartible inheritance in Bavaria and Nivernais before the sixteenth century.

Yver builds up a case to show that community property correlates with the *préciput* or the Paris–Orléans system of option while the complete lack of community goes with the total equality of the Normandy situation where forced recall prevailed. He further argues that the Normandy system is feudal, designed primarily for the aristocratic and bourgeois classes. He says little about the peasants, and without more detail on the actual practice, the argument remains unconvincing. In any event, as can be seen from the examples above, there is no European-wide correlation between conjugal community and systems where one son is advantaged, and between lack of community and forced recall.

In Bavaria forced recall was the early modern practice, yet here, unlike Normandy, unigeniture was the norm.[19] A book-keeping operation took place at the death of the parent or more often at his retirement. The land remained undivided and fell, together with the house and farm equipment, to one son, usually the eldest. The book-keeping made things appear as equal; the farm was valued at a certain amount, divided into equal shares, with the son who

---

[18] Le Roy Ladurie, *op. cit.*; Paul Hradil, *Untersuchungen zur spätmittel-alterlichen Ehegüterrechtsbildung nach Bayrisch-Österreichischen Rechts-quellen* (Vienna, 1908); Pflaumer-Resenberger, *Die Anerbensitte in Altbayern* (Munich, 1939).

[19] Pflaumer-Resenberger, *op. cit.*

got the farm obligated to pay the outstanding shares of his siblings in the form of marriage portions or dowries. The valuations took no account of the market value of the farm which indeed was usually much higher. It only took account of what was fair for the new farmer to pay. Since the arrangement was made by the retiring father, who would himself be supported by the farm for his remaining life, he did nothing to jeopardize the economic prosperity of the enterprise. The point is that forced recall in Bavaria went along with conjugal community, *de facto* inequality, and unigeniture.

Yver's argument regarding extreme equality in the Normandy case of forced recall is in itself misleading simply because the demography of the situation would create inequality. Marriage ages being what they were, there would often be cases in which the siblings were twelve to eighteen years in age apart. If elder children married early and young later, the temporal spread of dowry payments and portions would be even greater. In such a case the eldest child could have his portion to use for twenty to twenty-five years before the youngest received his and the former would not be obliged to return the increment that he had earned. If his portion had been partly in land and he had been impoverished and forced to sell, his father's patrimony would thereby have been reduced for the subsequent children. If his father's patrimony increased, he would share in the increment. Quite clearly this system favours the eldest, but in any event the siblings emerge as not quite so equal. With the book-keeping unclear we still do not know from Yver's account whether all sons got equal land or equal 'value'. In this regard the social values of the community are of crucial importance because legal arrangements were often by-passed by people set on doing so.[20]

There is also no reason why the conjugal community system and the systems of *préciput* or option should go together. All that Yver can demonstrate is that historically they do in some regions. Conjugal community appears to have appeared first in cities and spread out under the 'influence of the city'. What seems to be the case is that as peasants become more involved in market transactions, more funds are made available for the building up of movables or for making cash endowments. As brides begin to bring considerable endowments, their dowries are matched by those of their

[20] W. H. Riehl, *Die Familie* (Stuttgart, 1855).

husbands, often in exactly equal terms. This implies at least a community of movables and acquisitions. In Bavaria, where the universal conjugal community was the rule, the in-marrying spouse brought a considerable portion necessary to the economy of the enterprise. With that went the right to inherit the farm. Since conjugal community is the result of the growth of the urban market and the increasing participation of the peasant in it, it is not surprising that there are other changes wrought by the same forces. In the Paris–Orléans situation the system of *pre-mortem* inheritance, that is partible inheritance with limits, favoured the small peasant proprietor producing for a nearby urban market. In Bavaria the urban market was important but the city population not so large or dense as in the Paris basin. The large peasant enterprise remained dominant, but these developed the conjugal community based on large cash dowries.

It would be useful at this point to take a look at a concrete case of the establishment of a marital fund to see some of the ways in which family structure can be affected. For this we shall examine Nivernais in the period from the end of the Middle Ages to the eighteenth century.[21] In that region there were two basic systems of marital fund: the conjugal community and the *société domestique*. Basically the *société domestique* in Nivernais was a society of co-parceners including the parents of one of the newly married spouses, the siblings, and the in-marrying spouse. The latter was obligated to bring in a portion – usually of movable property – and this describes the totality of his or her fortune. It is in effect a compensation on the part of the new member for participation in the enterprise together with the enjoyment of its fruits. It bestows rights of enjoyment but no rights in property. There is no corresponding provision of a portion by the spouse already in the society and the property of the two spouses is in no way joined. If there are no heirs and the spouse already there dies, the in-marrying spouse must leave the society, taking her portion with her. She has no claims on the property of her husband. Similarly if she dies, her portion is returned to her heirs, that is, her family of origin. This type of arrangement was dominant in rural areas during the Middle Ages. Subsequently it disappeared, first in the cities, then in those rural regions close to the cities or where city influence penetrated, enjoying its longest life in the most rural

21 Gay, *op. cit.*

parts of the region. The arrangement fits a situation where the market has little or no influence, for there is in fact little liquid wealth that the in-marrying spouse can provide. In Nivernais there are examples of the exchange of sons and daughters to obviate the difficulty of providing movables.

The *société domestique* implies a number of things. To begin with, the links between the new spouse and the society into which she marries are fragile. By producing heirs the ties are strengthened because, having done so, she ensures her sustenance by the society for the rest of her life. At the same time the property she brought to the marriage now will fall to her children, thereby weakening the interests of her collateral heirs. A second characteristic of the arrangement is that the in-marrying spouse tends progressively to break her links with her family. At first the move is tentative, for her family continues to have an interest in her property. Unless she produces heirs, if she has been given a portion including immovables, she is recalled to the inheritance and movables are substituted. Producing an heir reduces the interest the family of origin has in her property, but increases her status within the domestic society. She will eventually supplant her mother-in-law as the dominant female; her portion becomes part of the property that will descend to the children. From this short discussion it can be seen that a marriage goes through a number of stages, and in this particular system the stages are quite gradual.

Along with the stages goes a progressive integration of property, in this case not of the couple but of the wider extended family. If, for example, the girl marrying in were a teenager, she would be making a break from her own family by being physically removed to a new location where different adults held authority over her. Her rights would be guaranteed by the fact that she brought a portion which also assured her status in the new unit; nevertheless she is a junior woman under the authority of her mother-in-law and perhaps her sisters-in-law. Her own family continues to have a direct interest in her, and that interest is guaranteed by the fact that they continue to have a claim on her property – a residual claim that will remain all her life, in however weakened a form. Bearing a child changes the girl's status to that of mother, with a consequent increase in duties and status within the family. The birth of a child signals the beginning of the change of generation (as does the coincidental marrying out of sisters-in-law) and ensures

110   DAVID SABEAN

the right of the girl to lifelong sustenance by the community. The
more children she bears – the more surviving heirs – the more
integrated and assured her place becomes. Finally she becomes
the senior woman with direction of part of the enterprise and
prepares to see her portion used to provide dowries for her
daughters and portions for her sons.

In Nivernais the other form of marital fund was a partial community composed of movables and acquisitions (*conquêts*). Both
spouses were obligated to bring a portion to the marriage, each receiving the right to survivorship of the other, irrespective of the
birth of children. Here then the integration of the marital fund is
immediate and begins with marriage, implying neo-local residence.
The system developed wherever the market influence penetrated
and fortunes became liquid enough for the establishment of considerable portions. It put primary stress on the break between
households and whatever ties that remain, or were built up, were
not based so strongly upon residual inheritance rights. The position
of the wife is one of more independence and it would be interesting
to discover if women tended to marry at a different age in areas
where the conjugal community was the norm. Since the influence
of the market is important for the creation of the conjugal community, and with market penetration comes the possibility of
greater mobility, one would expect there to be an increasing differentiation of the sibling group making the ties that bind them
more complex, often leading to total rupture.

Not much has been said about kinship-behaviour itself. Rather
the attempt has been to try to clarify some of the variables that
influence the way kin relate to each other. I have tried to emphasize
that the family must be treated as a temporal unit and that the
degree of integration of a household goes hand in hand with the
integration of the marital fund. One of the primary links between
households is formed by the residual rights in property stemming
from the fact that a sibling group is provided for out of the same
original marital fund. Where the establishment of new funds for
a new generation emphasizes the new unit as primary, as in those
areas where the conjugal community was the dominant form,
primary ties between siblings are thereby reduced. Where radical
differentiation between siblings takes place the ties may be broken
altogether. On the other hand, children may seek ties that, while
based on kinship, do not emphasize ties among siblings or between

father and sons. In areas where primogeniture predominates, peasant proprietors may stress cousin ties or the tie between father and eldest son. The landless may seek out kin outside the nuclear family for help. What ties already exist *in potentia* may be reinforced by marriage strategies or by the selection of godparents. Making any selection automatically excludes some other possibilities. It would be interesting to study the lines of fission in rural society – crime, conflict, village factions – in terms of family linkages, inheritance patterns, and the role of women and different forms of marital funds. What seems fundamental is the notion that different forms of property arrangements shape in an intimate fashion the total fabric of the family.

5. Peasant inheritance customs in the Midlands, 1280–1700

CICELY HOWELL

As an introduction to the history of English inheritance customs and the peasantry, this chapter deals with general trends over a long period of time. Its purpose is to set out the basic problems which the typical rural society encounters, and which inheritance customs are designed to meet, and, conversely, to show how situation and law mutually modify one another. Secure in the knowledge that the ground will be covered again by specialists, each in his own field, I have allowed myself a broad canvas, moving from the eighth century, which simply signifies 'a long time before the Conquest', and about which I can claim little specialized knowledge, through to the sixteenth and seventeenth centuries where I am on home ground. I have permitted myself the luxury of some grand generalizations, since one can only cover a thousand years in a single chapter if one passes over in silence most of the exceptions, which, though it would take a long time to argue, were only 'apparent exceptions'.

The virtue of an extended time scale is that it allows one to trace the continuity of one type of inheritance pattern through to its successor in the same area. The temptation otherwise is to set slightly differing customs alongside one another as representing different origins and different ethnic sources rather than different stages in the development of the same process. Does East Anglia, for example, owe its partible inheritance to the Frisians or to its abundant commons and fishing? Did the Frisians just happen to choose thinly populated coastal areas where partible inheritance could be continued, or did they refuse to allow unigeniture as a matter of tribal principle? One cannot answer this question by checking on the habits of the Frisians, but only by examining the whole gamut of inheritance patterns within their demographic and economic setting.[1]

---

[1] G. C. Homans, 'The Frisians in East Anglia', *Econ. Hist. Rev.*, 2nd ser., x (1957–8), pp. 189–206, and R. Faith's challenge in *Agric. Hist. Rev.*, 16 (1966), p. 24.

Peasant inheritance customs in the Midlands 1280–1700   113

'*The Authority of Custom and Long Use is not Slight*' Bracton,
De Legibus, fo.22.a.

The court rolls of the late medieval period and the probate records
of the early modern period shed abundant light on the inheritance
customs of the English peasant, and upon modifications of these
practices which were to have far-reaching results. However, many
of these customs ran counter to feudal legal theory, and are strongly
reminiscent of customary law as practised in the Scandinavian
countries, in Germany and in France, not to mention Wales and
Ireland, and indeed modern Russia.[2] Although English legal records
abound in references to customary law, few legal historians have
devoted much time to collecting and comparing customary practices. They have preferred to tell the story of the development of
legal, as against customary, theory and practice, a development
whose roots do not extend back much further than the twelfth
century, and which was in many respects at variance with the
customary outlook and practice of both magnates and smallholders
in medieval England. The law as a profession emerged in the
twelfth century and its practitioners rapidly created a corpus of
legal doctrine based on *raison d'état*, administrative convenience,
stratagems for dynastic survival, Roman law, canon law, and a
general desire to codify and to rationalize old practice in terms of
current doctrine. They freely admitted the existence of a parallel
system of local custom, and occasionally cited examples to illustrate
certain arguments, but they showed no interest in its rationale.[3]
Therefore, no contemporary discussion of the laws of inheritance,
as practised by the majority of Englishmen in the Middle Ages, has
come down to us. It is left to the social historian to reconstitute
the corpus of popular practice with regard to inheritance. What
emerges is a rich variety of patterns, behind which lie some fairly
straightforward principles.

The most fundamental of these principles was that family land
belonged to the whole family; every member had a claim to support
from it, from generation to generation. Responsibility for its

[2] F. Seebohm, *Tribal Custom in Anglo-Saxon Law* (London, 1902);
B. S. Phillpotts, *Kindred and Clan* (Cambridge, 1913); C. I. Elton and
H. J. H. Mackay, *Robinson on Gavelkind: the Common Law or the Custom
of Gavelkind*, 5th edn (London, 1897); L. Lancaster, 'Kinship in Anglo-
Saxon Society', *British Jnl of Sociology*, ix (1958), pp. 320–50, 359–77.

management could lie with a generation-set, or with a single representative, but the position was one of stewardship, not of ownership. This attitude is not the product of urban society, and barely survives in industrial societies today, but it is still strong in agricultural societies and was strong in England in 1700, and this in spite of half a millennium of official preaching to the contrary. However, so strongly did medieval lawyers argue against hereditary ownership of land, especially villein land, that the case against them must needs be outlined here with some care.

If we go back to a time when hereditary ownership of land was beyond dispute in Northern Europe, for example to that period when the early Irish laws were operative,[4] we find a society made

<hr/>

[3] L. Beauchet, *Histoire de la Propriété Foncière en Suède* (Paris, 1904), p. 1; L. Beauchet, *Loi de Vestrogothie* (Paris, 1894); A. Bergen, *The Law of the Westgoths according to the Manuscript of Aeskil* (U.S.A., 1906); J. A. Barnes, 'Landrights and Kinship in two Brennes Hamlets', *Jnl Royal Anthrop. Inst.*, 87 (1957), pp. 31–56; Radolphe Dareste, *Études d'Histoire du Droit* (Paris, 1889), pp. 349–50 for Icelandic law; A. Gurevič, 'Représentations et Attitudes a l'égard de la Propriété pendant le Haut Moyen Age', *Annales E.S.C.*, 27.3 (1972), p. 220; H. J. Habakkuk, 'Family Structure and Economic Change in Nineteenth Century Europe', *Jnl Econ. Hist.* 15 (1955), pp. 1–12; Sir M. Hale, *De Successionibus Apud Anglos: or a Treatise of Hereditary Descents* (London, 1700); I. Jutikkala, *The History of the Finnish Peasant*. Reviewed by F. Skrubbeltrang in *Scand. Econ. Hist Rev.*, xii, 2 (1964), pp. 165–80; L. M. Larson, *The Earliest Norwegian Laws; being the Gulathing and the Frostathing Law* (New York: Columbia Univ. Press, 1935); D. Herlihy, 'Land, Family and Women in Continental Europe 701–1200', *Traditio*, 18 (1962), pp. 89–120; Ernest Levy, *West Roman Vulgar Law* (Philadelphia, 1951); K. B. McFarlane, *The Nobility of Later Medieval England* (Oxford, 1973), pp. 71–6; F. de Schulte, *Histoire du Droit et des Institutions de l'Allemagne* (Paris, 1882); T. Shanin, *The Awkward Class* (Oxford, 1972); *Westgermanisches Recht*, Series ed. F. Beyerle and K. A. Eckhardt (Germany, 1936–72) for the Salic Laws, the Burgundian, Ripuarian, Lombard, Frisian, Saxon, Anglian and other *Leges Barbarorum*. (The text is in German and, unfortunately, the Latin original is not always supplied.) J. Yver, *Egalité entre héritiers et exclusion des enfants dotés* (Paris, 1966), with commentary by E. Le Roy Ladurie in 'Systeme de la coutume: structures familiales et coutume d'héritage en France au XVIᵉ siècle, *Annales E.S.C.* xxvii (1972), pp. 825–46, chapter 2 of the present volume; S. F. C. Milsom, *Historical Foundations of the Common Law* (London, 1969), p. 91; J. C. Holt, 'Politics and Property in Early Medieval England', *Past and Present*, 57 (1972), pp. 3–52.

[4] I have deliberately selected a post-Roman date and an area not directly influenced by Roman rule in order to circumvent the debate on the mutual interaction of Barbarian customs and Roman Vulgar law. (Ernest Levy, *West Roman Vulgar Law and the Law of Property*, Philadelphia, 1951). In fact, the two traditions had much in common, and the basic principle of family ownership as against individual ownership, is, as one would expect,

up of kindred groups each of which occupied its own territory or
fintiu. Membership of the kindred was defined by descent from a
common ancestor. Clearly, if this common ancestor was reckoned
from seven generations back, the kindred would be a large one,
if only four generations back, it would be small. Hence the importance attached to the number of generations. The Irish *der-
braithir* were confined to four generations, so that, when the fifth
generation was of an age to hold land, the second generation either
became heads of separate *derbfines* or the genealogy was tele-
scoped. Thus a man was left in no doubt as to who his kindred
were. Membership of the kindred gave him a claim to a share in
its land, both arable and pasture; this share varied in its exact
position and extent, as the total membership of the kindred was
redefined once in every generation. In some societies the landholders were restricted to members of one generation only; not
until the last of the senior generation passed away did the next
take control of the land. Such a system effectively reduced the
number of share-holders, though not the total number of persons
supported by the land. The latter system would seem to have preferred a few large shares to many small ones, though here we are
thinking in relative terms since we have little idea of the size of
territories or of the balance between arable and pasture.[5]

Flexible though the system was, it was peculiarly vulnerable to
the effects of population-growth on the one hand, and to loss of
territory in war on the other. The resulting population-pressure on
the land could be met by reducing the generation span of the kindred or by controls on marriage and on the age at marriage. The
kindred could be temporarily, or permanently, reduced to the extended or even to the stem family. Lateral descent was preferred
to lineal descent, in that a son inherited from his kindred rather
than from his father, and grandsons stood anything from seventh
to ninth in the line of succession, great uncles and their sons

the same. See C. W. Westrup, *Introduction to Early Roman Law, Part II,
Joint Family and Family Property* (Oxford, 1934), and *Part III, Patria
Potestas* (Oxford, 1939), pp. 233–47.

[5] T. M. Charles-Edwards, 'A Comparison of Old Irish with Medieval
Welsh Land Law' (Oxford University, D.Phil. Thesis, 1971); also *idem*,
'Native Political Organisation in Roman Britain and the origin of MW
brenhin' in Wolfgang Meid *et al.* (eds), *Antiquitates Indogermanicae* (Inns-
bruck, 1974); E. R. Norman and J. K. S. St Joseph, *The Early Development
of Irish Society* (Cambridge, 1961).

inheriting before them.[6] This follows logically on the principle that a permanent division of goods was only made upon the death of the landholder; those endowments which a landholder might make to one or other of his children during his lifetime were only of a temporary nature pending a definitive share when, upon the death of the landholder, the entire family inheritance was divided equally among all the heirs.

There is ample evidence however, that by the twelfth century, if not long before, the kindred had become so reduced in size and territory in many areas, that insecurity of tenure was becoming a serious problem. If there was only enough land to support one family, then clearly only one son could inherit it, and until that son could be sure of permanent possession he could not marry and have children. And so we find that although in some areas the old practice was continued of returning gifts made *inter vivos* to the hotch-pot – to use the traditional English phrase – upon the death of the landholder, in others the practice developed of permanently endowing one son during the lifetime of the landholder, and, with permanent possession, went, of course, the right of the son so endowed to transmit the land to his own son. Thus grandsons came to take precedence over senior generations.[7] In France this modification usually took the more subtle form of the 'option' by which a landholder could endow one or more of his children during his own lifetime, on the condition that they made no further claims upon the inheritance after his death unless they first returned to the hotch-pot that share which he had given them.[8] The practice was not unknown in England. Bracton, for example, noted that a daughter who had already received a *maritagium* could choose whether to return her share to the pot or not.[9]

Thus, in certain areas, unigeniture was slowly emerging where hitherto partible inheritance had been the custom. At the peasant level, where land was a source of livelihood rather than of political

[6] Seebohm, *Tribal Custom, op. cit.*, p. 276; *Laws of the Westgoths, op. cit.*, p. 49; Icelandic Law, *op. cit.*, p. 350; Phillpotts, *op. cit.*, 173–6, 184–5, 208, 209.

[7] Seebohm, *Tribal Custom, op. cit.*, p. 283; L. M. Larson, *The Earliest Norwegian Laws; being the Gulathing and Frostathing Law* (Columbia Univ. Press, 1935), p. 294; C. I. Elton and H. J. H. Mackay, *Robinson on Gavelkind, op. cit.*, p. 89.

[8] Yver, *op. cit., passim.*

[9] Bracton, *De Legibus et Consuetudinibus Anglie*, 2 vols, ed. S. E. Thorne (Harvard, 1968), fo. 76b, p. 223.

power, unigeniture is probably too definite a term. Bracton is specific in stating that, as late as the thirteenth century, primogeniture for socage holders did not entitle the eldest son to all the family messuages, but only to the first choice: if there was only one messuage, he should have it, but if there were more than one messuage, the remainder should go to the other children in order of seniority, and those who received no land should receive the equivalent in value in cash or kind.[10] The same principles held sway in gavelkind areas.[11] In other words, where unigeniture was permitted, and even enforced for the sake of the survival of the line, there was a marked tendency to revert to partible inheritance whenever circumstances permitted.

The areas which adopted the option or unigeniture coincide remarkably faithfully with areas of open-field cultivation, which happen to be also areas of widespread manorialization both in England and in France; I cannot speak for Germany. Homans used this correlation to support the thesis that unigeniture was the product of estate management and he may be correct.[12] Unfortunately, we know too little about population density in these same areas. It could be argued that unigeniture developed in areas of land shortage, which are also the areas most susceptible to the processes of manorialization. Partible inheritance continued to be practised over wide areas which were characterized either by sparse population, or by dense populations supported by fishing, small industries, and exceptionally rich pasture land. In other words, partible inheritance is found where there was enough land for all sons, or where land was not especially significant and the distinction between land and chattels not vital to the survival of the family.[13]

Unfortunately, our knowledge of the Celtic and Saxon countryside is so slight that precise knowledge of the degree and extent of manorialization will probably never be available. All we can say is that the small family holding was already normal in the

[10] Bracton, *De Legibus*, fo. 76a, p. 221.

[11] Elton, *op. cit.*, pp. 2–4.

[12] G. C. Homans, 'The Rural Sociology of Medieval England', *Past and Present*, 4 (1953), pp. 32–43. Also *idem*, 'The Frisians in East Anglia', *Econ. Hist. Rev.*, 2nd ser., x (1957–8), pp. 189–206.

[13] R. Faith, 'Peasant Families and Inheritance Customs in Medieval England', *Agric. Hist. Rev.*, xiv (1966), pp. 77–95; Habakkuk, *op. cit.*, p. 10; H. E. Hallam, 'Some Thirteenth Century Censuses', *Econ. Hist. Rev.*, 2nd ser., x (1957–8), pp. 340–61.

seventh century, that the kindred was already archaic, although it still formed the basic unit of society as far as social controls were concerned (and continued to do so throughout the medieval period), that some areas were already well populated, although primogeniture was not common,[14] and that large estates, run by serf labour, were a familiar feature.

Once the hereditary land of a family had been reduced to an area sufficient to support one family only, the composition of the household had to be tailored to fit the landholding. This was a simple economic and administrative necessity. However, the definition of a family cannot be changed as easily as a land boundary, nor can a family's attitudes. And so, when we come to study the composition of the peasant household in the thirteenth century we still find collaterals being supported by the heir to even the smallest of holdings, and in the sixteenth century we still find smallholders making equal provision for all their sons and daughters, while reserving the land to one only. We find peasants of villein status leaving their holdings to their heirs over countless generations, and distributing their chattels by will. The continuity in peasant attitudes from the tenth to the thirteenth century is evident and would not cause surprise were it not for the well-known fact that such attitudes run clean counter to feudal theory and to the corpus of legal doctrine elaborated in the twelfth and thirteenth centuries.

It is necessary, therefore, to examine more carefully the practice of manor courts in the period between Glanvill and Bracton, in order to see how far they were in fact affected by the developing theory of common law, and whether or not pre-Conquest attitudes could have survived two hundred years of attack.

Both Glanvill and Bracton accepted the view that a villein could not transfer property to his heir or be the heir of anyone. Neither paid much attention to what went on in church courts and in manor courts. The church taught that villeins, as well as freemen, should make wills (for the benefit of their souls), and probate of villein wills took place in the manor court, where villein land-transfers were also registered, subject to the custom of the manor. Custom, as to which member or members of the family should inherit, varied from region to region, but the fundamental right of the family, as such, to inherit was never questioned. In fact, a lord could force

---

[14] Faith, *op. cit.*, p. 79.

an heir to inherit. Many of the key phrases and certainly the subject of those local custumals which survive in England, such as the Customs of Kent and the Customs of Rotheley in Leicestershire are almost identical with the customary codes of Scandinavia, France and parts of northern Europe. Bracton was not writing about customs, he was writing about that new science, *lex*. He writes, 'Custom, in truth, in regions where it is approved by the practice of those who use it, is sometimes observed as, and takes the place of, *lex*. For the authority of custom and long use is not slight.'[15] His enthusiasm for *lex* has led him to an exaggerated vagueness about custom, which was nevertheless, the 'law' of every manor court in the country, and the only law which the majority of Englishmen made use of; it did indeed take the place of *lex*. It would be a mistake, therefore, to accept the *dicta* of Bracton, and still more those of Glanvill,[16] as reflecting the values and practice of law in England outside the specialized and limited area of the King's courts, which dealt only with the cases of men whose status and form of tenure made them of interest to the crown.

Moreover, the King's courts themselves recognized that custom replaced *lex* in certain circumstances. A recent detailed study of common law villeinage, analysed at some length the royal court's treatment of villein inheritance.[17] Its conclusion was the familiar one: that there was no villein inheritance at common law – 'the villein has no property of his own, and consequently cannot transmit property'.[18] But the author also admitted that, in practice, villeins left land to heirs and inherited land – and their right to do so was upheld in manorial courts, and he went on to say that the 'gap between legal theory and actual practice is wider (here) than at any other point in the system'.[19] Frequently the Justice in Eyre

---

[15] *De Legibus*, fo. 2a, p. 22.

[16] T. F. Plucknett, *Concise History of English Law*, 4th edn (London, 1948), p. 422, writes, 'Glanvill's distinction was good enough for the first arresting phrase of a treatise, but it bore little relation to the state of the law in his time.'

[17] P. Hyams, 'Legal Aspects of Villeinage between Glanvill and Bracton' (Oxford D.Phil. thesis, 1968). See also the same author's forthcoming book, *Kings, Lords and Peasants in Medieval England.*

[18] P. Vinogradoff, *Villeinage in England* (Oxford, 1892), p. 159.

[19] Hyams, *op. cit.*, pp. 118, 120. However, the common law distinction between free and villein tenants could on occasion be used by a lord to obstruct land transactions carried out by wealthy peasants, the object being, not so much to prevent the transaction as to extract from the villein actor a

upheld local hereditary customs. For example, in the Curia Regis rolls for Berkshire in A.D. 1212 it accepted that by local custom, a widow took the whole of the land which her husband had held, if he was a villein, but only one-third if he was a freeman.[20] In a Shropshire case for 1235 the justice upheld the custom that the land should pass to the youngest son while the chattels went to the wife and remaining children.[21] There are several references on the Winchester Eyre rolls for 1249 relating to East Anglia which accepted the argument that, if land had once been held in villeinage, it could not at a later date become subject to partible inheritance.[22]

Both Hyams and Levett have taken up the point of villein wills. Hyams found several examples taken from the plea rolls of the thirteenth century. Miss Levett found it a commonplace for the villein tenantry of St Alban's Abbey to make wills which were proved in the manor court, particularly between the years 1377–1420.[23] Her examples were drawn from several manors and refer to land as well as to chattels. It must be remembered that these were years of severe dislocation, when many families were seriously depleted in numbers, and the next of kin not obvious. Land on these manors was left to widows alone, to brothers jointly, to one daughter alone to the exclusion of three other daughters, and frequently it was sold, the next of kin being offered the right of pre-emption, and the money given to the church. This last was an accepted method of transforming material goods into spiritual resources which would benefit the family in afterlife, there being no remaining close kin to profit from the land itself.[24]

Wills were not copied out in extenso in the Merton College rolls for Kibworth Harcourt, Leics., but there are frequent references

high fine for settlement out of court. For example, in 1265 Earl John de Warenne fined the executors of a prosperous Sussex villager half a mark for the freedom to administer the dead man's goods, on the grounds that, strictly speaking, the man's land and goods should revert to the earl, since the man was his villein. The earl might not have won his case in court, but it would have cost his villein more than half a mark to take the case to court... Records of the Barony and Honour of the Rape of Lewis, ed. A. J. Taylor, Sussex Rec. Soc., 44 (1939), pp. 22, 23, 27, 29, 31, 32, 33 (1266).

[20] Hyams, op. cit., p. 119.

[21] Ibid., p. 132.

[22] Ibid., p. 118.

[23] A. E. Levett, Studies in Manorial History (Oxford, 1938), ch. iv.

[24] D. Whitelock, Anglo Saxon Wills (Cambridge, 1930); D. Herlihy, op. cit., Traditio, 18, pp. 89–120; R. Faith, op. cit., Agric. Hist. Rev., xiv (1966), p. 80.

to the executors of deceased tenants. Since it was the custom on this manor for the entire tenement to pass to the widow for her life, the executors had only to deal with the payment of debt and the disposal of chattels.[25] Similar references to wills appear on the Winchester Pipe Roll for 1208 in the guise of land taken up *de testamento* and *de legato* at Waltham, Downton, and Taunton.[26]

It would seem then, that in spite of the observations of Glanvill and Bracton, a villein's right to inherit both lands and goods was upheld both by custom and by the Church. Moreover, the King's courts would uphold custom in those areas and places where custom took precedence over *lex*. A lord when he held a manor court was providing a service; he helped to settle disputed claims and to register transfers. His was not a court held for the purpose of hiring and firing tenants. So we may conclude that in England, as on the Continent, villeins could devise their land *de jure* as well as *de facto*.[27]

Church law and customary law could clash, however. It is not clear how far back the Church's cognizance of wills extended, though it reached at least as far back as the Conquest,[28] The Church encouraged the free disposal of land; familiar with Justinian's *corpus juris*, it saw nothing outrageous in allowing the individual to alienate land from the family. By contrast, customary law, the older, the more deeply rooted, was specifically designed to prevent the alienation of land.

A fourth strand in the development of late medieval legal attitudes, was private estate practice. Customary law had little to say about slaves; they were men without land and of little or no status. Their masters were held responsible for their affairs, their well-being, behaviour, hours of work, and so forth. But the laws have plenty to say about the recently freed man, how long he should have held land before he could claim hereditary title to it, who were his heirs, and if he had no heirs, to which lord his land should revert. Estate practices and local custom tended to be easily confused, and by the late Middle Ages they were often treated as one and the same. Thus an estate custumal will often deal not

[25] Merton Muniments, Merton College, Oxford (= M.M.), 6407.6, 21, 29, and 6408.1.

[26] H. Hall, ed., *The Pipe Roll of the Bishopric of Winchester* 1208–9 (London, 1903).

[27] Hyams, *op. cit.*, p. 118.

[28] Levett, *op. cit.*, pp. 212–13; Hyams, *op. cit.*, pp. 123–6.

only with services and rents, but also with succession rules, the rights of widows, and warranty for sales, all taken word for word from customary law. With this down-grading of custom, one might have expected lords to usurp the right to frame laws. In fact, this does not seem to have happened, and the familiar phrase 'according to the custom of the manor' possibly carried greater weight than legal historians have attached to it.

If we can break away from our preconception of the medieval peasant as an eighteenth-century-type individual, holding land from a profit-orientated large estate for a term of years, and think of him as the representative of a peasant family, with hereditary rights to the land stretching back and forward indefinitely, then the customs governing inheritance assume considerable importance. The size of households, the size of holdings, the standard of living, the pattern of migration, all hinge to a considerable degree on local inheritance patterns.

Unfortunately, there is no satisfactory method of collecting data rapidly for a regional, let alone a nationwide, study. Attempts have been made to estimate the turnover of surnames from one rental to another for several estates within the same period, and to indicate thereby the degree of mobility into and out of estates, and the strength or weakness of peasant attachment to land.[29] The snag is that, just as the court rolls do not distinguish between sales and leases, so the rentals do not distinguish between owners and occupiers; they tend to list the occupiers, who were often lessees or the mortgagees. Moreover, since they only record the landholding group they do not indicate whether or not the men whose names no longer appear on a rental have actually left the village or not, or if the new names are genuine outsiders or simply sons-in-law or 'adopted' sons. Lastly, they were very often drawn up in a period of dislocation following high mortality, or estate reorganization. In fact, the drawing up of rentals might serve as a demographer's guide to exceptional mortality!

The only other short cut would be to take custumals, as for example the thirteenth-century custumal for the soke of Rotheley in Leicestershire,[30] or the better known Customs of Kent.[31] How-

[29] R. Faith, 'The Peasant Land Market in Berkshire during the Later Middle Ages' (Leicester University D.Phil. thesis, 1962); also A. Jones, 'Land and People in Leighton Buzzard in the later Fifteenth Century', *Econ. Hist. Rev.*, 2nd ser., xxv (1972), pp. 18–27.

ever, these custumals are rare, and full though they are, they do not tell us much about the structure of the household, or the size of the tenements which supported these households.

And so in the end one is driven to the detailed study of one estate. Hence this study of Kibworth Harcourt in south-east Leicestershire tracing the stability of families on their landholdings over four centuries. Figure 1 shows the length of time each family remained in the village of Kibworth Harcourt during the period 1280–1700 whether or not that family held land. Each millimetre square on the vertical axis represents one named village family, whose descendants are traced from father to son along the horizontal axis. Thus the horizontal axis indicates the length of time each family remained in the village and the decade in which it became extinct or left the village. Periods of plague (P) or high mortality have been indicated in order to show the cumulative effect of the late-fourteenth-century plagues upon continuity of tenure. The data is derived from the tithing lists of 1280 and 1686, the Poll Tax returns for 1377/79 and the rentals for 1300, 1340, 1372, 1440, 1484, 1500, 1593, 1679, 1686, 1693 and 1700. The remaining dates are based on biographical reconstructions of each of the families listed in the previous rent roll. These reconstructions were made from the court rolls for the fifteenth century and from the parish register and probate of wills for the sixteenth and seventeenth centuries.[32] Those families which did not hold land have also been indicated since they appear as a new category in the seventeenth century. So rapid was the turnover in families between 1410–40, that a separate chart had to be made for this period which is not reproduced here. The second gap, that between 1540–93, is due to lack of information. The figure throws into high relief the remarkable continuity of tenure between 1280 and the rental of 1340; every one of the 1280 surnames featured on the 1340 rental without exception, and only five new names were added – that they were added is in itself interesting, since in other parts of England village populations were already in decline by this date. What is more, the transfer of land from father to son can be traced

[30] G. T. Clarke, 'The Customary of the Manor and Soke of Rotheley in the County of Leicester', *Archaeologia*, xlvii (1882), pp. 89–130.

[31] Elton, *op. cit.*

[32] For details, see C. Howell, 'The Social and Economic Condition of the Peasantry in South-East Leicestershire, AD 1300–1700' (Oxford University D.Phil. thesis, 1974).

for these families in an independent source – the court rolls – and we can be certain that the 1340 rental was an accurate and up-to-date list of tenants and not – as can be the case with rentals – a fair copy of an out-of-date rental.

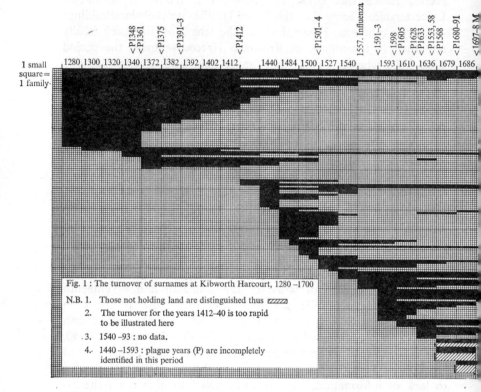

Fig. 1 : The turnover of surnames at Kibworth Harcourt, 1280–1700

N.B. 1. Those not holding land are distinguished thus ▨▨▨
     2. The turnover for the years 1412–40 is too rapid to be illustrated here
     3. 1540 –93 : no data.
     4. 1440 –1593 : plague years (P) are incompletely identified in this period

Figure 1. The turnover of surnames at Kibworth Harcourt, 1280–1700

In the plague years of 1348–9, 44 landholders in the village died. Only $4\frac{1}{2}$ bond virgates and $2\frac{1}{2}$ demesne virgates were not affected.[33] By the end of 1349 only one-fifth of these holdings was still without a holder, all the rest had been taken up by sons, many of them minors, by brothers and by nephews. There was no need for daughters to inherit. Here is a straightforward example of the phenomenon of which Arthur Lewis has given the classic exposition:

[33] See C. Howell, thesis, *op. cit.*, p. 47.

the phenomenon of an economy in which labour is so plentiful that its marginal productivity is negligible, or nil, or even negative; an economy in fact which has nothing to lose in productive power if its surplus manpower is removed, and indeed something, perhaps much, to gain.[34]

In 1354 there were more deaths and this time it was more difficult to find heirs; tenants were not finding it easy to keep up with rent payments, and the first examples occur of villeins fleeing the manor. Eleven more died in 1361, an outbreak of 'pestilence' occurred in 1376, and the 70s and 90s were conspicuous for their high average death-rate.

As plague followed plague at roughly ten-year intervals, one family after another became extinct in the male line. New names appeared on the court rolls, as land passed to sons-in-law or to adopted heirs. The size of households shrank from 5 to 3.96, while the average size of family holdings increased from 12 to 24 acres, and land in the hands of the lord was allowed to become *frysca et inculta*.

It was the custom on this manor for the usufruct of the entire holding to pass to the widow with reversion to the eldest son. The livestock and implements were divided equally among the remaining children. The novel situation of the late fourteenth century threw up two issues of considerable importance. The first was the question of equal division among heirs. According to Bracton, as we have already noted, if there was land for only one son, and, if primogeniture was the local custom, the eldest son should have it; if there were two or more holdings, then the eldest son should choose for himself one holding, the second son should choose another, and so on until there were no more holdings, the remaining children having to be content with the equivalent in movable goods.[35] In this, Bracton was enunciating a widely held principle, and one which was certainly followed by some families at Kibworth, such as the Polles. Around 1400, many men in Kibworth found themselves the possessors of more than one tenement. Had they decided to give one holding to one son, the other to a second son, within a generation or two the standard family holding would once again have been 12 acres. In fact, a significant number did not; they

---

[34] Quoted by A. R. Bridbury in 'The Black Death', *Econ. Hist. Rev.*, 2nd ser., xxvi (1973), pp. 590–1.
[35] *De Legibus*, fos 75b–76a, pp. 220–1.

passed all their land to one son. Almost certainly this was not a premeditated policy, but simply an *ad hoc* response to circumstances. There were fewer male heirs than usual, formerly inalienable customary land was now on the market and high wages provided the capital with which to purchase extra-familial land. Therefore, younger sons could acquire new holdings for themselves.

The second issue was the question of land transfer from one family to another. Customary land was hereditary land, and how could hereditary right be conferred upon a man and his heirs? Surely not by the simple payment of a sum of money? Most of the Barbarian Codes have a good deal to say on this subject. The most detailed, to my knowledge, are the Gulathing Laws of Norway. According to them there are two types of land, hereditary or odal land, and money land. Money land was a most unsatisfactory form of possession. At any time within twenty years of purchase, the seller's heirs could redeem it. After this initial twenty years the buyer's title became secure, but the land did not become hereditary land until it had remained in his family for five generations.[36] By contrast, land transferred by gift immediately became hereditary land. There were various types of gift; some, like the gift made by a king in repayment for service or hospitality, need hardly concern us in the peasant context, but the gift made in exchange for other land, the gift made to a son-in-law, and, significantly, the gift made to a foster son, are extremely interesting. Adoption could mean the legitimization of a bastard son with the consent of the heirs, but it could also represent a retirement arrangement in a case where there were no heirs. As the Gulathing laws put it, 'when a man takes another into his keeping for good or for ill and maintains him to fire and pyre, as the saying goes' (that is, until death), that man becomes the foster heir of the other.[37]

Now the average length of time for which a man held land in Kibworth was 27 years in the medieval period and 32 in the early modern. In the earlier period most Kibworth landholders continued as head of the household until death, although there are two or three examples of a father retiring early, and arranging a retirement contract with his son (or nephew or son-in-law), which contract

---

[36] Larsen, *op. cit.*, paras 270–94. It is also interesting to consider the *de donis* clause in the Statute of Westminster in this light.

[37] Larsen, *op. cit.*, p. 111. Also *Leges Langobardorum*, ed. Franz Beyerle (Witzenhausen, 1972), pp. 44, 45, 124, 132.

was duly recorded in the court rolls.[38] Figure 1, however, shows a sharp decline in hereditary continuity between 1350 and 1412, as one would expect after the Black Death and subsequent plagues. In such circumstances, one would expect to find a crop of retirement arrangements, if not with heirs then with foster heirs, as the survivors grew old and the enlarged holdings became too much for them.

This thought prompted me to make a more careful search of the Kibworth documents for retirement arrangements and the adoption of heirs. The search led me to re-examine the question of *ad opus* transfers at Kibworth which occur only between the dates 1359–1419. *Ad opus* is a very common term within the vocabulary of manorial records. Within the context of the surveys it is usually taken to mean 'holding for labour services' and in some cases as 'holding for either money rent or labour services at the option of the lord', a meaning which could also be conveyed by the phrase 'at the will of the lord'. But in the court rolls it appears in the form 'A surrendered this land *ad opus* B' and is used to distinguish this sort of land transfer from the routine 'A surrendered this land into the hands of the lord and B came and took it.' The distinction was clearly significant to villagers in the fourteenth century, but the precise nature of the distinction continues to elude the modern historian. We do not even know for certain whether these transfers dealt with sales or leases; in the Kibworth context they dealt with leases, but the terminology of manorial court records was by no means standardized from one estate to the next.

To add to the difficulties of the record interpreter, the phrase was also much used in the King's courts from the thirteenth century onwards but with a meaning quite inappropriate to a bondsman's status and economic resources. In professional legal parlance the term *ad opus* (derived from the Old French *oeps*, which in turn was derived from the Latin word *opus*) signified a 'use' – the device by which one person, or group of persons, held a parcel of land to the use of (*ad opus*) another, who, in the law French of the thirteenth century, came to be called the *cestui que use*. The earliest example of a bondsman availing himself of this device does not occur until 1504 by which date the tenurial basis of a bondsman's position had profoundly altered.[39]

---

[38] Howell, thesis, *op. cit.*, ch. vi. See also below, p. 128
[39] J. M. W. Bean, *The Decline of English Feudalism, 1215–1540* (Manchester, 1968), ch. iii.

Aware of this state of confusion and imprecision surrounding the term, I took the precaution of distinguishing between ordinary and *ad opus* transfers when tabulating the land transfers at Kibworth between the dates 1280–1700. It was, therefore, not difficult to re-examine the two categories. The following observations emerged. Transfers *ad opus* were only made between the dates 1359–1419 and then very frequently indeed. An *ad opus* transfer occurred only once within the history of any single tenement, on which occasion the tenement either passed out of the hands of an old, hereditary family to a newcomer, or the transfer formed part of a retirement contract between landholder and heir. Once land had escheated, that is, had become the responsibility of the lord for lack of heirs, it was never subsequently transferred *ad opus* by later tenants. Moreover, while land which had escheated to the lord passed very rapidly from one holder to another, land transferred *ad opus* usually remained in the hands of the taker for many years if not for generations. Lastly, the spate of *ad opus* transfers coincided not only with a period characterized by a shortage of heirs but also with a period when land was easily obtainable, especially vacant holdings in the hands of manorial lords who, in the hope of attracting tenants, were willing to waive entry fines and even to waive rents for the first few years. Why, one may ask, did incoming tenants prefer to take land *ad opus* from other peasant families rather than vacant tenements from the lord?

It is not difficult to posit a tenable hypothesis based on these observations. An *ad opus* transfer conveyed an hereditary title to the land from the holder of hereditary land to his or her 'natural' heir or an adopted heir, in return for maintenance on that land for the remainder of the grantor's life. Once land had escheated it was no longer hereditary land and, although this was not the case at Kibworth, a lord might regard this as 'estate' land which he could lease out for a term of years only, and whose rents and entry fines he could alter in a fairly arbitrary way. Hence the preference for hereditary land *ad opus* even if it meant supporting the grantor for his remaining days. If a man died as head of a household there was no need for an *ad opus* transfer, the land passed by custom to his natural or adopted heir. It was only if he wished to relinquish control before death that an *ad opus* transfer was necessary; it was thus essentially part of a retirement agreement, but it did also provide the opportunity for a man publicly to acknowledge an adopted 'son' as the heir to his land.

Maitland noticed a similar association of the *ad opus* transfer with a retirement arrangement at King's Ripton in 1301. In this instance one William the Chaplain granted his land *ad opus* the two sons of Roger and Catherine of Kellow on the understanding that Roger and Catherine would look after and support him for the remainder of his days, and would cultivate the land at their own cost.[40] The same sort of arrangement took place at Kibworth. In 1349 Robert le Yonge surrendered his messuage, one virgate of demesne land and half a customary virgate *ad opus* Robert Godyer in return for maintenance for himself and his wife.[41] This is an example of an *ad opus* arrangement between father and son, and for 1360 we have an example of an arrangement between a man and his adopted heir; John Maister surrendered a messuage and one and a half virgates *ad opus* his stepson Nicholas Gilbert upon the understanding that the latter would provide the old couple with board, lodging, and a small annuity.[42]

But why, one may ask, did the steward of a manorial court consider the phrase *ad opus* appropriate in the context of retirement agreements? J. M. W. Bean's recent work on the development of the use as a legal device in the royal courts goes far towards providing an answer. For the thirteenth century Bean found the legal usage of the term to be 'loose and ambiguous – in one case it covers an agreement to convey a marriage portion, in another security for a loan, and in others some sort of guardianship'. Pushing his researches further back, he discerned three trends. The first was the practice in Saxon and early German law of transferring land temporarily to another trusted person, to a guardian, for example, or to a friend, while away on pilgrimage; the second was the growth of the conception of a trusteeship; the third, and most immediate was the emergence of the executor in the late thirteenth and early fourteenth centuries as an agent who was responsible for the administration of the affairs of a deceased person after his death. The use came to be modelled on this institution and it is likely, he concludes, 'that it was the conception of the

---

[40] F. W. Maitland, *Select Pleas in Manorial Courts*, vol. ii (Selden Soc., 1888), p. 106.
[41] M.M. 6405, 23, Ed. III.
[42] M.M. 6407, 4 dorse.

executor as the personal representative of the deceased person that led to an increasingly powerful realization among contemporary landowners and their legal advisers that those who had hitherto held land to the use of another during his lifetime could continue to hold it after his death and employ it or its revenues as he had directed them before he died'.[43]

If we put ourselves in the position of the Steward of the court leet and court baron at Kibworth Harcourt, one Simon Pakeman, who was faced in the post-plague period with a large number of hereditary village families who were in danger of extinction through lack of heirs, and who wished to 'adopt' heirs to their land in traditional peasant fashion, it is not difficult to conceive of the phrase, *ad opus*, with its undertones of guardianship, trust, conveyance of land by legal arrangement rather than by hereditary right, as the most appropriate phrase to adopt in the abbreviated entries in the court rolls. Pakeman came from one of those 'recognized professional families which supplied the official land agent class of men both for the crown and its greater subjects'.[44] He held land himself at Kirby Bellars, was Steward of the Honor of Leicester and also of Leicester Abbey, he represented the shire in the parliaments of 1333–4, 1346, 1347–8, 1364–5, 1366 and 1368, he was a Justice of the Peace, and was frequently engaged on royal business.[45] His duties under the earl of Leicester would have brought him annually to Carlton Curlieu, Shangton, the Langtons, Smeeton Westerby, Stonton Wyville, Glooston, and Cranoe, all neighbours of Kibworth Harcourt, and it would be interesting to see if *ad opus* transfers were introduced on these estates as well, or, indeed, in Kibworth Beauchamp, since the earls of Warwick (Beauchamp) made extensive use of the new legal device in their own affairs.

If adoption into a family and its inheritance was indeed still a common practice in the fourteenth and fifteenth centuries, this makes a strong case for the continued peasant preoccupation with hereditary land. The case against peasant attachment to land rests on the very marked turnover of surnames on many manors during the early fifteenth century. A glance at Table 1 leaves one in no

[43] J. M. W. Bean, *op. cit.*, ch. iii, in particular pp. 129–32, 157.
[44] Levi Fox, *The Administration of the Honor of Leicester in the Fourteenth Century* (Leicester, 1940), p. 72.
[45] *Ibid.*, p. 35.

doubt that this was also true of Kibworth for the late fourteenth and the fifteenth century, but a more careful scrutiny will reveal a return to something like the old stability by the seventeenth. Many of the short-stay surnames in the latter century were landless men and many of the new names were those of sons-in-law. The return to stability in the seventeenth century is more clearly seen if one follows through the tenurial history of the copyhold tenements. For example, of the fifteen tenements taken on twenty-one-year leases in 1593–9, seven were in the same family in 1636, six had changed hands once, only one had changed hands twice, and the descent of the last cannot be traced. Taking the same fourteen tenements for the 1636–79 period, eleven remained in the hands of the same family or in the hands of a son-in-law, the remaining three had all belonged to the Brian family, who moved back to the neighbouring village of Smeeton Westerby during this period, and allowed their Kibworth lands to pass to in-laws, who were themselves men of the blood of the village. In other words, there was no turnover among copyhold families between 1636 and 1679.

TABLE 1   *The percentage of surnames surviving each forty-year interval*

1280–1340	100%				
1341 80	80%	1280–1412	23.6%		
1381–1412	77%				
1413–40	60%				
1441–84	48%	1412 1527	27%	1280–1700	8%
1485–1527	51.5%				
1593–1636	69.2%	1593–1686	57.5%		
1637–1686	75%				

To return briefly to the period of maximum turnover   the fifteenth century – the average outsider held land in the village for not more than 12 years. To take the turnover of new names at even ten-year intervals, would tend to underestimate the number of temporary landholders. Therefore, rather than try to estimate the degree of instability, I have attempted to measure the degree of continuity and stability, by giving the percentage of surnames which survived each forty-year interval (Table 1).

The sharp increase in the turnover of surnames coincided not only with the fall in the population level after the fourteenth-century plagues but, more significantly, with the extinction of hereditary landholding families. In such circumstances, the land might revert to common land and was shared among surrounding villages or it was appropriated by the lord, a phenomenon to which the many deserted village sites bear witness.[46] Alternatively, tenants who had no hereditary claim might be found to take up these holdings. The inflow of new tenants is reflected in the number of new names to be found on most court rolls during this period. Clearly, one cannot use the documents from this exceptional period to argue for or against peasant attitudes to hereditary land or the existence of a peasant land-market in normal circumstances. But the documents are crucial to the understanding of the legal position of peasant landholders in the sixteenth and seventeenth centuries. At Kibworth, demesne land became leasehold *without* hereditary right, while customary land became copyhold *with* hereditary right. On other manors, customary land was granted out on leases and without hereditary tenure, or, demesne and customary tenements were thrown together and granted out with no clear understanding as to hereditary rights, but, at a later date were claimed to be leasehold without inheritance because they included demesne land.[47]

The estate documents present us with a further problem of interpretation which may have some bearing on inheritance customs. The Poll Tax lists for the Kibworth region show that the majority of villages in the area had adopted the practice of tenure *ad voluntatem domini* in place of tenure *in bondagio*.[48] Kibworth Harcourt still held by the old tenure but change was in the air. The earliest reference to holding at will occurs in 1331 but the movement did not gather momentum until the 1360s. In 1358 Richard Malt, a newcomer, took up land 'at the will of the lord' which his predecessor, Henry son of Nicholas, scion of an 'old' family had held 'in bondage'. In 1360 John Joye took at will a tenement which his father had held in bondage, and there are half a dozen or so equally explicit examples of change. Unfortunately, we know nothing of the negotiations or motivation which lay behind these

---

[46] E.g. *Victoria County History Oxon.*, vi. Five such villages in Ploughley Hundred: Saxenton, Ardley, Cote, Tusmore, Bainton.
[47] Many examples in Ploughley Hundred, Oxon.
[48] P.R.O., E.179 133/29, 35.

changes in tenure nor do any differences emerge from the study of the court rolls. As Table 2 shows, the tide of change was running strongly in the last decade of the fourteenth century. By the time the court of recognitions was held in 1439, all unfree tenancies were recorded as being held at will.

TABLE 2   *The shift from holding* 'in bondagio' *to holding* 'ad voluntatem domini'

Decades	References to land held 'in bondagio'	References to land held 'ad vol. domini'	Decades	References to land held 'in bondagio'	References to land held 'ad vol. domini'
1359–69	34	7	1420–29	5	37
1370–79	4	3	1430–39	2	44
1380–89	6	4	1440–49	0	17
1390–99	7	20	1450–59	0	0
1400–09	0	8	1460–40	0	7
1410–19	4	16			

It is clear that the change signified something to those concerned, but it is not easy to discern in what precisely the advantage lay. Most of what we know of copyhold tenure is based upon the commentaries of lawyers and surveyors upon established practice in the sixteenth and seventeenth centuries. Most agree that copyhold tenure was derived from customary tenure in villeinage, but none venture to describe how it differed from it.[49] According to Holdsworth, there were in the fifteenth century no generally accepted formularies or categories for copyhold.[50] Hilton argued that the widespread adoption of rents *ad placitum* on the Leicester Abbey estates in the period 1340–77 was evidence of a peasant market at a competitive rate. 'The tenure *ad placitum*, unprotected by custom, was essentially a tenure whose terms were dependent on market conditions, on the balance between the demand for land and the needs of the lord for rent or for the land itself.'[51] Given

[49] Summarized by C. Calthorpe, *The Relation Betweene the Lord of a Mannor and the Coppy-holder his Tenant* (London, 1635), p. 89, and *passim*, edited by The Manorial Society, No. 10 (London, 1907). Also Bodleian MS., Viner 486.
[50] W. S. Holdsworth, *History of English Law*, vol. iii.
[51] R. H. Hilton, *The Economic Development of some Leicestershire Estates in the Fourteenth and Fifteenth Centuries* (Oxford, 1947), pp. 95–104.

the low value of land at the time, this would operate in favour of the peasant, which may explain why the initiative came from the landholders at Kibworth Harcourt and why the court of recognitions, held in 1439, confirmed the new tenure shortly after the reduction in rents agreed in 1427. But this explanation is not entirely satisfactory. Rents thereafter, far from reflecting market trends, became frozen; the rent fixed in 1427 still obtained in 1700. Moreover, land transfers ceased to be recorded in the court rolls, and, if the manor accounts are to be believed, no fines were taken until 1594. The hereditary principle remained firmly entrenched, and every transaction 'at the will of the lord' was also made 'according to the custom of the manor', the latter being the operative phrase. The change in 1439 seems to have been no more than an acknowledgement by the lord of an agreed drop in rents and an agreement to cease using the term *nativus*. Possibly the misleading phrase 'at the will of the lord' was inserted by lawyers to preserve the distinction between the jurisdiction of the lord's court and that of the king – it had to be made clear that the tenant was subject to the lord in matters tenurial, even when the tenant owed no more in rent than 14s. 0d. for 24 acres, a derisory sum in 1700!

The terminology was again altered by the statute of 13.Eliz.c.10, by which deans and chapters, parsons and vicars, colleges and hospitals were forbidden to lease their lands for longer than twenty-one years or three lives. Thereafter, the tenants of Merton College duly took out twenty-one-year leases at seven-year intervals 'according to the custom of the manor' but nevertheless continued to be classified as copyholders as distinct from the leaseholders of the demesne.[52] The custom of the manor had nothing to do with leasehold and the like but with hereditary right and so, predictably, tenements continued to pass from father to son in the same manner as before. At a much later date legally minded persons fused the two strands into a category known as copyhold by inheritance but without fixed fines.[53]

No discussion of peasant customs attaching to land and its

[52] Cf. *V.C.H. Gloucs.*, viii, p. 232. At Tredington, Glos., leaseholds for lives replaced copyholds but the manor court continued to treat these new leaseholds as copyholds.

[53] E. Kerridge, *Agrarian Problems in the Sixteenth Century and After* (London, 1969), pp. 37ff; M. M. Postan, *Cambridge Economic History of Europe*, i (Cambridge, 1966), p. 615; J. Bean, *op. cit.*, pp. 20, 22–5.

descent can avoid the question of the existence of an active peasant land market. The argument for such a market rests upon the assumption that sales of odd acres and rods of land are sufficiently significant to constitute a land market within the context of an agrarian subsistence economy.[54] Half an acre within an urban context represents considerable potential or actual wealth, either as building land or for market gardening. Half an acre within a fishing or pastoral area represents a useful supplement to a man's sources of income, what the two-acre holding is to the modern Humberside steelworker. But half an acre in open field country was an anomaly; it could not possibly be thought of as a subsistence unit; it was of value only to the widow or the craftsman, both of whom had other means of support. Land to a subsistence cultivator meant an area sufficient to support a household; a land market only had meaning when the unit of exchange was at least a quarter or a half virgate. It is interesting to note, for example, that three virgates at Kibworth, which became ownerless in the early fourteenth century, and were subdivided to provide small plots for cottars, were reassembled within a generation by these same cottars into standard full and half virgate holdings; in other words, into viable agricultural holdings which made sense within the village economy.[55]

The fact that these sales of half-acres were often accompanied by *cartae* serves to strengthen the case for the atypical nature of the transaction. A very small unit of land, the single acre, was being detached from a whole unit, a virgate, and added to another. This is one possible interpretation of the nature of the sale; the other, the more plausible, is that a small unit of land assarted from the waste, and hence the customary, hereditable, possession of no family, was being transferred, and since no village custom existed to sanction or uphold such transfers, recourse was had to the written charter, a form adopted from pre-Conquest times by Church and State to give authority to agreements of an unusual nature, for which no time-hallowed procedure existed, and which might, therefore, be challenged and disallowed at some later date. It could be argued that the alienation of small units of land could lead to

[54] M. M. Postan and C. N. L. Brooke (eds), *Carte Nativorum*, Northants. Rec. Soc., xx (1960). Challenged by E. J. King, *Peterborough Abbey, 1086–1310. A Study in the Land Market* (Cambridge, 1973), and by P. Hyams, 'The Origins of the Peasant Land Market in England', *Econ. Hist. Rev.*, 2nd ser., 23 (1970), pp. 18–31.

[55] Howell, thesis, *op. cit.*, p. 48.

the morcellation of virgates by the process of steady erosion. The fact that these transactions required the drawing up of *cartae*, however, indicates that they were so rare that no normal procedure was ever developed to deal with them in the manorial courts. The freeholders at Kibworth were periodically called upon to show their *cartae*, when a relief was paid, for example, or when a rental was being drawn up, the earliest extant record at Kibworth being the *Inquisiccio carta* held in 1291.[56] The business of producing *cartae* was always surrounded by some confusion, since no record of their content or sealing was kept in the Kibworth court rolls. The amount of land in question is consequently described as unknown, the services and rent as unknown, and an enquiry ordered forthwith. By contrast St Peter's Abbey, Gloucester, kept its peasant *cartae*,[57] as did Peterborough Abbey.[58] As Edmund King commented on the latter, the charters deal with very small holdings of one or two acres often accompanied by a licence to build, and the list of charter holders reads 'like a register of daughters and younger sons'.[59] Now the holders of the one-acre plots on St Peter's Abbey estates were also widows and younger sons. In other words these look like the dower holdings one comes across in most European peasant societies. At Peterborough and St Peter's they were treated as separate from the chief messuage, at Kibworth they were not. According to the later Kibworth wills, most widows held an acre in each field and house-space in the main house, but they do not appear as separate tenants on the court rolls.

The second argument for the existence of an active peasant land market is based upon the interpretation of the numerous transfers which took place every year as being sales. Such an interpretation leads to some curious situations; the membership of the peasant community at Kibworth was closed, outsiders were not encouraged, but within this closed group land changed hands with staggering rapidity. Yet the net result was that every man finished with the same land as his father had held before him. Thus A inherits a virgate in, let us say, 1300; he surrenders it to B in 1305, to C

---

56 M.M. 6389.
57 *Historia et Cartularium Monasterii Sancti Gloucestriae*, iii, ed. W. H. Hart (Rolls series 1867), and mss. in Gloucester Cathedral Library – Frocester Register B (1393) and ten volumes labelled 'Deeds and Sales'.
58 Postan and Brooke, *op. cit.*
59 King, *op. cit.*, p. 124.

in 1310, to D in 1314, and in 1320 he dies leaving one virgate to his widow, who then comes and surrenders this in court to her son. Clearly, these transfers cannot have been sales; they must have been leases. Another look at Table 1 will again show how rare a permanent alienation was before 1349, in spite of an average of two transfers a year recorded in the court rolls for the period 1280–1349. The practice of leasing land is perfectly compatible with the strong feeling that land should remain within the village community, and with the even stronger feeling that that land should not be alienated from the family. Yet it allows for the developmental cycle of the family, which at certain stages needs more land than at others.

So when we talk of a peasant land market, we must be sure that we are talking about complete subsistence units and about permanent alienations. The odd acre has significance for the townsman or the village craftsman or widow, but not for the peasant farmer. The lease made possible the retention of land within the family over many generations; the sale, on the other hand, destroyed this continuity.

But leases are the medievalist's nightmare! How do we know, when we read an extent, how many under-settlers there were? The suspected prevalence of sub-tenants has probably been exaggerated. Fortunately at Kibworth the evidence about them is unambiguous. Between 1300–10 or thereabouts, three virgates became tenantless due to lack of heirs. It was a period of acute land shortage, and so, very sensibly, the land was not offered to outsiders, but was broken up into small parcels and let to cottagers. In subsequent rentals these odd bundles of two acres, and five acres, and so on, are always identified as part of 'Robert Holke's virgate' or one of the other three. No indication is given in the documents, but this Robert Holke had been dead for some seventy years. Had only the 1372 rental survived, one might easily have been tempted to argue the practice of extensive subletting, hidden leases, lack of attachment to hereditary land, economic and social mobility, the emergence of the *kulak* and so forth. In fact, so unusual was the existence of odd, acre-holdings in place of virgate holdings, that this group was always given a special mention in the rentals and their ancestry traced to the last full virgate holders!

But, it may be argued, if partition could happen to a vacant virgate, how do we know that holdings, recorded as passing from father to son, were not in practice sublet or subdivided to persons other than family members? Once again the documentary evidence answers this question simply and conclusively. In the first place, as has been seen, the rentals consistently distinguished between normal virgates and disintegrated virgates and name the present tenants of the latter. Secondly, in the fifteenth century, when holders of tenements frequently absconded secretly during the night, a body of supervisors was set up to inspect abandoned holdings and to report upon the condition in which they had been left. Damages were charged against the late holder, and the man's pledgers were called upon to find the money and to complete the ploughing. On no occasion did they call upon sub-tenants to pay or to plough. Lastly, when land in the lord's hand was let, never more than two or three acres were let from any one virgate. In other words, the subletting of the odd acre was a commonplace within the system of fixed family lands, which could not be permanently alienated whatever the present size of the family. But the alienation of entire virgates could only happen in very exceptional circumstances such as the complete failure of heirs.

Up to this point the discussion of inheritance practice at Kibworth has been based upon the documentary evidence of rentals and court rolls. The discussion to follow will be based on the parish register and the probate records. The nature of the information yielded by these two very different types of source material is complementary rather than continuous. Therefore it may be useful to sum up the data deduced from the late medieval documents before entering upon a new line of argument.

The village community of the early fourteenth century was remarkably stable. Land passed from father to son and supported other, landless, members of the family. There was often more than one branch of a family in a village, so that if one line failed there were usually close kinsmen to hand. In the exceptional circumstance of a family becoming extinct the family could 'adopt' an heir if it did not wish the land to escheat to the lord. Whether or not a lord could veto an 'adoption' is not clear; in theory he probably could, in practice he was probably glad to be spared the trouble of finding a new tenant acceptable to the village. Merton certainly favoured *ad opus* transfers in the late fourteenth century when tenants were very difficult to find.

The drastic culling of village families which took place during the plague period made possible the accumulation of two or more units of family-land in the hands of one surviving line. This sudden increase in the size of holding, accompanied by a decrease in household size (since celibate adults and adolescent boys could now find work 'abroad') made possible the accumulation of savings in the form of cash or capital equipment which had seldom hitherto been possible. Children could be endowed with cash portions in place of land or maintenance on the land. Consequently, these large holdings were not subdivided in the next generation to provide as many children as possible with a minimum smallholding. Instead, the large holding was preserved intact, but every effort was made to improve its profit so that larger cash portions could be distributed among the children.

The high turnover of surnames on the fourteenth- and fifteenth-century rentals can be attributed to the temporary dislocation of the hereditary descent of land, rather than to a decline in the peasant's attachment to land. By the seventeenth century the old stability had been regained.

The principle source materials for the sixteenth and seventeenth centuries are the probate records and the parish register. These shed abundant light upon the retirement arrangements of the Leicestershire smallholder, a subject which was as central to the economy and life style of peasants then, as it is in rural economies today. They also illuminate the related topic of marriage portions and child portions which had far-reaching repercussions on the regional economy.

The descents of some fifty families, extracted from the register, provide a framework into which the wills of these same families can be inserted, and against which they can be interpreted. For example, one can discover the age of subjects mentioned in the wills by consulting the register, and by this means can state with certainty that at Kibworth it was usual for the eldest son to inherit, a point which the earlier court rolls do not make absolutely clear.

Two-hundred-and-seven wills were analysed. They all related to families living in Kibworth Harcourt, or, who had at one time lived in Harcourt and later lived in one of the other two villages of the parish, Kibworth Beauchamp and Smeeton Westerby. In the first stage of analysis the wills were grouped by family and examined under the following heads.

Date

Residue left to

Special arrangements for wife, if any

Number of children

Were child portions equal or unequal in value?

If unequal, who was favoured?

Legacies left to brothers and sisters;
     affines;
     cousins or kinsmen;
     nephews and nieces;
     grandchildren;
     godchildren;
     friends;
     servants

Specific mention of land

Legacies in cash only

Legacies in cash and kind (excluding land)

Money to be put out at interest

Legacies contingent upon obedience, marriage, etc.

Remarks

With the resultant charts before one, it was possible to select the more significant lines of enquiry, in particular, the deployment of the family's wealth upon aged dependants, young dependants, and persons who had a social but not an economic tie with the family, such as affines and godchildren.

The factual information thereby obtained for Kibworth could then be used to support a general discussion on the significance of dower arrangements in the life of the smallholder, the age of retirement and its repercussions on the age structure of the village, and the composition of the household; the manner of disposing of movable wealth among the next of kin, and the effect this had upon the potential for capital accumulation among peasant landholders. Lastly this survey shed light on the implications of an increasingly cash-dominated economy, even among smallholders, and upon the expectations of the younger generation, the majority of whom would migrate to other areas, taking with them a large portion of the hard-won wealth of the village.

I have not attempted to distinguish between the attitudes of labourers, husbandmen, and yeomen, the three groups represented in the wills, because it was found that practice varied from one generation to the next within the same family and economic group. The decisive factor was not class or family, but the age and family responsibilities of the testator at the time when he made his will.

Thus only those who had fulfilled their obligations, such as grandparents, widows, widowers, or those who had no such obligations, such as bachelors and single women, left legacies to the wider kin-circle, for example, to nephews, nieces, affines, cousins, grandchildren, and godchildren, 'neburs' and servants.

The wider kin-circle was thus relatively unimportant. By contrast, the distribution of land and goods between wife and children called for more detailed analysis, since the wills provided information on attitudes which could not be derived from the court rolls or the parish register. For example, it was the custom of the manor that the entire holding should go to the widow; from the wills we learn in what circumstances this custom was adhered to and when not. Likewise, it was the custom that only one son should inherit the land; the wills tell us in what sense he held the land, as sole owner or as family representative. Custom at Kibworth tells us nothing about the rights of the remaining children, whereas the wills are primarily concerned with them. The information derived from wills goes far towards bridging the gap between unigeniture and partible inheritance.

Accordingly, the sample was reduced to 193, by selecting only the wills of married men. These were divided into four categories: those wills in which the land was left to the widow alone, 29.5 per cent; those in which the land was left to the widow and a kinsman or son to be held jointly by them, 17.6 per cent; those in which the land was left to a son or daughter the wife being still living, 14.5 per cent; and lastly, those in which the land was left to a son or daughter the wife being dead, 16.6 per cent.

In the first category, those who left land to the widow alone, there were 56 wills. Of these forty testators left their property to their wife alone without any written condition safeguarding the interests of their heirs, and only fifteen of these were childless. The remaining sixteen inserted the type of limiting condition that one would expect: that their widows were to hold for life only, or for a term of years, or until the heir reached his majority, and were to forfeit the property if they remarried.

In the second category, those who left property to the widow and a kinsman to be held jointly, there were thirty-four wills. Of these, all without exception laid down explicit conditions. The wife was to hold jointly for life or until the heir was twenty-one, after which the heir was to guarantee her maintenance, unless she re-married. All except seven of these testators left at least some children under twenty-one.

Thus the tendency was to leave the residue to the wife, or to the wife and a kinsman, if the couple was childless or the children were minors.

In the third category, 28 testators left the land and residue to a son or daughter, the wife being still living. In every case specific arrangements were made for the maintenance of the widow; she was to have the use of a certain number of acres and, or, maintenance in the house, while seven were left a sum of money in cash to the order of £20 or so. These legacies in cash are particularly interesting, and will be discussed below. This category belonged to an older age group, in only six cases were all the children under twenty-one.

In the last category, thirty-two testators made wills in which the wife was not mentioned. In every case it was found that she had predeceased her husband. Seven of these testators left children all under twenty-one, of whom five left the property to the eldest son, the other two left it to be held jointly by all the children. Some or all of the children of the remaining testators were over twenty-one and the eldest son inherited. One case is significant. William Smith left four children and many debts. He instructed his executors to sell the copyhold in order to pay off the debts and to divide the proceeds equally among the two boys and two girls, giving to the youngest, a boy, an extra £5.

Thus the tendency was to leave the land to the son if some or all of the children were over twenty-one, and to make the heir responsible for the maintenance of the widow according to pre-scribed conditions.

The results of this analysis of the wills within the context of family circumstances can be summarized as follows:

In 33 cases where a man left children who were all minors, 42.4 per cent of these left the tenement and residue to the wife alone; 39.3 per cent left the tenement and residue to a wife and kinsman (usually a son); 18.0 per cent left the tenement and residue to a son alone (the wife being still alive):

In the 51 cases where some or all of the children were over 21: 29.4 per cent left the tenement and residue to the wife alone; 29.4 per cent left the tenement and residue to the wife and a kinsman (usually a son); 41.2 per

cent left the tenement and residue to a son alone (the wife being still living).
In the 18 cases of a childless marriage: 83.3 per cent left the tenement and residue to the wife alone; 16.6 per cent left the tenement and residue to the wife and a kinsman.

It has not been possible to trace in a sufficiently large number of cases, the subsequent history of these widows, due to the convention in the parish register of merely noting 'widow' in the burial entries. One cannot be sure whose widow she was. Therefore, we cannot tell how long a widow remained a charge upon a tenement, sometimes for over twenty years, or how soon she handed over effective control to the heir and 'went her way' as the wills and the old laws phrase it. The wills of widows seldom deal with land, and the court rolls show that widows often handed over the tenement to their sons after only a short interval, but we do not know what proportion these represented to those who did not.

It is quite clear, however, that provision for his wife was an important, one could almost say overriding, consideration in a man's mind when he felt that his own days were numbered. This raises an aspect of inheritance custom which is easily overlooked, partly because, without the wills, there is little one can discover about retirement arrangements, and partly, I think, because it is so often assumed that the life of the medieval peasant was brutish and short, and that old age was consequently not a very probable eventuality. The age of marriage in a region was determined by the age at which it was customary for a man to retire, or, if retirement was uncommon, the age at which landholders tended to die. It was also influenced by the nature of the retirement arrangements in the region. For example, if it was customary for the heir to buy the land from his father, as in the Scandinavian countries and in Ireland, then he had either to find some means of earning the necessary money, or he had to marry a woman with a large marriage portion. In such circumstances, the age at marriage tended to be high and fathers could only afford to provide one of their daughters with a suitable portion. The number of single women, in consequence, was large and the growth rate of the population was correspondingly reduced. This is not to say that the growth rate was necessarily low, modern Ireland being the classic example to the contrary.[60]

[60] W. G. Williams, *The Sociology of an English Village: Gosforth*

I have not come across evidence in England for the practice of the heir buying the inheritance; he succeeded to it, but at the father's pleasure. Therefore, there was no pressing need for him to marry a girl with a 'fortune'. Something should be said at this point about marriage portions. In modern parlance the word 'dower' is usually associated with the jointure or marriage portion which a woman brings with her to her marriage. The concept is derived from Roman and canon law and is relatively recent. The old word for this contribution was the '*maritagium*', and the word 'dower' had an older and quite distinct meaning. It was money or land which a free man gave to his wife at the church door at the time of his marriage. He was bound both by the common law and ecclesiastical law so to endow his wife. According to Glanvill, a free man could not endow his wife with more than one-third of his lands; later lawyers held that the dower could be more, but not less, than one-third.[61] However, we get nearer to common practice if we turn to the church manuals and rituals. Here we find the familiar formula, 'Wyth yis ryng I wedde ye, and wyth yis gold and sylvere I honoure ye, and wyth my gyfts I dow ye' (York). The last phrase varies regionally and a common alternative is 'with all my worldely catel I thee endow' (Norfolk, Wales).[62] Among villeins the dower was often quite literally 'all my worldely catel', and the widow by right took the entire tenement; this was certainly the case at Kibworth, though in other regions she was endowed with only a half or a third of the lands. Thus the dower custom in an area went far towards establishing the age-structure of that region and the retirement custom. A girl's *maritagium* or marriage portion at Kibworth was the same as her child portion, and the child portions of all daughters were equal, so that lack of a 'dowry' in the modern sense, was not the serious impediment to marriage that it was later to become.

However, the corollary of a modest *maritagium* was the absence

(London, 1956), pp. 46–52; Rigmor Frimannslund, 'Farm Community and Neighbourhood Community', *Scand. Econ. Hist. Rev.*, iv, no. 1 (1956), pp. 65–6; C. M. Arensberg and S. T. Kimball, *Family and Community in Ireland* (Harvard, 2nd edn, 1968), pp. 105–12, 135–6; Jutikkala, *op. cit.*, pp. 65–180; M. Spufford, *Contrasting Communities: English Villagers in the Sixteenth and Seventeenth Centuries* (Cambridge, 1974).

[61] G. D. H. Hall, ed., *The Treatise on the Laws and Customs of England commonly called Glanvill* (London, 1965), books vi, vii.

[62] W. G. Henderson (ed), *Manuale et Processionale ad usum Insignis Ecclesiae Eboracensis*, Surtees Soc., 63 (1875), pp. xvi, 19, 167.

of a substantial sum from a daughter-in-law in old age. A man had to put off retirement for as long as was physically possible, in order to provide for each of his children and ensure an income for himself and his wife. Meanwhile, his heir waited. At Kibworth during the late medieval period, the majority of transfers were from widow to son rather than from father to son *inter vivos*, and the number of retirement arrangements was remarkably few, as we have seen. Therefore, one can conclude that the heir had to wait until his father died. However, when one enters the sixteenth century and wills become available, one finds that a surprising number of heirs were already married at the time when their fathers were writing their wills. The old rule: no land, no marriage, would seem to have been relaxed. At what date this modification took place is not clear, but one can argue quite plausibly that the increase in the size of holdings, and the reduction in the size of households had made possible the three-generation family under one roof. Certainly at Kibworth it had become usual to allocate house-space under the same roof to more than one nuclear unit within the family. Thus an heir when he married was given house-space, but his father generally remained at the head of the household and farm. When the father died, the widow either remained at the head of the household, 'and she to have the ruling of my house', or she retired and was given house-space, usually a room with a hearth, and storage space in the yard. Thus John Carter, when he died in 1690, had been occupying seven rooms, his widow continued to occupy three of these until she died in 1711, while her son occupied the remaining four rooms. Thus, by the early modern period it was possible for a son to marry before he entered into possession of his inheritance. Nevertheless, he married late in life, so that the three-generation phase in the developmental cycle of the family was on average only 3.5 years and the generation interval rather long, thirty years. This brings us to the question of child portions.

When a man died leaving minors, he usually stipulated that his children should receive their portions when they were 16, 18, or 21 or when they married. However, if one turns to the wills of older men and of widows, one finds that children in their late twenties had still not received their portions and that the heir inherited the obligation to provide them. So the long generation-interval did not necessarily mean that a man had thirty years in which to accumulate the savings from which he could endow his children. The first few years would be spent paying off his siblings. The total amount to be raised and paid depended on his father's attitude towards the competing interests of his children as individuals, against those of the family inheritance.

In areas of land shortage the equal division of *land* among all sons could rapidly lead to the subdivision of family holdings until the minimum viable unit had been reached, beyond which it would be economically suicidal to subdivide. Younger sons could be expected to accept this as reasonable. But it does not follow that, because the land could not be divided among all the children, movables likewise could not be divided. We learn from the wills that the son who received the land did not receive the livestock and gear: these went to the remaining children. The heir could then either buy out his brothers and sisters, or could continue to support them on the tenement in return for the use of the livestock and the gear, at any rate for the first few years. In 1536 for example, Robert Smyth, who had only half a virgate and goods worth £13, left the land to his wife and eldest son and his goods to the other son and his daughters with the injunction, 'I will that my chyldren shall remain togyder in my house and live of my stok to the youngest be 16 years old.' In 1543, Thomas Stevenson of Smeeton, having made a similar division concluded, 'If any of my children depart or be married, their part shall be parted among the others.' We have already seen how, when William Smith sold his land, he instructed his executors to divide the proceeds evenly between sons and daughters alike, giving £5 extra to the youngest. These examples could be matched by many others and serve to illustrate one method of meeting the obligation to provide for many children without subdividing the land itself. In the days when most families in Kibworth held only half a virgate, this was probably the most common method of dividing the family inheritance. Seen in this light the sharp legal distinction between unigeniture and partible inheritance becomes somewhat blurred.

It is possible in the case of a small number of Kibworth families to examine in detail the relation between the size of the holding, the value of the movable goods and the value of the legacies over a number of generations, to which one can add further refinements such as the effect, if any, of current market prices on the value of legacies. Such an exercise can hardly be described as a short cut,

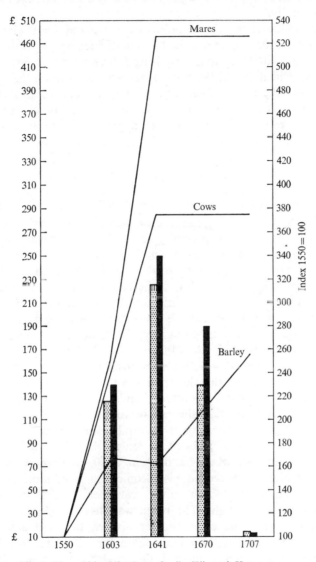

Fig. 2 : The wealth of the Carter family, Kibworth Harcourt
1550 – 1707 Cash legacies 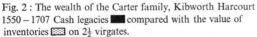 compared with the value of
inventories ▦ on 2½ virgates.

however, and only one sample has been worked through, for the Carter family.

One branch of the Carter family held two-and-a-half virgates of land from 1603–70; this was then subdivided among three sons. At the same time they may have leased three virgates from William Sheffield which had belonged to another branch of the Carters throughout the previous century. Wills and inventories survive for 1603, 1641, 1670, 1690, 1697, 1707, 1709, 1718. The chart (Fig. 2) shows the value of the movables as appraised for probate at these dates, against which is plotted the total value of the legacies to children at the same date. From 1603–41 the family invested heavily in cattle and horses, but always kept some 35 acres under the plough. Therefore, the market prices for mares and for barley at these dates have been added, using Leicestershire prices derived from inventories covering the whole county.

Figure 2 shows a steep decline in the family fortune after 1641. No reason is given, of course, but one can hazard the guess that the Civil War had something to do with it. The battle of Naseby was fought only a few miles to the south-west and tradition has it that Cromwell spent the night after the battle at Kibworth Beauchamp. Goodman Carter's cattle and particularly his mares would have been very much at risk. We shall never know, but his story may have read like the following for Mr Abberley of Stafford. 'Whereas Mr Abberley had eleven cows taken from him by the enemy, it is ordered that he shall have two heifers and a white cow remaining in the Committee's hands and one other which was taken away yesternight if she can be found, if the right owner of the cow have not the same.'[63] With livestock prices continuing very high it would be difficult to replace losses. In spite of this decline in fortune, when he died in 1670, William Carter left legacies which far exceeded his income and were more generous than his father's had been thirty years before when the family fortune was at its height. The result was disaster. Unable to meet his commitments, the elder brother divided the land among the claimants. Robert mortgaged his share for £172 and lost it, but the remaining brothers farmed the land jointly and only one married. The family survived as smallholders and carpenters until the twentieth century.

[63] D. H. Pennington and I. A. Roots (eds), *The Committee at Stafford, 1643–44* (Oxford, 1957), p. 182.

A simpler method, better suited for general surveys and regional comparisons is to work through the wills and inventories for a given parish, noting the nature and value of the legacy left to each son and daughter; if one works parish by parish one can be sure that at least within the parish the value put upon goods in the inventory is consistent, since the appraisers were drawn from the same group of men. This method deals only with the portions of younger and unmarried children but quickly yields a large sample.

I have used this method for the parish of Kibworth in order to plot the changeover from legacies in kind to legacies in cash. The figures also allowed me to chart the rise in the value of cash legacies and to compare this with the movement of prices in the Leicestershire area.

Figure 3 is based on the surviving wills from Kibworth parish, and for each block of years the percentage of portions worth £1–£4 each has been tabulated against the percentage of portions worth £5–£8 each and so on. Thus in the period 1520–60, eleven children received portions worth £5 each and one child received £6, but only one person, a relative, received as much as £30 in cash. By contrast, in the period 1681–1720, nine relatives received £5 to £6 each, whereas three children and two relatives received £200–500

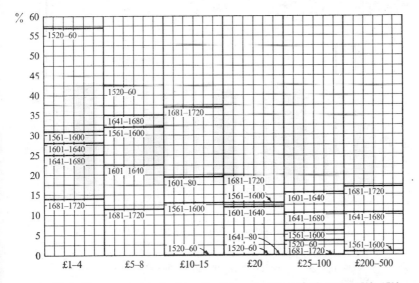

Fig.3 : The movement in the value of cash legacies, Kibworth Harcourt, 1520–1720

each. Thus in the mid sixteenth century 55 per cent of those who left legacies in cash left legacies worth only £1–£4, and only 3.57 per cent left a legacy worth more than £20. By contrast, in 1681–1720, the majority, 37.14 per cent left legacies worth £10–15 per legatee, 14 per cent left legacies worth £1–£5 each, and 17 per cent left legacies worth over £200 each. It is clear that there was an overall upward movement in the value of cash portions over the period 1520–1720.

However, Figure 3 leaves out of account those persons who left no legacies in cash, and also the value of the legacies in kind which children received in addition to their cash portions. Hence the need for Figure 4 which shows the proportion of legacies made wholly in cash to those made partly in kind and partly in cash. By the sixteenth century, the legacy wholly in kind was so rare as to have little statistical significance. As an indicator of the rate at which a virgate holder could accumulate surplus cash, the column to the left-hand side of Figure 4 has been added: thus in the year 1490, a virgate-holder could expect to save a net total of 42.7s.[64] The column for 1636–41 is misleading since it antedates the Civil

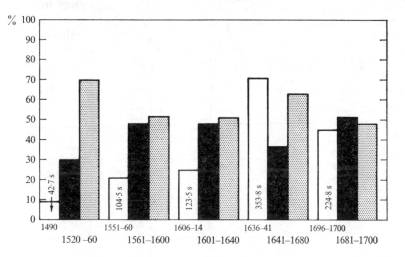

Fig. 4 : The relative percentage of portions in kind to portions in cash, Kibworth Harcourt, 1480 –1700 Portions in kind ▨
Portions in cash ▇ Cash surplus per virgate per annum (showing the savings potential at each period, in shillings) is shown in the left hand column.

[64] Howell, thesis, *op. cit.*, ch. v.

War, while the period covered by the wills spans the Civil War and Interregnum which were ruinous for many graziers like the Carters. The high profits of the 1630s were not sustained during the middle years of the century, hence the drop in the number of cash legacies and the increase in the number of legacies worth £5–8.

Taken singly, Figures 3 and 4 are misleading; they must be studied as a pair. Figure 4 for example, shows a rise in the proportion of cash-only legacies between 1560–1600 and thereafter indicates a fairly steady proportion of around 48 per cent; what it does *not* show is that the *value* of cash legacies continued to rise steadily, so that by 1681–1700 the 52 per cent of cash legacies were worth around £20 each, as against the 48 per cent of cash legacies in 1551–1600 which were seldom worth more than £5 each. On the other hand, Figure 4 corrects Figure 3 by making it plain that a hard core of poorer villagers continued to leave portions in kind supplemented by very small cash sums; the nominal 1s. left to children who had already received their portion has been discounted throughout. A figure which showed no portions in cash at all would indicate a highly improbable village structure in which there were no poor, and no old people with family heirlooms, furniture, and stock to leave to heirs. Concealed in the 'portions in kind' column of Figure 4 are also many small amounts of cash. One must also take into account the increase in quality as well as quantity of stock and gear. Figure 2 and the index figures on the right hand side of the graph show the steep rise in the price of mares and cows before the 1630s and the variations in the price of the staple crop, barley. From the inventories one learns that a plough was valued at little more than 5s. to 10s. throughout the sixteenth century, and a cart anything from 5s. to £1. Unfortunately, it is not possible to tabulate the rise in the value of legacies in kind since so many items are impossible to value on a comparative basis; without seeing the items concerned, how can one evaluate one second-hand chair, a brass pot or an old grey mare? My impression is, however, that over the period 1520–1720 the gap widened between those leaving few and inferior goods and those leaving high grade stock and well-furnished homes.

Taken together, the two figures allow one to make the following observations. By the sixteenth century testators had begun leaving money portions to their younger children in place of livestock and gear which were left to the heir. These cash legacies were worth more than what children would have received in kind, and reflect the growing prosperity of yeomen and husbandmen during the inflationary years of the sixteenth century. Thus, where a boy might have received a cow and a cart, he now received £5, and what is more, the cow and the cart remained on the holding to the benefit of the heir, thereby improving his chances of making a surplus and being able to endow his own sons generously. Therefore, a large number of cash-only legacies indicates a period of profitable farming for husbandmen and yeomen. A large number of mixed legacies, of gifts in kind supplemented by cash, indicates more uncertain conditions. For example, the number of portions in kind was high before 1560, dropped to 50 per cent in the period 1560–1640, rose during the Interregnum and fell to below 50 per cent by 1700. Those who continued to leave legacies in kind represented the hard core of smallholders who could never hope to save as much as £10 to endow two sons. As prices rose, the number of legacies in kind rose among the very small holders; as prices fell, the value of cash legacies increased. Not every family adopted the practice of leaving cash legacies: some persisted over generations in distributing the entire surplus, including the livestock and gear once in every generation, without ploughing any of the surplus back into the land. Ultimately, these families either perished or accepted the principle that the heir must be allowed to take over the land as a going concern within the context of commercial as against subsistence farming, and that the heir must be allowed to embark upon long-term agricultural improvements.

Thus the hard core of small property holders is conveniently and clearly revealed during the period of high agricultural prices after 1636. They group themselves at one end of the spectrum as leaving legacies predominantly in kind, and they were joined as the century wore on by a proportion of the middle group who had previously left legacies of £10–20 to each of their children. At the other end of the spectrum one can see a growing number of larger property holders, men who could leave £200 or more to their children. The number at the centre grows thinner as the process of polarization continues. The parting of the way between husbandman and yeoman can be seen taking place, the one to remain the humble villager, the other to become the local squire. Thus Parker, the half-virgater of the fourteenth century, the 'good nebur' and appraiser of wills of the sixteenth, became the 'gentleman' at the

Old House by 1679. Robert Lount, whose father's goods were worth £22 in 1627 was worth £274 in 1709 and left £300 to one grand-daughter, £200 each to his other two grand-daughters, and £400 to the fourth. He still ran the farm personally, but his sons-in-law did not.

Younger sons left home with up to £20 apiece; trade, the professions, the universities, lay open to them. If the matriculation lists of Brasenose College, Oxford, or, the school for Puritans, St John's College, Cambridge, are reliable indicators, then these sons of yeomen farmers, and men of *'mediocris fortunae'* were not slow to take advantage of the opportunities thus opened to them.[65] Kibworth boys went to Kibworth Grammar School, founded in the fifteenth century, and then to St John's, Cambridge.[66] There was always an educated curate resident in the parish, even in the fourteenth century, and by the seventeenth century they had a 'schoolmaster' and, in addition, a nonconformist school, presided over in the eighteenth century by Philip Doddridge and by Dr John Aiken, the friend and biographer of John Howard. Other sons went into trade and commerce, and the village had strong links with Market Harborough, Leicester, Northampton and London. It was spawning a middle class, and itself became a comfortable village ruled over by the Rays and the Parkers, who had made their way in the legal profession, and Haymes and Fox, who owed their prosperity to successful farming. Some of the other old families were less well off, but their sons inherited the skilled crafts of their fathers, and when they left home they took with them these skills. They were willing recruits for industry but they were not 'raw' recruits.

The effect of this shift from legacies in kind to legacies in cash, not only ensured the continuance of large farms but stimulated long-term improvements in agricultural practices, and provided the motivation for commercial, rather than subsistence, farming. Grassland management was brought to a fine art in south-east

---

[65] L. Stone, 'The Educational Revolution in England 1560–1640', *Past and Present*, 28 (1964), 41–81; J. Simon, 'The Social Origins of Cambridge Students 1603–1640', *Past and Present*, 26 (1963), 58–67; L. Stone and A. Everitt, 'Social Mobility in England 1500–1700', *Past and Present*, 33 (1966), 16–55; M. Spufford, 'The Schooling of the Peasantry in Cambridgeshire', *Land, Church and People*, J. Thirsk, ed. (Reading, 1970), pp. 112–49.

[66] B. Elliott, *A History of Kibworth Grammar School* (Market Harborough, 1957).

Leicestershire, so that it became one of the best fatting pastures in England, without, incidentally, finding it necessary to abandon open-field farming.[67]

It affected the quality of the migrants who left this area of impartible inheritance once in every generation. They were not recruits for the industrial proletariat; they swelled the ranks of the emerging English middle class.[68] This is an important qualification of the formula; primogeniture generates long-distance migrants who will provide the raw recruits for industry. Very small holdings will send out penniless and unskilled sons, but large holdings and small craft businesses will send out educated or skilled sons to join the professional and managerial sector. From the wills we can learn the average size of money portion received by younger sons in a particular region, and this will probably give us a more reliable indicator to the pattern and quality of migration than the type of inheritance custom alone. So long as sons received equal portions in kind, the difference between partible and impartible inheritance was not very great, but once the shift had been made to cash portions, areas of primogeniture tended to become associated with large farms and large portions, areas of partible inheritance with dual economies, smaller or poorer farms and small portions. The migrants from the former joined the middle class, those from the latter joined the vagabond class of the pre-industrial era, for whom there was seldom sufficient employment, and became the labour reserve for industry, once the industrial revolution had got under way.

To sum up: so long as land remained the sole source of family income, it was regarded as family property and was expected to support all adult members, either by supplying each with a share of land, or by supporting one nuclear family and a number of celibate adults. This led to accepted minimum-size holdings and the characteristic medieval pattern of uniform holdings in any given region; in one parish all the standard half-virgate holdings will be 12 acres, in another they will all be 24, the agreed minimum which younger sons would not challenge. The sudden drop in population after the plagues made possible an increase in the size

[67] R. M. Auty, Part 57: 'Leicestershire', in *The Land of Britain*, D. Stamp, ed. (London, 1937), pp. 254–7.

[68] Habakkuk, 'Family Structure and Economic Change in Nineteenth Century Europe', *Jnl Econ. Hist.* 15 (1955), pp. 1–12; A. Redford, *Labour Migration in England* (Manchester, 1927).

of holdings and provided the opportunity to generate cash savings. Cash savings enabled the new large holdings to be preserved, and furthermore rendered it unnecessary for adult kinsmen to be maintained on the holding. They took their portion and left, thus initiating a landless, migratory sector in society, which had not existed, on an appreciable scale, in the Middle Ages. Since they had received their portion they did not return, and the effective kin-group shrank in size. This is true of England but not of France, or of any area where child portions continued in kind, bringing children back at regular intervals to collect their sack of potatoes or to claim maintenance. The nature and value of child portions is, I suggest, as vital to our understanding of rural society and economy as the type of inheritance custom governing the distribution of land among heirs.

6. Peasant inheritance customs and land distribution in Cambridgeshire from the sixteenth to the eighteenth centuries

MARGARET SPUFFORD

Inheritance customs can be studied on their own by those interested in the workings of the family and of kinship groups. Yet the way the family chose to dispose of its land amongst its sons could have much wider repercussions. It could transform land distribution and the size of holdings, particularly in a time of mounting population pressure like the sixteenth century. This essay therefore explores the relationship between inheritance customs and the changes in the distribution of land that took place in this period in Cambridgeshire. The sources on which it chiefly draws are estate surveys, which demonstrate the latter,[1] and contemporary wills, which show the way the tenants proposed to leave their land after their deaths, and therefore the effects inheritance customs might be expected to have on land distribution.

As well as looking at the actual provision made in the wills, and the actual changes in landholding between the sixteenth and early eighteenth centuries, I have also attempted a brief preliminary examination of the social and economic status of those tenants who made wills which still happen to survive. It is obvious that if the will-making section of the population was socially slanted within the village, the provision made for sons within the group of will-makers might also be idiosyncratic, and not reflect general village custom. The background of the documents therefore deserves

---

[1] Manorial surveys do, of course, neglect subtenants, and therefore have the considerable drawback of concealing the bottom of the iceberg, the really poor and landless in the community. C. J. Harrison, 'The Social and Economic History of Cannock and Rugeley 1546–97' (University of Keele, Ph.D. Thesis, 1975), pp. 82–7, indicates the magnitude of the drawback for his particular area. Harrison shows that in a Field Book of 1554, 64 per cent of manorial land was sublet and suggests that, if this degree of subtenancy at Cannock is in any way typical, field surveys cannot be used to show land distribution 'except when one is certain that there was little or no subtenanting, or when full evidence on subtenanting survives' (p. 87).

attention. Further, I have looked at the burdens placed on the eldest or the inheriting son, even in cases where primogeniture, or unigeniture seems to be the custom, for the amount of strain placed on the main holding by provision for other siblings seems very relevant to its survival, although it may be concealed in the form of bequests of cash or stock.[2]

The three communities in Cambridgeshire, worked in depth, were carefully chosen for their contrasting geographical and economic settings. The village of Chippenham lies on the Cambridgeshire chalk uplands, which are typical of many chalk areas. The village of Orwell lies between the river valley and a clay upland region which is typical of the Midland Plain of England. Willingham, on the other hand, lies right in the fen near the river Ouse, and represents many other villages of the same kind.

Detailed examination of the surviving wills from these villages[3] shows that even in an area such as Cambridgeshire, which was nominally one of primogeniture, the provision made by fathers in their wills in the form of fragments of land and of cash sums for younger sons, and of dowries for daughters, as well as maintenance for the widow, all came out of future profits of the main holding. They did not come out of the savings, if any, of the testator.[4] They therefore amounted to a very considerable burden on the main holding and on the inheriting son. For this reason, the distinction between primogeniture and unigeniture on the one hand, and partible inheritance on the other, is a very blurred one. This burden seems to have assisted the breakdown of holdings of 15 to 45 acres, which were recognizable late medieval holdings of half a yardland to one-and-a-half yardlands, in the arable upland areas of Cambridgeshire in the sixteenth and seventeenth centuries. Inheritance customs had a different effect in the fens, where

[2] Margaret Spufford, *Contrasting Communities: English Villagers in the Sixteenth and Seventeenth Centuries* (Cambridge, 1974). The material on inheritance customs and the changing distribution of land in this paper is more fully represented in the relevant sections of this book. All detailed documentary references will be found there. The investigation into the economic status of the makers of wills in Willingham, however, is new.

[3] Cambridge University Library, University Archives, Consistory Court of Ely, original wills.

[4] M. K. Ashby, *The Changing English Village 1066–1914* (Kineton, 1974), pp. 116, 163. Cambridgeshire custom was in no way unusual. Similar unrealistic provisions were made by testators in the Gloucestershire village of Bledington in the same period.

smallholdings were much more viable because of the resources of the fen common for grazing stock.

The way provision for younger sons and daughters placed a burden on the main holding can be demonstrated clearly from the wills from Orwell. The surveys of land for Orwell are not as good as they are for Willingham and Chippenham. However, they are just good enough to show that in Orwell, as in Chippenham, tenants with traditional farms of half a yardland or a yardland were squeezed out, in the late sixteenth and seventeenth centuries, whilst the number of cottagers increased radically, and the men with an acreage larger than normal profited. But the surviving Orwell wills are excellent, and do much to transform the somewhat bleak figures setting out the distribution of land in the early seventeenth century, and to interpret the economic framework of the villagers' lives in personal terms.

The first fifty original wills which survive for Orwell are dated between 1543 and 1630. Half-a-dozen of the men who left wills before the 1630s had married sons, for whom they usually made no provision. Edmund Barnard, who died in 1575, provided for his sons, Hugh, and Robert, his youngest, but John, who already had four children, got only a relatively small bequest of grain. Frequently these men were widowers. If one or more of their sons had been able to marry, the implication is that a proportion of older men had already divested themselves of parts of their holdings before they came to make their wills.[5]

The twenty-two wills which were of most interest were those of the men who had more than one son to provide for. The provisions in these showed quite clearly that the farmers of Orwell were almost equally divided on the issue of whether to leave all their land to one son or not. Ten of the twenty-two left the holding entirely to one son, but tried to provide for the others with cash sums, and often with bequests of stock and grain as well. The other twelve tried to give their younger sons at least a toe-hold on the land, by leaving them a small part of their holdings.

Even where primogeniture was the rule, as much as possible seems to have been done for the other children. Some of the wills show how the cash to set them up in life was provided, and incidentally give some idea of the degree of financial strain that must have been placed on the family holding by this provision. Richard

5 See below, pp. 165, 173.

Kettle, yeoman, made his will in 1560. One of his sons, Arthur, was already married, and his father merely cancelled Arthur's debts to him. Richard Kettle had two other sons, John and William. He left his copyhold to his son John, but only on condition that John paid William a sum of £9 15s. 0d. out of the profits of the holding at the rate of 30s. 0d. a year. If he failed to keep up these payments, the holding was to pass to William 'according to ye Lawdable custome of Orwell aforesaid'. It is obvious from similarly detailed directions given in the wills that it was indeed the custom of Orwell that the tenement, not the father's savings, if any, usually bore the weight of providing for the younger children.

This sort of provision went right down through the lower strata of Orwell society. William Sampfield, labourer, started life as a servant in the household of William Higney, a yeoman who died in 1558. When William Sampfield made his own will 30 years later, he left his cottage, garden, and orchard to his only son, who was, however, to pay 13s. 4d. a year out of the holding for four years after he reached the age of twenty-two, to be divided equally between his two sisters. He was to give house-room to his mother as well. It is difficult to conceive how a labourer's cottage could bear such an annual burden on top of the rent when the wages of agricultural labourers were steadily losing purchasing power.

The most extreme example of such a procedure was provided by Robert Barnard, a labourer, who died in 1615, in the middle of the decade when wages were at their lowest, in real terms, between 1450 and 1649. Robert Barnard had a cottage and croft, and had also, by the end of his life, acquired three acres of arable to dispose of. He left this holding to one of his sons, who was not, according to his will, his eldest. The condition on which he left it was that a portion of £2 a year should be paid out of the holding to each of Robert's other six sons and single daughter in a specified order.

The burdens placed on holdings which were negligible by Midland standards, by such provisions, and which in any case can only have made a marginal yearly profit must have been immense. It is difficult to escape the conclusion that the anxiety shown by fathers, whether they actually practised primogeniture or not, to provide for all their sons, must have been one more factor which put the smaller holdings at risk in crisis years.

Fathers everywhere in Cambridgeshire seem to have laid this burden of provision for the younger members of the family on the inheriting son. The effect varied according to the economy and farming practices of the parish concerned.

Chippenham was an arable parish. Its light, chalky soil was kept in good heart by the sheep of its lord's foldcourse. It had a couple of hundred acres of heath-common, and another couple of hundred acres of fen-common. The inventories show a shortage of stock amongst the villagers, who were almost completely dependent on their rye and barley harvests.

TABLE 1   *Landholding on the chalk and in the fen (percentages)*

Customary acreage of arable	Chippenham		Willingham	
	1544	1712	1575	1720s
250 acres and over	0	6	0	0
90–250 acres	3	8	1	0
74–84 acres	5	0	0 ⎫	
52–68 acres	7	4	0 ⎬	1
1½ yardlands (approx. 45 acres)	7	0	0	0
1 yardland (approx. 30 acres)	9	0	4	4
Half-yardland (approx. 15 acres)	9	2	26	13
Under half-yardland	6	6	20	37
Total (over 2 acres)	46	26	51	55
2 acres and under, and landless	53	74	49	45
Total tenants (percentages)	99	100	100	100
Total tenants (actual numbers)	66	49 about	107	153

When the place was surveyed in 1544, nearly one-third of the landholders held more than the medieval standard of subsistence holding. In the thirteenth century, almost half the tenants had held a half-yardland of between twelve and fifteen acres; now only 9 per cent of them did so. But half the inhabitants of the villages in the year 1544 held a house and croft only, or a house and up to two acres. So the proportion of the wage-labourers, as well as of the prosperous, had much increased.

When the survey of Chippenham made in 1544 was annotated painstakingly just under a hundred years later, in 1636, the way in which land was distributed had again changed radically. The larger copyholds of two yardlands and upwards were not affected;

nor were the minute holdings of less than six acres which helped to support the more fortunate cottagers. But the middle range of sixteenth-century holdings, from a half-yardland, or approximately fifteen acres, to one-and-a-half yardlands, or forty-five-odd acres, had, with one single exception, disappeared completely. In 1636, the only remaining conventional holding was the yardland of 30 acres which Nicholas Cheesewright had held in 1560, and which his descendant John still retained, although he also had over seventy acres of leasehold. John Cheesewright's thirty-acre holding was the only medieval unit which survived as a reminder of the past.

In Chippenham, then, the most critical period for the small owner was not the first half of the eighteenth century, as Johnson, or more lately, Habakkuk, have supposed.[6] The small farmers of Chippenham had already suffered by 1636 and at some point between 1560 and 1636 they had been forced out. Certainly, the process continued after 1636. It was completed by the lord of the manor's action in the late seventeenth century, when he bought up most of the remaining copyhold land in the village. But this remainder was all concentrated in the hands of five men, and the three holdings which were described in detail in the court rolls were between 120 acres and 155 acres each. A reconstruction of landholdings in Chippenham from the map of 1712 (see Table 1) is in many ways simply a further proof that changes had already taken place by 1636. It adds nothing new. The small farmer had long gone out of business in 1712, and he had not reappeared in Chippenham, nor was he ever to do so again.

Instead, the figures for 1544 and 1712 show that the proportion of landless cottagers in Chippenham, or those with only a couple of acres, rose sharply from 53 per cent in 1544 to 74 per cent in 1712; tenants with thirty to forty-five acres disappeared; and the 3 per cent of men with over ninety acres in 1514 were replaced by 14 per cent of tenants with 90 to over 250 acres.

This picture accords very well with that painted by Le Roy Ladurie of changes in the distribution of land in Languedoc between the fifteenth and eighteenth centuries. Of St Thibéry between 1460 and 1690, he writes:

[6] A. H. Johnson, *The Disappearance of the Small Landowner* (Oxford, 1909); H. J. Habakkuk, 'La disparition du paysan anglais', *Annales, E.S.C.*, 20 (1965), pp. 649–63.

The great landowners progressed, the small ones proliferated, and the middle ones, caught in the squeeze, retreated prodigiously. It was the medium-sized holding, which was literally ground to pieces in the sixteenth and seventeenth centuries, that bore the brunt of the process of atomization.[7]

When he examined the economic position of peasants in the corn-growing north of the Beauvaisis,[8] the limitations of his material allowed Goubert to work in detail only on the period after 1660. He found exactly the same type of polarization that I have presented here: he described the corn-growing plateau of Picardy as a 'bleak countryside, with a monotonous type of farming, (where) peasant society appeared only in brutal contrasts. At the social peak was the large farmer, flanked by five or six *laboureurs*; down below was the wretched mass of *manoeuvriers*; between them nothing'. Goubert deduced by inference, although he was not able to prove it, that these contrasts between social groups were not so marked in the period between 1600 and 1635 when the pace of polarization was probably highest in Chippenham. But the crucial factors were the same. For the peasants in the cereal-growing part of the Beauvaisis they were the years of bad harvests between 1647 and 1653. In Chippenham they were the bad harvest years of the 1590s and thereafter. In Goubert's words, 'Crushed by debt, the small peasants had to give up a large part of their land to their creditors.'[9]

The timing, then, was similar in Languedoc, different in Picardy but exactly the same machinery was at work:

The more substantial *laboureurs*, those who had surplus crops to sell, sold them at considerable profit since the prices of cereals had risen two, three, or even four times. Thus enriched they bought up lands from their debtors among the small peasants.[10]

The reasons for the transformation in the distribution of land in Chippenham between 1544 and 1712 were more complex than those in Languedoc, where a straightforward explosion of popu-

[7] Emmanuel Le Roy Ladurie, *The Peasants of Languedoc*, trs. John Day (Urbana, Illinois, 1974), p. 22. This is based on the paperback edition by Flammarion (Paris, 1969). The pattern of development was the same in Lespignan, 1492–1607. Serignan 1453–1550, Montagnac 1520–1660, and St André de Sangonis, 1665–90; pp. 85–8, 91–4, 248–50, 314–16.

[8] Pierre Goubert, 'The French Peasantry of the Seventeenth Century', *Crisis in Europe*, ed. Trevor Aston (London, 1965), pp. 141–65.

[9] *Ibid.*, p. 163.

[10] *Ibid.*

lation, accompanied by true partible inheritance, seems to have been responsible.[11] Detailed examination[12] suggests that the bad harvests of the sixteenth century and particularly of the 1590s, combined with the sixteenth-century price rise, had much to do with the vulnerability of the small owner. The lever by which the small owner was forced off the land was, I suspect, indebtedness, what Goubert has described as 'the endemic burden of peasant debt'.

The existence of a widespread money-lending system in rural society, which permitted a man to stave off the immediate effect of a bad harvest, and by borrowing, to prevent a foreclosure on his holding when he was unable to pay the rent, makes impossible a neat correlation between years of bad harvest and court surrenders. Borrowing and credit appear to have underpinned the whole of rural society. The wills and inventories of Chippenham people make it plain that it was normal practice for retiring yeomen and even husbandmen to divest themselves of their farming goods and stock, and then lay out their money on loans and mortgages. Thus, it is fair to assume, they lived off the interest. But the most enterprising engrossing yeomen built up their holdings by acquiring mortgages while they were still farming. Twelve copyholds of between a half and one-and-a-half yardlands disappeared in Chippenham between 1544 and 1636; and five of these fell into the hands of fellow copyholders, farming on a larger scale. Here, then, were the 'coqs de village' of peasant origin, who also played such an important role in the sixteenth century in Languedoc.[13] They were headed by Thomas Dillamore, who had 199 acres and two roods of customary land. On his deathbed he very properly inserted in his will a passage, which was not common form, thanking God 'for my worldly state wherewith it hath pleased God to blesse me'.

These farmers of large copyholds had all collected fragments of other holdings. Dillamore held land which had been in the possession of no less than fifteen men in 1544; his nearest rival, John Francis, had pieces of holdings which had been in seven tenants' separate possession.

Inheritance customs played the same part in Chippenham as they did in Orwell. Fathers in Chippenham attempted to provide

[11] Le Roy Ladurie, *op. cit.*, pp. 51–5, 91–4.
[12] *Contrasting Communities*, pp. 61–2, 65–92.
[13] Le Roy Ladurie, *op. cit.*, p. 94.

for all their sons. They thus increased the indebtedness of their inheriting sons, by expecting them, as was the custom, to provide for the whole younger family, and the widow.

A dozen men who died leaving wills in Chippenham between 1520 and 1680 provided in them for more than one son, and therefore give some opportunity for examining the way in which the pattern of land distribution was affected by inheritance. Only two of the twelve men left their holdings outright to one son, and made no attempt to set other sons up with any toe-hold on the land at all. The remaining seven either attempted a true division of land amongst their sons, or handed on the bulk of the holding to one, and attempted to provide small tenements for the others, sometimes by deliberate purchase.

The effect that even semi-partible inheritance could have is illustrated clearly by an entry in the court rolls of 1632, dealing with the holding of the Shene family. This was a tenement of one-and-a-half yardlands which eventually fell to Thomas Dillamore. In 1636, the annotations on the survey made it plain that Dillamore and John Bentley had both acquired parts of the holding. The court rolls explained the reason. After the turn of the century, wills were regularly read in the court and often quoted. In April 1632, John and Thomas Shene, sons of Thomas Shene, who had died since the last court, came and read his will. He had left 4 acres of arable to John, who was admitted for an 8s. 4d. fine, and 'my house and all the rest of my lands' to Thomas, who paid the steep fine of £12, and sold it before his death in the following year to Thomas Dillamore. In 1634, John Shene surrendered his four-acre inheritance to John Bentley, who then acquired his interest in the holding.

The granting of a portion of land, which was not in itself adequate for support, to a younger son, merely weakened the main holding and made the engrosser's task easier. As the wills show, these small bequests of land were common. On the other hand, the engrossers themselves divided their holdings.

The most interesting case of the subdivision of a holding was that of Thomas Dillamore, the arch-engrosser who died in 1637. His will is in itself most revealing. He died as his will stated 'not sick, but aged in body'. He had married twice, and had had one son, another Thomas, by his first wife, and six by his second, as well as four daughters, who were left dowries of £100 apiece, huge by the current standards. Thomas Dillamore had not only engrossed holdings in Chippenham, but had also acquired by mortgage a holding in Woodditton which must have been very considerable since he expected the fine on it to be as much as £40. He had also bought a house and at least a half-yardland in the nearby parish of Fordham, and another acre or so in Freckenham. His dealings thus covered at least four parishes. The most considerable part of the holding went to Thomas, the eldest son by his first marriage, who got all the land in Chippenham. Some of it, indeed, had been transferred to him already;[14] one of the few entries in the Chippenham court rolls, which throw any light on Thomas Dillamore's business transactions, show him acquiring part of the Hill's half yardland and an odd 5 acres in 1598, and immediately transferring it to his son. In the following years he transferred 74 acres and various odd messuages which he had acquired in 1588 to Thomas, junior, who by then was married, forty years before his father's death. Again, we have a son established in the active lifetime of his father. As well as all the Dillamore acquisitions in Chippenham, Thomas also got a part of the land his father had acquired in Woodditton, although the bulk of this went to another son, Robert. The land in Fordham and the residue went to a third son, Colin, who was executor with his mother, and was to inherit after her death. On the whole, then, although Thomas Dillamore divided up his land, he did so on a parochial basis, and established three sons on adequate holdings. The provision made for two of the others was a mystery; they were probably already established elsewhere, for they were left 5s. and 10s. apiece. Another was left £10, and the last, obviously still a very small child, an annuity of £4 during his mother's life. Even so, the total cash bequests which the widow and one son were responsible for paying out amounted to over £450, and since none of the Chippenham land was in their hands, the residue must have been extremely large in contemporary terms.

In Chippenham, therefore, a great effort was made to establish younger sons with land. With smaller holdings than Dillamore's, the tendency must have been to weaken farming units and make

---

[14] For the distortions created by using a will alone as the only source for inheritance customs, see the excellent discussion in Alan Macfarlane, *The Family Life of Ralph Josselin: An Essay in Historical Anthropology* (Cambridge, 1970), pp. 64–7.

them less capable of weathering bad harvests and surviving as viable economic concerns. Even when there was no attempt to provide younger sons with land, the effort to provide them with a cash sum to start them off in life often had a weakening effect on the holding. Sometimes the burden placed upon the tenement was obviously preposterous in economic terms. The constant social effort to provide some at least of the younger members of the family with land must in the end have given more opportunities to the engrossers, whether they were lords of the manor or larger copyholders. On the other hand, the very same care shown by the more substantial yeomen, and the willingness of men like Thomas Dillamore to subdivide their holdings, must have acted as a brake on the development of the really large farms. There is no doubt, however, from the proven disappearance of the middle-sized farms, that the economic forces pressing such people off the land into the increasing ranks of wage-labourers were stronger than the constant endeavours made by the community to provide land for as many of its sons as possible.

If the effect of inheritance custom on the arable upland was to weaken the main holdings, what happened in the fens? The arable of the parish of Willingham only accounted for a quarter of its acreage. The rest was made up of fen-grazing, reed beds, willows, and two fen meres. The Willingham economy depended a great deal on stock raising and milk production, fishing, and fowling. In the late eighteenth century it was among the villages said to have large herds of cattle and rich pastures as well as good arable.

The late sixteenth-century wills provide ample evidence of emphasis on cattle and on cheese making. Bequests of stock were important in the wills. Henry Graves, a half-yardland holder who died in 1590, leaving a wife carrying a child, left her outright 'six milk cows of the best' at her choice, and his 'milking yard' along with the rest of his land for 21 years until his child came of age. A half-yardlander in Willingham, unlike Chippenham, was a wealthy man with a relatively large holding. The less land a man had, the more the fen common meant to him, so long as he had some right on it. There were men in Willingham who depended totally on the fen, and were not simply using it to supply the deficiencies of their smallholdings or their earnings as labourers. The will of William Pardye, made in 1593, was succinct. He was a waterman, and he left his only son John, two cows, 'all my lodge as it standith . . . with the fodder that is upon the same lodge, my boat in the fen, my boots, and a pair of high shoes'.

When the changes in the distribution of land which took place in Willingham in the sixteenth and seventeenth centuries are considered, it is therefore essential to bear in mind the existence of men like William Pardye, who held no land and had few goods, but could eke out a living with a boat, a pair of boots, a pair of high shoes and a couple of cows.

The way in which land was distributed amongst the Willingham community changed very markedly between 1575 and the early eighteenth century. The pattern which evolved was completely different from that of the other villages examined. In 1575 the 'typical' holding was still the half-yardland and its attendant house and croft in the village. Nearly half of the landholding tenants held a half-yardland which varied in practice between 16 and 25 acres, although it nominally contained 20 acres.

Between 40 and 50 per cent of the villages of Willingham in 1575 held only a house and a couple of acres. In all sixty-seven of the tenants named in the survey held under a half-yardland, and therefore in medieval theory held less than enough land for subsistence. However, the complete geographical distinction between Willingham, with its enormous acreage of fen, and the other open-field communities discussed here, must be remembered. The common rights, which in 1575 went with all the holdings and most landless houses in Willingham, completely changed the value of the arable holdings, which would, indeed, have been insufficient to provide a living in an upland area. A half-yardlander in Willingham was a wealthy man.

In the six generations between the survey made in 1575 and that of the 1720s, the breakdown of the medieval half-yardlands as recognizable units, was accomplished – just as it had been in Chippenham. But the results of this redistribution of land were quite different. The proportion of the landless or near landless with up to 2 acres dropped from 49 per cent to 45 per cent – whereas at Chippenham it had risen from 53 per cent to 74 per cent. The large farm never emerged as the dominant unit in Willingham. The most striking single change was the rise, in the seventeenth century, of the proportion of tenants who were more than cottagers, but still held less than half a yardland. The proportion of men with between two and sixteen acres went up from

20 per cent in 1603, to 37 per cent in the 1720s. The resources of the fen common enabled men to live on smaller and smaller holdings.

Inheritance customs were the same as in Chippenham or Orwell. Men with more than one son behaved, in their wills, exactly the same way as their counterparts in those villages. Only one of them left his cottage outright to his eldest son, who was still to find cash sums to set up his brother and pay his sister's dowry out of the holding. The others either divided their holdings between their sons, or attempted to keep the main holding intact but to provide younger sons with an acre or two, or a cottage.

The smaller and more negligible the holding, the more likely the dying man was to divide it between his sons, like Mathew Ewesden, who split his lease between his wife and two eldest sons. The men who held a half-yardland all tried to keep it intact. The integrity of the holdings was maintained but they were not built up, although the tenants of half-yardlands in Willingham were in a position to acquire land, simply because these acquisitions went to provide for the younger sons, and so to increase the number of smallholders.

Since the main holdings were kept intact, at least in the few wills of half-yardlanders which survive, and since also the number of men leaving more than one son was so small, the tendency to divide holdings can hardly be treated as significant, or as the main cause of fragmentation. Inheritance customs were no different in Willingham from Chippenham or Orwell. Well-to-do fathers in all three villages tried to set up their younger sons with cottages or fragments of land. The only difference between the villages was that cottagers in Chippenham or Orwell were very much less likely to live on their holdings than they were at Willingham. The well-meaning attempts made by families in these parishes to establish younger sons on the land therefore tended to weaken traditional holdings still further, and provided more opportunity for the engrosser to purchase small parcels of land in bad years. At Willingham the smallholdings created for these purposes were much more viable economic units. It was more feasible to live on a fragment of land in the fens. Therefore, the same tendency of fathers to try and establish younger sons on the land probably had a more lasting effect at Willingham than at either Chippenham or Orwell, where the consequences offered a positive opportunity to the engrossers.

The burden placed on the main holding when inheriting sons were made responsible for their brothers' and sisters' portions has been demonstrated. So has the habit of providing younger sons with a cottage or an acre or two of land: it could establish a new family in the fens, whereas in the uplands it weakened the main holding and left it more likely to fall victim to the engrossers. A forest settlement might well see changes in land distribution like those in the fens.

An outstanding problem remains. Who, in village society, made a will? Were the will-makers exceptional men, whose behaviour followed patterns which were not typical of their societies in general?

It is generally assumed that only the more prosperous in village society made wills.[15] This seems an important assumption to test. There are opposing generalizations in print, one to the effect that only the richer in village society made wills, and the other contradicting this. There are no figures demonstrating either view conclusively.

I examined the forty-nine wills which survive from Willingham from the last quarter of the sixteenth century. These are the years immediately following the survey of Willingham land made in 1575.[16] Some testators who died before the end of the century can easily be identified with tenants holding land in 1575. Others, who cannot yet be connected to a particular tenant of 1575, still made such specific bequests of, for instance, stock, that they must have had common rights. Others left such specific acreages to their several sons, that their minimum acreage is calculable. Others left only their tools, and are readily identifiable as landless craftsmen. Others again left stock and small acreages, very carefully described. They are often men who had appeared in the survey of 1575 as landless, and must therefore have acquired this small acreage between the survey and their deaths. The approximate wealth, disposable goods, and economic standing of the men making wills

---

15 Most recently tentatively suggested by R. S. Schofield, 'Some Discussions of Illiteracy in England, 1600–1800', not yet in print, when he suggests that wills are 'socially selective, with a bias towards the upper social classes' . . . 'Wills., for example may have been made more frequently by the richer men in each occupational group.'

16 About 45 per cent of the tenants who held land, or a commonable house, in Willingham in 1575, made a will, or were represented by a will, in the next 28 years. I do not know how many non-commonable houses, or subtenanted divided houses there were in Willingham in 1575, so that this figure of will-makers is a maximum.

in Willingham at the end of the sixteenth century can, therefore, be compared with the economic standing of the whole village community in 1575.[17] It is possible to see whether the will-makers were evenly distributed through society in this particular village, or whether, as the general assumption suggests, only the comparatively wealthy made wills.

TABLE 2   *Wills and status in Willingham*

	Tenants in Survey of 1575	Makers of Wills, 1575–1603	Percentage of landholding group
Half-yardland and over	33	7	(21%)
2 acres to half-yardland	21	8	(38%)
With under 2 acres of arable including landless	At least 53	34	(64%)
Totals	At least 107	49	(46%)

The results of this comparison are startling. The forty-nine will-makers in Table 2 were indeed distributed through the whole of village society in Willingham. But they were not evenly distributed. All the groups holding land were represented by wills, but landless men, or men who held a cottage with rights of common, or up to two acres of land, were most heavily represented. Sixty-four per cent of this group of tenants (nearly two-thirds) made wills. Thirty-eight per cent of the men with between 2 and 16 acres, or up to half a yardland (over one-third) made wills. Only a fifth of the most prosperous group in Willingham society, the half-yardlanders and yardlanders left wills.

This is a very curious picture which does not coincide at all with the generalizations usually made. A family reconstitution of Willingham is now in progress,[18] and when it is completed, it will be possible to associate most of the wills made by 1700 with specific tenants, and so correct the impressionistic element in the

[17] This sounds an artlessly impressionistic method of comparison. In fact, all the court roll entries for Willingham land have been checked as well, and all entries relating to testators added to the information in these wills. I am satisfied that I have fairly accurate figures for their acreages at death.
[18] By Miss G. Reynolds.

figures and provide a much bigger sample of will-makers. Meanwhile, it is possible to say that, although all groups in the village produced wills, at the end of the sixteenth century it was the poorer groups that produced most wills.

TABLE 3 *Makers of Wills at Willingham 1575–1603*

16	had two or more adult sons to provide for.
17	had unmarried daughters, children under age or unborn children to provide for.
5	were childless and had no obvious heir.
11	had no obvious domestic reason for will-making.
—	
49	

But it is also possible to look at the will-makers in another way, by identifying their family responsibilities. If the family circumstances described in the wills are taken into account it turns out that of the forty-nine making wills, a third had two or more sons to provide for and seem to have been making a will for this reason. The second and subsequent sons were being set up with subsidiary holdings which their fathers had managed to acquire, or with cash sums, or stock, or tools. Another third of the will-makers had unmarried daughters to provide for, or children under age, right down to those with only unborn children. The most pathetic example of the latter was Henry Greaves, who in 1585 left to his wife his copyhold half-cottage on the Green 'and after her death to my child, be it man or woman, if it please God she be with any'. A small number, five of the forty-nine testators, were either unmarried or childless and made a will because they had no obvious heir.

Under a quarter of the testators had no obvious family reason, in the form of a child under age to provide for, to make a will. So, in all, over three-quarters of the testators made a will, not because they were rich or poor, but because they had to provide for children who were not yet independent. This reason lay alike behind the wills of George Crispe, the man who held over ninety acres of free and copyhold land in Willingham in 1575, and died leaving sons aged three-and-a-half and one-and-a-half, between whom he divided his land; and Mathew Ewesden, who appeared as a landless cottager in 1575, and acquired a piece of leasehold land by the time he died in 1595. He left half the profits of the lease to his wife, and half to his two eldest sons, as well as leaving to his two sons his eight sheep with which to renew the lease. His boat and fishing nets went to his second son, the residue to his first.

If over three-quarters of the makers of wills in Willingham had to provide for children, I suggest that this need to provide for a young family must have been the dominant reason behind the making of a will. Again, the family reconstitution now in progress will check the exact demographic status of the testators.

There are obviously other reasons as well. I have tried to show that more wills were made in Willingham by the landless and near landless than by the more prosperous tenants. Over two-thirds of the surviving wills were made by this group. If it is true both that the poor made more wills, and that the main reason for making a will was for a man to provide for children under age, then it looks as if poor men may have died younger, or married later, leaving more young children. This is an important question for the historical demographer to resolve.

All sorts of other motives also probably operated. The half-yardlanders who left comparatively fewer wills had holdings which were to some extent regulated by the custom of the manor.[19] Many of the comparatively numerous men who had up to a couple of acres and left wills had held only a landless cottage with rights of common in the 1575 survey. By the time they died, they had often acquired a lease of a couple of acres, or a bit of fen, or the subtenancy of a second cottage. Like Mathew Ewesden, they were concerned with dividing up this bit of leasehold or the extra sub-tenancy, which was not controlled by manorial custom, in order to establish their under-age children as well as possible. They must have been making wills partly because they were dealing in frag-ments of land outside the customary framework. One of the motives of their will-making must have been care for their relatively pre-carious holdings.

Altogether only a maximum of 45 per cent of the tenants who were in Willingham in 1575 made a will during the next quarter-century. To make a will was, therefore, less normal in village

---

[19] Most of the half-yardlanders who did make wills were concerned with the disposal of exactly the same sort of fragments of leasehold and freehold land, and of subtenancies, as their less prosperous brethren.

society in the sixteenth century and seventeenth century, than not to make a will. Those who did seem to have been more influenced by the need to provide for under-aged, or unestablished children than any other motive. This in itself suggests that will-making was atypical, and that more men did not make wills than did so, simply because their children were already established in their lifetimes. We know very little about peasant retirement. It seems probable that inheritance normally took place gradually during the lifetime of the father, not at his death. Thus it was with the vicar of Earl's Colne in Essex: Ralph Josselin's

> retirement can, in one sense be dated from the wedding of his first child, Jane, in 1670, when he was fifty-five. At that time he began to break up his estate amongst his children . . . Retirement, nevertheless, was a gradual process . . . He was never left dependent on the support of his children or others.

Josselin's affairs were complicated by the early death, at twenty-nine, of his eldest son, John. Even so, before this he had supported John through an apprenticeship and had set him up in a shop of his own, after first attempting to arrange a marriage and buy a farm for him at the end of his apprenticeship. John's independence in no way depended on his father's death.[20]

Thomas Dillamore of Chippenham, who had set up his own son Thomas forty years before his own death, and had almost certainly provided for the two sons who only got five shillings and ten shillings apiece at his death, was therefore in no way exceptional. Examples have been given of fathers who died leaving married, settled sons both at Orwell and at Chippenham. Half-a-dozen men in Willingham died leaving married, established sons, as William Biddall did. He had been tenant of half a yardland of arable and marsh in 1575, and died, in 1586, leaving five sons, and a daughter. Two of his sons, including the eldest, who inherited the half-yardland, were married with children of their own when he died.

Marriage in Willingham did not in any case have to wait until the family tenement became available on the death of the father. Examples of men who came into court and surrendered holdings

---

[20] Macfarlane, *op. cit.*, pp. 98, 118–19. The independence of Josselin's second son was not nearly so secure, but this seems to have been because his relations with his father were always strained. Even so, he was able to marry and eventually to set up his own house, even without his father's consent (pp. 120–3).

to their sons are not uncommon in the court rolls. Half-yardlanders 'retired' in this way, and so did men who held only a messuage and its appurtenances. The sixteenth-century court rolls of Cannock and Rugeley in Staffordshire show similarly that 'transfers of land from father to son during the lifetime of the father were quite common' and also that 'such occasions were often the occasion for making settlements on the junior members of the family'.[21]

We do not know how often retirement became complete in old age. The most explicit statement I have yet seen on the total retirement of a man comes from another Cambridgeshire village, Little Gransden. It was made in the deposition of William King, a yeoman of Little Gransden, who was aged, he reckoned, about 'fourscore and twelve years, or thereabouts' in 1646-9, when his evidence was taken in a lawsuit,[22] obviously as the oldest inhabitant. He had been bailiff and rent-collector and had lived there for sixty years. He retained a phenomenally clear memory. He was said to be neither a freeholder, nor a copyholder, in Little Gransden. He had been, in his time, farmer of four different farms there, but, it was explained, 'his wife being dead, and his children grown upp, he now liveth as a soujourner with one of his sonnes'. The word 'sojourner' was used by the translators of the Authorised Version of the Bible, who included Jeremiah Radcliffe, D.D., rector of Orwell itself, who was buried there, and John Richardson, Regius Professor of Divinity in the University of Cambridge, inheritor of a half-yardland at Linton. The Bishop of Ely, Lancelot Andrewes was another. These were men who knew their Cambridgeshire well, although of course, the word was common currency in the rest of the country as well. They used 'sojourner' to cover the wandering and rootless, and classed sojourners with the fatherless.

In the Authorised Version of the Old Testament, King David used the term to cover the spiritual condition of all his people: 'We are strangers before Thee and sojourners, as were all our fathers. Our days on the earth are a shadow, and there is none abiding!' In seventeenth-century Cambridgeshire, once a man retired and had given up all his land, he was a sojourner, although he might live in the house that had once been his own. There he had, by right, no abiding place. The existence of completely retired

[21] Harrison, 'The Social and Economic History of Cannock and Rugeley, 1546–97', op. cit., p. 50.
[22] P.R.O., E134/24, Car.I/Hil.2.

old men was not peculiar to Cambridgeshire. There is a splendid example in the case of a cottage weaver in Oxfordshire, who, on the marriage of his son, caused a clause to be inserted into the agreement establishing the new couple in his cottage for both their lives, providing that the father had meat, drink, firing, and all his domestic needs for his lifetime, and that his new daughter-in-law was 'serviceable' to him. This arrangement held even after the death of the son, and the daughter-in-law's remarriage. She remained 'serviceable' and her father-in-law by her first marriage had house-room for as long as he lived.[23]

Examples of the 'old folks at home', including the males, being provided with bed, board, and access to the fire, can be multiplied in Staffordshire and Warwickshire in the fifteenth century, just as they were in Cambridgeshire wills of the sixteenth century.[24] We should perhaps be more aware of the existence of some of these old men, who did not have to make wills, sitting in the chimney corner, and sleeping in the little low chamber off the hall, grateful for the house-room provided by the inheritors of the holding.[25]

Inheritance customs need much more detailed investigation. This can only be done by combining wills with both demographic data from parish registers and details of land transactions from court rolls. The combination should show whether it was normal, as I suggest, to settle land on children at appropriate ages for them,

[23] Ashby, *op. cit.*, pp. 165–6.

[24] I am indebted to R. H. Hilton for raising this point in discussion after this paper was delivered, and taking the trouble to send me a few of his examples. I suspect that such examples could be multiplied from medieval court rolls all over the country. There appears to be a total conflict between the evidence of the Cambridgeshire wills, that widows, and even retired men were frequently given upkeep in the inheriting son's house, and Peter Laslett's opinion that three generational families did not exist in England, or were at least highly abnormal. I suspect that the conflict is more apparent than real, and have tried to resolve it in *Contrasting Communities*, pp. 114–118.

[25] The description of the circumstances is that of Leonard Woolward of Balsham, a retired yeoman who made no pretence of farming his land any more. He had handed over the occupation of his twenty-odd acres of freehold to his son. The description is possible because Leonard did in fact make a will, because he wished to leave an acre or so from the main holding to his daughter. If he had followed the pattern which I suggest was 'normal', and had provided for them at their majority, before his retirement, no will would have been made, and the physical conditions of his dependence would remain unknown. Because the will was idiosyncratic, it was disputed (*Contrasting Communities*, pp. 182–3).

and so whether will-making was mainly necessary to men who had not lived long enough to complete the process. It should also show how gradual such 'retirement' was, and how often men lived on after complete retirement to become pure dependants.

In the particular villages which I have studied, I have been able to show how the attempt by fathers to provide all sons with fragments of land, cash, or goods in kind, still placed a burden which could be crushing on the inheritor of the main holding, even where unigeniture was the custom. I have shown how this 'partition' weakened holdings, and assisted the disappearance of the middle-sized holdings in a time of population growth while multiplying small ones which were not economically viable, except in the fens. This growth in the number of smallholdings in the arable corn-growing parishes gave the engrossers, the 'coqs de village', their chance. I have suggested, and gone some way to prove, that men who made wills did so primarily because they had dependent children to provide for. More of the makers of wills seem to have been men with very small holdings, which were not secured by custom, as were the traditional copyholds. Lastly, I have suggested that relatively few men made wills because the normal process was for a man to establish his children as they came of age to be independent, and that a fathers' gradual retirement began with the first marriage amongst his offspring. It proceeded to total retirement and to dependence on a married son in an unknown number of cases, both because every child was dead or independently established, and because physical disability and old age had set in.

7. The European debate on customs of inheritance, 1500-1700

JOAN THIRSK

Any discussion of the inheritance practices of the upper classes in the sixteenth and seventeenth centuries calls for a preliminary survey of the considerable body of European literature on primogeniture produced at the same time. Most of it takes the form of legal treatises, and is part of a genre of legal dissertations that attempt to sum up present law and custom. But it may be possible to learn more from them than this. They are a quite new literary form in the sixteenth century, and they contain more than factual statements on the law of primogeniture; they include arguments for and against primogeniture, and some brief observations on its consequences. Do they shed any light on assumptions, expectations, or changing practices?

This brief essay does not dig very far below the surface. Many of the treatises are not available in English libraries. One needs to have deeper knowledge than the present writer concerning the testamentary preferences of the upper classes, especially in Spain, France, and Germany, before the treatises were written, in order to judge actual practices against the lawyers' statements on practice; specialists in the study of the European nobility and gentry are needed to illuminate these aspects of the question. But it may broaden our perspective if the debate is summarized, and some suggestions are offered concerning its significance.

The treatises are lawyers' statements about inheritance practices, but the writers were not simply lawyers. Some were administrators in government, and hence were intelligent observers and thinkers on the practical consequences of current practice. They necessarily had opinions, and the writing of such essays could not be divorced from practical considerations.

However, it is necessary to be cautious when interpreting these treatises. Mary Dewar has some sobering remarks on what should, and should not, be read into Sir Thomas Smith's description of the workings of the English Commonwealth (*De Republica Anglorum*, 1565),[1] and the same cautionary words could be uttered

[1] Mary Dewar, *Sir Thomas Smith. A Tudor Intellectual in Office* (London, 1964), pp. 111–13.

with regard to the many treatises *De Iure Primogenito*. Stimulated by his personal observations of French governmental institutions (he was in France on government business in 1551, 1562–6, 1567, and 1572) Sir Thomas Smith planned to describe the government of England in order to make clear 'the principal points wherein it doth differ from the policy or government at this time used in France, Italy, Spain, Germany, and all other countries which do follow the civil law of the Romans'. He wished to illustrate those 'points wherein the one [country] differeth from the other, to see who hath taken the righter, truer, and more commodious way to govern the people as well in war as in peace'. In Smith's work, says Miss Dewar, 'we are listening to a learned civilian expounding the formal structure of English society, not the experienced Secretary analysing the realities of power'. Smith was, of course, an experienced Secretary of State, perfectly capable of analysing the realities of power, yet that experience was firmly kept out of his text. Later historians have claimed for Smith a special place in the development of the concept of the sovereignty of Parliament, reading into his words meanings which were not there. We may be tempted to read more into the writings on primogeniture than is really there.

Nevertheless, primogeniture was practised in many different European countries, and it prompted comparisons. Like the constitution, it demanded to be judged by its long-term practical consequences. The writers of treatises strove, like Sir Thomas Smith, to separate theory from practice. They described the rule of primogeniture formally, but did not describe reality in detail. How much, then, do contemporaries betray in their writings of their concern for inheritance customs?

The first noticeable fact is that civilians in the sixteenth and seventeenth centuries wanted to write on primogeniture when no one pontificated on it in the fifteenth century. This is surely significant. Moreover, by the very fact that they were writing down something on the law, they were pressing for its acceptance and promoting conformity. They admitted that primogeniture was not observed by everyone; it therefore had to be justified. No matter how hard kings and princes were trying to commit their descendants and their subjects to primogeniture, moral pressures were being ignored. English writers explained how primogeniture was evaded in England. Nevertheless, they wrote in the conviction that primogeniture was the right and proper practice for great families. Every

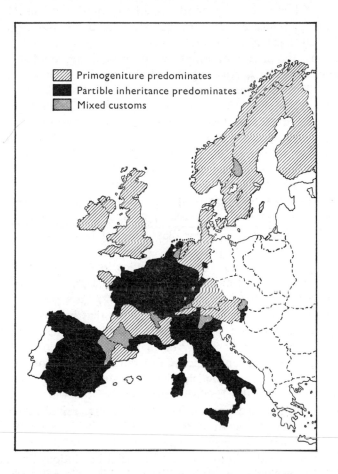

Figure 1. Inheritance customs in Western Europe (after Wilhelm Abel, *Agrarpolitik*, by permission of Vandenhoeck & Ruprecht)

Note This is the only attempt of its kind to map inheritance customs and the results are of course extremely generalised. Every country could show refined regional distinctions.

treatise went out of its way to justify it. No writer hammered his argument home, but by gentler methods of debate, usually by question and answer, each spoke with authority, and helped to harden attitudes in its favour.

Among the first authorities on primogeniture, quoted by all subsequent writers, was André Tiraqueau, of whose early life little is known except that he was born at Fontenay-le-Comte, capital of Lower Poitou, and spent most of his life there as *juge-châtelain* and then as *lieutenant*. He first attracted attention with an essay written at the age of thirty-five on the marriage laws, that went through twelve editions. His treatise *On the Nobility and the Law of Primogeniture* was written some time after 1524, and first published in 1549. It had gone through ten editions by 1580 (Tiraqueau died in 1558), and the fifteenth edition appeared in 1622.[2] The popularity of the work tells us something about public, perhaps not exclusively upper class, interest in the subject. What prompted Tiraqueau to write it?

He was a lawyer holding public office in a country town that was noted for its select company of able jurists. Rabelais was a friend. Tiraqueau's first treatise on marriage laws, set beside the later work on primogeniture, clearly shows that he observed most and reflected most on the fortunes of noble families. Tiraqueau had been born in 1488; it may be that he had some knowledge of the damage inflicted on French noble families in the course of the Hundred Years War. English historians dwell on the handsome fortunes made by the English gentry out of the war, but it was at the expense of the French. The Black Prince raised £20,000 by selling prisoners of war from Poitiers.[3] It is probable that Tiraqueau studied at Poitiers. He may have heard something of this experience from the other side. At all events, the social institutions that determined the survival of noble families were his main preoccupation.

Tiraqueau achieved such a reputation that he was appointed by Francis I a counsellor in the Paris Parlement in 1531; he must have been about sixty years old by then. He is said to have won the respect of Francis I and Henry II for his efficiency as a reformer and his equitable and humane administration of the law.

[2] For these and the following remarks on Tiraqueau's life, see Jacques Brejon, *André Tiraqueau* (Paris, 1937), *passim*; *Biographie Universelle*, under Tiraqueau.

[3] G. A. Holmes, *The Later Middle Ages, 1272-1485* (Edinburgh, 1962), p. 162.

His other legal treatises included one on legal punishment (proposing measures for mitigating sentences especially for crimes of passion), and another on petty offences (aimed at reducing the costs of litigation). He was evidently a wise and learned lawyer and, incidentally, a family man; some writers credit him with twenty, some with thirty children. But all in all this biographical information is insufficient to explain Tiraqueau's interest in the law of primogeniture.

In any case, Tiraqueau is not the first writer on the subject. Cooper identifies a fifteenth-century Italian jurist, Martini Garrati da Lodi,[4] and all sixteenth-century writers knew of Jean le Cirier, who wrote *Tractatus Singularis de Iure Primogeniturae vel Maioricatus* in 1521. He too was a counsellor in the Paris Parlement, though little seems to be known of his history.[5] The form of the essays by both Le Cirier and Tiraqueau was the same, and it set the pattern for all that followed. They first recited all the Biblical instances of inheritance practices, and decided that the Hebrews partitioned their estates, but that convenience led the Jews in the end to prefer the eldest son. Then followed a series of questions relating to primogeniture in practice: who is the eldest son? – who is the eldest of twins? – should the eldest succeed to the whole patrimony? – what is the correct way to treat adopted sons, bastard sons, etc.? Le Cirier's work passed through a number of editions, of which the British Library has those of 1521, 1549, and 1584. When Tiraqueau's treatise followed, it was much more popular, and more frequently cited.

Two Frenchmen, therefore, stimulate, if they do not start, the literature, but after that it was taken up enthusiastically by the Spaniards. A treatise on primogeniture in Spain was published in 1571 by Christian de Paz de Tenuta, another in 1575 by Melchior Palez a Meris, and another by Didacus de Simancas also in 1575. More Spanish essays followed in 1611 and 1612. German writers began to take an interest in the early seventeenth century: the first was Johannes Mehlbaum's *De Iure Primogeniturae* in 1611, followed by two more in 1614 and 1615. Fifteen treatises by German authors are bound together in one volume in the Bodleian Library.[6]

[4] See also below, p. 236.
[5] Mehlbaum described Le Cirier as a counsellor in the Paris Parlement. He does not appear in biographical dictionaries.
[6] The Bodleian Library reference to this volume is Diss. H. 129. The

Starting with Mehlbaum, they run on to the last publication in 1740. The German essays clearly describe a changing situation, which is not made explicit in the French literature. They report on the spread of primogeniture among the German principalities. It was ordained among Electoral families by the Golden Bull of Charles IV in 1356. Other princes gradually adopted it, or strove, not always successfully, to tie down their successors to adopt it. By natural law, said Mehlbaum, all free men should succeed equally; the children are all the offspring of the same parents. But the division of a kingdom is the worst misfortune that can befall it, and so, amongst the ruling class, it has become the custom to favour the first-born. It is difficult to say what is just and what is unjust in any absolute sense, says Mehlbaum; it depends on the circumstances. Primogeniture has become a strong custom because it has fewest drawbacks. Yet as he admitted, usage differed everywhere. His manner was to coax gently. His discussion was calm and temperate, without passion.

Tiraqueau had taken the same line: the customs of Poitou were one thing, other customs differed. But primogeniture was essential for the preservation of families. Despite certain injustices, it was necessary to tolerate primogeniture because of the common benefit that resulted from it. It prevented the morcellation of property. At the same time French and German writers all stressed in primogeniture the father's duty to provide for his younger sons. Their food should be provided and sometimes a small estate. Elder brothers were far from being the absolute heirs. They held a privileged place in the family, but they had serious obligations towards their younger brothers.

The writers of all these treatises sounded complacent about the growing strength of primogeniture. Clearly they approved of the trend, and by their writing they forwarded it. The stability of the state depended on the existence of well-rooted, well-endowed families commanding authority. The lawyers looked with satisfaction and pleasure on the rock-like solidity of great estates and great noble houses. Superficially all these essays by citizens of different countries in Europe seem to constitute a unified whole, speaking with the same voice, in the same style, and with the same aims. Yet in practice the workings of primogeniture cannot

European literature as a whole is listed in J. S. Pütter, *Litteratur des Teutschen Staatsrechts* (Göttingen, 1783), iii, pp. 754ff.

have been the same in all Continental countries. The French were among the first writers on the subject to be widely read; were they defending primogeniture because of some mild questioning of its wisdom? There is nothing polemical in these treatises. But, as Jack Goody points out in his paper, in every society, there is always tension between the equality pushing up from below and the inequality thrusting down from above.[7] The tensions will be weak or strong at different times, and the literature will flourish or wither accordingly. In view of Professor Le Roy Ladurie's description of the growing strength of egalitarian sentiment in France among classes below the nobility,[8] should we interpret the literature on inheritance as a response to mild upper-class apprehension – to put it no stronger – concerning the expediency of primogeniture?

In Germany, on the other hand, the argument in favour of primogeniture plainly had a purpose to bring all principalities into line, establish primogeniture as a rule of inheritance, and so enable princely power to be consolidated along with the stability of the state. The German treatises had an aggressive propagandist purpose, whereas the French may have been written in a more defensive mood. Such an interpretation of the literature, however, must be tentative.

In England, it seems fair to say that primogeniture was noticeably gaining ground among the gentry in the early sixteenth century. The preservation of estates in noble families had been made more effective since the early fourteenth century by means of joint feoffments and family trusts. Within this more secure legal framework, elder sons were advanced, but younger sons were also provided for.[9] These tendencies favouring the eldest son had been somewhat weakened in the later fifteenth century by the use of recoveries to bar entails, but the use made of this device did not challenge the growing primacy of primogeniture. The supporting literature written by jurists in France and Germany, however, did not yet exist in England. What was heard in England at a notably early date in the sixteenth century were rumblings of a controversy against its harsh consequences. It was plainly presented in Thomas Starkey's *Dialogue between Cardinal Pole and Thomas Lupset,*

---

[7] See above, pp. 26–7.
[8] See above, p. 50.
[9] G. A. Holmes, *The Estates of the Higher Nobility in Fourteenth-Century England* (Cambridge, 1957), pp. 40–1, 53–4, 57.

written about 1532–4. Starkey, it should be emphasized, wrote part of it in Italy when he visited Padua in 1533–4.[10] Its argument on customs of inheritance strongly suggests that his travels and discussions in Europe had revealed differences between the workings of primogeniture in England and other countries.

Starkey criticized primogeniture for the injustice of disinheriting younger sons.[11] He was saying this at a time when European writers were underlining the fact that younger sons were *not* disinherited thereby. Was English and Continental practice moving in different directions? Cardinal Pole in the *Dialogue* expressed vehement disapproval: 'utterly to exclude them [i.e. younger sons] from all as though they had commit some great offence and crime against their parents is plain against reason and seemeth to [di]minish the natural love betwixt them which nature hath so bounden together'. Primogeniture, he concluded was a 'misorder in our politic rule and governance'. The defence of primogeniture fell to Lupset, who claimed that good order and peaceful rule in the realm were promoted by it. People needed heads and governors to temper their unruliness. 'If the lands in every great family were distributed equally betwixt the brethren, in a small process of years the head families would decay and by little and little vanish away. And so the people should be without rulers and heads . . . [whereby] . . . you shall take away the foundation and ground of all our civility. Besides that you shall in process of years confound the nobles and the commons together after such manner that there shall be no difference betwixt the one and the other.' Thus primogeniture preserved a class of people with authority. Pole conceded Lupset's point that the nation needed governors and heads, but he wanted some compulsory legal provision for younger children. This was taken for granted in France, Flanders, and Italy, Lupset pointed out, and hence you never saw younger brothers begging as you did in England. Evidently in England things were working out differently from the theory as accepted on the Continent. Moreover, in England primogeniture had penetrated more deeply into the ranks of society below the nobility. Pole accepted the expediency of this custom of inheritance for princes, dukes, earls,

---

[10] G. R. Elton, 'Reform by Statute: Thomas Starkey's Dialogue and Thomas Cromwell's Policy', *British Academy Proc.*, liv (1968), p. 169.

[11] T. Starkey, *Starkey's Life and Letters*, ed. Sidney J. Herrtage (*Early English Text Soc.*, No. 12, 32, 1878), pp. 108–13.

and barons, but he did not think it tolerable among 'all gentlemen of the mean sort. For this bringeth in among the multitude over-great inequality which is the occasion of dissension and debate'.

In short, Starkey's *Dialogue* seems to bring out two different stages in the development of primogeniture: having taken firm hold in England, it was failing to preserve a just balance between the claims of elder and younger sons; also, it was tending to spread down the social scale to 'gentlemen of the meaner sort'. The two developments were doubtless linked with one another. As lesser gentlemen espoused the idea of primogeniture for the sake of building up their family's status, so some had to neglect the younger children for lack of means to provide handsomely for all. In other European countries where primogeniture was just as strong, for example, among the nobility of France, this extreme development had not occurred.

The difference in the rigour with which primogeniture was adopted in England and other Continental countries seems also to be brought out in the comments of travellers from abroad. They over-stated the facts of the English case, but in so doing, they tell us something more of their own prejudices. Lupold von Wedel, travelling in England in 1584 and 1585, said that the eldest sons of the nobility inherited all, while the younger took up some office or pursued highway robbery.[12] An anonymous Italian author in Mary's reign described primogeniture as the preferment of the eldest son leaving the other sons 'with no help from the eldest brother whatsoever'. Though land bought in the father's lifetime was sometimes conferred on younger children, this happened very rarely.[13] Continentals thought the practice in England very harsh compared with what they knew at home.

The literature on primogeniture in England after Starkey was

---

[12] Gottfried von Bülow (trans.), 'Journey through England and Scotland made by Lupold von Wedel in the years 1584 and 1585', *Trans. Roy. Hist. Soc.*, NS. ix (1895), p. 268.

[13] See C. A. Sneyd (ed.), *A Relation . . . of the Island of England*, Camden Soc., vol. 37 (1847), p. 27, for the evil effects of primogeniture in England; also C. V. Malfatti, *Two Italian Accounts of Tudor England* (Barcelona, 1953), p. 64, though this text seems to be derived from Thomas Wilson's account of primogeniture. See also *Cal. S.P. Venetian*, iv, p. 345 (1551); vi, p. 1670 (1557). These pitying comments on the plight of younger brothers depict a deteriorating situation as the century wears on. Finally in *Cal. S.P. Venetian, 1632–6*, p. 370: 'Equally cruel, not to say unjust, is the law that only one among brothers shall inherit the paternal property.'

186   JOAN THIRSK

slow to accumulate. People were not galvanized into action until they experienced the practical problems of younger sons of gentlemen almost begging in the streets. Then for several decades they offered solutions that had nothing to do with changing the laws and customs of inheritance, but were much more practical and down-to-earth: they suggested new careers. The settlement of Ireland was recommended in 1566 by Sir Humphrey Gilbert as a means of providing for younger sons.[14] Their misfortunes were referred to by Sir Edwin Sandys in a Parliamentary speech in 1604, and his concern in the matter must surely be linked with his active promotion of the Virginia Company and encouragement of younger sons in that enterprise.[15] On the other hand, it must be remembered that some experiences were pulling men towards another point of view: the Island of Jersey petitioned the Crown in 1617 for liberty to entail estates, 'the island being much weakened by partitions of lands'.[16]

When the debate took on a much more angry tone in the 1630s, it reverted to a discussion of law and custom and focussed clearly on the gentry class. The inheritance customs of classes below the gentry did not give rise to controversy: practices were as varied as the circumstances of families. Primogeniture in the original sense of advancing the eldest son, but nevertheless providing for the others, was common, perhaps the commonest custom among yeomen and below, but it did not exercise a tyranny. Among the nobility primogeniture was most common, but it seems to have been deemed by common consent the most acceptable practice for family and for state reasons. It reduced strife among brothers when the eldest automatically took the leading position; it maintained the status of the family; and it preserved a class of rulers in society. In general it did not cause excessive hardship to younger sons because the nobility had the means to provide adequately for all. The hardships were felt most keenly among the gentry because their means were not sufficient to provide decently for younger sons. Standards of living had risen sharply among the gentry in the course of the sixteenth century and elder brothers had greater expectations, and could not spare so much for their

[14] D. B. Quinn, *The Elizabethans and the Irish*, Folger Shakespeare Library, Folger Monographs on Tudor and Stuart Civilization (Washington, D.C., 1966), p. 107.
[15] J. R. Scott, *Joint-Stock Companies* (New York, 1951), pp. 123–4.
[16] *Cal. S.P. Domestic, Addenda, 1580–1625*, p. 582.

younger brothers. Younger brothers in their turn required more if they were to maintain social equality, or something approaching it, alongside their elder brothers.[17]

The debate that resumed in the 1630s now produced academic studies similar in form to the Continental treatises. John Selden interested himself in the origins of laws of succession, and wrote *De Successionibus* in 1631, using the Bible to establish the inheritance practices of the Hebrews. His earlier work, *English Janus* (1610), had tried to identify the earliest inheritance practices in Britain. He had decided that partition among sons was usual at the beginning of settlement, and that it remained the custom of the Saxons. It was allowed to continue in Kent after the Conquest, by permission of the Norman kings, and it continued in Wales. Nowhere in all this, however, did Selden make any allusion to the practical issues raised by contemporary customs in England or Europe.[18]

The polemical treatise that was widely read and acclaimed was John ap Robert's *Apology for a Younger Brother*, published in 1634.[19] The author was overwhelmed with indignation at the injustice dealt out to younger sons of gentlemen. Like the academic writers, he drew on Biblical examples to show that equal shares had been the more favoured usage in the early history of man. He did not make comparison with Continental conventions: indeed, he disclaimed all knowledge of other writings on the subject. But he made it clear that the practice of primogeniture was now thoroughly debased among the English gentry. It gave the bulk of the property to the eldest, and an education or an apprenticeship did not save the younger children from sometimes open poverty. Not surprisingly, this polemical literature increased in quantity during the Interregnum when preferment at court and in the church became impossible and trade was depressed.

The sympathy of many members of Parliament for younger sons raised hopes of a change in the law of primogeniture in the 1650s, but hopes were disappointed. In one sober and judicious appraisal of the problem by John Page, one-time Master of Chancery and doctor of civil law, replying to the angry polemics

17 For a general discussion of this period, see Joan Thirsk, 'Younger Sons in the Seventeenth Century', *History*, liv, 1969, pp. 358ff.

18 John Selden, *Opera Omnia*, ed. D. Wilkins, ii, part 1 (London, 1725); *Tracts written by John Selden* (London, 1683).

19 Thirsk, *op. cit.*, pp. 364ff.

of John ap Roberts, we see it again presented as something arising out of the debasement of the original concept of primogeniture.[20] It was never envisaged that primogeniture would leave younger sons with a mere pittance. But this was the way things had worked out.

Another dimension had been introduced into the English debate in the second half of the sixteenth century by the experience of colonization first in Ireland and then in America. The plan for New England in 1623 had been commended because it would find 'worthy employment for many younger brothers'.[21] Those younger brothers had now established themselves as landowners in a new country, and so the question arose: how was land to be transmitted after the first grants? An influential book in shaping opinion was H. Lloyd's *History of Cambria*, first published in Welsh in the thirteenth century, and now translated into English and added to by David Powell in 1584 (reprinted in 1602 and 1697). Powell argued that partible inheritance destroyed the Welsh nobility by causing the partition of estates and exacerbating strife between brothers. It was wholly appropriate in places where population was small and land plentiful. 'Partition is very good to plant and settle any nation in a large country not inhabited; but in a populous country already furnished with inhabitants it is the very decay of great families, and (as I said before) the cause of strife and debate.' When Silas Taylor, a one-time captain in the Parliamentary army, published in 1663 *The History of Gavelkind with the Etymology thereof* he quoted these words, and added in the margin, 'I could wish that those renowned English plantations in America would examine of what avail this in probability and policy may be to them and in particular the most famous plantation of Virginia.'[22] His advice came too late, however. By this time Virginia had formally adopted primogeniture.[23] In New England, on the other hand, Powell's point of view on the virtues of partible inheritance when settling a large, new country carried more weight. John Winthrop who had served as an attorney in the Court of Wards for 2½ years before going to New England, disliked primogeniture, and had been responsible for a petition to Parliament

[20] John Page, *Ius Fratrum, the Law of Brethren* (London, 1657), *passim*.
[21] *Hist. MSS Commission*, lxxiii, City of Exeter MSS, p. 167.
[22] Silas Taylor, *The History of Gavelkind* . . . (London, 1663), p. 27.
[23] C. Ray Keim, 'Primogeniture and Entail in Colonial Virginia', *William and Mary Quarterly*, 3rd ser., 25 (1968), pp. 545ff.

in 1624 which enumerated primogeniture among a number of 'common grievances'. He believed it to be 'against all equity'. The Massachusetts legislature subsequently adopted partible inheritance, though it did give the elder son a double share.[24]

The idea of giving the elder son a double portion came from Biblical sources, and leads to a third theme in the debate on inheritance, namely, the positions taken by Catholics and Protestants on the issue. All writers had turned first to the Old Testament for wisdom and guidance, but in fact the Biblical instances were numerous and varied, and did not all point in one direction. In the end, Protestants took up different positions. The attitude of an English Puritan is expressed very firmly in William Gouge's work *Of Domesticall Duties*.[25] A father should love his children equally, but nevertheless give his first-born a greater patrimony than the others. Joseph, the first-born 'of the true wife' had a double portion. There is an excellency in the first-born, as Jacob declared in his words to his eldest son: 'thou art my first born, my might, and the beginning of my strength'. 'Houses and families by this means', Gouge continued, 'are upheld and continued from age to age'. The stability of the Commonwealth consisted in preserving such houses and families. Nevertheless, younger children should be trained for a calling or given land other than the main inheritance. Provision of this sort was essential, and training in a calling was perhaps preferred, since it benefited the state to have trained people who expected to work for their living rather than encouraging young men to live easily on a piece of inherited land.

In Germany Protestant princes read their Bibles carefully and came to a different conclusion. The tradition in favour of partitioning estates among princely families had been strong in the Middle Ages, and although primogeniture gained ground in the sixteenth and early seventeenth centuries, there was much resistance to it. The testament of Duke Johann Wilhelm of Sachsen-Weimar in 1573 weighed up the *pros* and *cons* of primogeniture and partition and decided that partition was God's will, the exact portions of each brother being settled by lot. Philip von Hessen declared

[24] *Winthrop Papers, I, 1498–1628* (Massachusetts Hist. Soc., 1929), p. 306; G. L. Haskins, *Law and Authority in early Massachusetts* (New York, 1960), p. 170.

[25] W. Gouge, *Of Domesticall Duties. Eight Treatises* (London, 1622), pp. 575–9. I wish to thank Dr Roger Richardson for this reference.

in his will that it fell heavily on his conscience to prefer the first-born to the other sons. Some Protestant rulers feared that by espousing primogeniture they would drive their disinherited children into the arms of the Catholic church, for it alone offered the refuge of a monastic life.[26] Religion was so closely bound up with politics that it is perhaps not surprising that Protestants came to such different conclusions.

The literature summarized in this essay reveals contrasting view-points on different customs of inheritance, and a pressing concern for their political and social consequences. It is a mirror of the political and social anxieties of the seventeenth century. At the same time, it underlines the fact that primogeniture was not one rule of inheritance, but two. In England it was so strictly operated that younger sons were often left with a pittance or nothing. On the Continent it was not understood as a rule for endowing the eldest son with the family estate, and when Continental lawyers defended it in noble families and urged it upon landowners, they had in mind a system that preferred eldest sons and yet dealt justly with younger sons. Thus interpreted, it seemed to be wholly advantageous to families and to the state. English landowners, especially the gentry, however, had too readily pushed it to ex-tremes, and so were the first to experience the disadvantages of their excessive zeal. The English debate by the middle of the seven-teenth century was charged with passion against primogeniture, whereas it was a calmer issue in other European countries.

This seems to be the message of the literature. But it should be stressed that the view of it given here is partial. It has concentrated on the academic debate on the Continent, while considering the polemical debate in England. Was there a polemical, popular literature attacking primogeniture in Europe? Did primogeniture in practice in France, Germany, Spain and elsewhere diverge from the seemingly moderate definition officially expounded? These questions have not been explored, though the second of these is illuminated by Mr Cooper's essay. A preliminary survey of the literature does no more than fill in a background, and by giving

[26] Joseph Engelfried, *Der Deutsche Fürstenstand des XVI and XVII Jahrhunderts im Spiegel seiner Testamente, Inaugural-Dissertation . . . der Eberhard-Karls-Universität zu Tübingen*, 1961, pp. 118–26. I wish to thank Dr Henry Cohn for drawing my attention to this thesis.

a glimpse of contemporary opinion, draw attention to controversial features within it.

As far as England is concerned, an explanation is required for the evident abuse of primogeniture in the sixteenth and seventeenth centuries. It may well have been caused by the greater fluidity of English society at this time, compared with the Continent. This dispersed aspirations and *mores* of the nobility too rapidly through the next lower rank of society, fostering pride in family and habits of conspicuous expenditure that could not yet be borne by all gentry on the average gentleman's income.

The English debate about primogeniture, of course, was far from being at an end. In the eighteenth century the aspirations of the gentry filtered down to the next class below, and produced yeomen who followed the rule of primogeniture and, in order to make assurance doubly sure, settled their estates.[27] Primogeniture gained ground among the middle classes and provoked another controversy, centring upon that class, in the nineteenth century, More treatises were written, and fresh comparisons were sought in European experience.[28] Yet another illuminating body of literature was assembled of great value for the study of inheritance practices in Europe in the nineteenth century.

[27] John V. Beckett, 'Landownership in Cumbria, c. 1680–1750' (University of Lancaster, Ph.D. Thesis, 1975), pp. 149–50. I wish to thank Dr Beckett for allowing me to quote from his unpublished thesis.

[28] See, *inter alia*, G. C. Brodrick, 'The Law and Custom of Primogeniture', *Cobden Club Essays*, 2nd ser. (London, 1872); C. S. Kenny, *The History of the Law of Primogeniture in England* (Cambridge, 1878); Eyre Lloyd, *The Succession Laws of Christian Countries* (London, 1877).

8. Patterns of inheritance and settlement by great landowners from the fifteenth to the eighteenth centuries[*]

J. P. COOPER

The view that descent of land among great landowners by male primogeniture, settled by some system of entail, was a distinctive feature of western European society goes back at least to Montesquieu. Its origins lie in the sixteenth-century jurists' apologies for primogeniture described in Thirsk's paper. Pipes has recently written

> . . . primogeniture . . . was unknown to antiquity; neither the Romans, nor the German barbarians know of it and it also remained uncommon among Islamic cultures . . . With the spread of feudalism and conditional land tenure it gained wide acceptance in Europe . . . Primogeniture survived feudalism . . . for two reasons. One was the growing familiarity with Roman law; Roman law knew no conditional ownership and tended to sweep aside the many restraints imposed by feudal custom on the eldest heir, transforming what had been intended as a kind of trusteeship into outright ownership. The other was the growth of capitalism which enabled the younger sons to earn a living without necessarily inheriting a share of the parental estate. Primogeniture, however, never struck root in Russia, because all the necessary conditions were missing . . . It has been a firm principle of Russian customary law to divide all property in equal shares among male heirs . . .

Elsewhere Professor Pipes makes an explicit comparison with the strict settlements of English landowners and remarks 'The Russian

* I am greatly indebted for information and advice to Dr J. R. L. Highfield of Merton College, Dr Christopher Clay of Bristol University, Dr P. J. Jones of Brasenose College and Mr Christopher Thompson of Birkbeck College. They are of course not responsible for errors and misinterpretations in this paper.

I am also indebted to the following owners for allowing access to their collections: the Trustees of the Chatsworth Settled Estates (and Mr Wragg, the Keeper of the Collections), the Duke of Rutland, the Marquess of Bath (and his former Librarian Miss Coate).

landowning class never developed entail or primogeniture, two institutions essential to the well-being of any nobility . . . ' 'The meshing of . . . landed wealth with administrative functions enabled the western European nobility to resist royal absolutism in its most extreme forms.'[1]

Professor Pipes' account of Roman law and still more of feudalism may be open to criticism, but certainly English lawyers from Sir Mathew Hale applauded the common law rule for descent of land by primogeniture for ensuring socially useful occupations for younger sons of landowners, who would otherwise have 'neglected the Opportunities of greater Advantage of enriching themselves and the Kingdom'.[2] On the other hand the indestructibility of entails 'would put a stop to commerce and prevent the circulation of the riches of the kingdom', according to Lord Keeper Guildford in 1683, and conflicted with the common law's supposedly innate principle favouring freedom of alienation so that in Blackstone's words 'Property best answers the purposes of civil life, especially in commercial countries, when its transfer and circulation are totally free and unrestrained.'[3] Sir John Dalrymple, believing this principle prevailed in the sixteenth century, added it to the Harringtonian interpretation of the Civil War.

A commercial disposition had brought in the necessity for allowing an unbounded commerce of land; the landed men, the monied men found their views equally hurt by entails. The lawyers in their writings had been long inveighing against them, and the judges by their judgements had long been discouraging them.

Perhaps these various ranks of men did not foresee, in all their consequences, those important effects which quickly followed from the dissolution of entails and from the transition of property consequent on it. Perhaps too it would be urging too far in favour of a system, to say, that this dissolution was the sole cause of the great alterations which have since happened in the constitution of England; yet so far it is obvious and certain, that added to the dissipation of the church lands by Henry

---

[1] R. Pipes, *Russia under the Old Regime* (London, 1974), pp. 41–2, 176–7.
[2] Sir Mathew Hale, *The History of the Common Law of England*, ed. C. M. Gray (Chicago, 1971), p. 142. Maitland believed that 'our primogenitary law . . . obliterated class distinctions'. F. Pollock and F. W. Maitland, *A History of English Law*, 2 vols (Cambridge, 1898) ii, p. 274.
[3] Sir William Blackstone, *Commentaries on the Laws of England*, 5th edn, 4 vols (Oxford, 1773) ii, p. 288.

VIIIth and the alienation of crown lands by queen Elizabeth, the dissolution of entails produced that transition of property from the lords to the commons which so soon after made the commons, when possessed of almost all the land property of the kingdom, too powerful for both the nobility and the king . . . [4]

The English as conquerors and colonizers in Ireland had long regarded the propagation of the common law as the aim and justification of their efforts. Under Henry VIII the claim was no 'comen folke in all this worlde maye compare with the comyns of Ingland in ryches, in fredome . . . What comyn folke . . . is so power . . . so gretly oppresid . . . as the comyn folke of Irelande?' because 'all the noble folke', English and Irish, preferred extortion to being 'obedyent to the Kinge's lawes'. There was outrage that partible inheritance with equal shares for bastards had destroyed marriage.[5] Sir John Davies in 1607 declared ' . . . the customs of tanistry and gavelkind being absurd and unreasonable as they are in use here . . . shall be clearly extinguished. All the possessions shall descend and be conveyed according to the course of the Common Law. Every man shall have a certain home and know the extent of his estate, whereby the people will be encouraged to manure their land with better industry than heretofore . . . to bring up their children more civilly, to provide for their posterity more carefully.'[6] Bishop Aylmer had complained 'In Civil lawe the children succede indifferentlye in their father's patrimony *in feudis* the sonnes and in other sons and daughters.' 'For nothing soner destroieth greate houses, than the devision of thinheritance, as it appeareth in Germany . . . '[7] This was the aim of the Irish parlia-

---

[4] J. Dalrymple, *An Essay towards a General History of Feudal Property in Great Britain*, 3rd edn (London, 1758), pp. 167–8. Harrington saw this as an incidental factor, operating once nobles became courtiers and increased their expenditures, racked rents and sold lands 'the riddance thro the Statute of Alienations being render'd far more quick and facil than formerly it had bin thro the new invention of Intails', *The Oceana and other Works*, ed. J. Toland, 3rd edn (London, 1747), p. 69 cf. p. 303. Dalrymple may have been influenced by Denzil Holles' pamphlet of 1676, which asserted that Henry VII had 'made way by laws and other means for the Nobility to make alienations . . . and from this time the lands began to come into the hands of the People', *Somers Tracts* (London, 1748) iv, p. 121.

[5] *State Papers Henry VIII*, ii (London, 1834), pp. 10–11; iii, pp. 326–7, 348.

[6] *Ireland under Elizabeth and James I*, ed. H. Morley (London, 1890), p. 379.

[7] J. Aylmer, *An Harborowe for faithfull and Trewe subiectes* (Strasbourg, 1559) Sig. K[4ᵛ].

ment in 1704 when it enacted that all lands of papists in fee tail or fee simple 'shall descend to all and every the sons of such papists by any way inheritable to such estate, shere and shere alike . . . ' (2 Anne cap. vi cl. 3).

If Montesquieu approved entails and primogeniture as means to preserve noble families, themselves essential to true monarchies, he also expressed the republican tradition, partly derived from Harrington, that such devices were inimical to republican regimes which required more or less egalitarian partible inheritance.[8] This latter became part of the republican tradition within the Enlightenment, expressed in Jefferson's panegyric on the abolition of entails and primogeniture in Virginia as preventing 'the accumulation and perpetuation of wealth in select families' and 'substituting equal partition, the best of all Agrarian laws', being necessary parts of 'a system by which every fibre would be eradicated of antient or future aristocracy and a foundation laid for a government truly republican', 'an opening for the aristocracy of virtue and talent'.[9] The effects of the Virginian laws were probably slight,[10] but those of the French revolutionary legislation abolishing entails and freedom of testamentary disposition[11] were much greater.

Indeed their supposed effects on agriculture and the distribution of land were a major preoccupation of political economists in the nineteenth century. Tocqueville's emphasis on the extent of peasant proprietorship before 1789 seems to have concentrated historians' attention on the peasants to the near exclusion of other groups. Even work on peasant customs of inheritance has owed more to legal than to economic historians, while the latest quantitative

[8] *De L'Esprit des Lois* (ed. L. Parelle, Paris, 1826), Bk ii c. 4; v c. 9, c. 8. *Oceana* imposed compulsory partible successions on those with over £2,000 a year in land, but those with under this amount were free to do as they pleased. Harrington also held 'when the Law commands an equal or near equal distribution of a Man's Estate in Land among his Children . . . a Nobility cannot grow', *Works*, ed. Toland, pp. 102, 105, 303.

[9] *The Writings of Thomas Jefferson*, ed. P. L. Ford (New York, 1892) i, pp. 49, 68–9. For the bills, see J. R. Pole. (ed.), *The Revolution in America 1754–88* (London, 1970), pp. 546–9; cf. William Pinkney's speech, p. 564.

[10] D. Malone, *Jefferson the Virginian* (London, 1948), pp. 251–7.

[11] P. Sagnac, *La Législation Civile de la Révolution Française* (Paris, 1898), pp. 224–5. In 1793 the Convention decreed 'la faculté de disposer de ses biens, soit à cause de mort, soit entre-vifs, soit par donation contractuelle en ligne directe, est abolie; et que, en consequence, tous les descendants auront une portion égale sur les biens des ascendants'. This was of course modified by the *Code Civil*, *ibid.*, pp. 343–54. Entails were later restored, by Napoleon, see below p. 276.

studies of nineteenth-century fortunes have excluded the effects of inheritance.[12] Debates about the existence of feudalism in the eighteenth century, or the relationship between the development of capitalism and the Revolution seem to have been equally successful in diverting attention from aristocratic systems of inheritance which so aroused contemporaries. In England since the sixteenth century law reformers had been concerned to improve the lot of younger sons under the common law rules of inheritance. In the nineteenth century this concern was added to attacks on strict settlements as against freedom of alienation and produced the campaigns for free trade in land. The more radical campaigners took inspiration from the American and still more the French Revolution. So much so that, as dogmatic an exponent of free trade as McCulloch, could contradict Adam Smith and defend perpetual entails as 'the only solid bulwark of a hereditary aristocracy', their abolition would 'be very apt to bring about the ruin of the nobility; a consummation which could not be effected without still more serious consequences'.[13]

As generalizations such propositions may seem self-evident. Partible inheritance destroyed five Muscovite boyar families so that some descendants 'in the third and fourth generation actually sank to the level of slaves'.[14] Yet partible inheritance did not destroy Chinese lineages.[15] Differing conceptions of kinship, property and the relationship of the family to the state are obviously relevant. Ultimately in Europe the growth of the state can be seen as killing kinship, conceptions of property become less communal and more individualistic, while social relationships move from status to contract. Maine's insight that primogeniture was political in origin remains valid for many anthropologists, if less so for

[12] A. Daumard, *Les Fortunes Françaises au XIX⁰ Siècle* (Paris, 1973). Professor Daumard admits that such effects could and should be studied, pp. 113–14. It is more surprising to see the same method of global estimates of wealth by social categories, without analysing family inheritances, being used by G. Garnier, *Paysans du Beaujolais et du Lyonnais 1800–1970* (Grenoble, 1973).

[13] J. R. McCulloch, *A Treatise on the Succession to Property* (London, 1848), p. 79. A. Smith, *The Wealth of Nations*, ed. E. Cannan (London, 1961) i, pp. 407–9.

[14] R. Pipes, *op. cit.*, p. 176.

[15] M. Freedman, 'The Politics of an old state: a view from the Chinese Lineage', in J. Davis (ed.), *Choice and Change: Essays in honour of Lucy Mair* (London, 1974), pp. 68–88 provides a convenient summary of his own and other recent work, see especially pp. 69–71.

historians.[16] but to present such conceptual and structural differences in terms of a universal unilinear evolution through historical stages is an even more distorting legacy of the Enlightenment[17] in historical than in sociological analysis; a classic example is Maine's misreading of the Indian village community as aboriginally communistic.[18] Concern for kinship can coexist with unextended families, communal ownership with recognition of individual property rights; even in societies with strongly structured lineages, systems of partible inheritance can, as in the Mâconnais in the eleventh century, produce the same results as primogeniture.[19]

A more useful analytical concept seems to be that of the developmental cycle, whether applied to households,[20] or systems of inheritance. Rajput lineages changed from partible inheritance to impartible inheritance with primogeniture and in some circumstances back again, without significant changes in the social and economic environment. The lineages themselves changed their character as their relations with central political authorities changed.[21]

Thirsk's paper shows that in western Europe from at least the early sixteenth century there was a growing legal and political literature favouring primogeniture. This preceded or coincided with the development among great landowners of legal forms of

[16] R. G. Fox, *Kin, Clan, Raja and Rule* (Berkeley, Calif., 1971), pp. 83–4.

[17] Barnave, a keen student of Adam Smith, presents the notion of stages corresponding to dominant forms of wealth and property, so that Montesquieu's monarchy becomes only a transitional form, still dominated by landed wealth, the domination of industrial and commercial wealth leads to popular monarchy, or republican democracy. *Power, Property and History: Joseph Barnave's Introduction to the French Revolution*, ed. E. Chill (New York, 1971), pp. 91–4, 109–12, 122; *Introduction à la Révolution Française*, ed. F. Rudé (Paris, 1960), pp. 64, 66.

[18] For the historical assumptions about the priority of joint rights, joint family and egalitarian village community, largely shared by Durkheim, see 'The "Village Community" from Munro to Maine', L. Dumont, *Religion, Politics and History in India* (Paris, 1970), pp. 112–32.

[19] G. Duby, 'Lignage, noblesse et chevalerie dans la région mâconnaise. Une Revision'. *Hommes et structures du Moyen Age* (Paris, 1973), pp. 414–415. See below p. 254.

[20] As in the papers by Berkner and Howell in this volume.

[21] R. G. Fox, *op. cit.*, ch. 3: 'A developmental cycle has no end, except one brought on by such a massive social rearrangement that the traditional circularity is irrevocably broken.' 'Joint villages' and 'severalty villages' are themselves products of the cycle, so that there is no absolute priority, each can derive from the other, pp. 126–8.

settlement which entailed their lands on a succession of tenants for life. As we shall see, such forms of settlement were legally possible from at least the early fourteenth century in parts of France and Italy, in Castile from the late fourteenth century, in Germany in the sixteenth century.[22] The questions are how prevalent they were and what effects they had. It is difficult enough to establish what the law allowed, far more so to relate this to what men actually did, or how far their intentions were sustained by the courts. Yet materials for a preliminary comparative survey do exist. A tentative outline of the main developments can be attempted for England, the formal legal position is perhaps clearer for Castile than elsewhere, my ignorance of both law and reality in France and Italy is such that comparisons might seem pointless. But the work of others does allow some demographic comparisons with noble families in France and more with those in Italy. Some suggestions about the effects of these various forms of settlement on family fortunes, as well as on family structures, is possible. The relationship of great landowners to the economies of the various countries and above all to their governments is perhaps the surest conclusion of this paper. For the rest it is mainly a map of ignorance, an invitation to others to explore.

Customary systems of law continued to change even after the customs were codified, as in sixteenth-century France, and within each custom the rules applicable to nobles differed from those for commoners. In the later Middle Ages there was a widespread tendency for the head of the family to acquire greater powers of testamentary disposal of his property, ignoring customary rules.[23] Great landowners might bind their successors and limit their freedom of action, so that each could choose rules of inheritance for his family. While there were norms followed by most families and in some cases the practices of the great came to be imitated by their inferiors, there could also be differences within the same legal categories. Thus in Poland the middling and lesser nobles continued to follow partible inheritance while the magnates en-

---

[22] See below p. 255. This is a gross oversimplification of the German situation, in so far as it refers to the development of *fideicommissa* only and ignores the *Stammgüter* (noble estates descending to a single heir) and the earlier usages of primogeniture among the princely houses before c. 1250.

[23] See below p. 266.

tailed their lands from the late sixteenth century.[24] In England the habits of the greatest landowners probably differed from those of the middling and lesser gentry by the sixteenth century. Before looking further at the way customs of succession developed, it is desirable to avoid two elementary confusions of which many people, including myself, have been victims. The first is to think of primogeniture as excluding females, the second to think of entails as always being in tail male. In settling estates such exclusion was possible, as was tail general (including females after males in the direct line, but giving them priority over remoter collateral males) and settlements of this kind were common in Castile. Again the English common law rule of primogeniture in the descent of land in fee simple did not exclude females, though males of remoter degree took priority over females. The rule excluding the half-blood could give priority to females.[25]

Fortunately we are not concerned about the origins and spread of these rules before 1300. However, some general points may be ventured. The rules are generally thought to have begun with the ruling groups and to have spread downwards. If ultimately they became the basis for individualistic conceptions of property rights they were accompanied from the thirteenth century by the development of entail which limited individual ownership by rules of descent designated by the original donor in the interests of a lineage. The coming together of primogeniture and entail again probably begins with great families and is related to a development, peculiar to England, of the disassociation of titles of dignity from the possession of specific fiefs and territorial jurisdiction. The origin of entail is clearly connected with the development in the thirteenth century of the alienability of land given as a marriage portion (*maritagium*) once issue was born of the marriage, although the donor had originally intended it to be secured to the wife, or even to the heirs of her body. Professor Milsom remarks we know more about the beginnings of entail 'than about its history between the

---

[24] B. Baranowski *et al.*, *Histoire de l'Economie Rurale en Pologne jusqu'à 1864* (Wrocław, 1966), p. 44; P. Sczerbic, *Promptuarium Statutorum et Constitutionum Regni Poloniae* (Brunsbergae, 1604), p. 129 has an ordinance of 1589 giving the Chancellor Zamoyski power to will his real and personal estate, or part of it, as an inalienable perpetuity.

[25] The full rules of descent are given in Blackstone, *Commentaries*, ii, pp. 200–40, ch. 14. A concise and clear summary is in A. W. B. Simpson, *An Introduction to the History of the Land Law* (Oxford, 1961), pp. 54–9.

fourteenth century and the sixteenth. We do not know in point of law how secure it was, or was thought to be; nor do we know in point of fact what use was made of it, or how long individual entails actually lasted.'[26]

These are salutary warnings, though perhaps historians are marginally less ignorant of the points of fact than legal historians are of the points of law. An examination of Appendix II nos. 1 to 14 shows that grants in tail male were the predominant, though by no means the only, form of grants to younger sons. K. B. McFarlane showed that all the original earldoms in fee had been extinguished before the end of the fourteenth century; new creations of earldoms, as of other titles, including baronies by patent, were in tail male, in conformity with the prevailing form of settlement of the main inheritances of noble houses. He also stressed that the fourteenth century saw the rise of feoffments to uses, so that a testator could in effect bequeath his land by will. 'The result was a marked improvement in the prospects of younger sons. There were few who received no share in their father's lands. Without wishing totally to disinherit his heir a landowner felt at liberty to distribute his tenements among his sons in varying proportions.' This tendency was checked by the growing proportion of land which had been entailed and by the settling of estates, when eldest sons were married.[27]

Fathers in seeking settlements when their daughters married would want provision for female issue when male was lacking. This was most easily met by settling land (usually the jointure of the wife) in tail general.[28] A rather later development, which became

[26] S. F. C. Milsom, *Historical Foundations of the Common Law* (London, 1969), p. 147.

[27] K. B. McFarlane, *The English Nobility in the Later Middle Ages* (Oxford, 1973), pp. 80–1, 272–4, 276–8.

[28] For example the prenuptial contract of Elizabeth daughter of Lord Audeley in 1473 settled her jointure in tail general, that of Anne, daughter of Viscount Lisle in 1486 settled a lesser part in tail male, the rest in tail general; Nottingham University, Mi D 4794, 4798; 1536 settlement in tail general on Richard, son and heir apparent of Walter, Lord Ferrers, and his wife *Hist. Ms. Comm. Hastings*, i, p. 313; in 1531 a settlement of most of the Hastings lands, valued at £1,700 a year, was made in reversion on Francis, heir of George, earl of Huntingdon, in tail general on his marriage to the eldest daughter of Lord Montague, J. Nichols, *History and Antiquities of the county of Leicester*, 4 vols (London, 1795–1815), iii, p. 570. A settlement in reversion of the whole jointure in tail male was made on the marriage of Sir Henry Fynes, son and heir of Lord Clinton and Say in 1555, Brit. Mus. Harleian MS. 3881, fo. 46.

standard practice in the strict settlement, was to specify portions.[29] Thus great families normally had lands settled in both tail male and tail general, as well as some variable amount unentailed. McFarlane argued that most entails were allowed to run their course, even when they could have been barred from the later fifteenth century onwards. In general this is probably true enough, leaving their lands, as did Lord Clifford in 1536, to go 'after the olde cours of Inheritance thereof . . . as mouche thereof as hathe bene of olde tyme entayled to the heyres males or to the heyres generall' of his ancestors; 'according as thcy ought to do of right', 'I desert not my heirs; wherefore in my reason I offend not', as others had put it earlier.[30] Yet some, like Lord Bergavenny in 1515, were not prepared to see their younger brother inherit at the expense of their daughters.[31] Before the Statute of Uses in 1536 the potential power to dispose of land as the individual chose was at a peak. This was not peculiar to England; freer testamentary disposition combined with the influence of Roman law to produce in many countries the paradoxical growth of both *patria potestas* and perpetual cntails.

The Statutc of Usca itoolf and othor oontemporary writinge, echoed by a chorus of Cokc and his contemporaries, denounced uses as making the titles of purchasers and tenants uncertain, defrauding creditors of their due, widows of their dower and the

---

[29] The prenuptial contract of Alianor, sister of Henry Lord Clifford, in 1526, for her marriage to Sir Ninian Markinfield, provided for one daughter 200 marks and more than one equal shares in 300 marks. Bodleian Library MS. Dodsworth 74, fo. 116. My impression, based on inadequate evidence, is that such provisions were rare earlier in the sixteenth century, but became commoner by its end.

[30] 27 Henry VIII *cap.* 36, *The Statutes of the Realm* (London, 1817), iii, p. 588; Will of Sir Ralph Shirley 1514, *Testamenta Vetusta*, ed. N. H. Nicholas (London, 1826), ii, p. 542; *Stonor Letters and Papers 1290–1483*, ed. C. L. Kingsford (Camden 3rd ser., xxix, 1919), i, p. 104, c. 1469, H.S. 'thow I do make my wyffe the joyntur of my taylend I dyseryte not my heyres: wer ffor yn my reson I offend not'.

[31] The contract for the marriage of his daughter Jane to Henry, Lord Montague, settled land of 1,600 marks a year on Jane in tail general, remainder to her father's right heirs, land which had been entailed on the heirs male of his father and his mother, except lands which were not entailed to them or their ancestors in general tail to the value of 200 marks a year. If Bergavenny had a son (as he later did) he would pay a portion of 2,000 marks. *Minutes of Evidence . . . on the petition of William Selby Lowndes . . . to determine the abeyance of the barony of Montacute* (London, 1861), pp. 304–9. Cf. Appendix II, no. 13 (a) and (b).

crown and other lords of their feudal incidents. They were the cause of most of the litigation before the courts, while judges' opinions changed daily.[32] The main factor in changing the judge's interpretation of the law was pressure from Henry VIII in 1536. There were also views around 1530 hostile to entails. Christopher St German wrote

> . . . that tailed lands should from henceforth either be made so strong in the law that the tail should not be broken by recovery . . . nor otherwise; or else that all tails should be made fee simple so that every man that list to sell his land, may sell it by his bare feoffment . . . and then there should not be so great expences in the law, nor so great variance among the people, nor yet so great offence of conscience as there is now . . . [33]

A draft bill of 1529 or 1530 provided that all entails should be abolished, except those on noblemen's lands which henceforth could only be alienated with royal license. Whatever the bill's provenance, nothing came of it;[34] but it does offer some confirmation of the nobility's presumed cherishing of entails and of awareness of the notion, shared by Thomas Starkey, that nobles should have privileged modes of inheritance which had real importance in other countries.[35]

The decision against Lord Dacre's will in 1535 and the Statute of Uses (27 Henry VIII cap. 10) in 1536 destroyed the long-established ways in which landowners had settled their estates to pay

[32] W. S. Holdsworth, *A History of English Law*, 13 vols (London, 1922–1952), iv, p. 454 n. 2; Appendix III(3) pp. 577–80; J. M. W. Bean rightly observes that these 'complaints should not be taken too seriously' for the subjects 'any disadvantages in the administration of the law were much more than outweighed by the advantages'. *The Decline of English Feudalism 1215–1540* (Manchester, 1968), p. 289 n. 1.

[33] *Doctor and Student*, 16th edn (London, 1761), p. 95, Dialogue I, *cap.* 32.

[34] The bill is in Holdsworth, *op. cit.*, iv, Appendix III(1), pp. 572–4. E. W. Ives argues that it was not an official bill and was not connected with the agreement made between the king and the nobility (*ibid.*, pp. 574–7), 'The genesis of the Statute of Uses', *Eng. Hist. Rev.* lxxii (1967), pp. 676–82. But Bean argues that the bill was an official draft; is inextricably connected with the agreement and that both belong to 1530, *op. cit.*, pp. 258–69. Neither these views, Holdsworth's, nor the documents are reconcilable with L. Stone's statement 'In the early sixteenth century the peers refused the offer of inalienable entails included in the first draft of the Statute of Uses . . .' *The Crisis of the Aristocracy* (Oxford, 1965), p. 182.

[35] T. Starkey, *A Dialogue between Reginald Pole and Thomas Lupset*, ed. K. M. Burton (London, 1948), pp. 108–9, 174.

their debts and provide for their younger children after their deaths. The Statute did allow all devises of land by those who had died before 1 May 1536 to stand. From then until the passing of the Statute of Wills (32 Henry VIII *cap.* 1) in 1540, landowners found, as its preamble put it, ' . . . by daily experience . . . they shall not be able of their . . . movable substance, to discharge their debts and after their degrees set forth and advance their children and posterities'.[36] The Statute allowed two-thirds of land held by tenants in chief to be devised and all lands in socage. The general effect on great landowners was that a third of their lands went in wardship to the crown if the heir was a minor, and could not be diverted from the heir, at least a third would go to his widow in dower or jointure and another third could be devised to pay debts and provide for younger children, or for any other purpose. Another act allowed a tenant in tail in possession to bar the entail by fine, so that he could disinherit his son and make the land subject to his debts and sales. Even more important was that empowering him, or life tenants, to make leases for twenty-one years or three lives, reserving accustomed rents, which were valid after the grantors' deaths.[37]

The Statute of Uses had destroyed the means whereby great landowners had traditionally regulated their inheritances, but not their will to do so. *The Use of the Law* (wrongly attributed to Bacon) noted

Since these notable remedies provided by the Statute to dock entails, there is started up a device called perpetuity; which is an entail with an addition of a proviso conditional, tied to his estate, not to put away the land from the next heir; and if he do, to forfeit his own estate.[38]

Bacon himself, in Chudleigh's case in 1594, said ' . . . for sixty years past, infinite of these assurances have been made and that by the most learned and the most mighty who have endeavored to perpetuate their families . . . '[39] It has long been held that elaborate settlements limiting estates to unborn persons were only found from 1557 which was the year and form of settlement called in question

---

[36] Ives, *art. cit.*, pp. 687–97; Bacon, *op cit.*, pp. 273–301.
[37] 32 Henry VIII, *cap.* 36; *cap.* 31.
[38] *The Works of Francis Bacon*, ed. J. Spedding *et al.*, 14 vols (London, 1857–74), vii, p. 491.
[39] *Ibid.*, p. 623, Chudleigh's Case.

in Chudleigh's case.[40] Provisos and conditions to restrain alienation and the discontinuance of entails in settlements or wills were common in the fifteenth century and continued after 1536, but they usually voided the estate and did not put in the next in reversion.[41]

This newer kind of perpetuity was certainly being used by great families by the 1560s.[42] They seem to have become more frequent and elaborate in the next twenty years. Another reason for believing that the amount of land settled in this way grew is that the disposal of the monastic lands involved many families in sales, purchases, exchanges with the crown or others, which would have been hindered if large parts of their lands had been subject to perpetuities. Our examples include typical occasions for such settlements; that of the Spencer lands was the marriage of Sir John Spencer III to the heiress of Sir Robert Catlin; that of the third earl of Rutland was to tie that part of his lands going to his brother and heir male away from his daughter and heir general; while the

---

[40] J. Williams, 'On the Origin of the Present Mode of Family Settlements of landed Property', *Papers read before the Juridical Society*, i (1855–8), pp. 45–9, based on inspection of Harleian, Cottonian and Additional Charters in the British Museum. But the will of John Fitzherbert made in 1517 settled Norbury and other lands in tail male to his brother with remainders, with the proviso that if any heir attempts to alienate any of the property, the heir presumptive is to succeed, J. C. Cox, 'Norbury Manor House and the FitzHerberts', *Jnl Derbyshire Archaeological and Nat. Hist. Soc.*, vii (1885), p. 231.

[41] V. infra Appendix II, no. 8. Covenants not to discontinue lands, or disinherit daughters in 1445 and 1446, T. Barrett-Lennard, *An Account of the Families of Lennard and Barrett* (n.p., 1908), pp. 59–62. The will of Thomas, Lord Burgh, in 1550, settles land on his eldest son in tail general on condition that he and the heirs of his body 'by any means, crafts, or pollecie shall not aleyn, bargain, sell, discontynue, or otherwise put away the reversion . . .' on pain of re-entry by Burgh and his heirs, Public Record Office, Registers of Wills of the Prerogative Court of Canterbury [hereafter P.C.C.] 27 Coode. V. supra n. 40.

[42] Edward, first Lord North, in 1564 left two-thirds of his estate settled in tail male with specified remainders, with powers to incumber for the life of the person charging, to charge no more than a third with jointure and to make leases for twenty-one years or less. If a life tenant did more, his interest ceased and went to the next in succession, P.C.C. 7 Morison. In January 1558 George, Lord Cobham, made a similar entail of nearly half his lands on his numerous sons and daughters, with a proviso that on any act of discontinuance the next in remainder should enter as if the doer had died without issue, P.C.C. 58 Mellershe. In September 1557 William, Lord Dacre of the North, settled his lands in tail male with a clause of perpetuity, *The Household Books of Lord William Howard of Naworth*, ed. G. Ormsby (Surtees Society, lxviii, 1878), pp. 379–80, 385–6.

earl of Sussex's perpetuity was made on his brother and heir male, when he himself was childless, as was Sir Edmund Brudenell's in 1583.[43] More exceptional was that of Sir Richard Cholmley in 1579 who

> loved his son Francis so entirely, as if he had married with his approbation . . . he had left his whole estate freely to him without an entail . . . if he would marry any but Mrs. Jane Boulmer, who though of good family had no good fame . . . [who] would make her husband so dispose the land as not a foot should come to any of his blood . . . [44]

The main forms taken by these perpetuities and the attitude of the courts to them has been traced by Holdsworth.[45] The main form of conveyance had been upheld by the decision in Scholastica's case in 1572, but was condemned by the judges in Mary Portington's case in 1613; other forms had already been invalidated in Corbet's case in 1600, other cases in 1595 and in Wiseman's case in 1585.[46] Thus uncertainty about the validity of these settlements had grown from Chudleigh's case in 1594. Bacon had then argued that the draughtsmen of these devices were hoping to exploit existing uncertainties of the law. But it should be recognized how eminent these experimenters were: three chief justices, an attorney general and a master of the rolls were parties to three of the perpetuities already cited.[47] Why had judicial opinion reversed itself after some forty years?

[43] M. E. Finch, *The Wealth of Five Northamptonshire Families 1540–1640* (Northamptonshire Record Soc., xix, 1956), pp. 51–2 (Spencer, 1566), 143–4 (Brudenell); Belvoir Castle Muniments Room 4, Case I, Settlement 70, 11 June 1577; *Evidence before the Committee of Privileges . . . on the Petition of Sir Brook William Bridges claiming . . . to be Baron Fitzwalter* (1842), pp. 435–45, 22 Dec. 1579.

[44] *The Memoirs of Sir Hugh Chomley Bart.* (London, 1787), pp. 10–11. The remainders put the third son before the second whose paternity was doubted by Sir Richard. Cf. Coke's *Reports*, i, fo. 86r.

[45] *History of English Law*, vii, pp. 205–11; cf. Simpson, *An Introduction*, pp. 197–209, Milsom, *Historical Foundations*, p. 395. Mary Portington's Case was in Trinity term 1613, Coke *Reports* pt v, fo. 35v. Both Holdsworth and Simpson date it as 1614.

[46] Wiseman's Case dealt with a device for making entails unbarable by granting a remainder to the crown. The settlement in 1581 on Edward, Lord Dudley, in tail male with remainder to the Queen, her heirs and successors, would not have been affected, as the lands had been granted in tail male by the Crown in 1554. Dudley Public Library, Dudley Muniments Box 6/6.

[47] C. J. Dyer, Sir William Cordell, Master of the Rolls were executors of North's will (n. 42 above); C. J. Catlin was a party to the Spencer settle-

A major argument of Bacon, Coke, Popham and others was that perpetuities were a means of evading the crown's feudal rights and forfeitures for treason, just as uses had been before 1536. The former seems to be more a polemical assertion of guilt by historical association than of proved intention, since many of them explicitly reserved the crown's rights.[48] The bill for the abolition of perpetuities which received one reading in 1598 asserted that, again like uses, they defrauded purchasers and prevented possessors from selling or exchanging lands and more generally 'engender discorde in all families where they light and drawe the whole kindred into faction, but doe also make Children disobedient and parents unnatural . . . '[49] The undermining of paternal authority was also invoked by Bacon and was a standard argument down to the nineteenth century. Another providential argument was put by Judge Dodridge in 1620 and approved by Sir Hugh Cholmley in 1655

God gave lands to men and if men could make lands continue in their families for ever this would be a stop to the providence of God who sets up and pulls down . . . at his pleasure . . . if perpetuities were established this would prevent all the power of disposition of lands by God.

With more self-interest Lord William Howard invoked providence to make the rights of heirs general undefeatable.[50]

At a more worldly level there are signs that perpetuities had created difficulties. The Spencer one of 1566 was the subject of a

ment, C. J. Wray, Cordell, the Attorney-General Gerrard were parties to both the Rutland and Sussex settlements in note 43 above.

[48] It was claimed that an act of treason would be discontinuance, so that the estate would go to the next in succession. This may have encouraged the use of such settlements in the uncertainties of Mary's last and Elizabeth's first years. I have not ascertained whether the settlements to uses by the earl of Oxford in 1562 and the duke of Norfolk in 1569 (N. Williams, *Thomas Howard Fourth Duke of Norfolk* (London, 1964), pp. 119–20) contained provisos of perpetuity. Norfolk's settlement in tail male probably did, but it is difficult to agree with Williams that it would enable evasion of feudal incidents, as it covered less than half his lands by value.

[49] Holdsworth, *op. cit.*, vii, p. 546.

[50] *Reports de Henry Rolle* (London, 1666), ii, p. 221, *Memoirs of Sir Hugh Cholmley*, p. 15: 'it is not good to be too solicitous in settling an estate, or thinking to perpetuate a man's name and family, but leave it to succeeding Providence . . . ' Lord William Howard, married to one of Dacre's heirs-general, saw her grandfather, William, Lord Dacre, as 'seduced by devilish instigation . . . to crosse Almighty God in his omnipotent course . . . attempted to settle his inheritance upon the heirs male of his house and to bar . . . his right heirs of their due . . . belonging unto them, both by the laws of God, of nations, and of this realme'. Surtees Soc. lxviii, p. 366.

private bill in 1597 empowering sale of any part of the Catlin inheritance 'for the advancement . . . of the younger children' of Robert, who succeeded his father Sir John III in 1600 and was created Baron Spencer in 1603.[51] In the same parliament William Pope obtained a private act to allow him to settle a jointure and sell lands to pay his debts, despite the perpetuity created by Sir Thomas Pope in 1554.[52] In 1584 the earl of Bedford in his will charged his heir to ratify all his conveyances to his younger sons and his wife and his leases not warranted by 32 Henry VIII cap. 31.[53] Bedford's settlement also seems to have been made under Queen Mary; later ones certainly gave full powers to lease which ought to have avoided such difficulties. Nevertheless this may well have been where they were most vulnerable to the changed attitudes of the courts. Gilbert, earl of Shrewsbury, wrote in 1607 of a case before Popham

. . . where the elder brother made leases out of a perpetuity according to the words of the book and he [Popham] advised the leasees to compound notwithstanding that he that made the entail thought that he had such power and so the words seemed to carry, but the Chief Justice said that his law or learning was not sufficient to pen a good lease out of such an entail . . . [54]

This shows that landowners were certainly aware of judges' opinions, but their impact on conveyancing was probably slower. The 1615 edition of West's manual contains five precedents for perpetuities, three more than in the first edition of 1590. Only one

[51] M. E. Finch, *op. cit.*, pp. 51–4. House of Lords Record Office, Main Papers, Bill, 7 December 1597. The sale of two manors in Dorset was ratified in 1606, Private Act 3 and 4 James I, *cap.* 7.

[52] Private Act 39 and 40 Elizabeth, *cap.* 15. His descendants went on selling lands, although this act was later construed as establishing the perpetuities on the remaining land, so that another Act was needed to ratify the sales, Bodleian Library MS. Carte 78, fo. 661.

[53] '. . . I being but tenant in tayle , , , have made divers leases, estates and grants of annuities . . . which by my heyrs after my decease may at their pleasures be avoyded or elce by my dethe *ipso facto* be voyd . . .' P.C.C. 45 Windsor.

[54] To Henry Cavendish, 4 January, Nathaniel Johnston, MS. Lives of the Earls of Shrewsbury, iv, p. 84, Longleat Library, ix. B.6. Unfortunately there is no indication of the form of settlement involved. Mildmay's case was in Michaelmas term 1605 in King's Bench where Popham was Chief Justice. A legal adviser of the earl of Huntingdon about this time claimed that leases for 99 years, determinable on three lives, were usually confirmed by fines, this could not be validly done by a tenant in tail and would cause a discontinuance, MS. Carte, 289, fo. 10.

might have been upheld by the courts by 1613 and survived in the *Perfect Conveyancer* of 1650, which reflects practice of the 1630s, since it could be construed as an executory devise.[55] The most immediate and widespread effect may have been on the validity of leases. As we have seen there were two forces at work, belief in the freedom of the testator, as exemplifying paternal authority, and perpetuation of the inheritance and with it the power and prestige of the lineage. Generally heirs seem to have accepted entails even when they might have barred them. The perpetuities created after 1550 mostly affected only part of an inheritance. As we have seen, older entails generally included some in tail general, while the third part, subject to the crown's rights by the Statute of Wills, would go to the heirs general. The general view was expressed by Edward, third earl of Rutland, in 1583 who, having settled most of his lands with the perpetuity of 1577 to go with the earldom in tail male to his brother, bequeathed lands to go with the barony of Ross to his daughter and heir general, 'for that one of my ancestors whose heir I am did marry the heir of Lord Ross . . . '[56] If perpetuities in tail male had endured for two or three generations the amount of land going to heirs general might have been diminished, or at least postponed, given the rate of failure in the male line.[57] As we have already seen Lord William

---

[55] T. West, *Symbolaeographia* (London, 1590), sects 25(F), 37(b); *The First Part of Symboleography* (London, 1615), sects 84 (25 above), 98 (37 above), 99, 281. 99 would have been void by the decision in Mary Portington's Case, the others by earlier decisions. Sect. 647, 'A proviso to bind lands by will' is a less elaborate version of *The Perfect Conveyancer . . . Collected by Four severall Sages of the Law, Edward Henden . . . , William Noy . . . Robert Mason and Henry Fleetwood . . .* (London, 1655), Pt i, pp. 165–7, 'The form of a perpetuity by will, or a Provisoe to restraine alienation etc.' For the indestructibility of executory devises, Holdsworth, *History*, vii, pp. 130–5; Simpson, *Introduction*, pp. 204–10, the attitude of the common law courts after 1620 seems to have been uncertain. 'All suits grounded . . . upon Long Leases that tend to the defeating of the King's Tenures, or for the Establishing of Perpetuities . . . are regularly to be dismissed upon motion, if they are the whole matter of the Bill and there be no special circumstances to move the Court [of Chancery] . . .', T. Powell, *The Attorney's Academy* (London, 1623), pp. 45–6.

[56] *North Country Wills* i (Surtees Soc., cxvi, 1908), pp. 117–18.

[57] Settlements usually had remainders to females after males and finally to the settler's right heirs. The earl of Sussex's settlement (n. 43 above) ensured that nearly all the lands in it went eventually to the descendants of his sister. More restrictive perpetuities in tail male were settled on younger brothers, e.g. that by Roger, earl of Rutland, on his brother Francis in 1602, (Belvoir Settlements 90), where the lands went on failure of Francis'

Howard in 1605 took a much more extreme view of the divine rights of heirs general.

Men had often, even usually, wished for some of their land to go to their heirs general; if they came from great houses this probably continued to be so. But already some settlements specified the size of daughters' portions, if there were no sons of the marriage, and this may have spread first among lesser families.[58] By the early seventeenth century it was common to specify daughter's portions in marriage settlements, though this did not necessarily exclude them from receiving more, or even inheriting land, and the coming of strict settlements did not change this. It was not solely love of their daughters, or dislike of their younger brothers, which might make men favour their heirs general. Lord Bergavenny in 1515 by settling land on his daughter as his heir general apparent did not have to pay a portion for her, unless he had a son. The second earl of Cumberland demanded payment for the marriage of his daughter, Margaret, one of the coheirs of Charles Brandon, duke of Suffolk.[59]

heirs male to Roger and the heirs male of his body, failing these to those of Thomas, first earl of Rutland, then to the heirs of the body of Thomas's grandfather, finally to the right heirs of Edward, the second earl.

[58] The Dudley settlement of 1581 secured £2,000 to a single daughter of the marriage, £4,000 to more than one, if there were no sons, Dudley Public Library, Box 6/6. The contract for the marriage of Eleanor Scrope and Richard Tempest of Bragsnall in 1564 specified that if there were only issue female they should receive 800 marks in all (Eleanor's portion was £400), Bodleian MS. Dodsworth 88, fo. 97v. The marriage contract of Thomas Cornwall of Burford, Shropshire and Anne Littleton in 1594 provided in the same circumstances 2,000 marks for one daughter, £1,000 each for two, 1,000 marks each for more (Anne's portion was £1,600), Birmingham Reference Library, Littleton Papers, 351709. In 1546 a Daubeney marriage settlement is on the son and his wife and the heirs of his body, in 1607 the family settlement was in tail male with £1,500 specified for heirs general, *Calendar of Antrobus Deeds before 1625*, ed. R. B. Pugh (Wilts. Arch. and Nat. Hist. Soc. Records Branch, iii, 1947), nos 95, 140. The 1590 edition of West's *Symboleography* gives two settlements of jointure and one of jointly purchased lands to heirs of the husband's body (sects 22, 30, 27(A)), and two to raise portions, if there were no issue male (25(A), 28). The 1615 edition repeats these and adds another raising portions (Sects 81, 86, 88; portions 82, 85, 87). *The Perfect Conveyancer* (1650 [1655]) gives one example of reversion after the jointure to the heirs of the husband begotten on the wife (pt ii, p. 39), another to the husband and his heirs for ever (p. 46) and a settlement in tail male, specifying portions, if there were no issue male of the marriage (pp. 279–95).

[59] The Duke of Northumberland had offered 4,000 marks for her marriage to his son Gildford, if 'all those lands which be not allredie intailed to the heir male should discend' to her. Cumberland himself offered to settle £1,000 a year on her, if he had no son, in return for 3,000 marks, 1,000 of

On the other hand settlements in tail male of most of the estate, especially if reinforced by perpetuities, would mean that the heir general would have to receive cash not land, as the third earl of Cumberland had intended his daughter, Lady Anne Clifford, to do.

Despite the widespread desire of peers to settle major parts of their estates in tail male with perpetuities, no clear trend to the disadvantage of heirs general emerges in the second half of the sixteenth century. The Statute of Wills made it seem that at least a third was what the heirs general might expect. This could be related to the habit of settling jointures in tail general, since a minimum jointure should have been the equivalent of the right to a third by way of dower. It is clear that the Statute of Wills guided the arbitration between the heirs male and general of Giles, Lord Chandos in 1602.[60] The third earl of Rutland left his daughter about a third. Given the fact that heiresses usually married the sons of powerful men, they seldom lacked influence and advocates. Quite apart from the extreme, but not unprecedented, cases, such as Ferdinando, earl of Derby's, attempt to disinherit his brother, or the third earl of Cumberland's attempt to settle all his lands on his brother and away from his daughter, disputes and litigation were inevitable. Edward, third earl of Rutland, had attempted a secure and reasonable settlement, but Burghley married his eldest son to the heir general and began a prolonged dispute with the heirs male.[61]

Although the court's reversal of their tacit acceptance of perpetuities from the 1590s onwards certainly provided new ways of disputing recent settlements, the inheritances of most great landowners had been subject to forfeitures, attainders, regrants, resumptions, recoveries, restorations in blood, exchanges and partitions, so that technical flaws could nearly always be alleged or

which would be repaid if he had issue male, in negotiations with the earl of Derby. Bodleian MS. Dodsworth 88, fos. 103–105v. She married Derby's heir in 1555.

[60] For Chandos, see *Econ. Hist. Rev.*, 2nd ser., viii (1956), pp. 379 n. 1, 380 n. 2. The inquisitions at the death of the fourth earl found just under a third settled on Lady Roos; Belvoir, Case 39, extent 13 August 1588.

[61] B. Coward, 'Disputed Inheritances', *Bulletin of the Institute of Historical Research*, xliv (1971), pp. 204–11. For Cumberland *Econ. Hist. Rev.*, 2nd ser., viii (1956), p. 380 and n. 4. Equally spectacular determination to disinherit a younger brother was shown by Marquess Berkeley, though he had no issue, under Henry VII, while Thomas, Lord Berkeley, who died in 1417 favoured his daughter as heir general. R. T. Spence, 'The Clifford earls of Cumberland 1579–1646' (London Ph.D. thesis, 1959), pp. 218–24.

found. The flaws in the title deeds of Henry, Lord Berkeley, may have been more recent and obvious than most. They were exploited when he and his wife refused to marry their daughters (before they had a son) to the two Sidney brothers, nephews of the earls of Leicester and Warwick. Leicester's influence at Court was used to overawe jurors and protect his theft of Berkeley's muniments. When Leicester was dead and Berkeley had friends again at Court, first Hunsdon, then Henry Howard, earl of Northampton, verdicts and awards went in his favour.[62] Again there may have been technical flaws in the perpetuity in tail male which William, Lord Dacre, made in 1557, but there is no doubt that his second son's claim to the barony, after the death of his nephew in 1569, was valid. It was rejected and most of the lands went to the heirs general, Norfolk's wards, whose marriages to the duke's sons had already been arranged.[63] Even in eclipse Norfolk was far more powerful than Leonard Dacre. In 1583 Oswin Ogle, fourth son of the fourth Lord Ogle, unavailingly petitioned the Privy Council that his nephew Cuthbert the seventh lord ' . . . havinge no heyres male goeth aboute to cutt your poor suppliante from the benefitt of that whereby he is now Lord Ogle, for he the said Lord Cutbert continued the entail which was like to be cutt off . . . [that the Council] maintaine the entaile in the heyres male . . . '[64] Lord Ogle married his elder daughter to the younger son of the earl of Shrewsbury, Edward Talbot, and settled his estates on her and her sister, who later married Charles Cavendish, the earl's stepson, and transmitted the whole inheritance to her son, the first Duke of Newcastle.

Leonard Dacre and Oswin Ogle had no friends at Court; Henry, Lord Berkeley, had had them from 1554 to 1570 by his marriage

[62] J. Smyth, *The Lives of the Berkeleys*, ed. Sir J. Maclean, 2 vols (Bristol and Glos. Arch. Soc., Gloucester, 1883–5) ii, pp. 288–309, 314–32, especially 305–8, 326.

[63] Lord William Howard claimed that the livery and attournments to complete William, Lord Dacre's entail had never been properly executed (Surtees Society, lxviii), pp. 378–80. Leonard Dacre was denied time to search for proofs in 1569, N. Williams, *op. cit.*, pp. 117–18. Edward IV's award in 1473 between the heirs male and general, of Thomas Lord Dacre, which in allocation of lands favoured the heirs male, had put the barony in tail male, *Collectanea Topographica et Genealogica*, v (1838), pp. 319–20.

[64] Cuthbert was the elder son of a second marriage of Robert the fifth lord, Oswin's eldest brother, whose son by his first marriage, Robert, the sixth lord, had died without issue in 1562, when his sisters of the whole blood had claimed to be his heirs, Sir H. A. Ogle, *Ogle and Bothal* (Newcastle, 1902), pp. 64, 68–9.

to Norfolk's sister, but then he had to wait a generation for the Howards to come into their own again. Even so he had to compromise with the Sidneys and this was the usual result of conflicts between heirs male and heirs general. The crown was forced to arbitrate by the fact that both sides could win allies at Court (as with the Derby inheritance) and by fears of local disturbance, as much as by the obscurities of the law. From the twelfth century to the disputes over the Thynne inheritance after 1639 the crown was called upon to intervene. Perhaps the most important change of the epoch of the strict settlement is that such disputes were left more completely to the slow process of the courts, whose rules on what settlements could achieve had become clearer by the time of Lord Chancellor Nottingham. Family councils might still be hindered by personal and political animosities. It was the resulting pressures on money and time, added to those from more securely entrenched reversionary interests rather than the harnessing of court favour and faction, that now brought men to arbitration, ratified and subjected to some process of judicial scrutiny by private acts of parliament. Before looking at the effects of strict settlements, we must see how younger children were treated when there were no problems of arbitrating between heirs male and heirs general.

Younger children need to be considered together, although it is often easier to collect information about provision for daughters than for younger sons. The general lines of development are from provision in land to provision in money, but the chronology is different. Clearly it happened earlier for daughters with the cash portion replacing the *maritagium* after 1300. Stone sees a change for the younger sons first in the later sixteenth century to leases for years or two lives, then in the early seventeenth century to annuities and rent charges.[65] This ignores an appreciable number of cases, though certainly a minority of the total, where younger sons were given cash portions. These became the prevalent form for sons as well as daughters by the eighteenth century, when there was no real distinction between capital sums and annuities.[66]

[65] L. Stone, *The Crisis of the Aristocracy* (Oxford, 1965), p. 180, '. . . the outright grant of land to younger sons was being superseded . . .'. Earlier on that page such grants are said to have been mostly in tail male.

[66] Portions would be expressed as capital sums, usually remaining as mortgages on the estate, which the beneficiary could turn into a capital sum by assigning it. I am grateful to Christopher Clay for pointing this out. For

Habakkuk has argued that 'daughters were more important than younger sons, for they were the means by which the great landed families made their alliances, and, like most landowners. Nottingham endowed his daughters more generously than their younger brothers', so that it is desirable to see when, if ever, this became true. If we add Stone's conclusion 'that in the seventeenth century parents were devoting a very much higher proportion of their incomes to marrying off their daughters than were their grandparents in the sixteenth' and Finch's observations that 'the provision for Spencer younger sons shows no similar increase' to that for daughters,[67] it also seems desirable to discover whether this was achieved by sacrificing provision for younger sons.

It is also important from at least the mid sixteenth century to distinguish between great landowners, whether peers or not, and lesser ones. Much of the literature of complaint about the fate of younger sons seems to be concerned with the middling and lesser gentry. Cliffe writes of the Yorkshire gentry in the century before 1642: 'Among the richer gentry it was not unusual for them [younger sons] to be given parcels of landed property for their financial support. More frequently, however, a younger son was granted a life annuity . . . '[68] Provision by grants of land may have been commoner in south-west Wales, where there was a native tradition of partible inheritance.[69] This had also been true of Kent, but by 1640, though traditions of founding separate establishments

earlier examples see Appendix II, nos 5, 16, 17, 24(b), 26, 29, 32(c), 33–5, 37, 39, 40.

[67] H. J. Habakkuk, 'Daniel Finch, second Earl of Nottingham: His House and Estate', *Studies in Social History*, ed. J. H. Plumb (London, 1955), p. 157; Stone, *op. cit.*, p. 642; M. E. Finch, *op. cit.*, p. 60. But, while Sir John Spencer II probably treated his three surviving younger sons more generously than his daughters (Sir John I had no younger son), William Lord Spencer in 1636 provided at least as much for his younger sons, as for his younger daughters, see Appendix II 24(a), (c). Thus the increase in portions gave the daughters equality with their brothers.'

[68] J. T. Cliffe, *The Yorkshire Gentry 1540–1648* (London, 1969), pp. 83–4; individual examples of settlement of land are given, pp. 370, 374, but it is not clear whether they were limited for the recipient's life, or were in tail male.

[69] This is the impression given by the few instances from wills cited in H. A. Lloyd, *The Gentry of South-West Wales 1540–1640* (Cardiff, 1968), pp. 50–2. Professor Glanmor Williams shows that in Glamorgan the gentry who could afford it, and especially those who had made new acquisitions, provided land for their younger sons, while those of the poorer gentry might have to make do with leases, *Early Modern Glamorgan, Glamorgan County History* (Cardiff, 1974) iv, pp. 94–5.

for younger sons lingered, primogeniture among the gentry 'was rapidly becoming universal'.[70] Ferris considers that even the great gentry families in Dorset by 1640 generally granted only life estates to younger sons, though some got portions in cash. There were still rare instances of partible inheritance, while many cadet lines survived from earlier times.[71] Blackwood has found that in seventeenth-century Lancashire the normal provision was by modest annuities. Lancashire may be particularly significant, since in the early sixteenth century the gentry were more geographically isolated and even less likely to marry outside the county 'and the second rank of gentry consisted mainly of cadet branches of leading families', which suggests that some younger sons had been endowed with land in the later Middle Ages.[72] For most areas we can only guess at the gentry's habits around 1600, without any clues as to how they had developed.

However, it is clear that in the fourteenth and fifteenth centuries grants of rent charges and lands for life to younger sons were made by both greater and lesser landowners. As we have already seen, if land of inheritance was given it was most commonly in tail male. In the fourteenth century the lords Berkeley founded at least two important knightly families by such grants, the Berkeleys of Stoke Gifford and Uley and the Berkeleys of Beverstone. Such grants continued into the epoch of strict settlements, including the odd variant, used by the Russells, of granting a rent charge in tail male. The great attraction to the head of the family was the prospect of the land returning, if the cadet line died out in the male line, and this continued to happen into the eighteenth century.[73] The

[70] A. Everitt, *The Community of Kent and the Great Rebellion* (Leicester, 1966), p. 47; cf. C. W. Chalkin, *Seventeenth Century Kent* (London, 1965), pp. 202–3, it became usual to provide sons and daughters 'with portions of at least a few hundred pounds'.

[71] J. P. Ferris, 'The Gentry in Dorset on the Eve of the Civil War', *Genealogists' Magazine*, xv (1965), pp. 104–7.

[72] B. G. Blackwood, 'The Lancashire Gentry 1625–60' (Oxford, D.Phil. Thesis, 1973), pp. 42–3: the average of his sample of fifty-four annuities is £23, with only five over £50. But his evidence may not cover the greater gentry adequately. C. Haigh, *Reformation and Resistance in Tudor Lancashire* (Cambridge, 1975), p. 89. There was a very considerable number of cadet branches of gentry families in seventeenth-century Devon, W. G. Hoskins, *Devon* (London, 1954), p. 87.

[73] J. Smyth, *The Lives of the Berkeleys*, i, pp. 248, 349–53; see below Appendix II, nos 22(c), 24(c), 40, 41–4. The Somersets, earls and marquesses of Worcester and dukes of Beaufort, from the early seventeenth to the early eighteenth century frequently endowed younger sons with landed estates

other possibility was that a cadet line would become the heirs male, as happened with the Berkeleys both in the fifteenth century and in the sixteenth century and with the earls of Rutland in the seventeenth century. Grants of fuller estates, tail general or fee simple, did occur, but were rarer and seem to have become rarer still from the sixteenth century, though powers to grant fee simple estates were reserved in at least one strict settlement.[74]

The best prospect for founding a cadet line lay in marrying an heiress. But only the younger sons of the wealthy and powerful could hope for this, hence the bequests of wardships, or of money to buy marriages. Thus the ending of sale of marriages without the consent of the wards' families after 1611, followed by the abolition of the Court of Wards itself, probably damaged the prospects of younger sons. At all times those more interested in maximizing income than in founding families could seek to marry widows. It is observable that one younger son, not necessarily the second, might be particularly favoured. The extreme cases of depriving eldest sons for the benefit of younger ones usually came about as a result of second marriages. Spectacular examples were the founding of the baronial house of Grey of Ruthin with three-quarters of the estates of the original Grey of Wilton line in the early fourtenth century, the favouring by Ralph Nevill, earl of Westmorland, of his children by his second Beaufort marriage in the early fifteenth century,[75] and the division of his estates by Sir Thomas Thynne of Longleat in favour of the sons of his second marriage in 1639.

There are many examples where fathers were more generous to their younger sons than to their daughters.[76] The fact that testators usually left the same amount for an unborn child, whatever its sex, suggests that equal treatment was the norm, or the minimum for sons, as it became in strict settlements. Indeed it would be tempting to argue that, whenever circumstances permitted, fathers were liable to be more generous to their sons than their daughters. Habakkuk rightly remarks that the extent of provision for younger children 'varied very widely according to parental affection and

and on at least one occasion included an existing cadet branch before the main line in the remainders in settlements in tail male on a younger son.

[74] See below Appendix II, nos 4, 9(a), 10, 11(a), (b), 13(c), 15, 19, 22(a), 34 for grants wider than tail male; 42, powers to settle in fee simple.

[75] R. I. Jack, *The Grey of Ruthin Valor* (Sydney, 1965), pp. 1–3. K. B. McFarlane, *The Nobility of Later Medieval England*, pp. 67–8.

[76] See Appendix II, nos 4, 9(a), 12, 16, 19, 26, 31, 32(c), 33, 34, 36.

the circumstances of the family'. Moreover it was easier for a landowner before the regime of strict settlement to economize on their provision than on almost any other large item of expenditure.[77] Given the opportunities for individual whims to express themselves, individual instances may be no basis for generalization. Yet one generalization may certainly be put that new men were particularly likely to be generous to their younger sons. This is related to another generalization covering even more centuries and places, that a man's new acquisitions, his 'conquests', were at his free disposal and were peculiarly appropriate for the endowment of his younger sons. Again when a man married an heiress, his younger sons, or at least one of them, often benefited. Thus the endowing of younger sons was a demonstration of wealth and success as much as the commanding size of daughters' portions. For established families it showed their power to continue building up wealth and to command favour; for the newly risen it asserted and demonstrated their success.

Perhaps the best known sixteenth-century example is Burghley's endowment of his second son, Robert. The Lord Keeper Sir Nicholas Bacon's fortune was more modest, but he had four sons for whom to provide. Nathaniel, the second, married an heiress, and had Stiffkey and two other manors bought for him. Edward also married an heiress, but seems to have been given much less land. Anthony had about £400 a year land of inheritance in possession and in reversion after his mother and £100 from leasehold land. Francis, the youngest, was the worst provided for, having land bought for him for £1,300, as well as a manor and some leases, in all £200 to £300 a year, yet even this was about four times as much as the highest portion given to his three sisters.[78] Francis Rodes, justice of the Common Pleas, was another follower of this legal tradition whose most spectacular exemplar was Coke, with Lord Keeper Coventry a much more modest one.[79] The first Lord Rich

[77] H. J. Habakkuk, 'Marriage Settlements in the Eighteenth Century', *Trans. Roy. Hist. Soc.*, 4th ser., xxxii (1950), p. 19.
[78] A. Simpson, *The Wealth of the Gentry 1540–1660* (Cambridge, 1961), pp. 96, 98–9, 101–3. The daughters were given portions of £800, £666, and £866 between 1564 and 1572.
[79] Rodes provided a considerable estate and mansion for the eldest son of his second marriage and land for another, while annulling settlement of lands on another for untowardness. Two daughters were left 1,000 marks and £600 and four £500 each (two were already married or contracted), will 1587. *Nat. Register of Archives Report Marchioness of Crewe's*

was apparently prepared to endow his second son as generously as his first-born, and even his bastard son was to be provided with an estate of over £200 a year.[80] The first Sir John Thynne, servant of Protector Somerset and builder of Longleat, did not endow his sons so lavishly, but he was more generous to them than to his daughters.[81] The Thynnes' income continued to grow, when the second Sir John died intestate in 1604, his young son received more than either of his daughters; a fact of possibly wider significance, since this was an award made by mediators and confirmed in Chancery.[82] Even Sir Thomas Thynne, while favouring the sons of his second marriage and leaving his daughter £20,000, still left the younger son of his first marriage some land. An even stronger tradition of generosity to younger sons prevailed in the Petre family.[83]

If substantial endowment of younger sons continued in some families long after the first foundation of their greatness, it may also be found in long-established families. We have already seen this in the Beauchamps and the Staffords in the fourteenth and fifteenth centuries, perhaps the most striking example in the sixteenth century is that of George, earl of Shrewsbury who settled on each of his two youngest sons lands of £2,000 a year, so that, as their elder brother earl Gilbert claimed, they

. . . by most vilde means, did not only procure unto themselves a greater porcon of my father's lands than he left to my present

Muniments, CM372, J. Hunter, *South Yorkshire* (London, 1831) ii, p. 130. C. W. James, *Chief Justice Coke His Family and Descendants* (London, 1929), pp. 78–125. Coventry left lands to his second son, the amount of provision for his three other younger sons is not clear from his will. His three youngest daughters got £4,000 each, P.C.C. 1 Coventry.

[80] See Appendix II no. 22(a), the bastard was the grandfather of Sir Nathaniel Rich.

[81] The minimum given to at least three sons was to be £1,000 each; three others were given leases of at least £100 a year for 100 years inheritable by their eldest sons. An elder daughter got £1,333, two younger ones £666 each: Longleat, Thynne Papers 50/50, 156; 51/5, 30.

[82] Their portions were £2,000 each. The younger son was offered a lease of Thame rectory for the lives of himself, his wife and eldest son, or in default of sons, his eldest daughter, on condition of paying any receipts over £400 to his brother. But in 1640 it was valued at £600 and the widow was paying only £30 rent: *ibid.*, 58/13, 34–7, 59/41; unboxed papers no. 1857.

[83] *Ibid.*, 59/2–4, 83–93; 85/13–24. Over £20,000 in gold and silver was found at Longleat after Sir Thomas's death in 1639. See below Appendix II, no. 32.

possession . . . but also caused the most of that which descended to me to be so intangled with inteyles and such conditions of forfeiture as have not been seen and can hardly be performed . . . [84]

More fraternal harmony prevailed in the endowing of Sir Francis Seymour, the younger brother of William, third earl of Hertford, with lands in tail male worth over £400 a year with further land in reversion;[85] as also when Henry lord Windsor in 1589 was solicitous to augment the manor which his younger brother, Andrew, had received from their father. The Somersets, earls of Worcester and dukes of Beaufort, carried on a tradition of substantial landed settlements on younger sons beyond 1700.[86]

Most of these examples are of provision by those who could afford to be generous, though not all of those with encumbered estates necessarily economized on their sons.[87] Nevertheless when a father negotiated the marriage of his heir apparent, he might be under strong pressures from the bride's family to limit provision for his other children and particularly of land for his other sons. The articles in 1531 for the marriage of Francis, son and heir of George, earl of Huntingdon, with Katherine, eldest daughter of Lord Montague, empowered the earl to make life estates of lands of 100 marks a year each to his three younger sons. Each of them had lands of £73 a year in reversion after the earl specified in the final contract of 1534. This was broken by the earl selling and mort-

[84] To the earl of Essex, July 1594, E. Lodge, *Illustrations of British History*, 3 vols (London, 1791), iii, p. 61. As early as 1568 and 1571 Gilbert's father had offered to settle £2,000 a year each on these two younger sons. This was before the death of their eldest brother made Gilbert the heir and his subsequent quarrels with his father. £2,000 a year was duly settled on Edward when he married the Ogle heiress. R. White, *Dukery Records* (Worksop, 1904), pp. 339–40, see above p. 211.

[85] Sir Francis married an heiress who brought him over £200 a year in land. After their grandfather's death he and the earl sold land to pay his and their debts. Francis and his son compounded for an estate of £900 in fee in old rents and about £800 in life interests. His elder brother, later Duke of Somerset, settled £10,000 for his youngest son's portion and £6,000 for his daughter's, *Hist. MSS Comm.*, 58 (1968), *MSS of the Marquess of Bath*, iv, *Seymour Papers 1532–1686*, pp. 203, 269; Private Act 21 Jac. 1 no. 39; P.R.O. S.P. 23/191/785.

[86] *V. infra* Appendix II, nos. 19, 41; for settlements on the second and third sons of the fourth earl, see W. R. B. Robinson, 'The earls of Worcester and their estates 1511–1642' (Oxford, B.Litt. Thesis, 1956), pp. 132–4.

[87] The earls of Hertford were heavily in debt, see above, n. 85. The duke left principal debts of over £23,000 in 1660 against cash and credits of over £3,000, Longleat, Seymour Papers Box V/124–6.

gaging lands in it, so that in 1538 Lord Montague and his mother took control of much of the earl's land undertaking to pay over £11,000 of debt, while allowing him £240 a year for life and reducing the younger sons' reversions to £40 a year until this was paid.[88] When Francis, the next earl, agreed terms for the marriage of his son and heir with Northumberland's daughter in 1551, he promised ultimately to settle lands of almost £2,000 a year on them, reserving powers to pay debts, raise portions for his daughters and a rent charge of £40 for each younger son. However, he willed each of his three youngest sons lands of £60 a year for 80 years to him, and any future wife. Francis had bought his second son, George, an heiress for £500 and settled land of 100 marks a year on them in tail male; she later inherited land of some £130 a year.[89]

Though the earls of Huntingdon were in financial difficulties before Mary's reign, they remained powerful. All of the two earls' younger sons who lived to adult years married and five of the six were knights of the shire. But sheer numbers of children could strain the resources of lesser families. Thomas, Lord Wentworth, in 1544 had already married one daughter with 200 marks and left the same portion to eight others, while seven younger sons had annuities of £10 a year.[90] The same pressures operated when Dudley, later fourth Lord North, heir of a 'half-decayed family, with a numerous brood and worn-out estate' was negotiating the marriage settlement of his eldest son in 1666 and providing for four daughters and five other sons. Only one of his daughters got a portion commanding a marriage with a leading gentry family and two of the sons received less than the worst provided daughter. Even this required sale of some land and was the price of matching the eldest son to a young widow with £1,200 a year jointure.[91] If some fathers, like

---

[88] Despite these restrictions the earl's second son, Thomas, married Winifrid, Katherine's sister, probably after the attainder of their father Lord Montagu. They were restored in blood as his co-heirs under Mary. Brit. Mus., Harleian MS. 3881, fos 31r, 33, 35v.

[89] *Ibid.*, fos 43v, 47v; 4774, fo. 142; P.C.C. 8 Loftes. Earl Henry left each of his daughters £1,000. Francis' annuity was increased to £100 by his eldest brother who apparently helped him and his two younger brothers in other ways. C. Cross, *The Puritan Earl* (London, 1966), p. 32.

[90] P.C.C. 35 Bucke, proved 27 November 1551; P.C.C., F.38, Bucke.

[91] Roger North, *The Lives of the Norths* (ed. A. Jessopp, 3 vols, 1890) i, pp. 401–3, 405, iii, p. 312; Bodleian MS. North, b.12, fos 347, 353–4; P.C.C. 69 Hale. The daughters' portions were £2,500, two of £1,500 each, and £1,000. Dudley probably got about £500 and Montague about the same to set up as merchants; they each received annuities of £50 a year, while three other

Sir Francis Henry Lee of Ditchley, were undeterred by burdens of jointures and debt from generosity to a younger son (see Appendix II, no. 37), probably there were more who under such pressures followed Dudley North's example.

The examples in Appendix II were mainly chosen in order to illustrate the persistence of provision in land for younger sons. They are certainly not meant to be a representative sample. Stone believes

that the outright grant of land to younger sons was being superseded by the grant of a period of years, or more commonly for the two lives of the son and his bride . . . In the early seventeenth century increasing familiarity with professional occupations for younger sons made fathers prefer to give them annuities and rent charges rather than property, even for two lives.[92]

The first statement is supported by references to eight wills between 1560 and 1633. But Appendix II below gives eight examples of grants of land 1558–1600 and sixteen after 1600 (half of them before 1650).[93] If all Stone's examples scarcely establish a trend, further examination shows that only four of the wills provided leases and only two of these have leases for two lives, while four provided grants of land and one money to buy land.[94] The evidence

brothers each got £100 a year. Their father's will also ordered land to be sold to pay debts and the surplus to go equally among the younger sons. £2,200 a year was to be settled on the eldest son, with £200 present maintenance and another £200 on the death of his grandmother. I am indebted to Mr Grassby for providing and confirming some of this information. The total of the younger children's provision, excluding the cost of their education, would be at least 23 per cent of the value of the settlement on the eldest son at twenty years' purchase.

[92] L. Stone, *The Crisis of the Aristocracy*, pp. 180–1. In fact earlier examples of grants for the lives of a younger son and his wife can easily be found, e.g. the duke of Buckingham's case in 1504, *Year Book 20 Henry VII*, Michaelmas, fo. 10, plea 20; 1528, will of Sir Henry Willoughby of Wollaton, *North Country Wills*, ii (Surtees Society, cxxi, 1908), p. 121.

[93] Appendix II, nos. 13(c), 21(b), 22(a), (b), (c), (d), 23, 24(a), 26 before 1600; 24(b), 27–8, 30, 31(a), (b), 34 before 1650; 36, 37, 39–41, 43, 44 (two). To the examples after 1650 may be added Thomas, Lord Grey of Grooby, who in 1657 willed £4,000 to each of his daughters and that if his wife bore a son, he should have £500 a year in land in fee simple, P.C.C. 151 Ruthen.

[94] Stone, *op. cit.*, p. 180 n. 3, cites the following: P.C.C. 8 Loftes, Francis, earl of Huntingdon 1560 (see above p. 219 and n. 89) two leases for two lives and one in tail male; 66 Dixey, Henry, earl of Derby 1593, one lease for two lives; 33 Leicester, John, Lord Stourton, two leases to his two brothers; 67 Drake Sir Francis Knollys 1595, three leases, 20 Peter, 1573, Edmund, Lord Chandos eight manors granted in reversion after his wife in tail male. 12 Welles, William, Lord Windsor 1558, see Appendix II, no. 21(a). 46 Meade, Thomas, Lord Gerard, 1617, grants land to two younger

for a general change to annuities and rent charges is equally feeble, the more so as so many examples can be found before 1558. It may be plausible to suppose that they did become more common, but this remains supposition. Many examples of greater provision for younger sons than for daughters before 1558 could be produced, but these would be an unreliable basis for presuming a sixteenth-century trend towards favouring daughters at the expense of sons.

As far as the size of portions given to daughters is concerned, there may be enough examples in Table I of Appendix I to establish a general trend. For purposes of comparison Stone's findings have been reproduced in Table II. It will be seen that he has achieved better coverage of the first half of the seventeenth century. On the other hand Table I provides more examples for the periods before 1600 and after 1649. Before 1450, especially for 1401–50, it is obviously overweighted with large portions, and this is even more true for 1675–1729. The averages in Table III for knightly families give a better idea of the portions provided by the poorer peers in the fifteenth century.[95] Given this overweighting of the very wealthy, the best basis for long-term comparisons is given by the averages of earls and above, though it must be admitted that the fall between 1525–49 and 1550–74 may well be less representative of reality than the rise of the general average.

However, comparing the averages of earls and above for 1451–1500, or 1475–1524 with 1600–24 these show a fourfold increase, slightly less than the index based on food prices in Table II, substantially more than the index of industrial prices in Table I, Appendix I. As against this Stone's index of the general average of portions increases by 7.6 times between the same dates, substantially more than his index based on food prices, whereas the general average in Table I increases 4.7 times, only slightly more than the food index. In Table III the average for knightly families, comparing 1451–1500, or 1501–50, with 1551–1600 almost trebles, which is more than the increase for earls and above in Table I, comparing 1475–1524 with 1575–99, but similar to the average for

sons to them and their heirs for ever. 70 Seager, 1633, Richard, Lord Lovelace, left £3,000 lent to the East India Company in trust to his son to be used 'in raising a stocke or purchasing land', as well as the assignment of a thirty-year lease of tithes beginning in 1615. His daughter's portion was £4,000.

[95] The average of peers below the rank of 1451–1500 is not very far above that of the knightly families, see n. 4 to Table I.

all peers. The increase in the last two columns of Table I for earls and above from £6,250 for 1650–74 to £10,050 for 1675–1730 is remarkable, as is the apparent doubling of the average portion since the first half of the seventeenth century, given that rents and food prices stopped rising in the 1660s and incomes from land were depressed. However Clay has shown that the price of freehold land increased substantially from about 1690 to the 1720s, perhaps by as much as a third.[96] This and the long-term fall in interest rates may have encouraged great landowners to put heavier mortgage charges on their estates, but obviously more evidence is needed before we can describe the phenomenon accurately, let alone investigate its causes.

Imperfect as the evidence in Appendix I undoubtedly is, it does confirm that there was a sustained rise in the average size of portions from around the middle of the sixteenth century onwards and throughout the seventeenth century, outlasting the rise in food prices and rents. This did attract contemporary comment. The Jesuit Robert Persons writing in Seville in 1596 was concerned about the fate of younger sons lacking any right 'to a reasonable Portion at least of their Parents' Substance' and the opportunities for ecclesiastical promotion, provided by the Roman church, while the parents lacked the resources of nunneries making them

the better able to provide for the Marriage of their other Daughters . . . in which point notwithstanding, seeing that the excesses of our times in giving great Dowries, is growen to be at such a height, that it impoverisheth oftentimes the Parents; it seemeth a point worthy the consideration whether it were not expedient that the Parliament should limit the quantity of Dowries according to the State and Condition of every Man; which no doubt would greatly ease the Nobility and Gentry . . . [97]

---

[96] T. H. Hollingsworth, *The Demography of the British Peerage* (Supplement to *Population Studies* xviii, no. 2), Table 32, Marriages of completed fertility: cohort born 1575–99, mean size 5.49; 1675–99, 4.17, difference −24 per cent; 1700–24, 3.77, difference −31.3 per cent. Table 66, English males only, mean family size: cohort 1575–99, 5.15; 1675–99, 3.55, difference −31 per cent; 1700–24, 3.5, −42 per cent. C. Clay, 'The Price of Freehold Land in the Later Seventeenth and Eighteenth centuries', *Econ. Hist. Rev.*, 2nd ser., xvii (1974), pp. 173–89. For some discussion of the relationship between growth of portions and other demographic factors, see below, p. 291.

[97] [R. Persons] *The Jesuit's Memorial for the Intended Reformation of England*, ed. E. Gee (London, 1690), pp. 227–30.

Harrington for different reasons wished to limit portions to £1,500 'in Lands, Goods and Monys', without limiting heiresses and widows. Sir William Temple took the same view as Persons, but believed that it was only fifty years before, thanks to the allurements of City fortunes, that marriages came to be made

> . . . by men's avarice and greediness of portions . . . which has since ruined so many estates by the necessity of giving great portions to daughters, impaired many families by the weak or mean productions of marriage . . . I know no remedy for this evil . . . but a law providing that no woman of what quality soever shall have the value of above 2000 pounds for her portion in marriage, unless she be an heiress; and that no such, above the value of 200 pounds a year, shall marry to any but younger brothers.

Temple thus links the grievance of younger brothers with the competitive increase in portions without explicitly claiming that this had sacrificed younger sons' interests. Sir Josiah Child in 1668 believed portions had increased over four times in 60 years, attributing this to increasing national wealth, itself due self-evidently to his nostrum of falling interest rates.[98] Persons, like others dealing with the plight of younger sons, complains of eldest brothers' impartial neglect of both brothers and sisters. He points out that England was exceptional in usually giving the husband or his father full control over the wife's portion, while elsewhere he only had the usufruct of it. Yet in practice the portion was often used to provide for younger children.

Ap Robert, the leading apologist of the younger brother, believed that his plight had worsened, since elder brothers had become more spendthrift and grudging. Much of his argument was devoted to exalting paternal authority and urging fathers not to be inhibited by entails and family custom from disinheriting profligate and spendthrift heirs.[99] But Sir Christopher Wandesforde and other

[98] *Oceana and other Works*, 3rd edn (London, 1747), p. 102. 'Of Popular Discontents', *The Works of Sir William Temple Bart* (London, 1770), pp. 61–2; 'noble families would not be exhausted by competition with those of meaner alloy in point of fortune'; J. Child, *Brief Observations* (London, 1668), p. 7.

[99] J. Ap Robert, *The Younger Brother his Apologie* (Oxford, 1634), pp. 29–31, 35–7. Chapter 8 is headed 'That Unthriftinesse is one knowne name of many hidden sinnes and is alone sufficient cause of disherison, proved by the Law of God and Man'.

224 J. P. COOPER

writers of advice to eldest sons continued to exhort them to be as parents to their brothers and sisters.

Be so far from grudging at those small shares which I have cut out of my estate for them; that if by any Accident they come short, you may support and relieve them: let your House be always open to receive them . . . as Part of your Family . . . I do by the Authority of a Father require you in Case my Purposes to them be prevented; so to provide for them, that the World may see that you express your Duty to your Father by the Regard you have to the Rest of his Children.[100]

Many eldest sons obeyed such exhortations. Yet even among great houses some were grudging and obstructive. Edward Stafford, third duke of Buckingham, covenanted to settle two manors on his brother Henry in tail male when he married, but after the marriage in 1504 granted them to Henry and his wife only for their lives.[101] The case in 1681 which led to Lord Chancellor Nottingham's decisive formulation of the basic rule against perpetuities as a rule against remoteness of vesting and helped to make the strict settlement secure in the courts, had arisen because Henry, duke of Norfolk, had thwarted his father's intention of endowing his younger brother with a substantial estate in tail male.[102]

For the reforming defenders of younger sons there was also the example of the Dutch for one of the causes of their greater prosperity was held to be 'the dividing of their Estates equally to their children whereby Trade is (as it were) continued in a Line without Interruption; the contrarie being customarie with us'. Worsley's view was repeated by Sir Josiah Child and held responsible for the 'inconsiderable assistance of fortune' left to 'most of our youngest

[100] Written in 1636, *A Book of Instructions* . . . , ed. T. Comber (Cambridge, 1777), pp. 84–5.
[101] Henry Stafford was created earl of Wiltshire in 1510. The Year Book (see above, n. 92) confuses the identity of his wife, who was the widow of Thomas, first marquess of Dorset, who died in 1501. For the legal significance of the case, A. W. B. Simpson, 'The Equitable Doctrine of Consideration and the Law of Uses', *Univ. of Toronto Law Journal*, xvi (1965), pp. 11–12.
[102] The settlement was drawn by Orlando Bridgeman, the deviser of trustees to preserve contingent remainders, in 1647 and settled part of the Dacre inheritance on Henry; when he succeeded his eldest brother, who was *non compos mentis*, it was to go to the next younger brother Charles; *Lord Nottingham's Chancery Cases*, ed. D. E. C. Yale (Selden Soc. 79, 1961–2) ii, p. 905, *ibid.* (73, 1957) i, pp. lxxxiv–lxxxix; H. H. S. Causton, *The Howard Papers* (London, 1862), pp. 190–7.

sons of Gentlemen . . . who are bound Apprentices to Merchants'.[103] Most of the reformers were preoccupied with the gentry so that they tend to say little about inheritance among townsmen. The custom of London favoured partible inheritance in so far as the personalty was divided into three equal parts after paying debts and funeral expenses; one went to the widow, one was shared equally among children who had not already received their portions and one could be willed freely. This had long made the widows of wealthy Londoners even more attractive matches than their daughters.[104] Within these limits fathers could favour one son, who was often the eldest, but the tendency to equality of treatment could also extend to the distribution of land. A striking example is provided by Sir Thomas Leigh's endowment of his three sons, assisted by his childless former master Sir Rowland Hill. Humble, Lord Ward, may also be seen as acting in this tradition;[105] but, as we have seen, such behaviour is also typical of successful lawyers and other new men. Similar customary rules about children's shares in personal estates were not confined to towns; they applied also to the province of York and to Wales and had applied to the province of Canterbury 'sometime before the mid-sixteenth century'. Such rules must have benefited younger children, and their disappearance lends support to the thesis that the position of younger sons had worsened, though Sir Henry Finch, unlike Coke, still held that the right of a widow and children to their reasonable portions was the general law of the land in 1627.[106] But not only did the reformers' campaign for partible inheritance of land fail, like most

[103] Benjamin Worsley, *The Advocate* (1652) in *Seventeenth Century Economic Docs.* ed. J. Thirsk and J. P. Cooper (Oxford, 1972), p. 510; *Brief Observations concerning Trade* . . . (London, 1668), p. 3.

[104] S. L. Thrupp, *The Merchant Class of Medieval London* (Chicago, 1948), pp. 266–7; see below, Appendix I, Table III n. 3.

[105] Leigh died in 1571, T. Dugdale, *Baronage of England*, 2 vols (London, 1675–6) ii, pp. 464–5; S. Shaw, *History of Staffordshire* (London, 1798) i, p. 158; for Ward, see Appendix II, no. 36. Sir William FitzWilliam (died 1534) endowed his four younger sons with land, but John Isham, poorer than any of those mentioned, gave his two younger sons only leases and annuities, Finch, *op. cit.*, pp. 24–5, 102.

[106] T. F. T. Plucknett, *A Concise History of the Common Law*, 5th edn (London, 1956), p. 745. Holdsworth thinks this had happened during the fourteenth century, *History*, iii (4th edn, 1935), pp. 550–6; Finch, *Law and the Use thereof* (London, 1627), pp. 175, his *Nomotechnia* (London, 1613) does not contain this; cf. M. M. Sheehan, 'Influences of Canon Law on Married Women's Property Rights in England', *Medieval Studies*, xxiii (1963), pp. 120–3.

of the reforms of the Civil War and Interregnum, but the customs of partible inheritance of personalty were weakened. R. Grassby has shown that London merchants moved away from partible inheritance in the later seventeenth century and 'increasingly adopted the inheritance customs of landed society'.[107] In 1692 and 1696 testators in the province of York and in Wales were freed from the customary restrictions on their freedom on the grounds that widows, by claiming a third in addition to their jointures, reduced provision for children. In 1724 the enforcement of the custom of London was abolished, as it was alleged to discourage men of substance from becoming freemen.[108]

This victory for unfettered testation and individual control of property can also be seen as the culmination of the process of asserting paternal power. But it does not tell us what men normally did.[109] Returning at last to consider the effects of strict settlements on great landowners, we can see that there had been no effective movement towards giving younger children rights to a share of their father's property; indeed legislation reduced such rights. In this context such settlements might seem a triumph for eldest sons over both paternal power and their younger brothers. But Habakkuk points out that whereas earlier provision for many younger children might be subjected to the father's retrenchment or the heir's discretion,

The provision under the strict settlement was usually more generous, because it was specified at the marriage, after solemn family conclave in which considerable weight was given to the views of the grandparents, who were likely to be concerned to achieve a proper balance of interests between the younger children of the marriage, on the one hand, and the parents and the

107 I am indebted to Mr Grassby for lending me a chapter on family and inheritance from his unpublished work on London merchants.

108 4 William and Mary *cap.* 2 (the city of York was excluded, but covered in 1704 by 2 and 3 Anne *cap.* 5), 7 and 8 William III *cap.* 38; 11 George I *cap.* 18. These customs still applied in cases of intestacy.

109 'The rule of Primogeniture and the power of testation have not eradicated the principle of a Legitim. Even among the upper classes of this country . . . the lands which are settled on an eldest son are always charged with portions for his brothers and sisters; portions too which are made to carry interest at a higher rate than that which the rental of the land returns.' C. S. K. Kenny, *The Law of Primogeniture in England* (Cambridge, 1878), pp. 56–7. Nassau Senior testified that of thousands of wills and settlements made by him 'not one in a hundred was based on any principle but that of equal partition', *ibid.*, Appendix, n. E.

eldest son on the other . . . According to the eighteenth century traditions on the origin of the trustees to preserve contingent remainders . . . their main purpose [was] 'to secure in family settlements a provision for the future children of an intended marriage, who before were usually left at the mercy of the particular tenant for life'. So far as the provision for younger sons was concerned, the important change was less in its scale than in its form.[110]

However, as we have seen, marriage settlements from the later sixteenth century frequently made provision for daughters, if there were no sons of the marriage. Henry, Lord Scrope's settlement on his eldest son and his wife in 1590 specified portions for daughters and lands of £100 a year for the advancement of younger sons during their lives.[111] By the 1620s and 1630s marriage settlements might give powers to provide for daughters and sons of the marriage. For example the settlement by the earl of Warwick on Lord Rich in 1632 specified portions for daughters and gave Rich power to make grants of annuities, or in fee tail, or in fee simple to his younger sons after Warwick's death from lands worth about £900 a year.[112] If marriage settlements which only specified provision for daughters are quite common before 1642, they can also be found on into the early eighteenth century in strict settlements, as can the discretionary power to provide for sons given in Warwick's settlement.[113] As we have seen land continued to be

---

[110] H. J. Habakkuk, 'Marriage Settlements in the Eighteenth Century', *Trans. Roy Hist. Soc.*, 4th ser., xxxii (1950), pp. 16–17.

[111] Pub. Rec. Office, S.P. 15/22/35. Rowland Dutton of Dutton, Cheshire, willed by powers under a marriage settlement of 1601 portions of £400 each to six daughters and an annuity and lease of lands for life to a younger son, *The Duttons of Dutton* (London, 1901), p. 177.

[112] Essex Record Office, D/DcW T 25, 29 June 1632. I am indebted to Christopher Thompson for details of the settlement and valuations. Private Act 3 Charles I, no. 15 empowered Dutton, Lord Gerrard, to grant up to 200 marks a year to each younger son, to raise £5,000 for his daughters' portions and to make jointures.

[113] The precedent from Bridgman's *Conveyances* of 1692 only provides for daughters and does not mention sons, Holdsworth, *History*, vii (2nd edn, 1937), pp. 547–59; see below, Appendix II, no. 41, settlement of 1703; 31(d), settlements of 1680 and 1700; Oliver St John 1656, Beds. Record Office, D.D.J. 124; William Lord Kingston, Private Act, 9 Anne *cap.* 10 are other examples, though they seem to be less common than those which either empower or specify provision for younger sons. The ones empowering rather than specifying are rather commoner among the quite inadequate number of examples known to me before 1720.

settled on younger sons in tail male and powers to do this were included in Manners and Russell settlements. Much more investigation would be required to show when the eighteenth-century norm of equal provision for younger sons and daughters became predominant. As far as younger sons are concerned, unless fuller investigations show that provision for them had normally been either less or more generous than for daughters, the main long-term change brought by strict settlements was greater security. It is not yet clear that there were any significant short-term changes before about 1720.

Moreover not all a great landowner's land would usually be subject to strict settlement; the tradition of dealing freely with his own acquisitions and purchases survived. The younger son whose mother was an heiress might still get greater provision. Strict settlements could limit in advance the claims of heirs general, but, apart from the fact that unsettled lands might still descend to them, the charges put on the estate when it came to the heir male might be so great as to force him to sell at least some land. Thus the final result of the conflict of interests between heirs male and general could be much the same as in the later sixteenth and early seventeenth century. The means of arbitrating between them were different.[114] The abolition of military tenures in chief made it easier for those who wished to prevent land going to their heirs general. Settlements could also be used to direct inheritance through females to found cadet lines, who would perpetuate the paternal

---

[114] When the ninth earl of Derby died in 1702, there was prolonged litigation between his daughter and heir, Henrietta, and his brother and heir male, James, the tenth earl, until in 1715 they agreed to accept an Order in Chancery to determine their rights by arbitration, *Dingwall and Butler of Moore Park Peerage Case, Evidence* (London, 1870), pp. 87–99. When John Holles, duke of Newcastle, tried to disinherit his only daughter and heir, Henrietta, of the lands settled on her mother and her heirs by her grandfather, Henry Cavendish, duke of Newcastle, in favour of Holles' nephew Thomas Pelham, the duchess enlisted the support of the Lord Treasurer Oxford by offering Henrietta's marriage to his son. Harley was unwilling to give public support to the duchess' admittedly headstrong defiance of Chancery and generally acted with more circumspection than his Elizabethan and Jacobean predecessors had done. The eventual compromise came when Oxford was politically disgraced and the Pelhams in favour, but these circumstances do not seem to have affected the agreement to accept arbitration made before George I succeeded. A. S. Turberville, *A History of Welbeck Abbey and its Owners*, 2 vols (London, 1938) i, pp. 296–327; R. A. Kelch, *Newcastle A Duke without Money* (London, 1974), pp. 28–37.

name and arms of the heiress. Thus the last Lord Lexington settled his estate to go through his only daughter, wife of John, third duke of Rutland, to her second son Lord Robert and, when he died in 1762 without issue, to his younger brother Lord George, on condition that each took the name of Sutton.[115] Men were not necessarily concerned to expand great estates indefinitely for the benefit of eldest sons and were concerned to preserve their names.

Clay and Holderness have convincingly shown by general and local investigations that strict settlements did not prevent the break-up of large estates. Clay has also pointed out that the number of heiresses in the period from the 1670s to the 1740s was relatively greater, because the male replacement rate of the peerage had fallen below unity and continued to fall for three generations.[116] It may be that one result was to improve provision for younger sons, especially in concentrating endowment on second sons. Clay has given striking instances of this in the eighteenth-century history of the Petre family and Malcolmson has produced eight Anglo-Irish examples between 1743 and 1800. Whether there were relatively more such endowments in the eighteenth century than earlier requires further investigation.[117] But we can say that the demographic possibilities were greater down to the 1740s and that traditional propensities in endowing younger sons were not necessarily frustrated by strict settlements. As Squibb has pointed out there was a proliferation of requirements to take the settlor's name and arms as a condition of receiving an inheritance from the early eighteenth century, though he is wrong in implying that they were

[115] A. Collins, *The Peerage of England*, 7 vols (London, 1748) ii, p. 30. Charles, third son of the second duke of Devonshire married in 1727 one of the four daughters and coheirs of Henry Grey, duke of Kent (who married again in 1729 and had a son who died after a few months in 1733). His eldest son was Charles Cavendish, the scientist, who left an estate of £1,175,000 in 1810 to George Cavendish, third son of William, fourth duke of Devonshire, who had married the only daughter and heir of Charles, seventh earl of Northampton and was the grandfather of the seventh duke of Devonshire, *ibid.*, i, p. 330, G.E.C., *Complete Peerage*, vii, pp. 177–9, *Dictionary of National Biography*.

[116] C. Clay, 'Marriage, Inheritance and the Rise of Large Estates in England 1660–1815', *Econ. Hist. Rev.*, 2nd ser., xxi (1968), pp. 503–18, 517; B. A. Holderness, 'The English Land Market in the Eighteenth Century: the Case of Lincolnshire', *ibid.*, xxvii (1974), pp. 557–76.

[117] Clay, *art. cit.*, p. 505, below Appendix II, no. 31(d); A. P. W. Malcolmson, 'Absenteeism in Eighteenth-Century Ireland', *Irish Economic and Social History*, i (1974), pp. 28–30.

unknown before.[118] Not all of these were for the benefit of younger sons, like that of Lord Lexington, but many were. The phenomenon does not suggest any weakening of a sense of lineage, it had been common in Castile since 1500; what seems curious is that it should become general in England so much later.

The institutional and economic circumstances in which the strict settlement functioned are also important. It could only function effectively, given a market for mortgages in which there was a substantial demand for them as secure long-term investments. This in turn meant that the mortgagee needed to be able to assign the mortgage readily and to be protected by right of foreclosure, while the mortgagor was protected by his equity of redemption. The legal developments which made this possible had taken place by 1629;[119] their full exploitation probably came in the aftermath of the Civil War. In this context the strict settlement is a device for charging estates with annuities for jointures and mortgages for provision for younger children. The settlement could not be changed (except by private act) until the life tenant's eldest son came of age; the land could not be disposed of by a single person, acting alone, for perhaps on average around thirty-five years and up to more than twice this.[120] The life tenant's disincentives to invest in improvements or reduce encumbrances, were stressed by the critics

[118] G. D. Squibb, 'The End of the Name and Arms Clause?' *Law Quarterly Review*, 69 (1953), pp. 220–1, gives as his earliest known instance the will of Ralph, lord Grey of Warke who died in 1706. But the will of Henry, duke of Newcastle in 1691 contained the same provision and see below Appendix II, 21(c) for the settlement made by Lord Windsor in 1641. The only medieval attempt known to me is that of Ralph, last lord Basset of Drayton, who in 1389 left all his lands to his nephew Sir Hugh de Shirley in tail male. The will was disputed by Humphrey, earl of Stafford, claiming as heir and eventually Shirley retained only part of the lands. He never seems to have taken the name of Basset; F. P. Shirley, *Stemmata Shirleiana* (London, 1872), Appendix, pp. 34–43; *Cal. Ancient Deeds* (London, 1906) v, nos. A 11372, A 11357–8, A 11388; G.E.C., *Complete Peerage*, ii, pp. 3–4. William, last lord Latimer, left his lands to John, lord Nevill, his daughter's husband, and his heirs male or female. They were to bear Latimer's arms and pay 3,000 marks to his executors. *Testamenta Eboracenses*, i, p. 115.

[119] R. V. Turner, *The Equity of Redemption* (Cambridge, 1931), chs I–III; M. E. Finch, *Five Northamptonshire Families*, pp. 11–12, 32–4.

[120] A. W. B. Simpson, *An Introduction . . .*, p. 222–3. The figure thirty-five is calculated from the mean age of marriage at around thirty-two (eldest sons, however, married earlier than younger sons) and an expectation of life for men of thirteen rising to fifteen years at the age of fifty-five; T. H. Hollingsworth, 'The Demography of the British Peerage' (Supplement to *Population Studies*, xviii, no. 2), Tables 2, 42.

of strict settlements, especially in the nineteenth century. But compared with the perpetual entails in Scotland, which began to be
used from 1648 and were given statutory authority in 1685,[121]
continental *fideicommissa*, or Castilian *mayorazgos*, the strict settlement was remarkably flexible and adaptable to new circumstances.
Like sixteenth-century perpetuities it included powers to lease for
twenty-one years or three lives; properly drawn these powers now
included selling and exchanging land and borrowing for improvements, whereas elsewhere leases and incumbrances only lasted for
the life of the grantor. Even where the settlements were defective,
they could be changed comparatively cheaply and quickly by
private act of parliament.

From 1706 bills were referred to two judges and their report
was the decisive stage; the passage of the bill, once they had
approved it, was virtually certain, though amendments were sometimes made in committee. The Lords' Standing Orders ensured
that those in remainder should consent, unless they could be barred
by a recovery and that all interested parties had an opportunity to
oppose a bill. Once the parties had agreed, a bill would pass in
three or four months.[122] In a sense private estate acts were the
apotheosis of that process of settling matters by arbitration and
consent which so many law reformers had sought and which it
had once been hoped that Chancery might provide. The time taken
to pass bills was shortened in the later eighteenth century. Thus the
legislative powers of parliament were used to readjust settlements
to suit changing circumstances, with due regard to even remote
interests in remainder. In Castile great landowners could only
invoke the absolute power of the king in order to modify the force
of *mayorazgos*. In England there had long ceased to be any risk
that acts of Parliament would be used as Edward IV had used
them to favour his brothers, his son and his step-sons by disinheriting the widows and heirs at law of the Nevills, Mowbrays and
Hollands.[123] The need for the king's personal involvement in
securing arbitration in the inheritance disputes of great families

[121] E. Cecil, *Primogeniture* (London, 1895), pp. 56–61, J. R. McCulloch,
Succession to Property, pp. 52–7, 173–4.
[122] S. Lambert, *Bills and Acts Legislative Procedure in Eighteenth-
Century England* (Cambridge, 1971), chaps. 5 and 6 gives an excellent
account of the cost and procedure in estate bills. What is now needed is an
equally good account of the earlier history of private bills.
[123] C. Ross, *Edward IV* (London, 1975), pp. 190–1, 336–7, 348–9.

had survived at least until 1642. If the law relating to powers of settlement was clearer by 1685, the opportunities, and perhaps even the inclination, to use power and favour to influence legal proceedings became less.

Before the Statute of Uses unfettered freedom of disposition was possible, but probably most great landowners abided by family custom and tradition. Flagrant breaches would carry the penalty of subjecting the inheritance to the ordeal of prolonged litigation and dangerous political pressures. There was no general consensus favouring heirs male over females in all circumstances. The common law's defeat of perpetuities added further uncertainties to family disputes which would have occurred, whatever the state of the law. The strict settlement continued and made more secure the process of limiting the claims of heirs general, restricting, or postponing, actual inheritance of land by them. Strict settlements lasted, because of the strength of family tradition, or inertia; men usually renewed them when their eldest sons married, though adjustments might then be made. In the early eighteenth century the fall in mean family-size and in the male replacement rate and the proliferation of names and arms clauses may all have created favourable opportunities for younger sons. A growth of more lasting and more general opportunities open to patronage came about through places in government service and commissions in the army, which more than compensated for what was lost by the abolition of the Court of Wards.

In the first half of the seventeenth century a portion for a younger child was around one year's income of the father's estate, unless there was only one such child, when it might be considerably more, or unless there were very many children, or heavy debts, when it might be less.[124] If the average number of younger children was about three,[125] taking land at the conventional 20 years' pur-

---

[124] H. J. Habakkuk, 'Landowners and the Civil War', *Econ. Hist. Rev.*, 2nd ser., xviii (1969), p. 136; Stone, *Crisis of the Aristocracy*, p. 642. *The Trade of England Revived* (1681) '. . . the shopkeeping trade is both a convenient and easy way for the gentry, clergy and commonalty . . . to provide for their younger sons . . . For there are few younger sons, who are tradesmen that have much above one year's revenue of their father's estate for their patrimony', *Seventeenth Century Economic Documents*, ed. Thirsk and Cooper, p. 395.

[125] This is a rough calculation from Hollingsworth, *Demography*, Table 32, for the cohorts 1625–1724, after deducting children dead before fifteen and the percentages of childless marriages of secondary males in Table 36.

chase, the portions would then be 15 per cent of the capital value, at 18 years', 17 per cent. This may be thought of as a conventional minimum, since a maximum could be at least a third.[126] The portion received for the eldest son might be set off against this, but it was paid for by some immediate loss of income. If a family was to maintain its position, it was essential either to save or to make new acquisitions. Saving was the conventional wisdom of advice to sons;[127] if competition for patronage and heiresses seemed an easier and more exciting alternative, the penalty for failure was a mounting burden of debt. Greater landowners in England had some legal privileges, such as those conferred by the game laws and many more tacit ones conferred by power and patronage, but their privileges in matters of debt were less than those of most continental nobilities and were confined to the relatively small number of peers of parliament. Strict settlements were meant to protect family fortunes from spendthrift heirs, but they could only delay somewhat the ultimate sale of land to meet mounting incumbrances. Yet the indefinite postponement of such consequences and the sacrifice of the interests of creditors in order to preserve perpetual entails on great estates became a major feature of the economy and society of Castile in the seventeenth century.

The history of uses and of the perpetuity in England was effected by the exceptional characteristics of its highly centralized monarchy; no other monarchy in the thirteenth, still less in the sixteenth, century exploited prerogatives of wardship and marriage over its tenants-in-chief. The development of the Castilian *mayorazgo* illustrates the weakness of the crown in the fourteenth and fifteenth centuries. Entails in primogeniture existed from the late thirteenth century; some sixteenth-century jurists described the *mayorazgo*

[126] Irish Statutes 2 Anne, *cap.* vi, sect. 3 among the provisions restricting popish parents whose eldest sons became Protestants, allowed 'maintenances and portions' for younger children 'as well protestants as papists', to be ordered by Chancery, not to exceed one-third part of the inheritance. As the object was to favour the eldest son, this maximum was presumably placed low. Dudley, Lord North, provided for his seven younger children at least a quarter of the value at twenty years' purchase of the lands settled on his eldest son.

[127] *Wandesforde's Instructions*, ed. Comber, repeat Burghley's, 'the whole clear estate being divided into three parts, one third should be allowed for all personal and domesticall charges whatsoever, a third is to be reserved for provision of children's portions; and the last third laid up for purchases and other additions to the House'.

as essentially a fideicommissary substitution or entail, due to the influence of Roman law. Some seventeenth-century writers saw its origins in the undivided succession of the *casa solariego* in which some historians have seen Germanic influence of the *stammgut*. The latest account by Clavero dismisses such views, for failing to understand the distinctive features of the Castilian *mayorazgo*. These were not primogeniture and entail, but the overriding of rights under customary and written law, especially those of younger children to legitim, and that *mayorazgos* originally always concerned *señorios* (lordships)[128] and were incompatible with any grant by the possessor of *dominum utile* and so with the creation of perpetual leasehold (*emphyteusis*, whose nearest English equivalent is copyhold of inheritance). Undivided descent already prevailed in inheritances attached to titles, the *mayorazgo* was a means of attaching further property to such dignities and the new ones of duke, marquess and viscount created in the late fourteenth century. These went to a new nobility made up of cadets and bastards of the old high nobility and those risen from families of minor nobles, whose power and wealth were founded on grants of *señorios* by the crown, together with alienations or usurpations of its revenues and taxes.[129] Perhaps the most distinctive, and certainly the most enduring characteristic, of the fortunes of this new high nobility was the considerable part played in them by alienated royal taxes, especially *alcabalas* (sales taxes), from the fifteenth to the eighteenth century.[130]

---

[128] *Señorio* can mean territory as well as territorial jurisdiction and was a grant of dignity and of crown rights over subjects (*vassallos*), originally confined to nobles.

[129] Bartolomé Clavero, *Mayorazgo Propriedad Feudal en Castilla (1369–1836)* (Madrid, 1974), pp. 21–59, 116–17. This work gives an excellent and much-needed account of legal doctrines and characteristics and their development, it is less successful in describing the actual working of the institution and its consequences. Salvador de Moxó, 'De la Nobleza vieja a la Nobleza nueva', *Cuadernos de Historia anexos de la Revista Hispania*, iii (1969), pp. 1–210.

[130] J. R. L. Highfield, 'The Catholic Kings and the Titled Nobility of Castile' in *Europe in the Later Middle Ages*, ed. J. R. Hale et al. (London, 1965), pp. 381–3, 'The de la Cerda, the Pimentel and the so called "price revolution"', *English Hist. Rev.*, lxxxvii (1972), pp. 500–1, 509–11; A. M. Guilarte, *El Regimen Señorial en el Siglo XVI* (Madrid, 1962), pp. 148–9. 152–5, 438; C. Jago, 'Aristocracy, War and Finance in Castille. The titled nobility and the house of Béjar during the reign of Philip IV' (Cambridge, Ph.D. thesis, 1969), pp. 196–211; Salvador de Moxo, 'Los Señorios', *Hispania*, xxiv (1965), pp. 232–5. I am greatly indebted to Professor Jago for allowing me to use his thesis.

Early grants of *mayorazgos* either formed part of a grant of *señoríos* and other favours or empowered individuals to bind their existing properties. Thus Enrique II granted Huelva to Alfonso Pérez de Guzman in 1370 as a *mayorazgo* to his sons successively in tail male, failing them, to his daughters, with reversion to the crown if both male and female lines failed. In 1379 Juan I confirmed another grant of 1374 to Alfonso, empowering him to create three or more *mayorazgos* from his possessions to last a certain time, or for ever, with prohibitions of alienation, to be valid against any law or custom to the contrary. In 1401 Enrique III confirmed a testament by Diego López de Estúñiga creating several *mayorazgos*, and inhibited claims to legitim. In these early examples the terms are variable at the founder's discretion, but the license to ignore established customary or legal rights is explicit.[131] During the fifteenth century the invocation of the crown's absolute power becomes explicit, while paradoxically its actual power declined, one indication of this being the disappearance of the clauses of reversion to the crown, found in 1370. Already in 1432 the grant empowering Rodrigo Pimentel, count of Benavente, to settle his possessions is much more elaborate in general phraseology and in barring of claims to legitim in virtue of the king's 'deliberate will and royal absolute power'.[132] Where English nobles exploited uses to give themselves freedom in testation and to avoid the crown's feudal dues, Castilians obtained that freedom by direct concession from the crown.

The absolute power of the weakest of all the Castilian kings, Enrique IV, was invoked in 1460 to legitimate the bastard sons whether 'adulterine or abominable and incestuous or basely conceived' of Pedro Girón, master of the order of Calatrava, to suspend the imperial law prohibiting inheritance by bastards, and enable him to create *mayorazgos* for them to descend as he pleased with the provision that if a holder committed treason, or heresy, or other crimes, the *mayorazgo* would not be confiscated, but go to the

131 Nelly R. Porro, 'Concesiones Regias en la Institución de Mayorazgo', *Revista de Archivos, Bibliotecas y Museos*, lxx (1962), pp. 84–8 (1370), 88–90 (1379) with power to make property included inalienable for a limited time or for ever, 90–1 (1401).
132 Madrid, Archivo Historico Nacional 37, 741, no. 4514, fos 10 bis v.–14r. I am indebted to Dr Highfield for lending me his transcript, the testament using these powers was made 23 October 1440.

next in succession.[133] It came to be accepted that a royal grant of a town, or a title, implicitly included the power to found a *mayorazgo*. The legal effects of such foundations had also become clearer; the property was inalienable and the holder had no power to grant leases, beyond his life, assign it for dower, or portions, or to create *censos*[134] (in effect mortgaging it). If the holder needed to do such things, he would need a royal license and further invocation of the crown's absolute power. The consequences of this became important in the later sixteenth century.

The jurist Palacios Rubios in 1503 had reservations about *mayorazgos* which largely disappeared from the works of the late sixteenth century. A creation was only valid when made for just cause and while still providing for younger children, otherwise even if he obtained a royal license, the father sinned by not dealing equally with his sons. In cases of doubt, rights to dower and portions should have preference, unless they were explicitly excluded. By 1600 the prevailing interpretation was exactly the opposite, unless the deed of foundation explicitly reserved such rights, they were excluded by the doctrine of *favor del mayorazgo*.[135] Palacios doubted whether Law 27 of the Laws of Toro (1505), which gave power to entail a third and a fifth of a man's property, could create *mayorazgos* in the full sense of those created by royal license or immemorial custom and recognized in Laws 40 to 46. Law 27 came to mean that *mayorazgos* were no longer linked with titles, or *señoríos*, and no longer only founded by nobles. By 1575 creations in virtue of Law 27 were equated with the full *mayorazgo* which with its tacit exclusions was already held to be according to 'custom, the laws and constitutions' although a principal purpose of royal licenses in the fifteenth century had been to dispense with established custom and laws.[136] When Luis de Molina in 1573 produced the most authoritative of all the juristic treatises, he presented the *mayorazgo* as a particular instance of the general law of primo-

[133] Nelly R. Porro, *art. cit.*, pp. 92–9, 'aunque el tal crimen sea lege mayestatis o perduelionis o deserción o eresis o otro qualquier crimen mayor o mediano o menor', p. 97.

[134] Clavero, *op. cit.*, pp. 48–9.

[135] *Ibid.*, pp. 125, 129–30, 145.

[136] *Ibid.*, pp. 125–6, 145–7, 222–5. Diego de Covarrubias in 1556 held that bare mention of *mayorazgo* in wills or donations implies all the conditions 'según la costumbre, los leges y las constituciones', p. 139. In 1574 Diego Pérez still argued that foundations under Law 27 were not true *mayorazgos*, p. 141.

geniture, expounded by Tiraqueau, *primogenium apud Hispanos*, derived from canon, civil and customary law; the Laws of Toro themselves were merely declarations of common law (*derecho común*). By its nature it is perpetual and indivisible, cannot be alienated or mortgaged;[137] it exists for the public good, so that its conservation overrides the lesser private good which alienation to raise portions might serve.[138] Royal authority was no longer necessary to create *mayorazgos*, but it was essential if any changes were needed for those already in existence.

Molina's and other jurists' justification for giving preference to the interests of the *mayorazgo* was that it preserved the property of families whose continuance and power were necessary for the commonwealth. Thus the preamble to a foundation of 1581 declares that men can preserve the memory of what death corrupts by means of good customs to bind their property

> in order that in their absence their memory will endure among their descendants and successors, which memory would cease if such property continued free and unbound, because it is notorious . . . that free possessions . . . are consumed and damaged in many ways by prodigal successors who disperse them, or imprudent ones who do not preserve them, or pusillanimous ones who do not defend them, or by a multitude of heirs who partition them, so that . . . *mayorazgos* were instituted for the preservation of their memory and so that all the children, descendants and kin of that line may be favoured and assisted by the holder of the *mayorazgo* and can serve our Lord God and his natural kings and defend the honour of the house whence they descend.[139]

If this is conventional rhetoric, what was the reality? Dr Clavero stresses the limitation of the possessor of a *mayorazgo* legal responsibility for provision for younger children and widows; Domínguez Ortiz writes of the nobility of the seventeenth 'for many their own personal fortune counted for more than what might be left for their heirs. The incessant demands for authority to

---

[137] *Ibid.*, pp. 140–4, 218–21. For Tiraqueau, see Thirsk's paper.
[138] *De Primogeniorum Hispanorum Origine ac Natura* (Lyons, 1672), Bk. IV, cap. 6, no. 21, p. 443.
[139] M. Lasso de la Vega, Marquess de Saltillo, *El Señorió de Valverde* (Madrid, 1945), p. 143. Mayorazgo of Jorge Ruiz de Alarcón, xvi Señor de Valverde.

burden their patrimony with *censos* are a proof of this.'[140] This latter point is undeniable, as is the fact that their traditional way of life did not lead them to put thrift before splendour. Yet does it follow that the conventional declarations of founders of *mayorazgos* about preserving the fortune of the lineage and assisting its kin are meaningless?

Herlihy has argued that the wealthy minorities of the fifteenth century, and particularly the urban patriciates of Tuscany, had more children than the poor majority; thus pressure of numbers threatened members of élites with loss of wealth and status, and that this was not a new phenomenon.[141] One attempt to counter such pressures might have been through family cooperation and solidarity, such as the joint households, joint holdings and partnerships between brothers which, as we shall see, can be found in fifteenth-century Florence.[142] By emphasizing blood ties of common descent even the poor and depressed families could retain some of the power and prestige of a great house. This process was institutionalized to an extreme in the Genoese *alberghi*, where the clan included very poor families who could rely on the rich and powerful for support.[143] The higher nobility of fifteenth-century Castile, as Clavero acutely observes, practised legal monogamy and social polygamy. As their bastards seem to have been given both recognition and support, the pressure of numbers was increased.[144] The *mayorazgo* professed to ensure the preservation of the family's property and prestige, so that the resulting power would help the holder to provide for the younger children who had sacrificed their immediate legal rights in the interests of family

---

[140] A. Domínguez Ortíz, *La Sociedad Española en el Siglo XVII*, 2 vols (Madrid, 1963–70) i, p. 242.

[141] D. Herlihy, 'Three Patterns of Social Mobility in Medieval History', *Journ. of Interdisciplinary History*, iii (1973), pp. 642–7.

[142] See below, p. 279.

[143] J. Heers, *Le Clan Familial au Moyen Age* (Paris, 1974), pp. 160–1, 163–5, 171–2, 234–48, 253–9.

[144] Clavero, *op. cit.*, p. 98. The question of the recognition of bastards and provision for them deserves investigation and may throw some light on changing conceptions of blood relationships and family structures. Although Ireland and Castile may be extreme cases, a general, if superficial impression is that bastards were more numerous and had a more recognized place in noble societies of fifteenth-century Europe generally than in those of post-Tridentine Europe. In Franche Comté in the fifteenth century bastard sons (but not daughters) were given portions and accepted by the families of the lesser nobility, Heers, *op. cit.*, pp. 82–3.

solidarity. It will be seen later that renunciations by younger children were important in establishing entails in late medieval France.[145]

However, the *mayorazgo* was not necessarily confined to eldest sons; the confirmations of 1379 and 1401, discussed above, enabled each of the beneficiaries, founders to the great houses of Mendoza, dukes of Infantado, and of Zúñiga, dukes of Béjar, to found *mayorazgos* for four younger sons.[146] They were following the general pattern of the founders of great fortunes on which we remarked in England, of which other examples can be found in fifteenth-century Castile.[147] Often the main *mayorazgo* included ecclesiastical patronage which could be used for younger sons, but the provision of inheritances for younger sons did not necessarily cease with the founders of great houses.[148] Such foundations for younger sons often included conditions that if it reverted to the eldest branch for default of issue in the cadet line, the *mayorazgo* should go again to a younger son as soon as possible. If a man married an heiress, again as in England, the younger sons were likely to benefit, often

---

[145] See below, p. 258. Renunciations by the younger children were used to confirm *mayorazgos* with and without royal consent. Molina considered that the holder might add new conditions with the consent of the whole family and discussed under what conditions consent to founding and renunciations by younger children were valid, *op. cit.*, Lib. I, cap. 8, no. 26, Lib. II, cap. 3, pp. 46–7, 172–8.

[146] Francisco Layno Serrano, *Historia de Guadalajara y sus Mendozas en los siglos XV y XVI*, 4 vols (Madrid, 1942), i, pp. 289–92; C. Jago, thesis, p. 6.

[147] E.g. Juan Pachecho, first marquess of Villena, first duke of Escalona, founded two *mayorazgos* for his two younger sons, in 1457 and 1462, and provided portions for nine legitimate and two illegitimate daughters, nine of whom married. The smallest portion was two million *maravedis* (I owe this information to Dr Highfield); Pedro Fernández de Velasco, from whom the dukes of Frías descended, founded two for his two younger sons, *Archivo de los Duques de Frías*, i, *Casa de Velasco*, ed. Teresa de la Peña Manzuela, genealogical tree, following p. 526.

[148] E.g. 1572 the prince of Eboli, founded one of 8,000 ducats rent for his third son, Ruy Gomez de Silva, *Indice de la Colección de Don Luis de Salazar y Castro*, xxviii (1961), no. 44.487. 1484, Juan Manrique, count of Castañeda, founded a second *mayorazgo* for his second son, Juan; if his descendants failed in both male and female line, it reverted to the elder son's line. 1599, María Manrique, widow of Fadrique Enríquez, marquess of Villanueva de Rio, founded one for their second son, Antonio, remainder to their third son, if his descendants failed, to the eldest son's line, 'to be separated immediately when there are two sons', Luis de Salazar y Castro, *Historia Genealógica de la Casa de Lara*, 4 vols (Madrid, 1696) [hereafter Salazar, *Lara*], iv, *Pruebas*, pp. 94–5, 219.

by the founding of a *mayorazgo*.[149] Indeed part of the juristic doctrine of favouring the eldest son's *mayorazgo* was that before charging it in any way, the younger children should be provided for by the mother or grandparents, or from unentailed property.[150] Undeniably the endowing of younger sons did sometimes cause serious family quarrels,[151] but much the commonest occasion of litigation and uncertainty was provided by the rules about succession to *mayorazgos*. The attempts to enforce rules about holding of incompatible *mayorazgos* (in order to prevent accumulation by eldest sons) and about the carrying out of names and arms clauses, when foundations descended to females, can best be seen in the context of the general problems of succession.

The founder of a *mayorazgo* could choose the form of succession and by the seventeenth century an elaborate system of classification had grown up. But the regular system of succession had been in direct line by primogeniture with representation.[152] Founders could vary the terms, but the most usual ones seem to have favoured females before remoter males, equivalent to the English tail general (except that female heirs took individually by seniority not as coparceners).[153] Difficulties and disputes arose, because the terms of early *mayorazgos* were not explicit, or were ambiguous. For instance if the foundation was 'to perpetuate my memory', or with condition that any successor should bear 'my arms and names', it was claimed that this implied exclusion of females. Such doubts should have been resolved by a pragmatic of 1615, in answer to

[149] In 1580 the marriage contract of the duke of Maqueda with Luisa Manrique, daughter and heiress of the duke of Nájera, provided that if she succeeded to the *mayorazgo* of Nájera and had two sons, it was to go to the second, who was to take the name and arms of her father, if there was only a son and a daughter, it was to go to the daughter and she was to marry, sons or descendants of the duke of Nájera's brother, or his uncle, *ibid.*, pp. 343–4; 1518 María de Tovar, wife of Iñigo Fernández de Velasco, third duke of Frías, for her second son, Juan, *Archivo de los Duques de Frías*, i, nos. 335–6, 338.

[150] Clavero, *op. cit.*, p. 231, n. 40.

[151] Molina admits that some eldest brothers and fathers failed to make even minimum provision for younger children and tried to evade court decrees assigning *alimenta*, 'ut pluries vidimus fieri a maioratuum possessoribus in odium fratrum vel sororum', *op cit.*, Lib. ii, cap. xv, 72, p. 295.

[152] Clavero, *op. cit.*, pp. 211–18.

[153] Clavero, *op. cit.*, pp. 214 and n. 7, 241 and n. 56 claims that the regular succession excluded females until the mid sixteenth century. He seems not to offer completely convincing proof of this. In any case many founders explicitly included females.

the complaints of the Cortes of 1611 about the suits caused by such uncertainties and conjectures; it enacted that females should be preferred to remoter males, unless the founder had expressly, clearly and literally excluded them.[154] Even where females were excluded they ought to have portions charged on the *mayorazgo*, as in the English strict settlement.[155] The effects of female inheritance were likely to have been greater in Castile than in England.

The resulting concentration of property by marriage had already caused protests in the Cortes under Charles I. In 1534 he ordered that when two *mayorazgos* were joined by marriage, one being of 'dos cuentos de renta' or more, the elder son should take the greater and the second son or daughter the other. If there was only one child division would be postponed to the next generation. This law was included in the *Recopilaciones* and discussed by jurists, who agreed that it had never been observed.[156] The founders of *mayorazgos* had no greater success when they tried to insist that their names and arms should be perpetuated. By the seventeenth century it was generally held that the strictest conditions could be met by adding names and arms along with the entails to those already held,[157] so that the separation of the *mayorazgos* of two houses, by allowing a younger son to change his name as in the Lexington-Manners inheritance, or in that of Nájera,[158] rarely happened. Thus the *mayorazgo* drastically restricted the line of succession, not only in terms of provision for younger children,

[154] *Novissima Recopilación*, lib. x, tit. xvii, ley 8; Clavero, *op. cit.*, pp. 241–3, 213–14. It also settled doubts about succession by representation. Already in 1552 the Cortes had complained that disputes and uncertainties about female succession were of long standing and were subject to conflicting opinions and judgements, Juan Sempere y Guarinos, *Historia de los Vínculos y Mayorazgos* (Madrid, 1805), p. 288.

[155] Clavero, *op. cit.*, p. 241 and n. 55; Molina, *op. cit.*, Lib. ii, cap. xii, 51, p. 168, says this is the common opinion of jurists.

[156] Clavero, *op. cit.*, pp. 257–9, 150–3; *Novissima Recopilación*, Lib. x, tit. 17, ley 7. However, it was invoked in 1555 in a royal licence to separate the *mayorazgos* of Paredes and Nájera, Salazar, *Lara*, iv, p. 356. The seventh duke of Béjar had married Ana de Mendoza as her second husband, she brought the *mayorazgos* of her grandfather, the marquess of Mondejar, in Valencia (these included four originally settled by the third marquess on each of his four younger sons). The duke's marriage contract had assigned these to their second son, according to the law of 1534, but after her death the duke claimed that the law did not apply to Valencia, although he did buy property to form a *mayorazgo* for his second son; Jago, thesis, pp. 183, 214.

[157] *Ibid.*, pp. 256–7.

[158] See above, p. 229, n. 149.

but also by generally excluding remoter males. If this ensured a supply of heiresses, it seemed to contradict the institution's professed purpose of perpetuating the name and memory of the founder. When female succession occurred it nearly always produced disputes between families and prolonged litigation, just as the eldest brother's powers could produce bitterness and litigation between siblings. Yet the *mayorazgo* could also be an instrument as well as a rhetorical symbol of family solidarity, providing more than symbolical powers of patronage.

The necessary prestige and power was meant to be preserved by limiting the power of spendthrifts and by insuring the family fortune against individuals' crimes or misjudgements by clauses providing that if a possessor was guilty of treason, or other crimes carrying penalties of confiscation, the *mayorazgo* should go to the next in succession. Those incompetent to serve the family's interests, madmen, the deaf and dumb, hermaphrodites, professed monks or nuns, and more questionably, the blind, were excluded from succession.[159] Apart from ecclesiastical patronage belonging to the *mayorazgo* itself, the prestige and status of the possessor as a titled noble gave him expectations of *mercedes* from the crown for himself and his kin. The greater his services to the crown, the greater his claim on its patronage and his ability to further the careers of younger brothers or uncles, whether they were churchmen or soldiers. Perhaps the most sought-after perquisites of crown patronage were the places in the military orders which had been made more attractive from the early sixteenth century when the knights were allowed to marry. In the seventeenth century younger sons may have been more likely to go to the *Colegios Mayores* and in any case many of the newly created titled nobility were *letrados* and councillors who controlled entry to the colleges.[160] If a father did not have enough unentailed real and personal property to provide for his younger children, they had a right, enforceable in the courts, to *alimentos* (alimonies, allowances), which were supposed to be competent and were charged as rents on the *mayorazgo*, while

[159] Clavero, *op. cit.*, pp. 243–7, 267–9. The holder could disinherit his eldest son for ingratitude only if power to do so was included. The validity of exclusions for blindness and other physical defects was questioned by some jurists, including Molina. Exclusion of the mad and deaf and dumb was automatic, whether specified in the deed of foundation or not.

[160] R. L. Kagan, 'Universities in Castile 1500–1700', *Past and Present*, 49 (1970), pp. 65–9,

its capital value could not be touched. Sons each got an annuity, but their children inherited no rights to it, daughters had a right to raise their portions from the rents. The *alimentos* were acknowledged to be less than the *legitims* from equivalent unentailed property;[161] whether there were any rules for calculating them in relation to the *mayorazgo's* value needs to be investigated.

One way in which the eldest son was expected to help his sisters was by using the portion received with his wife to pay their portions. Pedro Manrique de Lara, count of Paredes, in his testament charged his son Antonio in 1539 to do this 'as other good *cavalleros, mayorazgos* of these realms are obliged and accustomed' and pay his sister 20,000 ducats.[162] This seems to help to explain the need for large portions and how competition for them increased their size in the sixteenth century. It was a process which carried considerable risks; if a wife died childless, her husband had to return her portion with increments to her family,[163] unlike England where he retained it. In any case it involved mortgaging the future, since if a wife had children it was usually laid down that her portion and dower from her husband should go to their children. Fathers solemnly charged eldest sons to cherish their sisters' and brothers' interests and to accept their father's debts (in the case of the second duke of Nájera in 1535 this was extended to the grandfather's debts as well).[164] The will to be generous to younger sons was still there, though testators often seemed to give priority to daughters in charging their eldest sons, but the means to fulfil this became less, as more and more property (including goods and chattels) became entailed

[161] Clavero, *op. cit.*, pp. 230–2. The eldest brother's duty to provide *alimentos* for his brothers and sisters, only began if their mother or grandparents could not provide sufficiently for them, Molina, *op. cit.*, Lib. II, cap. xv, 68–9, p. 294.

[162] Salazar, *Lara*, iv, p. 443; for another sister's portion see below n. 165. In 1530 Pedro Manrique, later fourth count of Ossorno, gave 10,000 ducats to his three sisters to supplement their share of the free property of their parents and another 10,000 ducats to his parents from the portion received from his marriage, *ibid.*, iv, pp. 186–7.

[163] E.g. marriage settlements in 1504 of Juana de Cardona, daughter of the duke of Cardona and Antonio Manrique, son of Pedro Manrique, duke of Nájera, and in 1629 of Bernardo de Silva, marquess de la Liseda with Aña Maria de Guevara, daughter of the count of Oñate, *ibid.*, iv, pp. 323–6, 114–17.

[164] Antonio, fifth count of Paredes, was charged to receive his younger brother 'en encomienda è cargo . . . è le tenga muy grand amor, pues ay tanta razon, è obligacion'; will of Antonio Manrique de Lara 1535, *ibid.*, iv, pp. 319–23, 444.

244 J. P. COOPER

and less and less was at the free disposal of the heir. He was compelled to raise portions for his sisters or daughters, or to provide
dower for his widow by creating *censos* on his *mayorazgo*, as
Antonio Manrique, fifth count of Paredes, did to raise a sister's
portion. As any creation of a long-term rent charge was invalid,
and could not bind any successor, a royal license was necessary.[165]
Such licenses can be found in the first half of the sixteenth century,
but they had certainly become of crucial importance in the fortunes
of great noble houses by 1580 and probably earlier.

By then the whole mechanism of marriage, the giving of portions,
security for their repayment in case the wife died leaving no living
issue, the granting of dower (*arras*) and maintenance to widows
had come to depend on this exercise of royal absolutism which
gave holders of *mayorazgos* rights and powers, explicitly denied
to them by law and by their foundation. By the same prerogative
the normal right of the holder of a *censo* to seize the property
charged in case of non-payment of the rent was changed to a right
to embargo the rents of that property. The result was that great
noble houses were carrying an ever-increasing burden of debt
without alienating land or rights; in some cases a major part of
their income was going in paying the rents of *censos*.[166] Their
dependence on royal favour was further increased from 1580 by
the grant of reductions of interest on the *censos* of great nobles.[167]
Jago has shown how such favours were multiplied after 1610,
despite the fall in the maximum legal rate of interest to 5 per cent
in 1607. As many ignored the provisions in the licenses for redemption of the capital of the *censos*, Philip II appointed a special
judge in 1596 to ensure that these were performed. Almost immediately grants allowing individuals to use the sums collected for
redeeming *censos* were made. In so far as this was not done and
creditors exercised their rights to distrain rents, some families were

[165] Faculty to sell *censo* to raise 4,000 ducats for Juana's portion by
Charles I in 1545, license in 1550 to Inigo Manrique to charge his *mayorazgo*
for restitution of his wife's portion and her dower, if his free property does
not suffice, *ibid.*, iv, pp. 449, 575.
[166] C. Jago, 'The Influence of Debt on the Relations between Crown and
Aristocracy in Seventeenth Century Castile', *Econ. Hist. Rev.*, xxvi (1973),
pp. 218–25. B. Bennassar, *Valladolid au Siècle d'Or* (Paris, 1967), pp. 264–
272.
[167] Bennassar, *op. cit.*, pp. 271–2; the normal rate was 7.14 per cent,
reductions to 6.25 per cent were general and there were some to 5.55 per
cent among those granted to eight families.

reduced to bankruptcy and provided the crown with yet another opportunity for dispensing favours. The formal declaration of limited bankruptcy (*concurso de acreedores*) meant the appointment of a judicial administrator who collected rents and paid creditors and an allowance to the debtor. The crown could favour individuals by allowing them to collect their revenues, despite distraints or allocations to creditors, or by appointing private judges to supervise repayment of their debts which ensured them a greater income than they would have got from a public *concurso*.

The burdens carried and the need for favours imposed on those in no danger of bankruptcy was still striking. In 1630 rents of *censos* took 25.5 per cent of the gross and 50 per cent of the net revenues of the duke of Béjar, one of the wealthiest and most careful of the Castilian grandees.[168] The crown helped to create further insecurity by contributing towards the marriage portions of favoured courtiers. It thus fed the competition which made portions over 100,000 ducats common for grandees by the seventeenth century, while at the same time refusing to license *censos* for more than 40,000 ducats for each portion. This meant that large parts of portions were in unsecured *censos* and provided occasions for innumerable law suits.[169] These suits and still more those over succession to *mayorazgos* provided further occasions on which influence and favour with the king and his councillors would be useful. The traditional justification for such favours was service done by noble families. Philip II's Castilianization of his empire created more opportunities for command and glory, some of which

---

[168] Jago, *art. cit.*, p. 227. Jago's thesis deals with the seventh duke's administration in detail.

[169] *Ibid.*, p. 225 and n. 1; A. Domínguez Ortíz, *La Sociedad Española*, i, p. 243, 110,000 ducats to the Constable's daughter from Philip III. For the huge debts of the family in 1629, 1635 and 1683, in the 1620s a *mayorazgo* of 5,000 ducats a year had been founded for a second son and 200,000 left for a daughter's portion, *ibid.*, pp. 370–1, 235–6. A law of 1534 reiterated by the Cortes in 1573, reissued again in 1623, limited portions for each daughter to two million *maravedis* for those with rents over 1.5 million *maravedis* a year, down to a million each for those with rents of 200,000 to 500,000. Jewels and clothes were not to amount to more than an eighth of the portion and no donations of fifths and thirds were to be made. Philip IV in 1623 restricted dower (*arras*) to a tenth of a man's free property and portions given to ladies in waiting (*Damas de Palacio*) to a million maravedis, as under Philip II, and ladies of the bedchamber (*de la Camera*) to 500,000, while no *mercedes* were to be given as part of their portions. All contracts and donations violating these laws were void. *Novissima Recopilación*, Lib. x., tit. 3, leyes vi, vii.

were profitable, but not all, as the fortunes of the dukes of Alba demonstrated. Although exempt from taxes, great nobles were expected to make real contributions in times of crisis, such as the *donativos* demanded in 1590 and under Philip IV and a host of other exactions of money and service in the 1630s. However much the balance had swung in favour of the crown since the fifteenth century, there was still a real interdependence between king and nobility. *Donativos* especially were occasions when most magnates sought privileges of raising the sums promised and additional ones through *censos* as well as privileges against their creditors.[170]

As the amounts of debt were already large by 1580, before pressures from the crown became severe, it has been argued that they may have been partly due to the failure of revenues to keep pace with prices. The evidence for this does not seem conclusive;[171] given that so much of their revenues came from *alcabalás*, which should have increased with rising population and wealth down to 1580, that some, but very variable proportions, came from dues in kind and that all leases were very short, a considerable lag behind prices might seem surprising. What seems more certain is that in the later sixteenth century it was comparatively easy to borrow and townsmen and clergy had savings to lend. This would be likely to encourage the tendency, which we have already noticed, to seek as large portions as possible, and certainly portions made a major contribution to the raising of *censos*. Portions were very

[170] *Ibid.*, pp. 232–4; by 1591 the grandees and titled nobles had offered Philip 703,000 ducats to be raised by *censos*, besides *censos* to be licensed for their own use. A. Dominguez Ortíz, *Politica y Hacienda de Felipe IV* (Madrid, 1960), pp. 298–300.

[171] A. Domínguez Ortíz, *La Sociedad*, i, p. 226, citing a speculation of Viñas y Mey about agricultural rents; more seriously, J. H. Elliott, *Imperial Spain* (London, 1963), p. 308, compares estimates of the incomes of thirteen families made by Marineo Siculo, published in 1539, which are assigned to the early years of Charles V, and by Nuñez de Salcedo in 1597, assigned to 1600. He concludes that their incomes 'had barely doubled over a period when prices quadrupled'. But Hamilton's index of general commodity prices rises from about 42 in 1520, to about 55 in the early 1530s, to 115 in 1595, 135 in 1600; his indexes of agricultural and [non-agricultural] prices rise from 35[45] in 1520, 50[60] in 1530, to 110[115] in 1595, to 140[140] in 1600, E. J. Hamilton, *American Treasure and the Price Revolution in Spain 1501–1650* (Cambridge, Mass., 1934), pp. 224, 260, Charts 9, 17. Thus the dating of the lists makes a considerable difference to the conclusion, but whatever dates are adopted, they do not support the view that prices, other than agricultural ones (those least relevant to aristocratic expenditures), had quadrupled.

much bigger in the early seventeenth century than a hundred years before, but there is not enough information to say whether they had risen faster than prices. Professor Jago has shown that the dukes of Béjar's income from rents and dues rose until 1630 and then began to decline and that this is probably typical of great estates in Castile and Andalusia. Thus the burdens of interest and of *alimentos* to members of the family, amounting in 1642 to about half the duke's gross income, had become a much heavier burden on his net income than they would have been in 1630.[172] As much of the debt before 1630, when the interest was already half the seventh duke's net income, had presumably been contributed to pay portions, Clavero's implication that the holders of *mayorazgos* could and did choose to provide for their younger children with a minimum of expense to the entailed estate does not apply here.

The debts of the dukes of Béjar charged by *censos* had risen from 272,415 ducats to over 450,000 in 1630, an increase of 65 per cent. The charge on their revenues would not rise proportionately because interest rates fell and they were exempted from repaying capital, but above all because their income was rising. When this changed to a decline after 1630, they would have been in real difficulties, quite apart from the exactions laid on them by the war. Until then they had been largely sheltered from the worst effects of Castile's economic difficulties after 1598 by the crown's concessions[173] which sacrificed monied interests to those of the aristocracy. Unlike the lesser nobility, the greater had devoted little of the capital raised by *censos* to building and improvements,[174] though these would have become decreasingly profitable after 1630. The crown sacrificed the capital of the holders of *censos* and *juros* and the accumulated savings of bullion to finance war. Bennassar argues that the use of *vellon* as the domestic currency enabled the government from 1622 to secure hoarded bullion for export by offering ever-increasing premiums for it in terms of vellon (up to 120 per cent in 1642). The reduction of interest on all new *censos* to 5 per cent in 1608 and on all existing *censos* in

---

[172] Jago, thesis, pp. 214–15, 224–5.

[173] Jago, *art. cit.*, pp. 231 and n. 4 (1600), 227.

[174] *Ibid.*, pp. 224–5. 1610–35 8.9 per cent of the total raised went on improvements by the titled, against 28.5 per cent by the lesser nobility. The former raised 58.1 per cent for services to the crown and 20.4 per cent for portions, though the 8 per cent for funding unsecured debts may include borrowing for the same purpose.

1621 came too late to save the peasant borrowers of the sixteenth century. Thus, the individual privileges granted to the aristocracy and the ability to pay interest on some *censos* in depreciated coin meant an expropriation of capital and wealth to pay for war which discriminated heavily against lenders. In 1643 the real income of some *censos* was put at a quarter of their nominal value.[175]

Long before the exactions of Olivares and the disasters of 1640 the effects of both *censos* and *mayorazgos* on Castile were strongly criticized by *arbitristas* (projectors of reforms). These writers often cited the petitions of the Cortes, which had shown particular concern about the question of debts and *censos*. As early as 1551 they had petitioned against 'persons of little quality and not very great fortune' founding *mayorazgos* and wanted to preserve the nobility by ending royal licenses to charge *censos*, and obligations for portions and dower on them. This latter was repeated in 1602; in the 1590s the deputies, representing the urban élites who were one of the major sources of loans, had shown increasing concern about their security.[176] In general they wanted to clarify the law about *mayorazgos*, especially about improvements and succession, and to shorten the procedures in disputed cases.[177] Thus the use of royal dispensing power and the uncertain results of litigation were the targets rather than the existence of *mayorazgos*. As Colmeiro pointed out long ago, most of the *arbitristas* recommended preserving existing ones, while restricting the creation of new ones, and deplored their foundation by lesser men.[178]

[175] B. Bennassar, 'Consommations, investissements, mouvements de capitaux en Castile aux XVIᵉ et XVIIᵉ siècles', *Conjoncture économique structures sociales. Hommage à Ernest Labrousse* (Paris, 1974), pp. 139–55, especially 154–5. But his assumption (p. 154) that all *censos* were paid in vellon is wrong; Jago found that 71 per cent of Béjar's in 1630 stipulated payment in silver, or a premium of 10 per cent in vellon, *art. cit.*, p. 228 and n. 7.

[176] Clavero, *op. cit.*, pp. 132–3, 148–9; Jago, *art. cit.*, pp. 222, 226.

[177] Clavero, *op. cit.*, pp. 132, 147; Sempere y Guarinos, *Historia de los Vinculos*, pp. 285–303. In 1573 and 1578 they sought unsuccessfully to have the proof of an 'immemorial *mayorazgo*' without formal foundation to be forty years' prescription. In 1610 they asked that decrees in favour of *alimentistas* should be executed without delay of appeal which was conceded in 1619, *ibid.*, pp. 299–300. For the earlier attempt to prevent accumulation of *mayorazgos*, see above, p. 241.

[178] M. Colmeiro, *Historia de la Economía Política en España*, 2 vols (1st edn 1863, reprint Madrid, 1965), ii, pp. 722, 727. Jovellanos in the eighteenth century took much the same line in allowing existing ones and opposing new creations, *ibid.*, p. 728, n. 17.

Like the Cortes, González de Cellorigo, one of the earliest and acutest of the *arbitristas*, accepted the traditional defence of *mayorazgos*.

... the greatness of these realms is founded on great and illustrious houses, as if on great and immovable pedestals, if they were divided the prop, which supports the monarchy and ensures its power ... would be lost. The royal house itself created these firmest of foundations and will be left without support, if they fail or are diminished, so that the Prince would be forced to create others *de novo*.[179]

On the other hand excessive accumulation was also dangerous and he wanted the law of 1534 to be enforced. He disapproved of their proliferation among those of mean condition and fortune and cited the petition of 1551 approvingly. He thought the prohibition of alienation and the law relating to improvements damaged agriculture. He wanted entails in primogeniture which allowed alienation, as he claimed existed in France.[180] Freedom of alienation would seem to follow logically from the Cortes' attacks on *censos* and other incumbrances on *mayorazgos*. Whether or not the Cortes saw this, it was advocated by two other *arbitristas*.[181] González also wanted to enforce limitation of the size of marriage portions and lamented the way in which 'the most honourable houses of Spain' 'had come to eat up the greater part of their rents' through licenses to raise portions.[182] Thus he would apparently only have approved borrowing, or sales, for improvements. He devoted far more space to attacking *censos* and *juros*, as destructive of productive investment, of the coinage and of

---

[179] Martín González de Cellorigo, *Memorial de la política necessaria y útil Restauración de la república de España* (Valladolid, 1600), fo. 58[r].

[180] *Ibid.*, fos 58[r], 58[v]. Law 46 of the Laws of Toro gave the successor to the *mayorazgo* the benefits of new buildings and repairs without paying anything for them to the personal estate of his predecessor. He cites Pelaez as his authority for France, but entailed property in France could not be alienated, though perpetual entails had been forbidden in 1566 (see below, p. 463). His proposals for increasing freedom of alienation were of 'a mild moderation'; to allow licenses to alienate for existing *mayorazgos*, when necessary, and not to grant new ones with prohibitions of alienation, unless 'the quality and substance of the persons' involved would 'justify such a concession'.

[181] Miguel Caja de Leruela, *Restauración de la abundancia de España* (1631); Gerónimo de Ceballos, *Arte real para el buen govierno* (1623); Colmeiro, *op. cit.*, p. 727.

[182] González de Cellorigo, *op. cit.*, fo. 19[r], cf. 61[r].

250   J. P. COOPER

incentives to honour labour and invention. In seeing them as a principal cause of the economic ills of Spain he has rightly won the attention of modern historians.[183] His chief remedy was the reduction of interest rates to aid redemption combined with public banks, for which a plan had been approved by the Cortes in 1599.

Although González anticipates the standard complaints of eighteenth-century reformers about the disincentives to agricultural improvement resulting from *mayorazgos*, he devotes little space to this and less to remedying them.[184] Utopian plans for wholesale agrarian reform and the sweeping away of *mayorazgos* by invoking the king's absolute power can be found in the contemporary, but unpublished, writings of Pedro de Valencia. He allowed that the king did not own the land as in Egypt and India, but he had universal lordship and jurisdiction over it 'to govern and direct its exploitation' which was to be used to redistribute the land in peasant family holdings to be held in perpetual leasehold or emphyteusis.[185] This anticipates and exceeds the deals of enlightened despotism, where González, though also full of praise for fruitful labour as the only creator of true wealth, founded his monarchy on great nobles rather than on peasant holdings.

The relationship of dependence between the great nobles and the monarchy had been reversed since the fifteenth century, but their interdependence was as great as ever and was still symbolized by the invocation of absolute power to override established property rights. In the fifteenth century this was done in instituting *mayorazgos*, in the seventeenth in restricting the rights of creditors against holders of *mayorazgos*. This latter can be seen not only as expressing the crown's determination to preserve great houses, / but also as an extension of customary privileges long enjoyed by the mass of the nobility in civil debts; the most important of which was that, unlike the English gentry, except the actual peers of

[183] *Ibid.*, fos 22ro–23ro, 4, 15vo; see especially P. Vilar. 'The Age of Don Quixote' in *Essays in European Economic History 1500–1800*, ed. P. Earle (Oxford, 1974), pp. 106–7.
[184] González de Cellorigo, *op. cit.*, fos 59ro–60ro; E. J. Hamilton, 'Early Spanish Banking schemes before 1700', *Journal of Political Economy*, lvii (1949), pp. 135–55, cf. *New Cambridge Modern History*, iv (Cambridge, 1970), pp. 39–40.
[185] J. A. Maravall, 'Reforimos Social-Agrario en el Crisis del Siglo XVII, Tierra, Trabazo, y Solaria Según Pedro de Valencia, 1555–1620', *Bulletin Hispanique*, lxxii (1970), pp. 26–38.

Parliament, they could not be imprisoned for debt.[186] On the whole the crown made few concessions to the demands of the Cortes for clarifying the law and simplifying litigation. This had the effect of making great nobles dependent on court favour in cases of disputed successions, as well as in seeking accommodations with their creditors. It also ensured prolonged and profitable business for the courts and the *letrados*, the mainstay of monarchical administration. In the eighteenth century a major theme of reformers was still the diversity of legal opinions and the prolixity of processes in these cases.[187]

The behaviour of the Castilian aristocracy can be seen as part of that general emphasis on the enhancement of paternal power which we mentioned earlier. For a large part of their burden of debt was accumulated in order to provide generously for younger children, especially for daughters, while restricting or denying their effective rights to legitim which were not controllable at the will of the father. Powers of disinheritance could also be applied to the favoured eldest son. For in 1559 the Cortes got the laws of Toro extended so that sons under the age of twenty-five as well as daughters could be disinherited for marrying without their father's consent. Otherwise the father could only disinherit if power was given to do so in the act of foundation.[188] Perhaps the most remarkable feature of the usual mode of succession chosen by the founders of *mayorazgos* is the emphasis on direct descent extending to include females to the exclusion of remoter males. As great houses, like the Mendozas, had successfully founded cadet lines, this was not due to lack of males bearing the family name, whose existence was fairly certain to ensure litigation over a female succession. A preferred strategy to perpetuate the name was to marry the heiress to one of the remoter males. Thus the fifth duke of Infantado whose sons died in childhood married his eldest daughter Ana to his second brother in 1581 in the hope of avoiding

[186] Execution could not be had against their houses, clothes, arms, horses and riding mules and they had a right to be given *alimentos competentes* in any *concurso* and bankruptcy proceedings by their creditors. Bernabe Moreno de Vargos, *Discursos de la Nobleza de España* (Madrid, 1636), fo. 65, no. 11; Joannes Arce ab Otalora, *Summa Nobilitatis Hispaniae . . .* (Madrid, 1613, first published 1553), p. 350.

[187] Sempere y Guarinos, *op. cit.*, pp. 303–4.

[188] Clavero, *Mayorazgo . . .* , pp. 133, 245. Clavero claims that such clauses were unusual.

suits about the succession. The only son of this marriage died young and the duke persuaded Ana to marry again at her own choice, her cousin Juan Hurtado de Mendoza, seventh son of the marquess of Mondéjar. After the fifth duke's death in 1601 a suit lasting 32 years was begun by Diego Hurtado de Mendoza, married to a daughter of another brother of the fifth duke and direct descendant of the first marquess of Santillana, the direct ancestor in the male line of the duke. By this second marriage Ana had only two daughters. The litigation was at first assisted by the marriage of the elder daughter of her first marriage to Lerma's second son. After the disgrace of Lerma, this proved an expensive investment, but the main inheritance went to Lerma's son who became seventh duke of Infantado.[189]

Unlike female inheritance in England which required division among coheiresses, the *mayorazgo* gave the whole to the eldest; thus Ana, sixth duchess of Infantado in her own right, excluded three married sisters. In Castile the concentration and institutionalizing of favour and patronage at court involved overriding legal rules despite protests from councils and law courts.[190] The crown connived at violations by the magnates of the laws of 1534 limiting the size of portions and the accumulation of *mayorazgos*, although the laws were solemnly repeated on into the eighteenth century. In England the legal rules about settlements were developed and institutionalized by the law courts; the means to vary or adapt them was through private acts of Parliament and family consent, not by royal prerogative and court influence. In England the amount of patronage available to the king's ministers had increased from the late seventeenth century, but patronage was no longer thought of as including dispensations from legal rules, or influence upon the courts, in favour of privileged individuals. Whereas the great nobles of France and Spain became more dependent on court favour for their economic survival in the seventeenth century, those of England became less dependent.

As was remarked initially a great strength of French legal history has been the study of customary law, especially in relation to peasant inheritance. The best recent textbook of the history of

[189] F. Layna Serrano, *Historia de Guadalajara y sus Mendozas*, iii, pp. 232, 341–4, 350; cf. above n. 156, for Ana's daughter by her second marriage.

[190] Jago, *Econ. Hist. Rev.*, 2nd ser., xvi (1973), pp. 231–2, 234–6.

private law remarks 'There has never been a serious study of the effects of entails (*substitutions*).'[191] For the present purpose it is a further misfortune that the fullest study of a group of nobles for any period is concerned with Brittany, one of the regions whose customary law did not allow entails.[192] There is general agreement that entails were used to set up rules of succession for great families. Just as the founders of *mayorazgos* might choose different rules for their descent, so each founder of an entail might choose an individual rule of succession for his family; their common characteristic was that they changed or suspended the rules of customary law, especially those concerning the rights of younger children. A further complication is that local customs themselves changed both before their codification in the fifteenth and sixteenth centuries and also as a result of the process of codification. If the law and customs prevailing at a given time are difficult to ascertain, their relationship to what men actually did requires detailed and devoted labour, producing studies such as J. Lafon, *Les Epoux bordelais 1450–1550* (Paris, 1972).

Given the presumption that the customs of great families each embody a potentially individual tradition, a great many would need to be studied before any reliable generalizations about the patterns of inheritance would be possible. My ignorance reduces us to considering a handful of random examples, while the obvious secondary literature on entails and noble inheritance is biased towards the south, the area of written law. It has been argued that the development of entails in the countries of written law was due to the need to give preference to eldest sons and protect family property in the absence of the preferential rights given to eldest sons (*droits d'aînesse*) and of *retrait lignagier* (rights of kin to buy back land alienated by a member of the lineage) found in the regions of customary law. There is a general functional resem-

[191] P. Ourliac and J. Malafosse, 3 vols (Paris, 1968), *Histoire du Droit Privé*, iii, p. 536. An important contribution has since been made by J.-M. Augustin, 'Recherches sur les substitutions fideicommissaires à Toulouse et en Haut-Languedoc au XVIIIᵉ siècle', Thèse Droit, Université de Toulouse, 1971 [hereafter Augustin, Thesis]. I am greatly indebted to Dr Augustin for permitting me to obtain a microfilm of his thesis.

[192] J. Meyer, *La Noblesse Bretonne au XVIIIᵉ siècle*, 2 vols (Paris, 1966). The other regions where *substitutions* were prohibited, or drastically curtailed, by customary law were Bourbonnais, la Marche, Auvergne, Sedan, Montargis, Bassigny, Nivernais, Normandy, Hainaut; R. Mousnier, *Les Institutions de la France sous la Monarchie absolue* (Paris, 1974), i, p. 68.

blance, but differences and complexities remain. The lands of written law also had local customary laws, some of which had originally included *retrait lignagier*, while in Lower Provence it was reintroduced in the fifteenth century.[193] Fideicommissary entails, originally derived from Roman law in the south, were copied in the north in order to strengthen customary *droits d'aînesse*, on the other hand the direct influence of Roman law on the custom of Paris in the sixteenth century increased the rights of younger children by introducing the notion of legitim.[194]

However, the existence of customs and legal rights of partible inheritance are not necessarily reliable evidence of what families actually did. Duby shows that in the Mâconnais from the early eleventh century succession by primogeniture developed. 'Undoubtedly all the sons possessed the same rights of succession, but they did not divide the inheritance at their father's death.' Only one of them married and had legitimate sons who later in their turn received the whole inheritance, less what their uncles had given to the Church for their funeral rites. Moreover a daughter in the absence of sons often inherited to the exclusion of uncles and male cousins. Thus the effects in restricting lineages to descendants to the exclusion of collateral males and in creating heiresses were the same as those of many, perhaps most, Castilian *mayorazgos*, but the result was achieved by family agreement and choice. From such choices the *droits d'aînesse*, originating in the higher nobility of castle owners spread, to become customary law applicable to all nobles.[195] Even so, in some customs, notably that of Paris, only fiefs carrying titles of dignity were not subjected to partition, and the rights of the eldest son would not suffice to prevent the whittling away of the original patrimony by partitions to provide for younger children.[196] In the south custom prescribed

[193] E. Jarriand, 'La succession coutumière dans les pays de droit écrit', *Revue Historique de Droit Français et Etranger*, xiv (1890), pp. 30–69, 222–68; P. Ourliac, 'Le Retrait Lignagier dans le Sud-Ouest de la France', *ibid.*, 4th ser., xxx (1952), pp. 328–55 shows that it existed beyond the boundaries of *Gallia Narbonensis*, while for Provence, see R. Aubenas, 'La Famille dans l'Ancienne Provence', *Annales d'histoire économique et sociale*, viii (1936), pp. 528–9.

[194] Ourliac and Malafosse, *op. cit.*, p. 472; Olivier Martin, *Histoire de la Coutume de la Prévôté et Vicomté de Paris*, 2 vols (Paris, 1922–30), ii, pp. 360–6.

[195] G. Duby, *Hommes et Structures au Moyen Age* (Paris, 1973), pp. 414–15, 344–5.

the equal partition of fiefs among sons on into the thirteenth century, while Roman law gave equal shares to all children on intestacy and rights to legitim when there was a will. Fragmentation of inheritances (despite the existence of communal holdings by brothers) and the desire of noble families to maintain their patrimonies produces a potentially stronger means than the strongest customary *droits d'aînesse* (those of Brittany and Normandy). The first stage in the process was common to both south and north in the thirteenth century, the exclusion of daughters who had received marriage portions, comparable to the replacement of the maritagium by the portion in England.[197]

Much more important was the development of entails. Fideicommissary entails appeared in testaments of great noble families in Languedoc from the twelfth century and were included in the customs of Montpellier in the early thirteenth century, though at first they were limited to one generation. But the limit to four generations imposed by Justinian in Novel 159 was ignored and perpetual entails were approved by Baldus in the later fourteenth century. Meanwhile they had already spread to Gascony, Provence and elsewhere. An examination of four thousand testaments from the Lyonnais 1301–1545 shows *substitutions* constantly present. In those of the nobility (*chevaliers* or *donzeaux*), they made excessively remote dispositions 'after their children, nephews bearing their name, then distant male cousins of flourishing estate (on condition of bearing their name and arms)'. Another study finds these nobles even less willing than non-nobles (*roturiers*) to provide land for their younger children. Many daughters and younger sons were put into religion, though those who were not might receive large and burdensome portions.[198]

[196] O. Martin, *op. cit.*, i, pp. 305–9. Females were excluded in collateral, but not in direct succession.

[197] Aubenas, *art. cit.*, pp. 523–8; J. Poumarède, *Les Successions dans le Sud-Ouest de la France au Moyen Age* (Paris, 1972), pp. 167–71, 183–9. For an example of male primogeniture being introduced into Gascon customs at the request of the nobility in 1295, *ibid.*, pp. 197–8. O. Martin, *op. cit.*, i, p. 303, ii, pp. 369–73.

[198] Poumarède, *op. cit.*, pp. 212–17; Augustin, Thesis, pp. 6–10; M. Gonon, 'Les Testaments Lyonnais', *Receuil de . . . la Societé d'Histoire du Droit . . . Anciens Pays du Droit Ecrit*, fasc. vi (1967), pp. 70–4; M.-T. Lorcin, *Les Compagnes de la Région Lyonnaise aux XIVe et XVe siècles* (Lyon, 1974), pp. 189–90, 186. Unfortunately I did not see Michel Petitjean, *Essai sur l'histoire des substitutions du ixe au xve Siècle dans la pratique et la doctrine, spécialement en France méridionale* (Dijon, 1975) until this paper

Perhaps the most famous example of the creation of a family law of inheritance in defiance of customary law is that of the d'Albrets. In the mid thirteenth century they were an old, but obscure family, practising partible inheritance. By the early fourteenth century by marrying heiresses and serving both the French and English crowns, they had become great lords. Amanieu VII had had three sons and four daughters. The daughters were married with portions and renounced all claims on their father's inheritance. The sons were emancipated and acknowledged their father's right to do as he pleased with his patrimony, renouncing their rights to legitim and under any local custom. Amanieu made the eldest son his universal heir by his will and assigned lands to his younger sons. The arrangements were then declared by local jurists to be in accordance with ancient family custom. The eldest son Bernard-Ezi II invoked the custom of Casteljaloux, 'his principal domicile', to justify similar arrangements for his nine children; one son and two daughters entered religious orders, two daughters were married with portions, the three other younger sons received land (much of it derived from maternal acquisitions) in the equivalent of tail male on condition of not claiming legitim or customary rights. The main inheritance was to descend through the eldest son in tail male, with provision of portions for heirs general, with successive remainders to the younger sons. If all the sons' male descendants failed, the main inheritance was to revert to the elder married sister and then to her son and that of the third son to the second daughter and then to her second son, each on condition of taking the name and arms of Albret. In case of refusal or failure, there were further remainders to other grandsons or nephews of Bernard-Ezi. The effect was to prevent female inheritance, except as a last resort, and to direct the younger sons' lands back to the main inheritance, if they failed in the direct line.[199]

While the main line of the d'Albrets flourished for another half dozen generations until it ended with the mother of Henry IV, the lesser nobility of the Bordelais do not seem to have adopted

had already gone to press. This very important work contains a full analysis (pp. 441–567) of the use of *substitutions* in Languedoc, Provence, Lyonnais (with an account of provisos for transmitting names and arms, pp. 486–7) and the two Burgundies.

[199] Poumarède, *op. cit.*, pp. 199–203; R. Boutruche, *La Crise d'une Société* (Paris, 1947), pp. 377–95, 492–518. Poumarède suspects that he invented the custom.

such measures until the later fifteenth century.[200] Equally significant is the case of Jean II de Lévis, seigneur de Mirepoix, who
received royal letters patent in 1333, allowing him to abandon the
custom of Paris which had whittled away his ancestors' patrimony.
He could now follow written law and was allowed to create an
entail, the eldest son keeping the whole inheritance, while paying
the younger children's legitims in cash. Entails in tail male were
made in 1341 and 1491, while in 1530 Jean V, made an entail,
forbidding any dismemberment of the house and any division or
alienation of the fief of Mirepoix, and stipulating that younger
children's portions must be in cash not land. On the other hand
the house of Chalon Tonnerre during the fourteenth century followed the custom of the Paris region and the Ile de France of
dividing the inheritance, the eldest son doing homage for the whole
fief, including the parts subinfeudated to his cadets. But in the
early fifteenth century the brothers of what proved to be the last
generation of the direct male line seem to have left their patrimony
undivided.[201]

Jurists often saw primogeniture as modelled upon the laws of
succession of royal houses. Another influence was likely to have
been the grant of appanages by the kings of France to their younger
sons which, unlike appanages in private law, were in tail male, not
in fee, and reverted to the crown on the failure of the male line,
leaving only portions in cash for the heirs general. This was the
strategy adopted by Bernard-Ezi II for his younger sons. A more
obvious and direct influence on the succession of a great house is
provided by the Bourbons; their original inheritance had been transmitted through females several times in the twelfth and thirteenth
centuries. In 1400 in order to secure the reversion of Auvergne on
the marriage of Jean, his eldest son to Marie, daughter of the duke

[200] R. Boutruche, 'Aux Origines d'une Crise Nobiliaire', *Annales*, 1939,
pp. 270–3, seems to imply a change reinforced by the new custom of 1521.
Cf. M. G. A. Vale, *English Gascony 1399 1453* (Oxford, 1970), pp. 156–8;
Lafon, *Les Epoux Bordelais*, pp. 229 n. 1, 300–1.

[201] O. Martin, *op. cit.*, p. 308; Augustin, Thesis, pp. 35–7; M. T. Caron
'Les Chalon Tonnerre: Destin d'une Famille Noble à la Fin de la Guerre
de Cent Ans (Unpublished thesis, 3ᵉ cycle, Paris X, 1971), pp. 33–4. Louis II
the last count had three brothers, one of whom married, another (the eldest)
was a Hospitaller. It was agreed in the marriage contract of their sister
Jeanne in 1400 that, if the youngest brother had no issue like his two
brothers already married, the succession should go to their sisters. In the
event the sisters were deprived of most of their inheritance by Charles VII
and the duke of Burgundy, *ibid.*, pp. 19, 29, 32, 35–41.

of Berry and Auvergne, Louis II, duke of Bourbon, agreed to settle most of his lands to go with Auvergne as an appanage, reverting to the crown if the male descent of the marriage failed. In fact when Pierre II died leaving only a daughter, the crown allowed the collateral heir male, descended from Jean I, to succeed.[202]

It may well be that the most important effect of fourteeenth-century entails was the exclusion of female succession which was fortified by renunciations. Thus the entails in the testament of Jean II de Chalon (Arlay), count of Auxerre, provided portions for heirs general, while giving priority to the male lines of his sons successively.[203] It was due to entails made by Jean I and II, counts of Armagnac, that Bernard VII in 1391 succeeded his brother Jean III who had only two daughters. Their uncle seems to have married them off cheaply (one renounced all her rights in return for a portion of 20,000 *livres*). Bernard's own daughter Anne married Charles II of Albret with a portion of 40,000 *livres* and renounced all rights to property of the house of Armagnac. On the other hand Bernard's son, Jean IV (d. 1450), did not restrict the rights of his daughter Isabella so completely, nor apparently the rights of his younger son in the way the d'Albrets or Lévis did.

If the Armagnacs provide a startling example of a fight to the death in which the main line literally destroyed the flourishing cadet branch of Fezensaquet and Pardiac,[204] some recognition of common loyalty to a lineage was more usual. Entails and re-nunciations sought to maintain patrimonies by explicit legal acts in which younger children sacrificed their customary rights for the

<hr/>

[202] A. Leguai, *Les Ducs de Bourbon pendant la Crise Monarchique du XVe Siècle* (Paris, 1962), pp. 35–8, 187–8, 191–4.

[203] Carolus Molinus [Charles du Moulin], *Opera* (Paris, 1612), iii, cols 2489–91. His third son was put before his second in one entail.

[204] *Archives Historiques de la Gascogne*, 1st ser., ii (1883), pp. 7–10, 112; C. Samaran, *La Maison d'Armagnac au XVe Siècle* (Paris, 1908), pp. 206–7, 342; Père Anselme, *Histoire Généalogique et Chronologique de la Maison Royale de France*, 3rd edn, 9 vols (Paris, 1726–33) iii, pp. 418–24, 427. Bernard VII had planned to marry his brother's widow Marguerite de Comminges, but was forestalled by Géraud, count of Pardiac, the descendant of a younger son of Géraud V, count of Armagnac, who married his eldest son to her. Pardiac's lands were eventually confiscated and granted to Bernard, whose younger son, Bernard, received some of them, as well as lands from his mother. When Jean IV's daughter Isabelle married Jean II, duke of Alençon, with portion of 100,000 gold francs, she renounced all claims to inherit, unless her parents died without heirs male. Charles, the younger son, received lands as legitim on his father's death, most of which came from the Pardiac lands.

benefit of eldest sons and the house. In the Mâconnais in the twelfth century the same result had been achieved by informal arrangements between brothers. In both eras a family's resources could be husbanded, or even increased, by some of the brothers and sisters entering the Church. The first testament of Bernard-Ezi II d'Albret had envisaged placing no fewer than five of his then twelve children in the Church.[205] While not all renunciations or vocations in religion were spontaneous and free, many were made out of an accepted sense of duty to the family's honour and fortune.

A remarkable example of an attempt to create an indivisible patrimony is provided by the public declaration by Alain VIII, vicomte de Rohan, in 1423. His land and the *comté* of Porhoet, inherited by his wife, and plate, jewels, and household goods were to be inalienable, not to be exchanged or mortgaged without the counsel of his closest relatives. Alain's half-brothers and his own sisters had already been provided for, but a younger brother seems to have accepted much less than he would have got according to the custom of Brittany which was one of the least generous customs in its provision for younger children. It is also probably relevant that the custom of Brittany did not allow entails. Alain IX had agreed to his father's declaration and seems to have provided for his children and to have dowered his wives from lands not in the settlement, though some were mortgaged. In 1527 the patrimony was finally split between two sisters when the last layman of the five sons of Jean II (son of Alain IX) died without issue.[206]

The Vergy family, seneschals of the county of Burgundy, used entails, renunciations and wills to limit and postpone inheritance by females and to concentrate the inheritance on to collateral males who would have been excluded in many Castilian *mayorazgos*, though they also used the device of marrying the female heir of the main line to a collateral male. Most of the younger sons and

[205] In his first testament of 1341 two younger sons were given land, two were to become priests, two knights of St John, four daughters were given portions, one was to enter religion. In the event two sons and a daughter died, one son became a Franciscan and two daughters nuns. R. Boutruche, *op. cit.*, pp. 387–8, 493–514, and see above p. 256.

[206] One of these daughters and heirs of Jean II married Louis de Rohan-Guemené of a cadet branch established in 1380. I am deeply indebted to Michael Jones of the University of Nottingham for providing me with this information. The declaration of 1423 is Bibliothèque municipale, Nantes, MS 1690, no. ii.

daughters who came of age married.[207] Some of the younger sons, notably Anthoine, son of Jean III (d. 1418), a leading servant of Philip the Bold, were very generously endowed with lands. Jean III's son, Guillaume, predeceased him and in 1399 he entailed some property on Guillaume's widow for life, then on her son Jean IV and his heirs male, remainder to Anthoine and his heirs male, remainder to 'the males of my house' and the nearest 'descended from my side [costal] and line' of whatever degree, provided he used '*mon Cry* and right arms'. This entail seems to have been ignored in the partition between uncle and nephew after Jean III's death, but it was invoked and increased by Anthoine in his will when he died childless in 1439.[208]

The Vergys' arrangements probably did not override customary law to the same extent as the d'Albrets', and certainly not to the extent of *mayorazgos*. The main instruments were renunciations by daughters, though some did not cover collateral succession, they probably became more complete later.[209] A principal occasion of conflict was diminished by two of the contenders lacking issue.[210] In 1452 Jean IV made an agreement, ratified by the duke, with Charles, grandson of a younger brother of Jean III, to settle their main inheritance in tail male with remainders to each other. They claimed that

> their predecessors were ever mindful to maintain the estate and honour of their name . . . by leaving their principal lordships successively to those bearing their name and arms . . . without allowing that . . . their lands . . . should go to daughters . . . or any not bearing the said name and arms, even though they ought to be their heirs . . .

Charles had also promised Anthoine who had died in 1439 that if his only son Anthoine left only a daughter (as in fact he did) he

[207] André du Chesne, *Histoire Généalogique de la Maison de Vergy* (Paris, 1628), pp. 200–70. They produced an archbishop of Besançon in the late fourteenth century (son of Jean II) and another in the early sixteenth (son of Guillaume IV).

[208] *Ibid.*, pp. 192, 206, 209, 272–5.

[209] The renunciation of Marie, daughter of Jean III, in 1390, did not apply if her brothers died without heirs male, Marguerite, sister of Jean IV, was heir to some of the lands, *ibid.*, pp. 267, 203, *preuves*, pp. 275–6, 328.

[210] Jean, count of Fribourg, the son of Jean III's daughter Marie and Jean IV challenged the entails and will of Anthoine, son of Jean III, in favour of Charles, seigneur d'Autrey and claimed as heirs of Anthoine by the custom of Burgundy, *ibid.*, pp. 262–3.

would marry her to a male cousin. Despite Philip the Good's demand for her to marry his nephew, Jacques, son of Charles II, duke of Bourbon, this was accomplished in 1469 when she married Guillaume IV, grandson of a younger brother of Charles' grandfather.[211]

The house of Montmorency faced the same problem when the eldest son of Guillaume (d. 1527) predeceased his father, leaving a daughter, who died young. When Guillaume arranged the partition of his and his wife's inheritances in 1522, another son Philip, bishop of Limoges, was also dead; the second surviving son, François, was generously provided for and the barony of Montmorency was entailed on his elder brother Anne, the future duke and Constable, in male primogeniture, with remainder to the male line of François, with a charge to pay 30,000 livres to any female heirs of Anne. Anne himself had four sons all of whom married and seven daughters, four married and three nuns. In 1563 he apportioned his and his wife's lands among his children. His eldest son François had much more land than in 1522 entailed to go with the duchy, with provision for appanages out of it for François' second and third sons, reverting back to the main entail, if they had no issue. There were successive remainders to Anne's younger sons, if male heirs of the eldest failed, with provision in land for female heirs. If his unmarried daughter had not been married, when Anne died, she was to have her legitim only. If any son disputed the arrangements, he was to receive only his legitim and customary share of goods, while his share of the partition would be equally divided among the others.[212]

---

[211] *Ibid.*, pp. 268–75, *preuves*, pp. 327–8. The daughter, Marguerite, married Guillaume IV in 1469 and died without issue in 1472 willing her property to him and his heirs male. His eldest son predeceased him leaving an only daughter so that the inheritance went to his second son.

[212] A. du Chesne, *Histoire Généalogique de la Maison de Montmorency et de Laval* (Paris, 1624), pp. 351–458, *preuves*, pp. 271–4, 290–4. The 1522 entail provided that if François' male line failed, the barony would revert to the female heirs of Anne. François had no issue. Some lands were also entailed on Anne for life with reversion to his second son (*ibid.*, p. 369, *preuves*, p. 291). The eldest son's daughter received 2,000 livres of rent in her marriage contract in 1518, but she died before the marriage (*ibid.*, pp. 376–7). The 1563 settlement provided that if the younger sons succeeded to the entail, free lands were allocated for heirs general of the eldest son; those of the younger sons were to have the lands settled originally on each younger son, which would go to the next youngest, if a younger son succeeded to the entail and had male heirs.

The Montmorencys increased their wealth, as well as their rank and status in the sixteenth century as a result of royal favour. Such favour provided honours and commands for the younger sons and contributed to the marriage portions given and received. Anne also added to his lands by purchase, so that he could afford both to add to the entail and to endow his younger sons generously. The problems of course came when families were no longer expanding their wealth and power.[213] Moreover, entails were not confined to great families. They were generally used by lesser nobles in the south from at least the fifteenth century and they were increasingly adopted elsewhere by nobles and non-nobles.[214]

The major problem caused by entails, as with uses in England, was uncertainty of title. The way in which they should descend was often disputed within families, as with *mayorazgos*, while purchasers and creditors found themselves deprived of their rights, if they bought entailed property or lent money on its security. From the fourteenth century there had been constant disputes about interpreting the common condition in *substitutions* of 'dying without legitimate male children' (*absque libero seu liberis masculis a suo corpore legitime procreatis*). For example if a man entailed lands on his brother so that if the brother died fulfilling this condition, the entail went to the testator's daughters successively under the same condition, what happened if the brother left a grandson by an only daughter? Many jurists in the fourteenth, fifteenth and sixteenth centuries held that the entail went to the brother's grandson, but many others held that it went back to the testator's

---

213 *Ibid., preuves*, pp. 276–7, 283, 289, 300–1, 303, 315–16; Anne received 50,000 livres with his wife and was promised as much more by Francis I; his eldest son married Henry II's bastard Diane with 50,000 *écus d'or* and his second son married the grand-daughter of Diane de Poitiers with 100,000 livres. Three of Anne's daughters received portions of 50,000 livres and the fourth 70,000. François' successor, Henri, gave his daughters by his first wife, his only son by her having died unmarried, 150,000 *écus* in 1593 and 1601. In 1609 a daughter by his second wife married Condé with 300,000 livres from her father, the reversion of 5,000 livres of land a year from her uncle and 150,000 livres from Henry IV. Louis, Duc d'Aumâle, *Histoire des Princes de Condé*, ii (Paris, 1864), pp. 442–5.

214 This refers to *substitutions graduelles*, intended to extend over several generations. By the seventeenth century *substitutions* were widely used by much poorer groups in Toulouse, including craftsmen and artisans, but these were limited to one or two degrees, charging a wife to render the entailed property to a son, or a son to a grandson, or were *substitutions compendieuses*, Augustin, Thesis, pp. 22–3, 31–2, 270–1, 340–9.

daughters.[215] With eminent authorities on both sides, it was usually worth disputing such inheritances.

Thus Guillaume de Vienne, knight of the Golden Fleece, in his will of 1434 apparently entailed Arc-en-Barrois on the border of Burgundy and Champagne on the male line of his son Guillaume, with various remainders. Guillaume junior's son Jean died without issue, leaving a sister as his nearest heir; two of those in remainder had left no male issue, so the entail went to a collateral Guillaume de Vienne of Montbis (d. 1471). His great grandson François made his sister's son Antoine de Bauffremont his heir, on condition of bearing his name and arms in 1537. This was challenged by direct male descendants of a younger son of Guillaume of Montbis. Litigation continued until after 1587, but eventually the de Bauffremont title was upheld. What is significant is the length of the litigation and the length of the entail. Charles Du Moulin gave his opinion that the entail had run out since it had exceeded the four degrees specified by Justinian's Novel 159,[216] though on another occasion he offered the opinion, more in line with accepted practice, that in the countries of written law there were no limitations on entails in the direct line.[217]

The outcome of the case may have been influenced by the legislation of 1566 limiting the length of entails. This was obviously in response to growing complaints about the inconvenience of entails and the Ordinance of Orléans in 1561, restricting future entails to two degrees after institution, spoke of it 'cutting off at the root numbers of suits'. The Ordinance of Moulins in 1566 restricted entails before 1561 to four degrees and provided that future ones

[215] For such a case arising from the will of Humbert Alamandi, seigneur of Aubonne and Coppet in Vaudois, in 1351, J.-F. Poudret, 'Consultation de Juristes et Coutumiers par le Comte Amédée VII de Savoie au sujet de l'interprétation d'une substitution fidéicommissaire', *Receuil . . . d'Histoire . . . des Anciens Pays du Droit Ecrit*, fasc. ix (1974), pp. 637–50. In 1390 the adepts of customary law supported the testator's grandson, the jurists his brother's grandson; for other jurists' opinions, *ibid.*, pp. 646–50.

[216] R. Filhol, 'Une Consultation de Charles Dumoulin relative à la seigneurie d'Arc-en-Barrois', *Revue Hist. de Droit français et étranger*, 4th ser., xxvii (1949), pp. 122–32. There was also a question of fact at issue, whether Arc was included in the original entail.

[217] *Opera* (Paris, 1612) iii, col. 2493, Consil. 51 '. . . ultra quantum gradum et in infinitum providere quod in linea directa usu receptum est in Insubria et Gallia, quae iure scripto regitur, ubi clare de mente et verbis constat'. This opinion was given in 1546, that in n. 215 is unfortunately undated. Arc was within the area of Burgundian customary law.

would only be valid if publicly registered within six months of their creation.[218] At the same time an edict laid down that lands attached to duchies created henceforth would escheat to the crown, if the holder died without heirs male.[219] Seemingly royal authority had drastically modified the way in which landowners, especially great nobles, had settled their estates.

The actual results are not easy to determine even in terms of how the courts reacted, still less in those of effects on family settlements, creditors and the land market. At first the limitation of four degrees seems to have been applied to new entails as well as old.[220] The Parlements disagreed as to whether degrees should be reckoned by heads (the number of individuals succeeding to the entail) or by *souches* (generations of a family succeeding). The Parlement of Paris by the early seventeenth century took the narrowest interpretation of two degrees by counting heads, that of Toulouse the widest one of four degrees by generations, despite the Code Michau's enactment of the former rule in 1629. The 1629 code's prohibition of making of entails by 'rustics' was only accepted by one Parlement, that of Dijon.[221] It was generally agreed that the provisions for registration ordained in 1566 were ignored, but the implication of the 1690 declaration is that the courts still treated such entails as valid.[222] The ordinances of 1566 did not apply in provinces, not then part of the realm, such as Béarn and Franche-Comté. Moreover, perpetual entails were allowed for *duchés-paires* and might be granted to favoured individuals by the crown.[223]

[218] Jourdan, Decrasy, Isambert, *Recueil général des Anciennes Lois Françaises*, 27 vols (Paris, 1823–33), xiv, pp. 80 (Moulins, art. 59), 204 (Orléans, art. 57).

[219] J. P. Labatut, *Les Ducs et Pairs de France au XVIIᵉ Siècle* (Paris, 1972), p. 61. An edict of 1582 stipulated that the lands attached to a new *duché-paire* must amount to 8,000 *écus* annual revenue.

[220] Ourliac and De Malafosse, *Histoire du droit privé*, iii, pp. 528–9.

[221] Augustin, Thesis, pp. 39–41; Bordeaux counted by heads and accepted four degrees. Mousnier, *Les Institutions de la France*, i, pp. 66–7.

[222] Laurens Bouchal, *La Bibliothèque ou Thresor du Droit François*, nouv. ed. Jean Bechefer (Paris, 1677), iii, p. 565; *Recueil des anciennes Lois françaises*, xx, p. 113.

[223] P. Viollet, *Précis de l'Histoire du Droit Français, Sources – Droit Privé* (Paris, 1886), p. 759. For an example, letters patent of 1701 confirming 'donation et substitution masculine graduelle et perpetuelle à l'infini en faveur des aînés de la Maison de Mailly-Néelle' of lands of 40,000 *écus* revenue attached to the marquisat of Néelle, to Louis Charles de Mailly, prince d'Orange, Anselme, *Histoire Généalogique...*, vii, p. 638. For entails by dukes and peers, Labatut, *op. cit.*, pp. 239–42.

This accorded with the traditional view that entails were part of the appurtenances of great noble houses introduced to 'preserve more enduringly the name, arms and property in the family and to avoid the property being lost and consumed by the prodigality, crime and disaster of daughters or undeserving heirs', to which was added the view that only property worth more than a certain amount should be entailed and would justify the expenses involved.[224] By the sixteenth century courts and jurists had created a system of presumptive interpretation which allowed the extending of entails or their virtual creation by presuming the intention of a testator or donor. This cherishing of entails certainly contrasts with the attitude of English common law courts and has some analogy to the doctrine of *favor del mayorazgo* developed in the sixteenth century. Cujas listed three reasons for presumption, an expressed preference for males over females, belonging to a family of ancient nobility, a family custom of making such entails, to which Du Moulin added prohibition of alienation, inclusion of conditions of taking the name and arms and the redoubling of conditions, 'if my son dies without issue, or his children without children'. To infer an entail Cujas required several of these, Du Moulin only one, while the Parlements differed in their requirements and constructions.[225] These conjectures were a notorious cause of litigation and uncertainty. In using them to infer entails, jurists were favouring the interests of the family against creditors, and often of the direct line against collaterals and ascendants, of males against females.

In so far as entails did preserve family property, they did so by restricting the power of the possessor of the entail to dispose of part of that property and so were a restriction on paternal authority. As we have seen this was at its greatest in the south, where

---

[224] L. Bouchel, *op. cit.*, p. 567, proposing a minimum of 2,000 *écus*, or 10,000 livres; Bernabe de la Roche Flavin had also proposed 2,000 *écus* in 1617, Augustin, Thesis, p. 209.

[225] J. A. Sallé, *L'Esprit des Ordonnances . . . de Louis XV* (Paris, 1771), pp. 272–4. The classic instance is where a father made a substitution if his son died without children, but if instead the son had children, would the property then be entailed on them? 'Si les enfants étant dans la condition, sont présumés compris dans la disposition'. The Parlement of Toulouse did not admit conjectures based on the family's nobility or on family custom, but any one of the others sufficed to put the children in the disposition; all four of the others were needed to presume a *substitution graduelle*, Augustin, Thesis, pp. 191–5.

freedom of testation was not limited as it was in varying degrees by customary law in the north and west. Just as entails had flourished in the south along with paternal power in testaments, so in the sixteenth century jurists favoured paternal power as well as entails. Professor Mousnier has argued that this was part of a process of transition from a wider conception of the family based on the lineage to a narrow one of the conjugal family, a household separated from the lineage; beginning in the thirteenth century this was completed in the seventeenth and eighteenth centuries. However this may be, there is no doubt that the theoretical exaltation of paternal authority led to an increase in legal powers, notably in controlling marriages of sons under the age of thirty and of daughters under twenty-five, on pain of total disinheritance, while the courts were eager to reinforce powers of discipline over recalcitrant sons.[226]

If the influence of Roman law by the sixteenth century had promoted the growth of entails and so a sense of property belonging to a lineage rather than to an individual, it not only reinforced paternal power, but also weakened the effects of renunciations by daughters married with portions, or of their exclusion by some customs. As we have seen, renunciations were one of the most important means of checking division of inheritances. As pacts concerning future succession, they were invalid in classical Roman law; their proliferation was due to doctrines of canon law. They conflicted with rights of legitim, another legacy of Rome. Already in 1346 Jean d'Armagnac in his will left his daughter a portion in lieu of all her right of inheritance; if she claimed a supplement to the portion as legitim, she was to be paid cash and would lose the benefit of the entails in his will. Normally a daughter renouncing at marriage, or excluded by will, could not claim legitim, nor could her children re-enter the succession if she predeceased her parents.[227]

---

[226] Mousnier, *Les Institutions de la France*, i, pp. 73–8, 56–60. The legislation belongs to 1556, 1566, 1579 and 1639 (when disinheritance was extended to the issue of marriages made without parental consent). Consent was also required for entry into religion until twenty for girls and twenty-five for men. Cf. Ourliac and Malafosse, *op. cit.*, iii, pp. 524–5.

[227] Poumarède, *Les Successions . . .* , pp. 168–77, 170 n. 26 (d'Armagnac's will), 176 n. 44 marriage contract of Gaston de Foix and Béatrix d'Armagnac, 1379, renouncing paternal and maternal inheritances, *legitima* and supplement.

By the fifteenth century Provence allowed a daughter to sue if she had lost heavily by renouncing. Bordeaux moved hesitantly in this direction in the sixteenth century. But the most startling change was at Toulouse where the custom of 1286 had excluded *filles dotées*. There by the late sixteenth century a daughter could claim a supplement, if the legitim of the father's estate was less than the portion given, even if she had renounced, provided that she had suffered considerable loss. The Parlement of Bordeaux took a more hesitant and contradictory line, while the Parlement of Paris decided a case in favour of the supplement in 1666 for Périgord and Limousin.[228] The customs of the centre (Berry, Orléans, Chartres) allowed actions for the supplement, those of the West did not. The right was generalized by the ordinance of 1735.[229]

As we have seen the legislative will to restrict entails was not enforced effectively until the eighteenth century and there was great variety in interpretation by the courts. The ultimate tendency was again restrictive, culminating in Daguesseau's ordinance of 1747, which confined entails to two degrees, disallowed conjectures and allowed some entails to be broken. Before pursuing the reaction against them, we must try to discern their nature and effects. The interpretations of the Parlement of Toulouse meant that entails might last two hundred years,[230] those of the Parlement of Paris might give only twenty or thirty years and at most the lives of a father, his son and unborn grandson, perhaps fifty years. The entail could then be renewed, but the property in it was tied up for about the same period as in an English strict settlement. These limitations and the variations of local customary law should have induced great noble families to settle major parts of their estates according to their own traditions of succession by securing royal grants of perpetual entails, but the extent to which this was done still requires to be investigated.[231] The proportion of entailed to

---

[228] J. Maillet, 'De l'Exclusion Coutumière des Filles Dotées à la Renonciation à succession future dans les Coutumes de Toulouse et Bordeaux', *Rev. Hist. de Droit Fr. et Etranger*, 4th ser., xxx (1952), pp. 514–544.

[229] Ourliac et Malafosse, *op. cit.*, iii, p. 492.

[230] Augustin, Thesis, p. 46. This is based on eighteenth-century expectations of life.

[231] Unfortunately Labatut's book gives scarcely any details of the entails used by the dukes and peers, still less the proportion of entailed property in their estates, though he does show that the property directly attached to the peerages was often half or less of their land, *op. cit.*, pp. 267, 285–8.

unentailed land, the way in which this varied over time, the relationships between the pattern of family settlement and local
custom are all further areas of ignorance. Professor Forster's study
of the Saulx-Tavanes could mark the beginning of the sort of studies
needed to dispel it.

Although this concentrates on their fortunes after entering the
ranks of the court nobility in the mid eighteenth century, it shows
a change from generous endowment of younger children in the
late sixteenth century to a policy of entailing the main paternal
inheritance.[232] Families long established among *les Grands* still
settled as much as possible of their property intact for the eldest
son, while leaving the other children their legitim in order to 'preserve the splendour and dignity of the house', as did the duke of
Bouillon in 1718, while the duke of Noailles traced his family's
entail in male primogeniture back to 1248. But 'the grandeur of
the house' could also be sustained by 'founding a second branch',
as the duke of La Rochefoucauld put it in settling the duchy of
La Rocheguyon on his younger son in 1715, though it probably
was much commoner to provide for younger sons out of the
maternal inheritance.[233]

Entails never overrode the rights to legitim in the way that was
allowed by Castilian jurists' interpretations of *mayorazgos*. But
the tendency had been there for the Parlements of the countries
of written law had originally held that if a father's testament included a younger son in an entail after his elder brother and failed
to institute him for his legitim, he had no right to contest it.[234] The
effects of reversing this view and of allowing daughters who had
renounced to sue for supplements weakened the effectiveness of
entails in concentrating the inheritance on the eldest son by the
eighteenth century and before.[235] For the entailed lands to continue
undiminished, it was essential for there to be free property also

[232] R. Forster, *The House of Saulx-Tavanes Versailles and Burgundy
1700–1830* (Baltimore, 1971).
[233] Labatut, *op. cit.*, pp. 240–1. The Noailles entail provided for descent
through a female, if the male line failed, provided her husband and their
eldest son took the name and arms without additions.
[234] Augustin, Thesis, p. 177; it is not clear whether this rule had been
changed before the eighteenth century.
[235] R. Forster, *The Nobility of Toulouse in the Eighteenth Century*
(Baltimore, 1960), pp. 134–6 gives an extreme case where a daughter
obtained 109,000 *livres* in supplements to a portion of 130,000 *livres* contracted in 1722. The supplements were still being paid to her son in 1772.

in the inheritance. For the heir had the right to subtract from the entail various costs such as repairs and legal charges, the legitim (including his own) and supplement of dower and restitution of portion to widows was also chargeable, if there was not enough free property available. If debts accumulated so that they exceeded the value of the entail it could be sold.[236] In certain circumstances legacies and debts in the succession could be subtracted from the entail.[237]

Augustin rightly remarks that the maintenance of entails largely depended on the good will of the younger children, who, instead of insisting on their legal rights of immediate payment of their portions, allowed payment by instalments, or even renounced for the sake of the head of the family. Moreover, as in twelfth-century Mâconnais, few younger brothers married, so that their portions usually returned to the family, while among the middling nobility only one daughter commonly married. Forster reckoned the average portion of a daughter of the middling nobility of Toulouse was between three and four years' income which seems high by English standards and helps to explain why so many remained unmarried.[238] As a third of the estate went as legitim (if there were four or fewer children), this would explain why it was apparently usual only to entail half the estate.[239] By the eighteenth century younger children at Toulouse were more favourably treated than by the noble customs of Brittany, Normandy, the Bordelais and much of western France[240] and approximately as well as by the custom of Burgundy,

---

[236] Augustin, Thesis, pp. 260–2, 303–7; M. Argou, *Institution du Droit François*, 11th edn corr. A. G. Goucher d'Argis (Paris, 1787), i, p. 367. The deductions (*distractions*) could be even greater if the beneficiary was allowed to claim the Trebellian and/or Falcidian quarters, but it was normal for testators to prohibit this, Augustin, p. 251.

[237] This would apply at the first creation of the entail, when the holder (*grevé*) took from the donor by testament. If the entail was made by marriage contract, which did not institute him as heir, or by donation, or by an earlier testament, the next in remainder of the entail might refuse a testamentary succession which would make him liable for heavy debts.

[238] Augustin, Thesis, p. 307; Forster, *Toulouse*, pp. 126–30, 132.

[239] Assuming three children (and the average family of children surviving to maturity was nearer four, *ibid.*, p. 128, Table VIII) and valuing land at twenty years' purchase, the legitim of each would be 2.1 years' revenue, so that the total cost of legitim and marrying one daughter with a portion of four years' revenue would be 9.5 years' revenue, or at three years 8.5; at twenty-five years' purchase the figures would be 10.9 and 9.9 respectively.

[240] J. Meyer, *La Noblesse Bretonne au XVIII Siècle*, i, pp. 121–7.

but their position had been potentially much less favourable down to the late sixteenth century and perhaps later for younger sons.

Augustin shows that there was a decline in the use of *substitutions graduelles* by the nobility after 1712, though he admits that many of the greater families continued to use them in the traditional way. What seems particularly significant is that whereas the high robe of the sixteenth and seventeenth centuries had imitated the old nobility in using them for their lands, new nobles were less likely to do so in the eighteenth century. Indeed no *substitutions graduelles* were made by the richest groups in Toulouse after 1765, though of course older entails remained in force and simpler forms, such as the *substitution compendieuse* remained fairly popular.[241] The Ordinance of 1747 restricted entails, empowered the courts to break entails made by testament for the payment of debts, though this did not apply to those made by donations and marriage contracts, and set up elaborate and expensive procedures for registration and supervision by the courts. But at Toulouse the decline of entails antedated the Ordinance, physiocratic demands for free trade and assertion of absolute rights of individual ownership, and the changes in religious practices which can be seen after the mid eighteenth century.

The turning point seems to have been the declaration of 1712, which at last enforced more effective registration of entails and made unpublished ones invalid. This in turn completed efforts which had been renewed in 1690 and 1704, as a result of complaints of defrauded creditors and purchasers who found they had no title. Such complaints had already been at the origin of the sixteenth-century ordinances; more recently Savary had warned lenders to beware of borrowers whose property was entailed, yet the ordinances had remained unenforced. Was it simply that increasing extravagance and indebtedness of the nobility had led to creditors being able to protect their interests through a bankrupt monarchy, itself dependent on manipulators of credit? Without claiming that luxury and extravagance diminished among the great nobility, the hypothesis

---

[241] Augustin, Thesis, pp. 23, 275–8, 282–6, 291–3, 308. The sketch given by F. Bluche, *La Vie Quotidienne de la Noblesse Française au XVIIIe Siècle* (Paris, 1973), pp. 204–9, is probably nearer to a generalization about the provincial nobility in which the decline of entails at Toulouse was exceptional.

that the situation had been roughly comparable to what apparently happened in Castile after 1630 is a tempting one in the present state of ignorance.

For there is increasing evidence for a decline in revenues from land from about 1680 in the south and somewhat earlier in the north. South of the Loire the crisis of the middle of the century had been less severe, but in both south and north, despite fluctuations, revenues in the first half of the century had recovered from the slump of the late sixteenth century and had sometimes reached new heights. The fall in the later seventeenth century was accompanied by increasing fiscal pressures, by the economic and demographic disasters of the 1690s and the first decade of the eighteenth century, and by falling production, population and volume of transactions. Agricultural production and revenues at constant prices fell by about a quarter between the 1670s and the second decade of the eighteenth century in most regions, with variations above this of up to a third and a half and below it to 15 per cent for the Parisian region. The only exceptions seem to be Alsace and Burgundy whose recovery from the devastations of the mid seventeenth century was not seriously interrupted. In Languedoc the number of notarial acts fell from 1690 and reached a minimum from 1709 to 1717.[242]

The pressure on the net revenue of nobles whose provision for their younger children usually required considerable borrowing and mortgaging must have been severe. As land values fell, even those who had never intended to defraud their creditors would find their income and their unentailed property inadequate security for their debts. At any rate the enforcement of the registration of entails in 1712 coincides with the nadir of agricultural rents and incomes in Languedoc and in most of France. If creditors got some solace from registration, solace for at least some of their debtors came with Law's system which enabled them to pay off mortgages and obligations cheaply and which raised the price of land.[243] Rents rose again after 1720 or 1730, while long-term interest rates

---

[242] E. Le Roy Ladurie and J. Goy, 'Première Esquisse d'une conjuncture du produit décimal et domanial. Fin du Moyen Age–XVIII° siècle', in J. Goy and E. Le Roy Ladurie (eds), *Les Fluctuations du Produit de la dîme* (Paris, 1972), pp. 362–7; E. Le Roy Ladurie, *Les Paysans de Languedoc* (Paris, 1966), pp. 528–37.

[243] P. Deyon, *Amiens capitale provinciale* (Paris, 1967), pp. 336–8.

fell. In the region of Toulouse the return on land was higher then than that on *rentes* by 1765 and probably much earlier.[244] Thus the decline of *substitutions graduelles* at Toulouse may be partly a response to the way in which they had probably impaired landowners' credit and ability to cope flexibly with the crisis of the last years of Louis XIV and were found inappropriate to the period of rising rents and land values after 1720. However, not all noble families, especially those belonging to the greater nobility, abandoned them. The region of Toulouse was one with an exceptionally highly commercialized agriculture and land market, based on grain production by relatively large farms, so that to generalize from its experience in the eighteenth century to that of other regions would be rash.

Even less precise information is available about how great nobles settled their estates in the eighteenth century, but, as we have seen, the presumption is that they continued whatever tradition of entailing existed in the family.[245] In the case of the Saulx-Tavanes most of their Burgundian estate was entailed on males before the creation of the duchy. After the creation of the duchy all except about 3,000 *livres* of the estimated gross Burgundian revenues were entailed. But the Norman lands, the maternal inheritance of the first duke, accounting for 27 per cent of receipts from land in 1788, were apparently free and were sold to pay debts in 1789–91. It looks as though the Saulx-Tavanes entailed a higher proportion of their land than provincial nobles at Toulouse. They had the resource of a considerable income from royal appointments and pensions, 47 per cent of their receipts from land in 1788, though this was doubtless more than counterbalanced by maintaining necessary splendour at Versailles. The main means of preserving an entailed patrimony throughout the eighteenth century and

---

[244] G. Frêche, *Toulouse et la region Midi-Pyrenées au siècle des lumières, vers 1670–1789* (Paris, 1974), pp. 568–72; land yielded over 4.25 per cent in 1765.

[245] J. Meyer, *La Noblesse Bretonne*, p. 127, says the greatest families, including the court nobility and some of the high robe, adopted the custom of Paris in their marriage contracts to regulate their successions, though he admits, notes 8 and 9, that this affected the common property of the marriage, not the inheritances. Unfortunately he says nothing more about the latter outside Brittany. For an example of a marriage contract establishing a community under the custom of Paris, and also containing entails in male primogeniture, see that of Mazarin's niece. G. Livet, *Le Duc Mazarin, Gouverneur d'Alsace* (Paris, 1954), pp. 15–16.

before was by marrying heiresses and disposing of their inheritances.[246]

Yet the Saulx-Tavanes only seem to have begun to follow or resumed a policy of concentrating their patrimony on the eldest son under Louis XIII. In the late sixteenth century they seem to follow the pattern of a Burghley in endowing younger sons.[247] Whether or not they were typical of the court nobility of the eighteenth century in the proportions of land they entailed, they were in their dependence on royal favour for a substantial part of their income.[248] At a lower level of wealth and status the careers of the eldest sons of the family of Gerrard de Béarn, whose lands were in Angoumois and Perigord, were linked with the army and the Court from the sixteenth century to 1789. From the sixteenth century the inheritance was concentrated on the eldest sons by entails and dispositions which provided the sisters with husbands from the local nobility, while only six out of twenty-one younger sons married. The value of their estates was 200,000 *livres* about 1600 and 800,000 in 1788. The estate grew by marriage and by exercising rights of *retrait lignagier*, while the Court connection did not produce crippling debts.[249]

At the level of the Saulx-Tavanes and above there were other families who also accumulated debts and failed to invest or use any of the perquisites gained at Court for productive purposes. But some of the greatest beneficiaries for pensions and places, the princes of the blood, Conti, Condé, Artois, Orléans, were directly involved in industry and mining. The most spectacular though scarcely typical examples of entrepreneurship and investment

[246] R. Forster, *The House of Saulx-Tavanes*, pp. 51, 107, 135–7, 217–18, 220.

[247] Forster, *op. cit.*, pp. 2–7; Marshal Gaspard de Saulx (d. 1579), the refounder of the family fortune, failed to take his own advice and endowed his younger children very generously.

[248] F. C. Mougel, 'La Fortune des Princes de Bourbon-Conty, Revenues et Gestion 1655–1791', *Revue d'Histoire Moderne et Contemporaine*, xvi (1969), p. 37; pensions were just under a third of the fortune in 1670 and 1753, over a fifth in 1783. D. Roche, 'La fortune et les revenues des Princes de Condé à l'aube du XVIIIᵉ siècle, *ibid.* xiv (1967), p. 45; offices and pensions amounted to 45 per cent of their total receipts. F. Bluche, *La Vie Quotidienne . . .* , pp. 98–105.

[249] J. P. Labatut, 'La famille Gerard de Béarn sons l'Ancien Regime', *Etudes Européenes Mélanges offerts à V.-L. Tapié* (Paris, 1973), pp. 322–8, 6 out of 21 younger sons married, 5 were *abbés* or canons, 5 were soldiers and 11 'vivent noblement sur les domaines'.

among *les Grands* are the prince of Croy with the Anzin company and the duke of La Rochefoucauld-Liancourt's multifarious interests in textiles and agricultural improvements.[250] Indeed it could be argued that at the end of the *Ancien Régime*, there was as much direct involvement in industry and mining on the part of the high nobility in France as in England and that in the textile and iron industries there was perhaps more.[251]

At the very end of the eighteenth century some of the greatest Castilian grandees had been concerned in projects for a company to build canals. But there was more evidence of enlightened theorizing than of active enterprise and productive investment.[252] They remained what they had become in the early seventeenth century, a court nobility, dependent on royal favour for their economic survival until rising rents and land values in the eighteenth century made their presence in Madrid more a matter of custom and choice than of sheer necessity. The similar dependence of the great French nobles had been visibly institutionalized at Versailles, but pensions and places of profit had played a vital part in the fortunes of great families, such as Montmorency, Condé and Noailles long before. Perroy observed that the duke of Bourbon, at the end of the fifteenth century, had receipts totalling about 90,000 *livres*, but that barely half of this came from his domains; 'all the rest came from royal gifts: regular pensions, offices . . . Throughout the century this had been so, as in all the princely appanages.' The dukes had maintained pressure on the crown to secure such grants by joining all the coalitions of princes between 1410 and 1484.[253] At Versailles the same ends could be pursued by court intrigues, by plotting with royal mistresses, rather than with rebellious magnates, though court factions did sway both domestic and foreign policies.

As we have seen the great nobles of fifteenth-century Castile had been less dependent on the crown, more able to annex its

---

[250] G. Richard, *Noblesse d'Affaires au XVIIIᵉ Siècle* (Paris, 1974), pp. 130–1, 134–6, 139–40, 190, 192–3, 202–5; F. Bluche, *op. cit.*, pp. 106–10.

[251] Great nobles ceased direct participation in the iron industry in England in the first half of the seventeenth century.

[252] A. Domínguez Ortíz, *La Sociedad Española en el Siglo XVIII* (Madrid, 1955), pp. 90–1; the Economic Societies were the resort of provincial nobles, R. Carr, *Spain 1808–1939* (Oxford, 1966), pp. 39–42; G. Anes, *Las Crisis Agrarias en la España moderna* (Madrid, 1970), pp. 289–91, 429–431.

[253] E. Perroy, 'L'Etat Bourbonnais' in *Histoire des Institutions Françaises au Moyen Age*, eds F. Lot and R. Fawtier (Paris, 1957), i, pp. 316–17.

jurisdictional powers and fiscal rights apparently lastingly for their own purposes, but their successors found themselves almost wholly dependent on court influence and ceremonials sooner than their compeers in France. From the late sixteenth century they were protected from the consequences of their own fecklessness to a greater extent than in France. There the interests of lenders were given increasing consideration by the monarchy and the courts from the late seventeenth century onwards, while earlier those interests had not been so deliberately sacrificed as in Castile. Large sales of land to meet debts were possible in France to an extent that was not apparently conceivable in Castile.

The preamble to the ordinance of 1747 invoked the assurance of liberty of commerce as requiring public registration of entails. It denied the traditional justification of long entails 'as preserving the patrimony of families and the lustre of the most illustrious houses'. Instead endless suits, renewed at each descent, about interpreting the founder's intentions, the rights of wives to dower and of subtracting charges, have often ruined families. The ordinance reduced entails to approximately the effective length of the English strict settlement, apart from the special privileges of great nobles. The length and multiplicity of suits are undeniable. Indeed, one of the singularities of French entails is that, unlike sixteenth-century English perpetuities or *mayorazgos*, an alienation by the possessor did not put in the next in remainder; he was left to sue the purchaser when the seller died.[254] The effect must have been to increase litigation and uncertainty of title. As we have seen, an entail of itself could not prevent a patrimony from diminishing, unless it was supported by adequate free property and cooperation by the younger children. The example of the ancient family of Rigaud de Vaudreuil shows that they had twenty seigneuries in the Lauragois in 1450, in 1789 they had only three. Yet a perpetual entail had repeatedly saved these three, including Vaudreuil itself, from executions and forced sales in the seventeenth and eighteenth centuries.[255]

Legal and enlightened opinion grew more hostile to entails and favoured eldest sons in the eighteenth century. Dagusseau thought that ideally entails should be abolished altogether, not reformed and restricted. It was increasingly alleged that they inhibited pro-

254 J. Brissaud, *A History of French Private Law* (London, 1912), p. 730.
255 G. Frêche, *op. cit.*, pp. 377–8.

ductive investment in land, but how far this can be substantiated is as yet unknown. However, the survival of entails and of *retrait lignagier* must have affected the land market and were incompatible with individualistic conceptions of property rights. The Convention in 1792 abolished *substitutions*, restricted donations, and imposed equal partitions of parental property among the children. The Civil Code restored the father's power to advantage one of his children, but limited the amount to between a quarter and a half of the inheritance, according to the number of children and allowed entails of one degree to the children, born or unborn, of a relative of the testator. The Code can be seen as a generalizing of the principles of non-noble successions according to the custom of Paris. But in 1806 and 1808 Napoleon restored and strengthened perpetual entails in male primogeniture under the supervision of the *Conseil d'Etat*. These were of two sorts, one granted by Napoleon to his imperial nobility out of lands in conquered territories. The other was founded on their own lands at the request of individual owners. Both were inalienable, could not be seized for debt and were perpetually transmissable without testament. They were finally abolished in 1849 and the neo-Harringtonian tradition, transmitted through Montesquieu, triumphed over entails and primogeniture.[256]

Long before equal partition of inheritances had been identified as a foundation of republican virtue, St Bernard had held that it was appropriate for merchants, though not for nobles.[257] The Fuggers applied this principle to their landed property in the sixteenth century.[258] Most of the French farmers general of the eighteenth century probably did likewise, though a minority favoured their eldest sons,[259] as we have seen London merchants increasingly

[256] J. Godechot, *Les Institutions de la France sous La Revolution et L'Empire* (Paris, 1968), pp. 436–8, 661–2; see above notes 4, 8, 11, pp. 194, 195. For the survival and revival of one province's nobles, C. Brelot, *La Noblesse en Franche Comté de 1789 à 1806* (Paris, 1972), pp. 119–50.

[257] L. de Molina, *De Primogeniorum Hispanorum Origine* (Lyons, 1672), p. 115.

[258] R. Mandrou, *Les Fugger propriétaires fonciers en Souabe 1560–1618* (Paris, 1969), pp. 75–81.

[259] Y. Durand, *Les Fermiers Généraux* (Paris, 1971), p. 374, n. 2; of 32 successions, four advantaged the eldest son, twelve favoured equality, while there is no clear evidence for the remainder, though nine had *substitutions* compatible with equality.

did in the later seventeenth century. In the early fourteenth century Cino da Pistoia had written 'In England the custom is that the eldest (*major natu*) has all the property, but in Italy that all the sons succeed equally.'[260] Fynes Moryson wrote of the late sixteenth century

> Never did I observe brothers to live in such unity as in Italy, so as the father being dead, many of them ordinaryly live in one house together, not deviding their patrimony, but having all goods in common or as they call it in brotherhood . . . and persuading one to marry for procreation, the rest living unmarryed and much respecting their brother's wife . . . while they live in this sorte, if any one spend wastfully, or give his daughters in marryage, all is supplyed of the common charge

and if later any one wishes to live of his own an equal partition is still made. He also noted that in the 'commonwealthes of Italy', in intestacy there was equal partition between sons, while in Naples and 'in the fees of absolute princes the eldest brother succeeds and the care to maintayne their sisters and dispose them in marriage lyes upon the brother's inheritance'.[261]

Moryson was himself a younger son and keenly interested in comparing rules of inheritance. His comments draw attention to two matters which continue to concern historians, the differences between communes and princely states in their laws of inheritance, and the way noble inheritances were affected. A tradition going back to Muratori and Giannone saw the spread of fideicommissary entails as due to Spanish domination and example. These allegedly began with great nobles in the early sixteenth century and spread downwards after 1600 at the expense of the *fratellanza* described by Moryson. Recently historians have interested themselves in the structure of families and of households. Nobles formed lineage groups which acted together to preserve their property from the eleventh century, or before; families did not divide their inheritances and held property jointly. Groups of kin could be joint holders of lordships and castles; lineages' connections in the male line with branches of the house made up the *consorteria*, which often had written statutes regulating their affairs from the twelfth century

---

[260] G. M. Monti, *Cino da Pistoia* (Città di Castello, 1924), p. 179. I am indebted to P. J. Jones for this quotation.

[261] *Shakespeare's Europe*, ed. C. Hughes (New York, 1967), pp. 155–6. Moryson spent most of his time in Venice, Padua and Tuscany, but had visited Rome, Naples, Genoa and Milan, pp. v–vi.

278   J. P. COOPER

onwards. The marriages of both men and women might be controlled and the *consorteria* usually had rights to repurchase property alienated to strangers by its members.[262] The noble *consorteria* was as important in towns as in the country. Herlihy believes that the free communes of the thirteenth century broke the effectiveness of such associations, only to see them take on new forms from the mid fourteenth century. Thenceforward common ownership of property disappears, but while small nuclear households became the focus of men's interests, the consciousness of bonds of kinship between them was still strong, perhaps stronger.[263]

However, Goldthwaite alleges that in fifteenth-century Florence concentration upon the private enjoyments of the nuclear household weakened 'the very concept of the family as a more extended social organization'. Patricians became relatively indifferent to living kin and dead ancestors, only the political crises of the late fifteenth and early sixteenth century made them seek a new and securer identity as nobles with inherited privileges. Proud of genealogies which guaranteed their status, they used fideicommissary entails from the later sixteenth century to preserve the name and glory of each family, making its property inalienable and indivisible and appointing a dynastic succession. Renaissance palaces which had been monuments to a private splendour, with no provision for wider family gatherings or public spectacles, were refashioned as monuments to proclaim dynastic pride and pretensions.[264]

It is certainly not true that common ownership disappears in either the fifteenth or sixteenth century; long-term ownership by groups of kin may have become rarer, but short-term communities of brothers, as part of a domestic household cycle were common enough, as was joint ownership of seigneurial rights and fiefs by noble families in *consortili*.[265] Whether even in fifteenth-century

262 F. Nicolai, 'I Consorzi Nobiliari ed i Comune nell'alta e media Italia', *Rivista di Storia del Diritto Italiano*, xiii (1940), pp. 116–47, 292–342, 397–477, especially 136–7, 424–34.
263 D. Herlihy, 'Family Solidarity in Medieval Italian History' in *Economy, Society and Government of Italy*, eds D. Herlihy, R. S. Lopez, V. Slessarev (Kent, Ohio, 1969), pp. 173–84.
264 R. A. Goldthwaite, *Private Wealth in Renaissance Florence* (Princeton, 1968); 'Florentine Palaces as Domestic Architecture', *Am. Hist. Rev.*, lxxvii (1972), pp. 987–1006.
265 Nicolai, *art. cit.*, pp. 134, 311; E. Gamurini, *Istoria Genealogica delle Famiglie Nobili Toscane et Umbre* (Florence, 1671), pp. 139–43; S. J. Woolf, *Studi Sulla Nobiltà Piemontese nell'Epoca dell'Assolutismo*

Florence patrician households were typically so unextended, so inward looking, or so indifferent to wider kin, as Goldthwaite claims, is extremely doubtful.[266] He may be on surer ground in claiming that the fideicommissary entails of the later sixteenth century and the granting of titles (though certainly not the granting of fiefs)[267] by the grand dukes of Tuscany do institutionalize what might be new rules of succession. As we shall see, these accompanied demographic changes, but how far the legal institutions caused the changes still needs investigating. Just as the history of the family in medieval Italy 'is one of continuous tension between divisive and cohesive tendencies', so to some extent these can be seen in the domestic cycle of fifteenth-century Florentine patrician families, analysed by Kent, moving between an extended family headed by a patriarchal grandfather, communities of brothers and conjugal households. In the course of his life an individual would usually have lived in two or three different types of household. The *consorterie* of Florence differed from each other in character and functioning; they were not so strongly organized as institutions, as the *alberghi* of Genoa, but they were legally recognized and defined entities. More generally individual members of a great noble family were expected to put the interests of the house (including not only living kin, but also dead ancestors and unborn descendants) before those of the immediate individual interests of any one conjugal family. The way in which this higher interest was defined and the legal means of pursuing it varied over time, as did the willingness of individuals to live up to what was expected of them, but this constant, if seemingly trite, convention

(Memorie dell'Accademia delle Scienze di Torino, Serie 4ª, n. 5, 1963), pp. 25, 84–90, 152.

[266] Much the most important work on this subject is the unhappily still unpublished thesis of F. W. Kent, 'Ottimati Families in Florentine Politics and Society 1427–1530. The Rucellai, Capponi and Ginore' (London Ph.D., 1971). His 'The Rucellai Family and its Loggia', *Journal of the Warburg and Courtauld Institute* xxxv (1972), 397–401 is a significant contribution, but gives little idea of the thesis's range of evidence and perspicuity in social analysis.

[267] S. Berner, 'The Florentine Patriciate in the Transition from Republic to *Principato* 1530–1609', *Studies in Medieval and Renaissance History*, ix (1972), pp. 3–15, 6; G. Pansini, 'Per una storia del feudalismo nel Granducato di Toscana durante il periodo mediceo', *Quaderni Storici*, xix (1972), pp. 131–86. There were only ten fiefs granted before 1609, none to Florentine patricians; altogether the Medici infeudated less than 5 per cent of the total *fuochi*, mostly in the Maremma.

inhibits the individual's power to control property and the development of a self-sufficient and self-regarding nuclear family. It did not prevent litigation, rivalry, political quarrels between members of the same lineage, but their occurrence does not demonstrate the demise of the traditional convention, the birth of a new one and of new social structures.

Italian laws, customs and communal statutes generally preferred males to females in successions and excluded females who had been given portions, though there were areas in the north and others under Byzantine influence in the south, where sons and daughters shared equally.[268] Fiefs descending by Lombard law were inalienable and divided equally between sons with exclusion of females so that, as we have seen, they were often held in common; those going according to Frankish law were indivisible, as were fiefs of dignity, marquisates and countships. Frankish law postponed female inheritance, transmitted the familial fief which was inalienable to the eldest son, while hereditary fiefs could be freely willed. As in France, by the twelfth and thirteenth century property owners were seeking means to hold patrimonies together and again lawyers responded. Testators' powers to bind their property were developed by using prohibitions on alienation and conditions to transfer the property intact to designated successors. Thus in 1260 Uberto, Marquess Pallavicino, if his son Manfred died without a male heir, left his castle and lands to the sons of his brother and if Manfred died without issue other lands were to go to his daughters *pupillariter et per fideicommissum*.[269] In 1287 the Roman family of Conti established a fideicommissary entail in male primogeniture on some of their lands *in infinitum et perpetuum*.[270]

By the fourteenth century jurists were construing tacit *fideicommissa* and developing rules for conjecturing the intentions of the testator. The dominant consideration was that anyone with a considerable patrimony would wish it to remain in the family for as long as possible. By the end of the fifteenth century this development was complete; the order of succession included only male descendants until the fourth generation, unless the testator had

[268] C. Giardina, 'Successioni (Diritto Intermedio)' in *Novissimo Digesto Italiano*, p. 740.
[269] I. Affò, *Storia della Città di Parma* (Parma, 1793) iii, pp. 406–7. I owe this reference to P. J. Jones.
[270] P. S. Leicht, *Storia del Diritto Italiano. Il Diritto Privato*, pt ii (Milan, 1943), p. 254.

directed that it should continue till the extinction of the family or the house. Prohibitions on alienation had taken example from Lombard law, in excluding females from claiming the Falcidian quarter and substituting portions for their legitim. As in France, devices for preventing all claims to Trebellianian and Falcidian quarters even by males were introduced. Trifone argued that the undivided *fideicommissum* was fully developed in Italy independently of Spanish influence and example, though he agreed that the spread of fideicommissary entails in primogeniture did owe much to Spanish power and influence.[271] His case is strengthened by the very considerable legal differences between the *mayorazgo* and the fully developed Italian fideicommissary entail: legitim, dower, and portions could be charged against the entail, whereas this required a royal license in Castile. However, what matters is practice rather than legal doctrine. Aymard believes that in Sicily the prohibition on alienation was only combined with the *fideicommissum* after 1500. Admittedly this is based on the history of one family which only achieved magnate status in the early sixteenth century, but he also notes that by 1550 the barons in the Sicilian parliament had ceased to demand greater freedom to alienate fiefs. They now supported primogeniture, the extension of Frankish law, regulation of marriage portions.[272] Goldthwaite has argued that Florence in the sixteenth century saw a change from the use of family *fideicommissa* to ones incorporating entails in primogeniture which were combined with the granting of titles and fiefs by the Medici.[273] Undoubtedly Spain by creating fiefs with titles of dignity assisted the spread of entails in primogeniture

---

[271] R. Trifone, 'Fideicommesso' in *Novissimo Digesto Italiano* (Turin, 1961) vii, pp. 194–9. M. Caravale substantially accepts this account, but claims that in the fifteenth century legal doctrine had not made such a complete fusion between the interests of the family and the *fideicommissum* as in the next two centuries, 'Fedecommesso', *Enciclopedia del Diritto*, xvii (Milan, 1967), p. 112, n. 42.

[272] M. Aymard, 'Une famille de l'aristocratie sicilienne aux XVIe et XVIIe siècles: les ducs de Terranova', *Revue Historique*, ccxlvii (1972), pp. 32–5. It is difficult to understand, given the doctrines of inferring entails and *fideicommissa*, why the prohibition of alienation was so beloved.

[273] Goldthwaite, *op. cit.*, pp. 271–2. While he is probably right about the relative prevalence and novelty of the undivided *fideicommissum* in the late sixteenth century it is impossible to accept his 'new attitude to property'. 'In the sixteenth century property slowly came to be regarded as an inalienable possession of the family . . .' For the relative unimportance of grants of fiefs in Tuscany, see above, n. 267, p. 279.

in Italy; but it can be argued that Spain was satisfying a demand in Naples and Sicily, not creating one. In Naples to transform fiefs held under Lombard law into indivisible ones required royal assent to subject them to an entail. There were constant demands for the right to entail fiefs which were partially met in 1595 and more fully in 1655 and 1666.[274]

In Milan all the fiefs were held by Lombard law. Spain first imposed male primogeniture on new grants of fiefs, then in 1601 and 1609 on titles and fiefs of counts and marquesses. The Senate was asked to introduce primogeniture for old fiefs and refused, but from 1618 the succession to old fiefs was changed, provided at investiture the eldest son compensated other heirs. The Spanish crown hoped to secure escheats, but there were very many grants of fiefs in the seventeenth century.[275] The duke of Savoy in 1648 allowed primogeniture to be applied to fiefs, whatever the terms on which they were originally granted, in order to avoid the discord and inconveniences of *consortili* and 'to maintain and increase the splendour of the nobility . . . the principal ornament of our crown'. The new grants were to be approved by the duke and Senate and the younger sons could only claim *alimenta*.[276]

In Venice legislation about *fideicommissa* goes back to the fifteenth century, but they seem to become general among the Venetian nobility after 1550. But it was exceedingly rare for them to be combined with primogeniture; they normally prohibited alienation and left equal shares to all the sons, apart from often giving the eldest special rights over the family palace, or some additional property. None the less since usually only one brother married and the others left their shares to their nephews, the result was much the same as that brought about by entails in primogeniture elsewhere. The demographic consequences of this will be considered more fully at a later stage.[277]

---

[274] Trifone, *art. cit.*, pp. 200–1.

[275] Giulio Vismara in *Storia di Milano*, xi (1958), pp. 260–3. In 1714 a third of infeudated land had been granted before Charles V, out of a total of about 900, 350 had been granted by Philip IV and later, and were mostly purchases.

[276] S. J. Woolf, *Studi*, p. 27; A. Pertile, *Storia del diritto Italiano* (6 vols, Turin, 1896–1903) iv, p. 153, n. 10, fixed this in the eighteenth century at a third or a quarter of the rents of the entail, if there were more than four claimants, or four or less, *ibid.*, p. 157.

[277] J. C. Davis, *The Decline of the Venetian Nobility as a Ruling Class* (Baltimore, 1962), pp. 69–71. Pertile, *op. cit.*, p. 158, n. 27.

The effect of entails was to restrict younger sons' chances of marrying and to a lesser extent those of daughters. In Naples and Sicily younger sons had only the right to a life annuity charged on the entail and to a share of their mother's property. The way the annuity should be reckoned was everywhere a source of much litigation, eventually in Naples the view prevailed that it should be the usufruct of the legitim reckoned according to the rules of Roman law.[278] But daughters' portions had to be paid in cash, but could be charged as *censos* on the entail. The widow's dower which might be two-thirds of her portion and in Piedmont could be taken in cash was also chargeable on the entail.[279] The raising of portions was a constant source of indebtedness. Median portions given by the Florentine patriciate nearly tripled in the sixteenth century and remained at the same level until 1750. There may have been even greater increases in Piedmont between the late sixteenth and mid seventeenth century; by the early eighteenth century a portion for daughters of greater noble families was about one year's income and rather more in poorer families.[280] The Sicilian dukes of Terranova's long-term indebtedness, a substantial part of which was due to portions and dowers, increased fivefold between 1580 and 1610 to over half the net revenues. Their income from land and dues tripled in the second half of the sixteenth century, and increased a little until about 1650. But before then the growth of long-term debt had put the estate under judicial administration. The real test must have come, as for other magnates in south Italy, when their revenues fell sharply and did not improve again until the mid eighteenth century.[281]

There is plenty of evidence of growing debts in Naples in the late sixteenth century and at least one spectacular example of the ruin of a great inheritance. Already in 1580 Niccolò Berardino Sanseverino, prince of Bisignano had over 700,000 ducats of debts; as his revenues in 1577 were 130,000 ducats and rose to 149,000 in 1590 this might have been manageable. But the prince was a spendthrift whose debts reached 1,641,143 ducats in 1590 with annual interest of 127,000. The crown appointed an administrator

278 Pertile, *op. cit.*, p. 157.
279 Woolf, *Studi*, pp. 154–5; use of *censos* was late in Piedmont, becoming common only after 1650.
280 *Ibid.*, pp. 156–7; Litchfield, *art. cit.*, p. 203; these figures are for portions received at the marriage of sons.
281 Aymard, *art. cit.*, pp. 56–61, 51–3.

and ordered the sale of 500,000 ducats of feudal property. Niccolò's son died without legitimate issue and after much litigation over the succession to the entail, much of the inheritance was sold. However, this outcome was untypical, most of the established nobility survived, despite their debts, and were joined by new-comers from Genoa and Tuscany who built their fortunes more from the crown's financial difficulties than from the lands of the older families.[282] The Roman barons fared much worse in 1596, when Clement VIII enforced seizures and sales of their lands, including those entailed, to pay their debts. The old nobility lost much land, Genoese, Florentines, and the new nobility of papal nephews were the gainers.[283]

The debts of the established nobility did not destroy them as a group in Naples, Sicily or Piedmont in the seventeenth century, but they did make them more dependent on the crown. Particularly in Naples and Sicily their long-term debts were a major source of unproductive investment for other classes, whose interests suffered from the protection afforded to noble debtors by royal authority and, in Sicily, by enforced reductions of the rate of interest. Nevertheless the impression remains that creditors' interests got more consideration than in seventeenth-century Castile. The length of entails was restricted in Piedmont in 1598 and in Naples in 1666 to four descents. Legal doctrine and decisions allowed that in cases of need property could be sold to pay legacies, debts and portions, despite prohibitions of alienation.[284] However, this was a tedious process and a reforming edict in enlightened Tuscany in 1747 limited entails to four generations and permitted the possessor to use capital for portions and for improvements.[285] In many respects, notably rights to legitim, to raise portions and assign dower out of the entailed property, Italian doctrine and law was much nearer to those of the non-Castilian kingdoms, especially

---

[282] G. Galasso, *Economia e Società nella Calabria del Cinquecento* (Naples, 1967), pp. 3–17, 42–56; F. Caracciolo, *Il Regno di Napoli nei secoli XVI e XVII*, i, *Economia e Società* (Rome, 1966), pp. 302–39, shows that the period of greatest alienations to pay debts by the old nobility was from 1560 to 1620.

[283] Pertile, *op. cit.*, p. 159, n. 30; E. Delumeau, *Vie Economique et Sociale de Rome dans la seconde moitié du XVIe siècle* (Paris, 1957), i, pp. 475–83.

[284] Trifone, *art. cit.*, p. 202; Pertile, *op. cit.*, pp. 153, n. 10, 162–7.

[285] I. Imberciadori, *Campagna Toscana nel '700* (Florence, 1956), p. 148.

Catalonia, than to Castilian doctrines of *favor del mayorazgo*.[286] The traditional discussion of the influence of the laws of Toro in Italian legal histories might be better directed towards considering the influence of Aragon.

If Spanish examples were followed by the founders of entails, the amount of female inheritance ought to have increased along with primogeniture, since, as we have seen, Castilian law favoured direct female descendants.[287] Given my ignorance about the common rules of succession chosen, speculation is pointless. The escheats resulting from granting fiefs in male primogeniture may have profited the treasury in Piedmont and Tuscany, but they were far outweighed by sales of domainal rights and jurisdiction in Milan, Naples and Sicily. If the so-far-accepted chronology of the spread of indivisible entails is correct, it occurred especially from the later sixteenth and early seventeenth century, though probably earlier in Rome and the south, when revenues from land were rising rapidly and more than keeping pace with prices. This rise was halted and often reversed in the seventeenth century, generally by about 1630 in the north and later in Sicily. Recovery and expansion of noble revenues did not happen until the mid eighteenth century in the south, earlier in some other parts. Italy became a primarily agrarian economy, an exporter of primary products, during the seventeenth century and the nobility and the Church dominated more than half the land or its revenues in most regions, except some of the poorer and more mountainous ones.[288] A much quoted nineteenth-century estimate claimed that three-quarters of the lands of Tuscany were bound by entails and ecclesiastical mortmain.[289] Already in the later seventeenth century the leading jurist, Cardinal De Luca, had admitted that entails in primogeniture had bad effects, wanted to limit them to three generations and praised

---

[286] B. Clavero, *Mayorazgo*, pp. 279–87 deals with the non-Castilian kingdoms.

[287] For the strength of legal doctrine against female inheritance, N. Tamassia, *La Famiglia Italiana nei Secoli Decimoquinto e Decimosesto* (Milan, 1910), pp. 292–4. For a fifteenth-century entail in male primogeniture, repeated in 1514, which gave preference to females over collateral males, when the direct male line failed, see G. Saige, *Documents Historiques Relatifs à la Principauté de Monaco* (Monaco, 1890), ii, pp. lxxviii–lxxxii; for an early sixteenth-century example, preferring males, Galasso, *op. cit.*, p. 13.

[288] S. J. Woolf, *Storia d'Italia Einaudi*, iii (Turin, 1973), pp. 23–32.

[289] E. Poggi, *Cenni Storici delle Leggi sull'Agricoltura* (Florence, 1845–1848), ii, pp. 223–4.

Clement VIII's *Bulla baronum* for favouring credit and freedom of contracts. However he concluded that their advantage outweighed their disadvantages.[290]

Faced with rising population and the need to increase both agricultural output and state revenues, fideicommissary entails became the target of enlightened reformers. Reforms by the state culminated in abolition in Piedmont and Tuscany. Piedmont had begun reforms earlier than Tuscany, where the legislation of 1747 is comparable in scope to Daguesseau's edict.[291] Muratori in 1742 had denounced *fideicommissa* as making the fortunes of lawyers by creating uncertainty and endless suits and for destroying credit. He was particularly hostile to their use by those with little property and wanted them limited and publicly registered, holding up Piedmont as an example.[292] The *illuministi* of the later eighteenth century, Beccaria, Longo, Vasco, Filangieri, denounced them for inhibiting freedom of trade, restricting the number of landowners, thus preventing profitable use of land and inhibiting investment of money and labour in it. Filangieri was particularly eloquent in denouncing primogeniture and entails as 'the cause of exorbitant wealth of a few and the wretchedness of the majority' – 'a family is reckoned unhappy the more children it has' – to abolish them would rid Europe 'of two institutions made expressly to reduce the numbers of proprietors and of mankind'.[293] Although physiocratic notions of free trade obviously influenced these writers, in their general denunciations of entails and concentration of property, there is no sign of the concern for avoiding morcellation which led some French agronomists to deplore partible inheritance customs and favour primogeniture, as the means of creating the large farms desired by the physiocrats.[294]

---

[290] I. B. de Luca, *Theatrum Veritatis et Justitiae* (Rome, 1670), x, p. 382, no. 13, he favoured entails to three generations, 'ob magnas ac inextricibiles lites exinde resultans ac etiam ob impedimentum libertatis commercii'; Trifone, *art. cit.*, p. 204.   [291] Trifone, *art. cit.*, pp. 204–5.

[292] L. A. Muratori, *Dei Difetti della Giurisprudenza* (Venice, 1742), *cap.* xvii.

[293] F. Venturi, ed., *Illuministi Italiani*, iii, *Riformatori Lombardi, Piemontesi e Toscani* (Milan, 1958), pp. 174–5 (Beccaria, *Elementi di Economia Pubblica*), 223–39 (A. Longo, *Osservazioni su i Fedeccommessi*, 1765), 785–90 (Giambattista Vasco, 1769); G. Filangieri, *La Scienza della Legislazione* (Milan, 1822), ii, pp. 40–2, first published 1780.

[294] A. J. Bourde, *Agronomie et Agronomes en France au XVIIIᵉ siècle* (Paris, 1967), ii, pp. 1039–40; after 1770 there was more defence of small holdings, p. 1042.

TABLE A

	Milanese patriciate[a]					Florentine patriciate[b]			Venetian nobility[e]
	Never married[c]		Survivors to 15 entering church[d]			Fathers born	Survivors, single at 50		Men who reached marriageable age, never married
	Male	Female	Male	Female	M + F		Male	Female	
1600–49	49.0	75.0	30.9	48.0	39.0	1500–99	48	30	51.0
1650–99	56.0	48.5	22.0	30.5	25.8	1600–99	60	55	60.0
1700–49	50.5	34.5	12.8	13.0	12.9	1700–99	38	14	66.0
1750–99	36.5	13.0	5.0	2.8	4.1				

Figures used in percentages.
[a] D. E. Zanetti, *La Demographia del Patriziato Milanese* (Pavia, 1972), pp. 83–4, Tab. iv, 1, iv. 2.
[b] R. B. Litchfield, 'Demographic Characteristics of Florentine Patrician Families', *Jnl. Econ. Hist.*, xix (1969), p. 197, Table 2.
[c] Percentage of those deceased at fifty and above, the dates cover groups of generations.
[d] The dates in the first column are for periods in which their fathers were born.
[e] J. C. Davis, *The Decline of the Venetian Nobility as a Ruling Class* (Baltimore, 1962), p. 72, Table 4.

That strict entails in primogeniture limited the number of marriages may seem a self-evident truth requiring no further investigation. But the fact that there is good demographic data at least for three urban patriciates makes it possible to consider what happened over two centuries or more. Table A shows much the same proportion of male celibacy until 1700 in Milan, Florence and Venice. In the next century it declines sharply for Milan and also for Florence, but in Venice it goes on rising. Unfortunately no details are given about the settlements used in Milan, though it seems to be assumed that entails in primogeniture had become normal by the early seventeenth century.[295] Accepting Professor Goldthwaite's assumption that this form of entail was only adopted at Florence in the late sixteenth century, the marriage pattern had already changed from that in the fifteenth century. For Professor Litchfield says that on average only one son and one daughter in each family married in the sixteenth century, whereas two or three sons had married in the fifteenth century, so that the change would seem to precede that from a family entail to primogeniture. Late marriage of men was already characteristic in 1450–99 and probably before. Average age of first marriage was static around twenty-nine to thirty years 1450–1549 and then rose by 3 years 1550–1599, rising by another 3 years in the seventeenth century; 1650–99 it was 6 years above the median for Milan yet the average size of the Milanese family was then about the same as the Florentine, which suggests that age of husbands at marriage did not of itself influence family size.[296] The rise in Florentine marriage portions of two and a half times in the sixteenth century did not outstrip agricultural prices, but if families were in the habit of giving five years' income as a portion, this would explain why only one daughter was married.[297]

As we have already seen, the Venetians continued to use the family *fideicommissum*, not primogeniture, but the practice of only one brother marrying was generally adopted by 1550 or before.

[295] D. E. Zanetti, *op. cit.*, pp. 51, 233.

[296] *Ibid.*, pp. 87 and Table IV/3, 176 and Table V/14, Litchfield, *art. cit.*, pp. 197–8, 199 Table 3, 200. Average family size in Florence 5–6, 1500–1700, in Milan 5.3, 1650–99, 7.2, 1600–49, when mean age of marriage was 30.9 and 30.3.

[297] Litchfield, *art. cit.*, p. 203. The decline in the size of portions after 1750 apparently coincides with the rise in the number of marriages. It would be of interest to know whether this is a result of the reform of entails in 1747.

What is remarkable about Venice is not just that the proportion of never-married men went on rising, but that of only sons who never married rose from eighteen to 64.7 per cent between the sixteenth and the eighteenth century. Moreover, the number of

TABLE B *Nuptuality of French Nobles and British Peers*

	Fifteen noble families of Toulouse,[a] children by generations, percentage never married		British peers' sons,[b] percentage never married of those at risk		
	Males (church)	Females (church)	Marriage epoch	All	Heirs	Younger sons
1670–1700	50.0 (15.6)	48.7 (27.0)				
1700–30	51.4 (31.4)	61.4 (25.0)	1728–52	34.6 [30.2][c]	16.7	41.4
1730–60	39.4 (15.2)	59.9 (22.7)	1753–77	25.7 [29.7]	12.6	31.7
1760–90	31.4 (nil)	28.0 (nil)	1758–1802	30.5 [29.6]	18.7	36.5

[a] R. Förster, *The Nobility of Toulouse in the Eighteenth Century* (Baltimore, 1962), p. 129, Table ix. The children who died young have not been included in the totals. The group is six sword and nine robe families.

[b] D. Thomas, 'The Social Origins of Marriage Partners of the British Peerage in the Eighteenth and Nineteenth Centuries', *Population Studies* (1973), p. 101, Table 2. Heirs are defined, if they were heirs at fifteen, and those at risk of marrying all those reaching seventeen, p. 100.

[c] [ ] Mean age at first marriage.

TABLE C *Brothers and sisters of Ducs et Pairs*[a]

	1589–1660		1661–1723	
	Brothers	Sisters	Brothers	Sisters
% Never married	–	34 (27)	–	42 (27)
% Laity	70 (39)	73 (58)	73 (33)	63 (40)
% Ecclesiastics	30 (17)	27 (22)	27 (12)	37 (24)
Total	100 (56)	100 (80)	100 (45)	100 (64)

[a] J. P. Labatut, *Les Ducs et Pairs de France au XVIIe Siècle* (Paris, 1972), pp. 108–9. Those belonging to the first period, would have entered the Church c. 1560–1630, those of the second period c. 1630–90. Unfortunately no figures are given for marriages of the laymen.

TABLE D   *Peers' children*

	Males		Females		Portions
Cohort born	Marriage epoch[a]	Percentage never married[b] [not married by 50]	Marriage epoch[a]	Percentage never married[b] [not married by 50]	Average proposed[c] £'s
1550-74	1574-98	2.5 [3.7]	1570-94	9.0 [9.0]	1550-74 850
1575-99	1599-1623	13.9 [14.9]	1594-1618	4.2 [4.2]	1575-99 2,250
1600-24	1624-48	22.9 [26.4]	1620-44	12.8 [15.0]	1600-24 3,550
1625-49	1651-74	15.0 [20.5]	1646-70	17.9 [17.9]	1625-49 5,050
1650-74	1676-1700	17.9 [21.1]	1671-95	15.1 [16.3]	1650-74 6,250
1675-99	1701-25	21.9 [26.2]	1697-1721	23.8 [23.8]	1675-1729 9,250
1700-24	1728-52	20.0 [25.8]	1722-46	26.3 [26.7]	

a T. H. Hollingsworth, *Demography of the British Peerage*, p. 25, Table 17; the median age at first marriage has been added to the cohort dates.
b *Ibid.*, p. 20, Table 11.
c From Appendix I, Table I.

childless marriages was 24 per cent, whereas at Florence and Milan it was 16 per cent.[298] A very inadequate sample of the children of twenty marriages of six Castilian noble families in the sixteenth century shows that as in Venice or Toulouse in the late seventeenth century (Table B) half the sons did not marry.[299] What is more surprising is that only a quarter of the daughters did not marry, a far lower proportion than at Milan before 1750, Florence before 1700, Toulouse before 1760, or among seventeenth-century dukes and peers (Tables A, B, C). All these other examples give proportions of around a half, though both Milan and still more Florence anticipate Toulouse in marrying off more daughters. The mid eighteenth century marked the start of a steep fall of entries of both sons and daughters into the Church. Once again the exception is Venice where the number of nobles in the Church increased from 123 in 1706 to 166 in 1760, although the number of nobles was declining.[300]

TABLE E   *Dukes' children never married (Percentages)*[a]

Cohort born	Males	Females	Born eldest son	Born younger sons
1330–1479	9	7 ⎫		
1480–1679	7	6 ⎬	4	9
1680–1729[b]	17	17		
1730–79	14	14 ⎬	8	20
1780–1829	16	12 ⎭		

[a] Hollingsworth, 'A Demographic Study of the British Ducal Families', *Population in History*, pp. 364, 374. Tables 17 and 32.
[b] Of those born 1700–1750, the number of never married among the sons of dukes and peers is estimated at between 17% and 27%. C. and L. Henry, 'Ducs et Pairs sous l'Ancien Régime', *Population*, xv (1960), p. 812.

Lack of entry into the Church is the obvious difference between the British peerage in Tables B, D and E and the other groups. Table D suggests an extraordinary state of affairs in the late sixteenth century. When (c. 1580–1620) the size of portions was rising fastest, both the proportion of daughters never marrying and the

[298] Davis, *op. cit.*, pp. 60, 72, 63; Litchfield, *art. cit.*, p. 198; Zanetti, *op. cit.*, p. 176.
[299] The families are Mendoza, dukes of Infantado and counts of Coruña; Manrique, marquess of Aquilar, counts of Ossorno, Señores de Villacis; de Molina.   [300] Davis, *op. cit.*, p. 67, n. 50.

mean age of their first marriages fall for the second cohort, though both rise again for the second and third cohorts. The proportion of males who married (and thus of younger sons) was extremely high and increasing for the first two cohorts, when the size of daughters' portions was increasing fastest. If the comparison with Table E can be relied upon, the proportion marrying rose above that found for the richest peers before 1500.[301] In Table D the Civil War does not produce a lasting interruption in the rise of the average size of portions, but there was a fourfold increase in the percentage of never-married daughters comparing 1594–1618 with 1646–70. The percentage for sons had already risen sharply by 1648, it then fell for the next cohort, then rose again to almost the same level for the eighteenth century.

The figures in Tables D and E are unfortunately not directly comparable with those in Table B, but part of the price of sustaining the rise in portions may have been an increase in the number of bachelor younger sons back to levels of 1624–48.[302] There was also a further long-term increase in the proportion of never-married daughters, reaching about 25 per cent in the early eighteenth century, accompanied by a further rise in the mean age of first marriages. The mean age of first marriages of men had risen from twenty-five to twenty-six [median 24.2] 1574–1623 to 28.07 1701–25 and 30.16 1728–52 [median 28.43] by about 15 per cent to a level comparable to those in Florence in the sixteenth and to Milan in the seventeenth century.[303] The mean age for women rose from about twenty to twenty-three by $3\frac{1}{2}$ years (some 17 per cent), increasingly above that at Florence and Milan. After 1750 the patterns converge, especially at Toulouse (Tables A, B). The trend would be even more marked at Milan, if the figures for 1800 to 1849 were included, since the percentage of unmarried men fell to eighteen and of women to 7.5, though childless marriages, 1750 to 1899, at 21.4 per cent were approaching the Venetian levels of the sixteenth and seventeenth centuries.

[301] D. Thomas shows that in the eighteenth century dukes and marquesses followed a pattern of 'rank endogamy' in marriage, art. cit., pp. 101–4.

[302] As the portions 1675–1729 come overwhelmingly from magnate families the better comparison would be with Table E, where the proportions of never married are lower than in Table A.

[303] As the Florentine and Milanese had very few younger sons marrying compared with the British and as younger sons were likely to marry later, the averages are not strictly comparable.

Tables E and C, because of their different bases of calculation exaggerate the gap between the daughters of English and French dukes in the seventeenth century, but nevertheless it was a large one. Table E also raises the question as to whether anything like the proportion of daughters entering nunneries in Tables A, B and C did so in pre-Reformation England. What little information is available would tend to suggest that the proportion of magnates' daughters taking the veil was small,[304] but the same could be said of sixteenth-century Castile. Whether the post-Tridentine church simply met an increasing demand or helped to create one requires investigation. But the extent to which the Catholic Church before 1750 supported noble family structures and fortunes clearly fulfilled all the expectations that Persons had offered to attract the nobility and gentry back to Catholicism in 1596.[305] By the eighteenth century the French dukes and peers apparently solved these problems by drastically reducing the size of their families from an average of 6.15 (1650–99), to 2.79 (1700–49), to 2.0 (1750–1799), while the average age at first marriage of both men and women fell.[306]

Given high infant mortality and the normal incidence of childless marriages, the French dukes were as well on the way to extinguishing their families as the Venetian nobility had been by their preference for celibacy since the seventeenth century. Levy and Henry believe that the fall in family size was due to deliberate contraception. Does this indicate a new conception of marriage and the family, or is it merely a new answer to the old problem of preserving inheritances, proof of the influence of the Enlightenment, or of Filangieri's thesis about primogeniture? In sixteenth-century Florence the adoption of entails in primogeniture seems to have followed the change in incidence of marriage, not to have produced it. Zanetti argues that the cumulative effect of entails was pushing the Milanese patriciate towards extinction from about 1750. His argument is based on the fact that the curve calculated for them then assumes the same shape that the curve of extinction

---

[304] The Beauchamp genealogies from the late thirteenth to the early fifteenth century record 29 daughters (not including two who died young) of whom 23 married and 5 (about 17 per cent) became nuns.
[305] See above, p. 222.
[306] C. Levy, L. Henry, *art. cit.*, pp. 820, 813.

calculated for the Swedish nobility takes. As the Swedish nobility had originally practised partible inheritance, and their curve is not a chronological one, Zanetti's view seems open to question.[307] What is incontrovertible is his observation that the demographic vigour of his families in the early seventeenth century was superior to that of any other known aristocratic group at the time, despite a policy of restricted marriage. This makes it all the more desirable to know how long that policy had been pursued.

At least in the case of British peers, we know that there was a drop in the generation replacement rate below unity and in mean family size in the late seventeenth and early eighteenth centuries, which coincides with the continuing rise of portions, when revenues and prices were falling or stable. In the case of ducal families, to whom the index of portions is most relevant, this applies to the cohorts of 1680–1729, with recovery after the mid eighteenth century. The rest of the peerage also shared the recovery, so that the regime of strict settlements did not increase the rate of extinction; it was accompanied by a decline in that rate until well into the nineteenth century.[308]

Denmark offers the example of a nobility with a tradition of partible inheritance which in the course of the seventeenth century suffered a catastrophic demographic decline. In 1660 the old aristocracy (those received before 1660) owned 97.4 per cent of the manors and in 1700 only 44 per cent, while only 54 per cent of the group were still manor owners and 41 per cent were military or civil officers, as against 5 per cent in 1625. Whereas they were reproducing themselves in 1625, in 1700 the reproduction rate even of manor owners was 0.81 and of the military officers 0.52. The total number of men and women was almost halved between 1660 and 1720; the main causes were the decline of frequency of marriage among the officers and a general rise in mortality, in a period when Denmark's population increased by perhaps three-quarters. War and economic difficulties undermined and indebted the nobility in the first half of the seventeenth century, when there was no absolute monarchy. When there was one after 1660 instead of subsidizing

[307] Zanetti, op. cit., pp. 71–2; M. Roberts, Gustavus Adolphus (London, 1958), ii, pp. 59–60. Moreover entails were weakened by the legislation of Maria Theresa; the proportion of sons marrying went on increasing, but the rate of extinction also increased.

[308] Hollingsworth, Peerage, pp. 34, 36, Tables 23, 25, 'Ducal Families', p. 367, Table 22.

them as courtiers, it provided for their extinction as army officers,[309] a new and involuntarily half-celibate military order.

As we have seen the traditional defence of entails and primogeniture had been that they preserved the property and name of great houses on which the political stability of monarchies was founded, while partible inheritance would undo them and promote social mobility. This mutability could be seen as providentially ordained so that it would be presumptuous, even sinful, to thwart it. Alternatively it could be seen as a positive duty to preserve a divinely ordained hierarchical ordering of society.

At a time when unbarrable entails and primogeniture had been spreading since the late sixteenth century through Europe from Austria to Poland and the English strict settlement was in the making, the Harringtonian alternative held that maintenance of wider distribution of property was the foundation of political stability. Variations of this view, fortified with either free trade or cameralist arguments, appeared to triumph with the Enlightenment and the French Revolution, though with an increasing emphasis on the virtues of peasant proprietorship. For fiscal reasons enlightened despots wished to promote substantial peasant proprietors, as Jacobins and Jeffersonian democrats professed to do for political and social reasons. The legal institutions of inalienable entails were eventually destroyed in France, Italy and Spain in the nineteenth century, but they survived in the Habsburg lands and Germany.

In France, Spain and Italy the price that great nobles paid for institutionalizing the preservation of their names had been a political one, of accepting ceremonious subjection, while others paid the economic costs. In Venice where they were the rulers, the price proved to be an accelerated self-extinction. The strictest form of

---

[309] S. A. Hansen, 'Changes in the Wealth and Demographic Characteristics of the Danish Aristocracy 1470–1720', *Third Int. Conference of Economic History*, iii (The Hague, 1972), pp. 91–122. Neither here nor in the English summary of his book *Adeles vae Edens Grundlag* (Copenhagen, 1964) does he mention the nobility's inheritance customs, for which I have relied on Fynes Moryson, MS Corpus Christi College, Oxford, p. 239, 'In succession generally the sonnes succeed to equall portions and have double parts with their sisters, yet among Gentlemen, if the father had but one lordshipp, the eldest son should have it, giving his brothers their equall portions in money . . .' This would explain some of the chronic indebtedness described by Hansen and E. L. Petersen, 'La Crise de la noblesse danoise entre 1580 et 1660', *Annales*, xxiii (1968), pp. 1237–61.

inalienable entail, the Castilian *mayorazgo*, had the effect of promoting female inheritance; an obvious point which needs investigating is whether the undivided *fideicommissum* had the same effect in Italy. Even the Castilian *mayorazgo*, despite its formal legal strength, was not necessarily successful in binding and stabilizing property in any conditions. It was introduced into Mexico in the late sixteenth century, but in Oaxaca the result was that unentailed Indian landholding was stable, but that of Spaniards was not and their estates became smaller and fragmented by the eighteenth century.[310]

As long as men gave priority to considerations of perpetuating family glory, the formal legal system of inheritance mattered less than the political and social power which enabled such families to have their way. The same results could be and were achieved by systems of inheritance which formally provided for partition, or community between sons, or primogeniture. Among great landowners, if there is any trend discernible in the centuries after 1300 in the countries with which we have dealt, it would seem to be more towards emphasis on a narrow definition of lineage, in turn fortified by policies of restrictive marriage, than an evolution towards a nuclear family. In Castile one aspect of the narrowing of the lineage was the preference of females over collateral males in inheritance; how common this transference of paternal inheritances and names through females became in France and Italy requires investigation. Marriage portions are the most general aspect of female inheritance. The fact they went on rising in England and stayed at a high level in Florence in the seventeenth century, when landed revenues stagnated or fell, would indicate that daughters received more of the family fortune. The numbers marrying did not fall in Florence; they did in England, but there the portion was payable, even if they did not marry, though there was a temporary fall in the size of families. The level of portions found at Florence and Toulouse (three to five years' income) would have made it impossible to marry more than one daughter without ruining the family. Once restricted marriages had become the custom, it would be difficult to end them without either financial sacrifice, or social derogation.

The conjugal household became more authoritarian, as fathers were endowed with greater formal legal powers to control their

[310] W. B. Taylor, *Landlord and Peasant in Colonial Oaxaca* (Stanford, Calif., 1972), pp. 45–6, 153–4, 200–1.

children's marriages and to disinherit them. Normally great English landowners provided as generously for their younger children as did most of the Continental systems we have considered and more generously than some, such as the noble customs of Brittany. Marriage contracts often provided for them out of maternal inheritances. But unless they did, before the rise of the strict settlement everything had depended on the father's pleasure. Whereas younger children had rights on both paternal and maternal property in most other countries, ironically the English strict settlement came to give less paternal power to disinherit than did the *mayorazgo* and fideicommissary entails.

Before then the power of English fathers may explain why Fynes Moryson thought their children were notably more deferential to them than elsewhere. Yet even the strictest entails needed family cooperation, if they were to be effective. Unless there was cooperation, there were endless opportunities for litigation provided by the need to conjecture and interpret the intentions of dead ancestors. The prevalence of suits does not necessarily prove the decline of solidarity; it may show rivalry between lineages; between nearer kin the outcome may be arbitration within the accepted tradition of that family's provision for younger children.

In the long run because magnates wanted to provide both for the glory of their house and for their younger children, entails in primogeniture made them more dependent on monarchies for patronage, pensions and privileges in dealing with their debts. English magnates came to depend not on absolute sovereign power of kings, but on acts of parliament to adjust their settlements, not so much on the perquisites of court favour, as on those of political patronage. The glory of the family was reflected both by the self-restraint of younger sons *and* the successful creation of cadet lines. But studies of individual families are needed, if we are to do more than throw out hypotheses and flog dead horses of legal doctrine, as I have done here.

The economic consequences of such entails cannot simply be assumed by citing the *latifundia*, poverty and underdevelopment of Andalusia, Calabria, or Sicily. While legal powers can be as important as the fact that Catalan *mayorazgos* were compatible with emphyteutic tenures and those of Castile were not, circumstances must be studied. McCulloch long ago pointed out that the number of entails in Scotland (where they were perpetual) nearly trebled between 1785 and 1846; in 1814 about one-third of the land by value was under entail and by 1847 about a half, including virtually all of 'many large and populous districts'.[311] Yet this was a period of remarkable agricultural improvement and general economic growth. As entails were always publicly registered in Scotland, there is an opportunity for a comprehensive study. In France the existence of *retrait lignagier*, and even in its absence elsewhere the general prevalence of seigneurial rights of pre-emption, were probably more of an impediment to the full physiocratic enjoyment of landed property than entails.

The stabilization of great family estates and their ability to provide for younger children and widows depended on long-term and short-term borrowing. Creditors had suffered in seventeenth-century Spain and in Sicily from loss of capital and income due to royal interventions, just as office holders in France saw their capital expropriated when the price of offices stagnated and fell in the mid seventeenth century. Nevertheless like royal administrations, magnate estates had their clients and beneficiaries. The earliest and most obvious ones were the lawyers and the courts. Perhaps especially from the later seventeenth century they were also rural merchants, farmers of seigneurial dues and tithes, *labradores* and *poderosos* in Castile, *gabellotti* in Italy, ruling oligarchies in towns (who were often lesser nobles). Such groups, whether noble or non-noble, themselves dominated the economic and political life of town and country, exercising the delegated power and authority of the magnates. Eventually they could dispense with such endorsements and act independently of, or in connivance with, central authority to a much greater extent than the magnates had been able to do in recent times. In the seventeenth century the inhabitants of great estates and seigneurial towns had often been protected against the full force of growing fiscal exactions by royal administrators and tax-farmers; this happened in Naples and Sicily, in Castile (except during the time of Olivares) and in France before the reforms of Colbert. From the later seventeenth century administrative reforms eroded such traditional benefits from magnates' protection, while legal reforms weakened entails and strengthened the position of creditors. Absolute monarchies founded on an effective nobility of service, as in Prussia, proved the ones most willing

311 J. R. McCulloch, *A Treatise on the Succession to Property*, pp. 55–7.

to continue to protect and subsidize noble family settlements and mortgages.

Concluding summary

We began with a long tradition holding that the modes of inheritance of great landowners helped to determine important characteristics of European and non-European states and societies. Constitution makers, such as Harrington and Jefferson, social analysts, such as Montesquieu and Maine, have believed that monarchies and republics required different laws of inheritance. Economists and critics of traditional societies both in the eighteenth century and since have blamed a multitude of economic, social and demographic ills upon entails. Another tradition from the Enlightenment has presented the evolution of societies, economies and laws of property from phases embodying communal, hierarchical and religious values to ones concerned with individualistic, competitive, nationalistic and secular ones. Without denying that some such long-term general process of modernization has taken place, we saw that analysing the legal rules or customs concerning inheritance may be a fallible guide to what men did or wanted at any given time. Nevertheless knowledge of legal doctrine and how it changed is an essential preliminary to any effective analysis.

Much more analysis in terms of developmental cycles has been done of families and households than of longer term changes in patterns of inheritance. The basic classification of families into joint, stem and nuclear derives from Le Play's studies of peasants. The joint family's obvious function among Asian and European peasants was to ensure continuity in the supply of labour. Both stem and joint families occur more frequently among the wealthier than the poorer and it is also claimed that equal partible inheritance usually accompanies joint families.[312] But stem and joint families are not confined to peasants, they can both be found within urban patriciates, in Genoa from the twelfth to the fifteenth centuries and in fifteenth-century Florence. What may seem a low percentage of joint and stem households at a given time does not mean that such households are not an important part of the develop-

---

[312] For an illuminating general analysis, see R. Wheaton, 'Family and Kinship in Western Europe: The Problem of the Joint Family Household', *Journal of Interdisciplinary History*, v, no. 4 (1975), pp. 601–28.

mental cycle of richer families. In the Florentine and Genoese patriciates the actual presence of married sons within the paternal household, so that it can be strictly defined as a joint family household (though this did happen) matters less than the continuation of property arrangements between brothers, the descent of the principal dwelling in the main line, the acknowledgement of membership of a wider agnatic lineage (*casa, consorteria*), enforcing *retrait lignagier* on its members' property and possessing a sense of identity both in participating in ceremonies and politics.

Magnate families in France or England might not, or could not, conform to the literal model of a stem peasant household with the married son and heir living in the same premises. Magnate households were mobile, not static and the married son and heir commonly had a separately organized household. Nevertheless inheritance by male primogeniture, whether or not ensured by entails, with younger children receiving portions, *alimenta*, or annuities, can be seen as analogous to the peasant customs necessary to support stem households and families. When younger sons marry and receive lands in tail male with reversions back to the main male line, the process can be seen as establishing a joint family interest in shared and conditional rights to property, without establishing a joint family household. If there is a phase in the cycle when property is held by brothers in common, the social and psychological bonds are closer. Nevertheless entails were all intended to exemplify the holding of property in common with those both born and unborn in the interests of a lineage and according to the more or less explicit directions of an ancestor, or the recognized customs of a family. What settlements of these kinds attempt is a stability and prolongation which mortality and other demographic factors deny to actual households. Joint family households are in precarious equilibrium, constantly threatened by fission.[313]

Strategically joint fraternal and stem households and entails usually go with a strengthening of the inheritances of patrilines at the expense of the property rights of females. The clearest example of this is the restriction of the wife's rights to dower under Frankish and Lombard law in twelfth-century Italy.[314] The exclusion of daughters who have received marriage portions from rights to

[313] *Ibid.*, p. 619.
[314] E.g. D. O. Hughes, 'Urban Growth and Family Structure in Medieval Genoa', *Past and Present*, no. 66 (1975), pp. 13–15.

share in the inheritance of their father's property in Italian and French customary and written law is part of the same process. Another aspect is the size of marriage portions given with daughters. Everywhere the trend was against giving land from patrimonies as marriage portions, but advantageous marriage alliances were still sought and everywhere there were complaints about the increasing sums given and demanded as portions. Ineffective, though repeated, laws were made to limit the size of portions in Venice from 1420[315] and in Castile from 1534 and were advocated elsewhere. Whether their real value rose faster than prices in fourteenth- and fifteenth-century Venice is unclear, but they did in seventeenth-century England and Florence and probably elsewhere. By or before the seventeenth century the practice of restricting marriages of younger children is strongly established in the patriciates of Milan, Florence, Venice and Genoa,[316] though of course it can be found, though not precisely measured in some nobilities much earlier than this. The effect of restriction of marriages in Florence may have involved a change from a situation where the joint family type of inheritance was a norm to which patricians aspired, to one where a stem type of inheritance prevailed (institutionalized by the change from the family to the undivided *fedecommesso*).

However it must be remembered that only about a quarter of the marriages in a given population would produce two or more sons, so that the possibilities were restricted. Moreover 17 per cent of the marriages would produce no heirs and 21 per cent only daughters.[317] If average family size fell, as it did with British peers and Venetian and Genoese patricians in the seventeenth century, the proportion of families with daughters only would increase slightly and there would be a much greater increase in that of families without heirs.[318] Thus in any system of inheritance these factors would influence the distribution of property. As, unlike the

[315] S. Chojnacki, 'Dowries and Kinsmen in Early Renaissance Venice', *Journal of Interdisciplinary History*, v, no. 4 (1975), pp. 571–600.

[316] E. Grendi, 'Capitazione e nobilità a Genova', *Quaderni Storici*, xxvi (1974), pp. 419–20.

[317] J. Goody, 'Strategies of Heirship', *Comparative Studies in Society and History*, xv (1973), pp. 16, 18. These are the probabilities with average family size of six children and 0.65 probability of a child dying before his father, corrected for 5 per cent of sterile marriages.

[318] *Ibid.*, if the average family size falls to four, the percentage of marriages with daughters only, corrected as above, would rise from 21.6 to 23.7 and of ones with no heirs from 17.0 to 28.5.

ancient Romans and others,[319] adoption was not used, the problem of female heirs became even more important as inheritance became more clearly patrilineal. If artificial creation of heirs by adoption was ruled out, recognition of bastards was another possible way of augmenting heirs. The fifteenth-century nobility of Castile, due particularly to the prohibition of marriage for members of the military orders, made considerable use of this expedient. It has been shown that the fifteenth century was the golden age for bastards of the great nobility in France.[320] Possibly this can be seen as a situation in which numbers of kin were still necessary to maintain a family's power, as well as wealth. What is certain is that the legal status of noble bastards deteriorated by 1600 in France and we would also expect the effects of the Counter-Reformation and reformed churches to tell against them elsewhere. Their decline may be seen as part of the process of restricting the numbers of families and kin.

The flourishing of French bastards might also be seen as a consequence of the thinning of lineages by a greater incidence of deaths in foreign and civil wars. The rate of extinction in the direct male line remained roughly constant in England in the fourteenth and fifteenth centuries; we do not know whether it did in France and the possibilities of younger brothers founding cadet branches may have decreased, while the potential incidence of female inheritance may have increased. The spread of entails, whether including or excluding females, would have favoured the concentration of landed inheritances, if only by inhibiting possessors, without children or with daughters only, from destroying their inheritances by alienations for riotous or pious uses. A superficial impression suggests that in England, possibly in Castile and even less certainly in France in the later Middle Ages the proportion of daughters of great families entering religion was less than in France and Italy from the later sixteenth century.

To return to the problems of female inheritance, a family might

[319] An exception is the creation of artificial agnatic kin by the recruitment of new families to Genoese *alberghi* who adopted the name and arms of the *albergo*.

[320] M. Harsgor, 'L'Essor des bâtards nobles au XVe siècle', *Revue Historique*, no. 514 (1975), pp. 319–54, cf. above, p. 238. Harsgor exaggerates the uniqueness of France by ignoring Castile. It would be desirable to investigate the position in Italy. Clearly bastards were relatively disadvantaged in England, though they seem to be frequently recognized by gentry families in Lancashire and Wales on into the sixteenth century.

wish to marry sons to heiresses while restricting the rights to land of its own daughters and widows. In England absence of *retrait lignagier*, equal partition among co-heiresses, and the relatively strong dower rights of widows might suggest weak links of wider kinship and of patrilineal succession. Yet the legal norm was male primogeniture and testators' powers to devise property could amount to an unrestrained *patria potestas*. That power, as in countries within the tradition of Roman law, was used to create entails. In England these gave priority to male descent of much of the inheritance, but might also provide for heirs who had only daughters by settling some land in tail general, while later strict settlements might give them exceptionally large portions in cash. In Castile, from the sixteenth century, *mayorazgos* tended to prefer female heirs in the direct line before remoter males. This might lead to devices, such as marrying uncles to nieces, but more often to a kind of adoption. If the line ended in a female, her husband was required to adopt the name and arms of her family and to transmit them to his heir. Similar dispositions occur in English and French settlements and sometimes they were used to transmit the mother's maiden name and inheritance to a younger son.[321] In Castile the intentions of *mayorazgos* were commonly frustrated, since the husband often only added his wife's name and arms to his own. In all periods and places a man who had acquired a great fortune or had greatly added to his patrimony, was more likely to endow younger sons generously.

In France there are signs of legal doctrine and decisions showing more favour to females in interpreting rights to legitim and to Falcidian and Trebellianian quarters; how far these affected the inheritances of great families needs to be established. The tendencies to narrow the line of patrilineal descent in favour of females is clearest in Castile, but they occurred in England and France;[322] whether they occurred in Italy needs investigating. The survival of consorterial arrangements would have preserved family names,

[321] An English usage which appears to start after the Reformation was to give one of the sons of an heiress his mother's maiden name as a Christian name.
[322] Already between 1298 and 1348 the dukes of Burgundy had avoided partitions of their lands by settling entails in male primogeniture in favour of their direct descendants, in which, if their direct male line failed, their daughters and grand-daughters and their issue were preferred before the settlors' own brothers; M. Petitjean, *Essai sur l'histoire des substitutions* (Dijon, 1975), pp. 555–8.

though not particular lines. There were still thirteen *alberghi* with communal property in Genoa in 1681. But the restriction of marriage to one son and one daughter in each generation meant that lines became extinct or ended in female heirs more frequently. The rate of extinction became high in the patriciates of Florence, Venice, Siena and Genoa.[323] In Catholic countries celibacy was institutionalized through the church. Although a quarter or more of each sex of the Genevan patriciate never married by the eighteenth century,[324] the proportion was around a half in Milan and Florence, 1600–1750. The sixteenth and seventeenth centuries saw a general increase in legal paternal power, especially in the control of children's marriages.

Restriction of marriages saved money, strengthened patrimonies and enabled large portions to be paid. Yet if entailed property survived for several generations it became increasingly burdened from at least the sixteenth century with long-term debts. Much of these arose through provision of large marriage portions and dower for widows. This increased the collective and individual dependence of great nobles on monarchies, except in England. As nobles' revenues stagnated or fell during the seventeenth century, their need for pensions, perquisites and protection from their creditors increased. When revenues increased again in the eighteenth century in Naples,[325] Spain and in some cases in France, there was no investment in improvements.

In France from the early eighteenth century the rights of creditors began to be more effectively protected as entails were restricted; the same process occurred in Piedmont and Tuscany. Meanwhile other factors undermined the system of restricted marriages. While the Venetian nobility's increasing preference for celibacy even among only sons would have doomed it to extinction, elsewhere the size of families and fertility of marriages declined. Here the French dukes and peers led, but the same phenomena are found in Genoa by 1700 and in Milan after 1750. From about 1750 also there was a decline in sons and daughters entering the church in

[323] G. R. F. Baker, 'Siena sotto i Medici e gli Absburgo-Lorena', *Rivista Storica Italiano*, lxxxiv (1972), pp. 591–611; Grendi, *art. cit.*, pp. 417–19.

[324] L. Henry, *Anciennes Familles Genevoises* (Paris, 1956), p. 52, men born 1650–99, 12.0 to 18.1 per cent, 1700–49, 25.8 to 30.8 per cent; women 25.5 and 29.3 per cent.

[325] P. Villani, 'Note sullo sviluppo economico-sociale del Regno di Napoli nel settecento', *Rassegna Economica*, xxxvi (1972), pp. 50–2.

Milan, Florence and Toulouse. Thus although entails were to survive into the nineteenth century in many parts of Europe, the demographic structures and religious and social institutions which had accompanied and sustained them were already changing drastically by 1800.

Appendix I. Marriage portions

Table I provides a slightly longer perspective to Professor Stone's findings (see Table II) and some slight analysis of the general averages. The inadequacy of the coverage of the fourteenth and fifteenth centuries is apparent. Given the dearth of examples, the judgements of experienced scholars are preferable to averages. G. A. Holmes writes: 'In most of the known contracts of the magnate class, the portion was about 1,000 marks of £1,000 . . . ': *The Estates of the Higher Nobility in Fourteenth-Century England* (Cambridge, 1957), p. 43. For the fifteenth century T. B. Pugh says: 'The daughters of a wealthy baron could expect marriage portions of at least a thousand marks . . . ' S. B. Chrimes *et al.* (eds), *Fifteenth Century England* (Manchester, 1972), p. 118, n. 11.

The proportion of instances from wills is much greater for the first half of the sixteenth century than for the seventeenth century. The average of sixty-three portions from wills and settlements in the first half of the sixteenth century was £900, and from twenty-six settlements £1,040.

It must be emphasized that the sums mentioned in wills, settlements and marriage contracts were not always paid. But it was not always a question of defaulting, sometimes higher portions were paid than promised in wills or enfeoffments to uses. For example, Mary, widow of the first marquess of Dorset, in her will of 6 March 1527/8 (P.C.C., 22 Jankyn) stated that the marquess had willed (c. 1501: J. Nichols, *History of Leicestershire* (London, 1795–1811), iii, p. 663; Sir William Dugdale, *The Baronage of England*, 2 vols (London, 1675–6), i, p. 720; *Cal. Close Rolls, Henry VIII*, i, no. 945) to four of their daughters £1,000 each (two other daughters were also married), which sums were not yet paid. Accordingly she assigned lands to raise the sums for three daughters already married; the contract for one, Cecil, is already mentioned in her father's will. Again, the earl of Derby in his will (proved 27 June 1524: P.C.C., 21 Brodfelde) said that he had been promised 4,000 marks with his wife by Lady Hungerford, but had received only 600. He willed that his wife should not have her jointure according to the marriage contract until the full sum was paid. His daughter Margaret was to have £2,066–13–4 owing but if Lady Hungerford

TABLE I *Marriage portions proposed by peers: figures in [ ] brackets are portions proposed by earls and above*

Portions in £	1300–50	1351–1400	1401–50	1451–1500	1475–1524	1525–49	1550–74	1575–99	1600–24	1625–49	1650–74	1675–1729
0–200		1	1	3	7	16						
201–499		3	4	11	3	6	6[1]					
500–999	5[2]	5[3]	6[1]	7[6][e]	14[3]	11[1]	7[5]	6[3]	7	1	3	
1,000–1,999	4[2]	3[2]	1	6[5]	7[6]	12[10]	18[12]	7[4]	9[1]	9[5]	3[1]	
2,000–2,999	2	3[3]		[1]	3[2]	[6]	1	3	3[1]	20[7]	6[3]	[1]
3,000–3,999			[2]					5[1]		13[4]	2	
4,000–4,999			[1]						6[5]	7[6]	3[1]	4[1]
5,000–5,999			[1]						2[1]	4[1]	4[3]	8[7]
6,000–6,999									[5]	3[2]	5[4]	7[3]
7,000–7,999										6[5]	[3]	[5]
8,000–8,999										9[4]	8[7]	[2]
10,000–12,999									2			16[14]
13,000–14,999												[1]
15,000–19,999										1		[3]
20,000–24,999											[1]	[1]
25,000												[3]
No. of portions	11[4][a]	15[8][b]	16[5][c]	28[12][d]	34[11]	51[17][f]	32[18][g]	23[8][h]	34[13][i]	73[34][j]	38[23][k]	51[41][l]
Average size to nearest £50	1,200 [900]	950 [1,400]	1,100 [2,400]	700 [1,150]	750 [1,150]	750 [1,450]	850 [1,000]	2,250 [2,000]	3,550 [4,650]	5,050 [5,400]	6,250 [7,800]	9,350 [10,150]
Peers below earl	1,200	500	500	300	550	400	900	2,350	3,000	5,000	3,900	6,100
Phelps Brown Industrial Index[m]	..	..	105	100	102	115	213	230	261	283	340	330 (1670–1700)

Notes to Table I

ᵃ Includes one portion of £800 and two of £1,000 given by Ralph Stafford before he was created an earl in 1351.

ᵇ Highest is 4,000 marks paid by Richard, earl of Arundel in 1364 to buy a marriage for his daughter Alice. The lowest is the £200 left by Philip, Lord Darcy in 1399 to his daughter Elizabeth from the money owing for the marriage of his son John *in perimpleacionem maritagii sui: Testamenta Eboracensia*, pt i, ed. James Raine (Surtees Society, iv, 1836), p. 255. The next lowest is 500 marks given by Lord Poynings in 1361: *Calendar Close Rolls, 1360–4*, pp. 257, 259–61.

ᶜ Highest is 6,500 marks given by Richard, duke of York with his eldest daughter Anne: T. B. Pugh in Chrimes *et al.* (eds), *Fifteenth Century England*, p. 118, n. 11. The lowest is 200 marks given by Lord Rivers, 1450: *ibid.* The highest known portions proposed in the fifteenth century were 10,000 marks each settled by Edward IV in 1475 on his two daughters: R. Somerville, *History of the Duchy of Lancaster* (London, 1953), i, p. 239. They are not included in the Table.

ᵈ The highest is the 4,000 marks paid to buy a marriage for Eleanor Percy by the executors of her father, the fourth earl of Northumberland: J. M. W. Bean, *The Estates of the Percy Family 1416–1537* (Oxford, 1958), p. 134. She had been left 3,000 marks in her father's will. The lowest is the 100 marks given by William, Lord Stourton in 1476 on the marriage of his daughter Margaret to James Chudlegh: J. Prince, *Worthies of Devon* (Exeter, 1701), p. 209, citing a copy of the covenants. One wonders if it only recorded the first payment of a series. The next lowest is by John, Lord Mountjoy, whose will (P.C.C., Logge, 211) left his daughter Constantine £100, with the proviso that if she wished to become a nun it should also be paid. It was more common to reduce the portion if the recipient entered religion, so perhaps this can be taken as a minimum for a nun. If both these exceptionally small portions are excluded, the overall average for twenty-two portions would be £775, and that of the twelve remaining below the rank of earl would be £350.

ᵉ These include three portions settled in 1457 by the third earl of Northumberland by an enfeoffment to uses of lands reckoned by Bean to be worth at least £1,000 a year: *op. cit.*, pp. 101–2. His three daughters were to have the proceeds of the lands for two years, while four years' revenue was to be devoted to his sepulture and founding three perpetual chantries, and six years' revenue to paying his debts: E. B. de Fonblanque, *Annals of the House of Percy* (London, 1887), i, pp. 547–8.

ᶠ The highest portion is £2,666. If the sixteen lowest portions (200 marks each left to his nine daughters by Thomas, Lord Wentworth in 1544; the 1,150 marks left between four daughters by John, Lord Scrope in 1548; and 300 marks to three daughters by John, Lord Ogle in 1543) are eliminated, the general average is £1,000 and that for peers below the rank of earl is £600. It should be noted that one of Lord Scrope's daughters received a portion of £400 on her marriage in 1564 (Bodleian Library MS. Dodsworth 88, fo. 97v.).

ᵍ The highest is £2,000 left by Edmund, Lord Chandos in 1572. The lowest is £400 to Eleanor, daughter of John, Lord Scrope.

ʰ The absence of any poor peers has inflated the average. The highest portion is £4,000, the lowest £1,000. I have not included the £8,000, £6,000 and £6,000 promised to the three daughters and co-heirs of Ferdinando, earl of Derby in 1595: B. Coward, 'Disputed Inheritances', *Bull. Inst. Hist. Research*, xliv (1971), p. 205. Elizabeth in 1603 married Henry, Lord Hastings bringing £4,000 immediately. This has not been included under 1600–24.

ᶦ Stone's is obviously a fuller sample for this period, though both are probably overweighted with the wealthier peers. The lowest portions are two of £1,000.

ʲ These include three portions of £8,000 each settled on Emmanuel Scrope, earl of Sunderland's three bastard daughters. The lowest is £1,000, the highest is £20,000 for Anne Bayning's marriage to Francis, Lord Dacre in 1641 before she became her father's co-heiress. But Lord Dacre's executors after his death in 1662 claimed that he had only received £10,000 of the portion: T. Barrett-Lennard, *The Families of Lennard and Barrett* (London, 1908), pp. 278, 296.

ᵏ The lowest is £2,000 the highest £12,000. The two portions of £15,000 each given by Cromwell, when Lord Protector, have not been included. They must represent some sort of maximum, in the difficult conditions of the 1650s, and may be compared with those proposed by Edward IV, cited in note c above. W. C. Abbott, *The Writings and Speeches of Oliver Cromwell* (Cambridge Mass., 1947), iv, pp. 602, 765. In 1639 Sir Thomas Thynne had left his daughter by his second marriage a portion of £20,000.

ˡ The lowest is £4,000 and the whole group is even more heavily weighted towards the wealthiest families.

ᵐ This index's base is 1451–75 = 100: *Economica*, xxiv (1957), p. 306. It is worth comparing its movement with that of the index of food prices, since it may have slightly more relevance to the changing cost of aristocratic expenditure than food prices. But its appropriateness for this purpose is very limited, since it does not include high-quality textiles.

---

did not pay, it was to be raised from the rents and profits of his lands.

On the other hand Thomas, duke of Norfolk, on his death in 1524 left his four unmarried daughters by his second marriage £300 each (N. H. Nicholas, *Testamenta Vetusta* (London, 1828), ii, p. 603). But the next year his daughter Catherine was contracted to Thomas Berkeley with a portion of £1,000, though the marriage never took place (J. Smyth, *The Lives of the Berkeleys*, ii, pp. 225, 252). In 1530 another daughter, Dorothy, married Edward, earl of Derby, with a portion of 4,000 marks and a jointure of 1,000 marks (22 Henry VIII, *cap.* 23: *Statutes of the Realm*, iii, p. 351). These two portions have been included in Table I, but not those willed by the duke. Again, Arthur, Lord Capell left four daughters £3,000 each in his will (Public Record Office, S.P. 23/223/24). In 1648 one of them married Lord Beauchamp with a portion of £10,000 (Longleat, Seymour Papers, Box V/58).

In general wills may tend to understate the amounts actually given in portions, because they often provided that, if a child died under age and unmarried, the portion should go to the survivor, or be equally divided among survivors. The same can be true of provisions in marriage settlements for children unborn but these

TABLE II   *Marriage portions offered by peers, 1475–1724*[a]

Portions £	1475–1525	1525–49	1550–74	1575–99	1600–24	1625–49	1650–74	1675–1724
0–499	5	9	2					
500–999	4	6	5	1				
1,000–1,999	1	13	7	7	3		3	
2,000–2,999			6	8	9	10	1	
3,000–3,999			1	2	8	6		1
4,000–4,999				2	14	25		5
5,000–5,999					2	13	3	
6,000–7,999					7	16	6	2
8,000–9,999						2	3	1
10,000–14,999					2	12	5	9
15,000–19,999						1		2
20,000–24,999							1	3
No. of items	10	28	21	20	45	85	22	23
Average size to nearest £100	£500[b] 3	£700	£1,300	£2,000	£3,800	£5,400	£7,800	£9,700
Portion index	100	140	260	400	760	1,080	1,560	1,940
Phelps Brown price index (to nearest 10)	110	170	290	400	500	600	630	620

[a] From L. Stone, *The Crisis of the Aristocracy, 1558–1641* (Oxford, 1965), Appendix XXXI, p. 790, by permission of the Clarendon Press.
[b] This figure excludes two very unusual portions of £2,666 received and then given by the Stanleys, earls of Derby. If these are included the average is £800.

play no part in Table I, also provision in such settlements was often increased later, e.g. Appendix II, nos. 36, 45.

Portions proposed for, or given with, those who were already heirs general have been excluded as far as possible, as they were likely to be exceptionally large. Conscious exceptions have been made in two cases; first George, Lord Chandos, whose will in 1654 provided his four daughters and heirs with £6,000 for the eldest and £3,000 each for the others. If his wife had borne a son, two daughters would have had £6,000 each and another £3,000 (24 Jan. 1654/5, *Baronies of Strange of Knokin and* STANLEY EVIDENCE (London, 1921), pp. 154–60). The second is Edward, earl of Bath,

TABLE III *Portions proposed by knightly families and wealthy Londoners*[a]

£	Knightly 1400–50	Knightly 1451–1500	Londoners 1451–1503	Knightly 1501–50	Knightly 1551–1600
0–100	4	4	3	11	
101–150	10	2			
151–200	6	3	4	10	1
201–250			2	15	
251–300	1	7		11	2
301–350		6	3	9	8
351–400	1	4	1	1	2
401–500	1			2	13
501–600	1			3	2
601–700		1	5		21
701–900		1			1
901–1,000			1		10
1,001–2,000					15
Total no. portions	24	28	19	62	75
Average in £	191	282[b]	348[c]	286[d]	859[e]

[a] This is compiled overwhelmingly from wills: Knights 1400–50, 2 settlements and 11 wills: 1451–1500, 3 settlements and 15 wills: 1501–50, 21 wills and 5 settlements: 1551–1600, 28 wills and 22 settlements.

[b] If the four lowest portions of 100 marks left to each of his daughters by John Shirley of Staunton Harold in 1475 are removed, the average would be £322.

[c] If the three lowest portions of £100 each left by Robert Gregory in 1466 (P.C.C., Godyn 116) are removed, the average would be £394. Gregory left his wife £400 as her part of his goods, and a son £200. The widows of Londoners were normally better endowed by the custom of London than their daughters. Geoffrey Boleyn, who left his three daughters 1,000 marks each, left his wife 2,000 marks and half his plate in 1463 (P.C.C., Godyn 4). Sir William Heryot in 1484 left his wife £1,000 and four sons and a daughter £200 each. Sir Edmund Shaw in 1487 left his wife as her part £2,000, and to his son and daughter £1,000 each (*Calendar Close Rolls Henry VII*, i, no. 794). Nicholas Wyfold left his wife £1,000 as her reasonable part of his goods and £100 plate, and his daughter 500 marks and 500 marks of plate (P.C.C., 60 Stokton). In 1464 William Marowe left two sons £400 each, three daughters 500 marks each, and to his wife £1,000 and 100 marks of plate. Like many of the others he also had considerable property in land (P.C.C., Godyn 4 and 85).

[d] If the five lowest portions of 200 marks each left by Sir William Pelham in 1538 to his daughters are removed, the average would become £300.

[e] The lowest portion is £300 left to his younger daughter by Edward Griffin, Mary's Attorney-General, who left her elder sister £500 and a younger son £5,000 in 1570. Only nineteen portions are before 1570. The portion of £4,000 willed by Sir Philip Sidney has been omitted; if it were included, the average would be £899.

who by settlement of 1632 and his will in 1637, left each of his three daughters and co-heirs £1,433–6–8 (*Minutes of Evidence Dynaunt, Fitzwaryn and Martin Peerage Claims* (London, 1915), pp. 251, 257). It might seem equally logical to exclude only daughters since they usually received exceptionally large portions, but they do form a very small minority of the cases. Moreover, eldest daughters were frequently given more than younger ones.

The selection of knightly families in Table III was made with the intention of including only apparently wealthy and important families, but it does include newly risen men who had made fortunes in the law. The individuals included were not all necessarily knights.

Appendix II. Some examples of provision for younger children

1(a) In 1360 John de Vere, earl of Oxford, provided his second surviving son, Aubrey, with six manors in reversion after his mother.

1(b) Hugh Courtenay, earl of Devon (d. 1377), left lands to each of his four surviving younger sons, in all between seven and ten manors, in reversion after their mother. G. A. Holmes, *The Estates of the Higher Nobility in Fourteenth Century England* (Cambridge, 1957), pp. 33–4, 47–8.

1(c) Thomas Beauchamp, third earl of Warwick (d. 1369), settled land of 400 marks a year in tail male on his younger son William, who was to become Lord Abergavenny: McFarlane, *op. cit.*, pp. 191–2. Richard, the fifth earl, who died in 1439, left provision in his will for endowing a younger son who was never born. He was to have the 400 marks a year of land which had come back to the head of the house on the death of the widow of William, Lord Abergavenny, in 1435 (his only son having died in 1422). In addition he was granted the manor and castle of Bathekyngton and the manor of Grovebury in Leighton Buzzard, the reversion of which the earl had received in 1429. P.C.C., Rous, fo. 147; *Victoria County History, Bedfordshire*, iii, p. 403.

2. Richard, earl of Arundel, by his will of 4 March 1392, left his younger son Thomas manors in reversion to him and his heirs male, default to the testator's right heirs. Until Thomas received £100 a year from the manors, he was to have an annuity of £100. His daughter was left 1,000 marks. J. Nicholas, *A Collection of the Wills of the Kings and Queens of England* (n.p., 1778), pp. 131–3.

3. Edmund, earl of March, in 1380 left his second son land of 300 marks a year to him and the heirs of his body, remainder to Edmund and his heirs, much plate and 400 marks in cash (*Ibid.*, p. 113).

4. Sir William Langford, 1411, wills to his daughter £100; to his third son Henry 10 marks a year land to him and heirs of his body, remainder to his second son; to that second son, William, the manor of Chale, Isle of Wight, to him and heirs of his body, remainder to

Henry and heirs of his body, remainder to Sir William and his heirs. *Fifty Earliest English Wills*, ed. F. J. Furnivall (*Early English Texts Society*, old ser. (xxviii, 1882), pp. 18–20).

5. William, Lord Roos, 22 February 1412, wills to his second son William lands for life, a third of his goods to three other sons, to maintain one until beneficed and the other two till *competenter marientur: The Register of Henry Chichele, Archbishop of Canterbury, 1414–1443*, ed. E. F. Jacob, 4 vols (Canterbury and York Soc., xiv, xv, xvi and xvii, 1937–47), ii, pp. 24–5.

6. Thomas Poynynges, Lord St John, 1429: lands to two younger sons in tail male. *The Register of Henry Chichele*, ii, p. 389.

7. Sir Henry Willoughby made his testament on 15 September 1443 and his will of lands on 16 January before, naming four daughters and six younger sons. Five of the sons were granted land in tail male with various remainders to each other. The lands settled on his heir were partly in tail male and partly in tail general. Three of the younger sons were to have lands of ten marks a year bought from the proceeds of his personal estate settled in tail male and, if there was enough, the other three were to have similarly £5 a year. Any child not advanced in his lifetime was to have 200 marks. There were also substantial legacies of plate to the four daughters and three of the younger sons (University of Nottingham, Middleton Collection, M in F6). Sir Henry married as his second wife Margaret, daughter and heir of Sir Baldwin Freville, by whom he had seven daughters all of whom married. His son and heir by his first wife, Richard, died without issue in 1471. His younger son Baldwin founded the Willoughbys of Grendon, Northamptonshire (*Historical MS Commission, Middleton*, pp. 505–7). His widow remarried and survived Sir Henry some forty-three years until 1491. The whole inheritance was worth about £650 a year net in 1498, excluding receipts from coal (A. Cameron, 'Sir Henry Willoughby of Wollaton', *Transactions of the Thorpton Society*, lxxiv (1970), p. 11).

8. William, seventh Lord Lovel, in 1455 left eight manors in four counties and Minster Lovel, Oxfordshire, to his second son William in tail male, with contingent remainders if he or any of his issue male discontinued the entail, the lands should go to the testator's right heirs; if William died without issue male, or if he or any of his heirs male became Lord Lovel the lands should go

under the same conditions to his two younger brothers successively and finally to his father's right heirs. He left four manors to his third son and four and half manors to his fourth son with similar conditions and remainders (*Lincoln Diocese Documents*, ed. A. Clark (*Early English Texts Society*, original ser., cxlix, 1914), pp. 81–6).

9(a) Humfrey Stafford, first duke of Buckingham, by his will in 1460 left to his son Henry and his wife, Margaret, countess of Richmond, and the heirs of their bodies, remainder to his own right heirs, lands of 300 marks per annum and of another 100 marks per annum to Henry for life, but if he died leaving issue, an heir apparent to Margaret, the 100 marks to remain to the heirs of the body of Henry. He had already made a similar settlement of 300 marks a year in land for the marriage of his son John to Constance, daughter and heir apparent of Henry Greene in January 1458 (P.C.C., Stokton, fo. 167: R. Halstead, *Succinct Genealogies* (London, 1685), pp. 196–9). In his will he mentions £1,000 owed to the earl of Shrewsbury which must be his daughter's marriage portion; his older daughter had £1,533 in 1452 of which some was still owing (McFarlane, *op. cit.*, p. 87).

9(b) Hugh, earl of Stafford, in 1385 left his three younger sons £100 per annum each for life out of lands in the hands of feoffees: N. H. Nicholas, *Testamenta Vetusta* (London, 1828), i, p. 119; G. A. Holmes, *The Estates of the Higher Nobility*, p. 53.

10. Sir William Vernon of Tong, 1467: to four daughters 500 marks each, to his son Richard the manor of Hasilbach for life, to his son Rauf the manor of Rowarth to him and his heirs and all 'my purchast lande' for life. (*Prerogative Court of Canterbury*, Godyn 193.)

11(a) Richard Fynes, Lord Dacre of the South, in 1483 willed one manor to each of his four younger sons and the heirs of his body with remainders to his eldest and then to the other sons.

11(b) Thomas, second Lord Dacre, in 1531 left £200 and two manors to his third son Thomas, and his heirs (T. Barrett-Lennard, *An Account of the Families of Lennard and Barrett* (n.p., 1908), pp. 184, 185 n. 6, P.C.C. 13 Hogen).

12 Henry Percy, earl of Northumberland, 1485: to son William 1,000 marks a year for life; to son Alan, clerk, 200 marks a year for life; to two daughters 3,000 and 2,000 marks. *Testamenta*

Eboracensia, pt iii, ed. James Raine jun. (Surtees Soc. xv, 1865), p. 306.

(13a) Sir George Nevill, fifth lord Bergavenny by his will of 1 July 1491 (P.C.C. Horne fo. 66ᵛ) gave to his younger son John at twenty-four, provided he did not become his heir, the manor of Worfeld in Shropshire in tail male remainder to the testator's next heir for ever. His sons Edward, Thomas, Richard were left the manors of Holkham (Norfolk), Claxhale (Suffolk), Otterley (Suffolk) respectively on the same terms. His son William was to have the manor of Bergwich (Norfolk) for life, but if he became a priest before the age of twenty-six he was only to have £20 a year until promoted to a benefice of 100 marks a year.

13(b) His son George, sixth lord Bergavenny, made his will 4 June 1535 (P.C.C. 35 Hogan) in which he provided for his mistress whom he married on his death-bed and her unborn child four manors in Sussex for their lives.

13(c) Edward, Lord Abergavenny (d. 1622), settled the manor of Newton St Loo, Somerset, on his second son Christopher Nevill who married Mary, daughter and co-heiress of Thomas Darcy of Tolston Darcy, Essex (D. Rowland, *A Historical and Genealogical account of the noble Family of Nevill* (London, 1830), p. 162). By his will he also settled land in Sussex on Sir Christopher for life, then to Sir Christopher's son, Richard, and his heirs for ever (P.C.C. 106 Savile). Richard's grandson succeeded to the barony as heir male in 1695. Newton had been bought in 1564 from the earl of Huntingdon for £2,600 (C. Cross, *The Puritan Earl* (London, 1966), p. 308) by Edward's father who became the heir of the entail created by George, the sixth lord (*G.E.C.*, i, pp. 34–5). He was the grandson of the fifth lord's son, Edward, whose second son was Henry Neville of Billingbere, Berkshire, who married the daughter and heir of Sir John Gresham.

14. Sir Robert Tailboys, in 1495, willed life estates in five manors to four younger sons: *Inq. Post Mortem, Henry VII*, i, nos. 1,037, 1,053.

15. Sir William Carew made his will 26 May 1501. (P.C.C. Moone, fo. 86ᵛ.) left to each of his three younger sons lands to him and his heirs for ever. If his second son, William, became a priest, his lands were to go to the youngest Thomas. If any younger son died with-

out issue his lands were to go to the survivors; if all so died, then to the eldest son. John, the eldest, was to receive the purchased lands in Norfolk and Suffolk, lands in Devon and Worcester went to his widow for life and then to the heirs of his body. In default 'of issue male to remayn to yssue generall and soo from heir to heir as long as any of myne yssue be on lyve, or any of their heirs', in default to turn 'agayne to the gifte of my moder'. His daughter received 100 marks, but it is not clear whether this would be her whole portion. Wychbold in Worcestershire, settled on William, remained with his descendants until at least 1562 (*V.C.H. Worcestershire*, iii, p. 60). John was the eldest son of a second marriage and the founder of the Carews of Crowcombe, Somerset (W. A. Copinger, *The Manors of Suffolk*, i, pp. 358–9).

16. Sir Henry Vernon of Tong by his will of 18 January 1514/5 left a daughter 800 marks portion, a younger son 500 marks and to another £1,000 to purchase land or get him a marriage. Two other younger sons already married are mentioned. (P.C.C. 8 Holder.)

17. 1523, Nicholas, Lord Vaux, left his younger son £1,000 to purchase lands to the clear value of 100 marks per annum or else to purchase him a wife that may dispend 200 marks of inheritance per annum and above, the remainder of £1,000 to be delivered to him at the age of twenty-four. He left three daughters £500 each, and had to pay £666 portions each to three other daughters. (P.C.C. 11 Brodfelde.)

18. Thomas West, Lord La Warre, by his will 8 October 1524 left two manors to one younger son and three to another in tail male. Three daughters received 500 marks each 'so that they be married to men of substance' by advice of their mother and eldest brother, if one entered religion she was to have only 100 marks. (P.C.C. 2 Porche.)

19. 1525, Charles, earl of Worcester leaves to his son George by his third marriage the reversion of various lands after the death of his mother some for life and others which the earl had of the gift of Richard, earl of Kent, to him and the heirs of his body. If George is disseized of these latter lands, he is to be given lands of equal value in tail male. The value for livery of only part of the lands granted his widow was £185-6-8. George also got a third of his goods and the earl's daughter a £500 portion. (P.C.C. 13 Porche.)

20. Sir John Harington of Exton in 1553 willed a manor to each of his four younger sons to the heirs and assigns of each for ever and £300 to the one of his four daughters, still unmarried (P.C.C. 1 More.)

21(a) William, Lord Windsor, in 1558 left his younger son William a manor and other lands to him and his heirs and another manor and purchased lands in tail male, to his only son by his second wife, Philip, a manor in reversion after his mother and four manors to him and his heirs male, remainder to William in tail male remainder to Edward, the son and heir. Another son Walter received two manors in tail male. Six of Lord Windsor's seven daughters married. Philip died young. William married a daughter of the earl of Worcester.

21(b) Edward, Lord Windsor, in 1572 left to each of his three younger sons a manor and lands to him and his heirs for ever in fee simple on condition that if the grantee and all issue male of his body died without issue male then the demise to cease and the grantor's heirs may enter. He left each of his daughters £1,000, of whom two died young and two married.

21(c) His eldest son Frederick died unmarried in 1585, leaving his brothers Edward and Andrew each an annuity of £50 and charging his brother and heir, Henry, to augment his sisters' portions which 'I myself have purposed'. In 1589 Henry conveyed the manors of Eton and Alderbourne to his younger brother Andrew. Although Andrew's son married Elizabeth, the daughter of Henry, her brother Thomas, sixth Lord Windsor who died childless in 1641 conveyed all his estates to her elder sister's son, Thomas Windsor Hickman (A. Collins, *Historical Collections of the Noble Family of Windsor* (London, 1754), pp. 50–8; P.C.C. 28 Pyckering and 1 Windsor; *V.C.H. Buckinghamshire*, iii, pp. 265–6, 297; G.E.C., *Peerage*, xii, pt 2, p. 799 n. (e)).

22(a) Richard, first lord Rich, according to the surviving evidence seems to have been prepared to endow his second son, Robert, as generously or more generously than his eldest son who predeceased his father, having no issue by his marriage. His third son was given a manor to him and his heirs in reversion after his father whom he predeceased, as did the fourth son, who was married. Nine daughters were also married. His bastard son had a manor entailed on him and his executors were instructed to purchase a ward with £200 a year in land for his wife.

22(b) Robert, the second lord, in 1579 settled some £140 a year in land on his second son in tail male, but again the eldest son died without issue in his father's lifetime. The third son Edwin received land of over £100 a year from his mother. Edwin was one of Essex's knights and bought land in Norfolk, while selling part of his land in Essex to his elder brother. His grandson became a baronet (F. Blomefield, *An Essay towards a Topographical History of Norfolk*, 2nd edn (London, 1805), v, pp. 54, 60, 78–9, 83–4, 103). In 1581 the second lord willed his daughter £1,500. His landed income was about £2,200 a year.

22(c) Robert, the third lord and first earl of Warwick, in 1597 settled land of £200 a year in tail male on his second son, Henry, in reversion after himself and terms declared in his will. In the meantime Henry received an annual pension of £100 and in 1612 property at St Bartholomew's worth some £300 a year. He was left the lease of a house, plate, stock of sheep and corn, and debts of £1,580 owed to the earl, if collectable, in his father's will in 1617. The third son Charles (d. 1627) received a similar reversion in tail male of land worth £120 a year in 1605.

22(d) Robert, the second earl, married a great heiress Frances Hatton as his first wife. In the settlement on the marriage of his eldest son in 1632, provision was made that if there were no sons of the marriage, an only daughter would get £13,000, two daughters £7,000 each, more than two equal shares in £20,000. Warwick retained power to appoint rent charges, make grants in fee simple or tail to his younger sons over lands worth over £700 a year. His second son, Charles, had lands of about £270 settled on him and the heirs of his body in reversion after his father. In 1641 on Charles' marriage to Mary, daughter of the earl of Cork, with a £7,000 portion, Warwick settled some £130 of this property on them jointly, the rest remaining in reversion. Henry Rich, the third son, died in 1637, without apparently getting any provision other than an allowance. Hatton, the youngest son, received some of his mother's Norfolk property, presumably after his father's death in 1658. (I am greatly indebted to Mr Christopher Thompson for the detailed information on which this oversimplified summary is based.)

23. Sir Henry Sidney by his will of 1582 left to his younger sons Robert and Thomas £50 a year each and land in tail male. Sir Philip Sidney in 1588 left his younger brother Thomas land of £100 a year in tail male, leaving his only daughter and heir £4,000. (P.C.C. 27 Windsor, *Letters and Memorials of State*, A. Collins, ed. (London, 1746), i, p. 110.)

24(a) Sir John Spencer of Wormleighton at his death in 1586 settled four manors, two parks and other lands bought by him on his three surviving younger sons, the two elder each shared the residue of his goods and the third got £500; all three shared a further legacy of £4,000. He also married six daughters the eldest of whom had £1,000 portion.

24(b) His grandson Robert, first lord Spencer, in 1625 left his two younger sons £2,500 and £2,000, the elder received land of at least £100 a year, the second an annuity of £100 and had a rent charge of £160 settled on him and his wife by his eldest brother.

24(c) In 1636 William, the second lord, left his two youngest sons (two were already provided for) £200 a year in land each settled on them and their future wives and the heirs male of their bodies with remainders to the eldest son. His eldest daughter had been given a portion of £6,000 and the four younger ones were left £4,000 each, as was the child his wife was carrying when he made his will (M. E. Finch, *The Wealth of Five Northamptonshire Families, 1540–1640* (Northants. Records Society, xix, 1956), pp. 57–60; P.C.C. 27 Gore).

25. 1592: Settlement made by Henry, Lord Scrope empowering the assignment of land of £100 per annum 'for the advancement of younger sonnes during their lyves', and £200 per annum for 'the advancement of daughters'; if one daughter, only £1,000; if more than one, 1,000 marks each. (Public Record Office, S.P. 15/22/35.)

26. 1596, earl of Pembroke left his second son £6,666, or lands of that value; to his daughter a £4,000 portion. (P.C.C. 39 Woodhall.)

27. Sir George Manners of Haddon 5 February 1608/9 willed to his younger son Roger the Manor of Whitwell, Derby, and rectory of Grynley, Nottingham to him and his heirs male and £500 towards stocking his grounds and setting up his house. (P.C.C. 82 Wood.)

28. Sir John Portman (d. 1612) by his will of 5 November 1606 left his four daughters a total of £4,700. He left each of three younger

sons a manor; to the two youngest, to them and the heirs of their bodies; to the second son, to him and his heirs in reversion after the death of his mother, with other lands for his life. (*Sales of Wards in Somerset 1603–41*, M. J. Hawkins, ed. (Somerset Record Society, lxvii, 1965), pp. 140, 142–3.)

29. Henry, Lord Gray of Groby, by his will of 20 June 1614 left £2,000 to his youngest son George to be put to increase for 7 years and made provisions to raise portions of unspecified amounts for his two other younger sons. (P.C.C. 107 Lawe.)

30. 1614, Sir William Wentworth of Wentworth Woodhouse left two daughters £2,000 each; to his seven younger sons went at least £700 a year, at least two of them received land of inheritance (one of them had land worth £200 in 1634), the rest may have had only life annuities of about £100 each. *Econ. Hist. Rev.*, 2nd ser., xi (1958), p. 228.

31. William, earl of Devonshire (d. 1628) settled on his only daughter an £8,000 portion and on his second son in reversion after his mother £2,000 per annum to him and the heirs male of his body, claiming that his father had settled more land on his second son. (Private Act, 3 Charles I, no. 3; Chatsworth House, Hobbes Papers, D5.)

32(a) John, first lord Petre, who died in 1613, settled lands worth £550 a year in the 1630s on his second son, John, and lands worth over £300 a year on his third son. John changed the remainders to his other brothers, settled by his father, to the third and other sons of his eldest brother.

32(b) William, the second lord (d. 1637), settled land and money amounting to £40,000 on four younger sons who lived to be adults, alienating land worth over £550; he also left his second son £1,000 and each younger son £500 in his will.

32(c) In 1638 Robert, third lord Petre, died, having settled lands of £1,441 a year for 30 years in trust to raise £35,000, of which £6,000 and £4,000 was for two daughters, £10,000 for his second son and £5,000 each for three younger sons, two of whom died under age. (W. R. Emerson, 'The Economic Development of the Estates of the Petre Family in Essex in the Sixteenth and Seventeenth Centuries' (Oxford D.Phil. thesis, 1951), pp. 229–31; J. J. Howard, ed., *Genealogical Collections Illustrating the History of Roman*

Catholic Families (London, 1887–92), i, pt i, pp. 71–2; M. J. Hawkins, ed., *Sales of Wards*, pp. 190–3; Public Record Office, S.P. 23/66/185.)

32(d) William, the fourth lord, made a settlement in 1680 providing £10,000 for daughters' portions, if he had no son, £5,000 if he did have a son. His will confirmed the £10,000 to his only daughter. In 1700 Thomas, the sixth lord (d. 1707), settled £10,000 for daughters' portions, if he had a male heir, if not, then £15,000. In 1705 this was increased to £15,000 and £30,000. He did have a son and left only one daughter, who also received £1,000 in her brother's will, but died unmarried in 1713, leaving her mother £10,000. Robert, the seventh lord (d. 1713), married a great heiress Catherine Walmsley and their settlement provided £20,000 if there were only daughters and £15,000 for daughters and younger sons with power to grant annuities up to £500 for each younger son. In the event there was only one posthumous son, the eighth lord, Robert James. His marriage settlement provided £20,000 for daughters and younger sons; if there were no sons, then £20,000 for one daughter, £30,000 for more than one. Catherine remarried Charles, Lord Stourton, and had no children by him. She died in 1788, when Dunkenhalgh and other of her Lancashire lands went to the second son of her grandson, the ninth lord Petre. (Essex Rec. Off.; D/D p. F71, F.92, F.100; Lancashire Rec. Off. D/D pt 37. I am indebted to Dr C. Clay for sending me particulars of these settlements. J. J. Howard, ed., *op. cit.*, pp. 75–7; *V.C.H. Lancashire*, vi, pp. 421–2.)

33. 1640, Sir Christopher Wandesford by his will left one daughter £2,500 and two younger sons £3,000 each; if the elder son became his heir, £6,000 was to be used to buy land for the other son.

34. By indenture of 8 June 1647, William, Viscount Saye and Sele, promised to settle land, purchased c. 1632 for at least £4,500, of the clear yearly value of £300 on Susan, sole daughter and heir of Thomas Hobbes, late of Gray's Inn, for life as dower on her marriage to John Fiennes, his third son, and then to John his heirs and assigns for ever. John was to settle fee simple land of £200 a year to the use of himself and the heirs of his body got on Susan, failing these to his right heirs for ever. The Viscount's youngest daughter Anne received a portion of £2,750 in 1648. Four other daughters were already married. The youngest son, Richard, had £3,380 secured to him in 1658.

In 1632 the Viscount had made a settlement of a term of 500 years to pay his debts, raise a portion for Anne, and give each of his five youngest sons 100 marks a year during their mother's life and after her death £100 a year to him and his heirs; the residue of the rents to go to his second son Nathaniel. This was cancelled in 1638 and another agreement made to raise £12,000 to pay debts and raise unspecified portions for younger children (Bodleian Library, MS North c.30/12; 28–9, 64, 71, 78; MS Rawlinson D 892, pp. 76, 82–90, 57–8, 61–4.)

35. 1653, Sir Thomas Pelham's will gave one daughter £5,000 and two younger sons £1,000 each: M. F. Keeler, *The Long Parliament 1640–1641. A Biographical Study of its Members* (Memoirs of the Amer. Phil. Soc., xxxvi, Philadelphia, 1954), p. 302.

36. Humble, first lord Ward, by his will of 1 July 1655, proved 11 November 1670, settled on his youngest son, William, in addition to what was already settled on him at the marriage of his eldest brother Edward, the Manor of Belbroughton and Fairfield and lands in King's Rowney, Dudley and Rowley to him and his heirs for ever. He was also left £1,000. The marriage settlement of 1 March 1647 had left Belbroughton and £250 a year of land un-entailed with full powers to Lord Ward to dispose of them. If Edward died without issue male, any daughter or daughters received £3,000. Lands other than Edward's wife's jointure were charged with an £80 annuity for the lives of Lord Ward's second son, his wife and their eldest son or daughter and £50 a year to each younger son for life. The same annuities were chargeable for Edward's younger sons, if he predeceased his father. £500 each was charged for Lord Ward's daughters' portions. His will left another £500 and the freehold of a farm to his daughter Theodosia, similar bequests to two other daughters having been erased. Belbroughton had been bought by Humble's father and conveyed to him in 1649. John Ward, grandson of William, succeeded to the peerage in 1740. He left Belbroughton and Fairfield to his younger son William, who was eventually heir of his eldest brother John (Dudley Public Library, Earl of Dudley's muniments, Box 2 bdle. 1, Box 3 bdle. 9; *V.C.H. Worcestershire*, iii, p. 15.)

37. Sir Francis Henry Lee of Ditchley, before succeeding to the baronetcy in 1658, had had settled on him as a younger brother land of inheritance of £130 a year and an annuity of £300 to which

his elder brother, Sir Henry, had added £100 of inheritance. Their sister received a £2,000 portion. Sir Henry left his two daughters and co-heirs £8,000 each, other legacies of £4,240, debts of £12,000 and a personal estate of £500. Sir Francis Henry in 1667 left his younger son Francis Henry £10,000, or at his choice land of £500 a year to him and his heirs. The estate was now burdened with two jointures amounting to £2,500 a year. In 1687 Francis Henry agreed to accept £6,000 only; having received the money, he refused to sign a release, although his elder brother, now earl of Lichfield, had previously given him over £500. The result was a Chancery suit in 1689–91. The estate had been worth about £5,000 a year in 1639. Sir Francis Henry in 1660 married an heiress who brought land of over £500 a year which had been sold after his death. In 1690 the estate was worth about £4,200 a year of which £2,500 went in jointures. (Oxfordshire County Rec. Office, Dillon Collection, xviii/m/122, 126; xviii/d/3h 2–5; xviii/k 8, 10–13, 6, 2.)

38. Thomas, Lord Leigh, by his will of 6 January 1671/2 bequeathed his younger son Charles £2,000 originally lent him to purchase land in Worcestershire, on condition of repaying a mortgage of £1,000 borrowed by Charles. He was also left the lease of Grovebury manor in Leighton Buzzard from the canons of Windsor with the right of renewal, on condition that he repaid £1,500 borrowed by Thomas from another of his younger sons, Christopher. The rectory of Leighton through the lease of a prebend of Lincoln had already been settled on Charles; the two together were valued for compounding at over £1,000 a year above the rents in 1649.

Charles by his will in June 1704 left his lease for lives after the death of his wife of the prebend of Lincoln to his nephew Thomas, second lord Leigh, with power to renew. He asked Lord Leigh to bestow it on his younger son Charles, referring it to 'his own judgment and the meritt of his said son's duty and obedience towards him'. This last Charles died without issue in 1749 having lived at Leighton Buzzard (*The Leigh Peerage*, 2nd edn, published by Henry Kent Causton jnr (London, n.d., c. 1834), ii, pp. 475–8, 495–6; i, pp. 4–5; P.R.O., S.P. 23/197/799, 763; *V.C.H. Bedfordshire*, iii, pp. 403–4, 408, 414.)

39. Robert Sidney, second earl of Leicester, in 1675 left his youngest son, Henry, the manor of Long Itchington, Warwickshire, worth £200 a year in 1636 to him and his heirs, £25,000 and all

his personal estate. His second son, Algernon, was left £5,000. The generosity to Henry was due to his father's quarrel with his eldest son. But Henry, later earl of Romney, made the second son of his nephew, Robert, the fourth earl, his heir (A. Collins, *Memorials*, i, pp. 146–7, 153, 174–5; Hist. MSS Comm., *De L'Isle and Dudley*, vi, pp. 531, 553–4.)

40. 1679, by his will Sir Henry Frederick Thynne left his daughter Katherine a £5,000 portion and his third son, Henry Frederick, £4,000. His second son, James, was left the manors of Buckland and Laverton in tail male, remainder to Henry Frederick in tail male, remainder in tail male to the eldest son and finally to the testator's right heirs. The manors were worth £800 a year before the Civil War.

41. In 1682 a settlement was made by Henry, first duke of Beaufort (d. 1700), to raise £10,000 for the only surviving daughter of Charles, marquess of Worcester (d. 1698), and £800 a year for life to Charles' second son, Lord Charles Somerset, but leaving no provision for his third son, Lord John. After the marriage in 1702 of Henry, the second duke, the manors of Wollaston and Tudenham, Gloucestershire, and the lordship of Gower and Kilvey were settled on Lord Charles for life in tail male, with remainders to his younger brother John, Arthur Somerset (son of the first duke who married the daughter and sole heir of Sir William Russell of Llanhern, Carmarthen) and to Henry, son of Lord John Somerset deceased (son of the first marquess of Worcester). They were given power to settle up to £2,000 a year as jointure for their wives. £400 a year for life free of all taxes were settled on Lord John who died in 1704. Lord Charles died in 1710 without issue, his lands would then have gone to Arthur Somerset whose only son died young, Henry Somerset had a son who died without issue.

The 1703 settlement provided £15,000 portion if the second duke had one daughter, and £20,000 to be equally divided among two or more. If he had no sons, additional portions of £5,000 to an only daughter, or £10,000 equally divided among two or more were to be given (Private Act, 1 Anne, Session 2, *cap.* 3, A. Collins, *The Peerage of England* (London, 1748), i, pp. 209, 212–14.)

42. 1683, first duke of Devonshire's second son Henry had £1,400 per annum for life at the age of twenty-four, to be increased to £2,000 on his marriage; his third son James £600 per annum in tail

male. Chatsworth Miscellaneous 18; Private Act, 3 and 4 Anne, *cap.* 27.

43. In 1669 William, later first duke of Bedford, settled £300 a year rent charge in tail male on his third son Lord Edward Russell, who married, but died without issue in 1714. His fourth son, Robert's, widow had a rent charge of £300 a year for life. William Russell, the son of George the sixth son, had £100 a year for life and a £200 a year rent charge in tail male. Lord James, the fifth son, had annuities of £300 a year for life. By the marriage settlement of 1695 Lord John Russell, second son of Wriothesley, the second duke, who later succeeded as fourth duke in 1732, had an annuity of £400 a year and his two sisters portions of £6,000 each. (Wriothesley's sisters received portions of £25,000 each.) The marriage settlement of Wriothesley, the third duke, in 1725, provided £10,000 for a single younger son or daughter, £20,000 equally among two or three, £6,000 each for four or more, with the survivors sharing any portion of those dying. It also gave power to assign up to £2,000 a year for life on younger sons and to settle any term of years, or estates of inheritance in fee simple or tail up to £2,000 a year (Private Acts, 10 Anne, *cap.* 4; 11 George I, *cap.* 29.)

44. In 1698 John, first duke of Rutland, settled land in Yorkshire worth over £900 a year in 1659 and 1679 in tail male on his younger son Thomas Baptist Manners who died aged twenty years without issue in 1705. In 1717 John, the second duke, settled the same lands with some others on his second son, Lord William Manners, in tail male, remainder to Lord Thomas Manners, his third surviving son, remainder to Lord Sherard Manners, eldest son of the duke by his second wife, remainder to the second son of that wife, remainder to his five daughters. The younger sons of the duke's heir, Marquess of Granby, were to have £500 a year for life, if not entitled to the immediate freehold; if only one daughter she was to get £10,000, two or three were to have equal shares in £20,000, four or more £5,000 each. (Private Act, 3 George I, *cap.* 6; Belvoir Acts, 1244 and Brief Declarations.)

45. In 1706 the agreement for the second marriage of William, first lord Cowper, provided the principal and interest of £2,100 in cash and a £300 Exchequer annuity for the portions of younger children. By his will in 1723, the year of his death, having been advanced to an earldom he increased this by giving his son Spencer

an annuity, increasing to £300 at the age of twenty-four, and £1,000 and to his two daughters £6,000 and £5,000. Thus finally each got an annuity of £100; the son also received £300 a year and some £2,500 and the daughters £7,500 and £6,500, so that the son was less well treated than the daughters. (C. Clay, 'Two Families and their Estates' (Cambridge, Ph.D. thesis, 1966), pp. 189–90. I am again indebted to Dr Clay for this.)

46. In 1707 the marriage settlement of Thomas Fane, earl of Westmorland, provided for one daughter only £5,000, for two £10,000, for four or more £20,000 equally divided, except the eldest was to have £500; any younger sons were to share equally with younger daughters. (Private Act, 5 George I, *cap.* 10.)

47. 1707, Edward Coke of Holkham left his two daughters £5,000 each and his two younger sons £200 per annum each for life. His wife's estate (about £660 per annum) went to the second son for life, charged with £500 each for the daughters and £2,000 for the third son (I am indebted to Dr R. A. C. Parker of the Queen's College, Oxford, for this information).

48. 1709, John Gower, Lord Stittenham, willed £6,000 each to two daughters; to three younger sons £200 per annum each for life and £2,000 each. (Private Act, 10 Anne, *cap.* 2.)

9. The grid of inheritance: a comment*

E. P. THOMPSON

The essays in this volume have told us a great deal about the sociological texture of given communities and about existent relationships within them, as exemplified by their inheritance practices.
We have perhaps learned less about process over time, since intentions in inheritance systems, as in other matters, often eventuate in
conclusions very different from those intended. If we anatomize
inheritance systems in a condition of stasis, it is possible for the
mind to assent to a fallacy which, in our waking hours, we know
very well to be untrue – that what is being inherited remains a
historical constant: 'property', 'ownership', or, more simply, 'the
land' – land which, after all, did pass on from generation to generation, which is still there for us to walk over, which may even carry
today much the same kind of crops or timber or stock as three
hundred years ago.

Of course we know that this constancy is illusory. In land what
is being transmitted through inheritance systems is very often not so
much property in the land as property in the usufruct, or a place
within a complex gradation of coincident use-rights. It is the tenure
– and sometimes functions and roles attached to the tenure – which
is being transmitted. Perhaps a little light may be thrown backwards upon what was being transmitted by considering aspects of
the decomposition of certain kinds of tenure in England in the
eighteenth century.

It is difficult to estimate the proportion of landholdings governed
by copyhold or by other forms of customary tenure in the years
from the Restoration to the mid eighteenth century – the period
which is generally accepted as the classic period for the accelerated

---

* These comments which arose in the course of the conference are based
upon work, some of which is yet to be published: for the forest areas of
Berkshire and eastern Hampshire, *Whigs and Hunters* (London, 1975) and
for some other aspects of eighteenth-century customs, 'Common Right and
Enclosure' in *Customs in Common* (forthcoming). In any case, many points
are proposed here as questions, requiring further research, rather than as
conclusions. My thanks are due to Jeanette Neeson and to editors and
contributors to this volume for reading this comment in manuscript and for
sending me valuable criticisms, some of which raised questions too complex
to answer in the context of this study.

328

decline of the 'yeoman'. We should remember that there are two different totals to be counted: the acres and the farmers. It is not difficult to find, in the early eighteenth century, manors in which the average size of customary holdings was small, so that the acreage of freehold or of land subject to non-customary economic rental greatly exceeded the acreage in copyhold, but in which the total number of customary farmers exceeded the number of freeholders or of tenants-at-will. The point is important, since the economic historian may find that the clues to expanding agrarian process lie in the 'free' sector, while the social historian may find that the psychological horizons and expectations of the majority of the farming community lie still within the customary sector.[1]

Without attempting any quantitative assessment it will be sufficient, for this comment, to emphasise that the survival of customary tenure into the eighteenth century was very considerable: in very many private manors: in Church and collegiate lands: in Crown lands, forest areas, etc.[2] It is also my impression that there was, from the 1720s onwards, some revival of careful court-keeping, and considerable activity in the field of customary law. This had nothing to do with some unlocated 'reaction' or with antiquarian sentiment. Customs of manors were scrutinized in new ways by stewards and by lawyers, whose employers saw property in new and more marketable ways. Where custom inhibited rack-renting, 'fringe' use-rights – timber, mineral-rights, stone, peat and turves – might assume even greater importance for the manorial lord anxious to improve his revenue. In general agricultural improvement and the enlargement of the market economy meant that customary use-rights had a more valuable cash equivalent than before, if only they could be prised loose from their sociological and tenurial context.

Despite the consolidation at law of rights of copyhold in the late

---

[1] Since much copyhold land was itself sub-let on economic leases, it may well be true that by the eighteenth-century leasehold at rack-rent 'had largely displaced all other tenancies': Eric Kerridge, *Agrarian Problems in the Sixteenth Century and After* (London, 1969), p. 46. But the number of occupying customary tenants remained substantial and they should not be allowed to be lost to view.

[2] Here I will use the term 'customary tenure' in a general (and sociological) rather than precise (and legal) definition. Copyhold need not be held according to the custom of the manor, while beneficial leases were not, at law, customary tenures although Church and collegiate manors were in fact often subject to customary practices. See Kerridge, ch. 2 for a lucid discrimination between forms of tenure, which (however) affords priority to legal definitions over customary practice.

fourteenth and fifteenth centuries, these were not of course absolute. If copyhold could be sold, mortgaged, bequeathed in any direction (although not according to the custom of all manors), it could still be forfeited for felony and for waste: and it was on occasion so forfeited.[3] Tenures unsecured by a will or by a clear lineage of heritable descent, according to the custom of the manor, could fall back into the hands of the lord. Where tenancies for lives were predominant, as in some parts of western England, the eighteenth century may have seen greater insecurity of tenure. Such tenures were copyhold (in the sense that they were held by copy of the court roll) but they remained tenancies-at-will and subject to arbitrary fines at the entry of new lives.[4] Perhaps such insecure tenures were increasing.[5] Where fines were truly arbitrary this could effectively enforce insecurity of tenure: thus at Whiston and Claines (Worcs.) it was reported in 1825 that 'the customary tenants have been copy-holders of inheritance until within these hundred years . . . But for many years past the tenants have been constrained to fine at the lord's pleasure; and some to let their inheritance be granted over their heads, for want of ability to pay such great fines as were required of them, or to try their rights with the lords.'[6] In other

---

[3] Thus the Court Baron of Uphaven (Wilts.), 20 October 1742; Rinaldo Monk's copyhold cottage forfeited to the lord, he having been convicted of felony and transported: P.R.O. T.S. 19.3. Forfeiture for waste (often compounded by a fine) is more common.

[4] In a copyhold of inheritance even a fine uncertain must be 'reasonable' – a definition which was set by common law at around two years' improved rental. But a copyhold at the will of the lord limited fines to no such legal rationality: R. B. Fisher, *A Practical Treatise on Copyhold Tenure* (London, 1794), pp. 81–2, 90. Six or seven years' improved rental might be charged in such cases, 'the only alternative left to the tenant is to pay the fine, or let the estate fall in'.

[5] R. B. Fisher who was Steward of Magdalen College claimed to be writing from practical knowledge of manorial usages in many parts of the country: Coke had been writing only of 'pure and genuine copyholds' but 'at this time of day there is a sort of bastard species . . . a copyhold tenure', i.e. copyhold for lives, which was to be found 'in a multiplicity of manors within the kingdom'. How far this 'bastard species' was of recent creation, how far it indicated a degeneration of 'pure' copyhold could only be established by many local studies: *ibid.*, pp. iv, 14–15, 90.

[6] Charles Watkins, *A Treatise on Copyholds* (4th edn, 1825), ii, pp. 549–550. It is difficult to set a date upon the customs which Watkins's editor assembled for the 100 pages of Appendix III to the 4th edition. Some customs cited date from the seventeenth century or earlier: but others, including most of the Worcestershire customs, appear to have been sent in by a correspondent in the attempt to describe contemporary or very recent practice.

Worcestershire manors there is an evident tension between 'custom' in the sense of practices and expectations, and custom as enforceable in terms of law. At Hartlebury the custom is 'to grant one life in possession, and three in reversion, and to alter and change at the will of the lord; when three lives are dropt the lord may grant the estate to whom he pleases; though the tenants claim the first offer'.[7]

But in general customary tenures in the eighteenth century appear to have been falling away through a process of attrition rather than through any frontal assault from landowners and the law. (Since many substantial landowners themselves had an interest in copyhold, through purchase or inheritance, the form of tenure was by no means coterminous with the interests of the yeoman or husbandman.) If the lord or his steward could see an advantage in bringing the land back into hand, either to set it out again in an economic leasehold or in anticipation of enclosure, they had opportunities to hasten on the process. Fines on entry or on surrenders could be forced up, based upon the improved rather than upon the customary rents, and these could hasten a copyholder's career towards indebtedness. The well-situated copyholder could claim equal security of tenure with the freeholder. But he could of course claim no *greater* security. Both were equally subject to those vagaries of economic or familial situation which could lead them to mortgage their lands and to heap debts upon the heads of their sons. And, when we discuss inheritance systems, we should not forget that one of their important functions in some peasant and petty tenurial societies was precisely to ensure security down the generations for the landlord's or moneylender's interest upon the farmer's debt.

---

[7] *Ibid.*, ii, p. 553. At Tebberton the custom as presented in 1649 was 'that the lord hath always used to grant the copyholds for three lives in possession, and three in reversion', the fines being arbitrary; but Watkins' correspondent notes that 'of late years the lord hath only granted for two lives in possession and two in reversion, which is no invasion of the ancient custom, as grants are entirely at the lord's pleasure'. A comment on the case of Broadwas perhaps generalizes the experience of insecurity in a number of Worcestershire manors: 'these servile tenures are inconsistent with the present times; and occasion ill-will to the lords, and uneasiness to many honest men': *ibid.*, ii, pp. 546, 564. It is interesting to note that the only instance of wrongful treatment towards copyholders which Kerridge, after his very extensive searches, is able to confirm as at least 'an allegation which found some support' concerns tenants of the Dean and Chapter of Worcester Cathedral forced, in the early seventeenth century, to take leases for years in place of copyholds of inheritance: Kerridge, *op. cit.*, p. 83.

Customary tenure is seen, very often, in its legal status only, as defined in case-law. But custom always had a sociological dimension also, and one recognized at law in the reservation 'according to the custom of the manor'. This can perhaps be seen most clearly in the in-between world of Church and collegiate tenures. Such tenures did not have the security of copyhold, nor can they be regarded as tenancies-at-will. The definition is not one at law but in customary usage. The historian of the finances of St John's College, Cambridge, comments (on the seventeenth and early eighteenth centuries):

> For some reason the College over a long period appears to have acted on the assumption that it was precluded from varying the rents of its estates. It is not possible to discover an entirely satisfying ground for this assumption. So far as is known it rests on no legal basis . . .[8]

But he goes on to show that successive Bursars found ways of overcoming their inhibitions from the first quarter of the eighteenth century; and the increase in revenue came first of all from fines.[9]

The reason for this situation lies less in law than in a certain balance of social relations. From 1576 ('Sir Thomas Smith's Act' of 18 Elizabeth) Church and college tenures were normally limited to three lives and 21 years, with renewals expected every seventh year. Undoubtedly Church tenures, as well as royal and manorial over-rights in forest areas, had been deeply shaken in the Interregnum. After the Restoration, the Church scrutinized all tenures and raised substantial fines upon those which were confirmed. These tenants, and their children, no doubt felt that they had paid for the security of a copyhold. Their tenure had (it was argued) 'by long Custom become Hereditary, purchased almost as dear as

[8] H. F. Howard, *An Account of the Finances of St. John's College, Cambridge, 1511–1926* (Cambridge, 1935), p. 47.

[9] See also R. F. Scott, *Notes from the Records of St. John's College, Cambridge* (St John's, Cambridge), Second Series, 1899–1906, no. xiv, who estimates that the usual fine for surrenders and renewals in the seventeenth century was one year's gross or extended rent: this was raised over the course of the eighteenth century to 1¼, 1½ and thence to two years. See also W. S. Powell in *Eagle* (St John's College), xx, no. 115, March 1898. By the nineteenth century the fine was generally 2.6 of the gross letting value: St John's College, Cambridge, calendar of archives, drawer 100 (70): Statement of Senior Bursar at Audit for 1893. I am indebted to the Master and Fellows of St John's for permission to consult their calendar and archives, and to the Librarian and Archivist for assistance.

Freeholds, from the Confidence reposed in their Landlords of Renewals on customary Terms'.[10] But the security of tenure was never endorsed at law. Church and college tenures remained as 'beneficial' leases, in which the right of renewal at a 'reasonable' fine was assumed but not prescribed.

That fines became less 'reasonable' after 1720 was a consequence of the Whig ascendancy, and the greed of the Whig bishops.[11] The raising of fines of course encountered resistance: a steward will report (as one reported to St John's from Windlesham, Surrey, in 1726) 'the Homage insisted that my demands were very extraordinary'.[12] On such a matter the homage could usually be overruled. But to overrule or alienate a homage was not quite as simple a matter as it may appear to our eyes – eyes which have long been habituated to seeing property-rights overruling functions and needs. These were the farmers, large and small, on the spot, and a distant corporate manorial owner found it necessary to work in

[10] Anon., *Reasons for a Law to oblige Spiritual Persons and Bodies Politick to Renew their Leases for Customary and Reasonable Fines* (London, n.d., c. 1736).

[11] Or so it is argued in *Whigs and Hunters* (London, 1975), Chapter 4, *passim*. The Church appears to have introduced new tables for the assessment of fines, computed according to the interest on the capital investment, the age of the life in being, the number of years lapsed since the last renewal, etc., at some time between 1715 and 1720. The rules demanded 1½ years' extended rental value for renewal of twenty-one year leases, and so in proportion for more or fewer years out: and, in leases for lives, two years' value be insisted on for one life out, and where two are void in proportion, or (preferably) conversion of a lease for three lives to a twenty-one-years' lease. These tables, known as 'Sir Isaac Newton's Tables', created great resentment among tenants: they raised fines, replaced personal and flexible negotiations by a uniform rationalized standard, and above all disallowed the tenants' claim to have established themselves by long precedent in tenures which in effect were customary, heritable and subject (like copyholds) to a fine certain. See St John's College calendar, drawer 109 (38), 'Rules agreed to by the Church of Canterbury at your Audit 1720, according to Sir I. Newton's Tables, thus allowing your Tenants 9 per cent which they think favour sufficient': also C. Trimnell to W. Wake, 4 July 1720, Christ Church College Library, Oxford, Arch. Wake Epist. XXI. For the case of the tenants (some of whom were substantial landholders), *Reasons for a Law, cit. supra* note 10; 'Everard Fleetwood' (Samuel Burroughs), *An Enquiry into the Customary-Estates and Tenant-Rights of those who hold Lands of Church and other Foundations* (London, 1731). For the case of Church and Colleges, see *inter alia*, Anon., *Tables for Renewing and Purchasing of Cathedral Churches and Colleges* (London, 1731).

[12] John Aldridge, 27 October 1726, St John's College calendar, drawer 109 (185). For other complaints at the raising of fines, all in 1725, see *ibid.* drawer 109 (80), (84), (92), (99).

some cooperation with them.[13] The steward of College or Church might encounter, on some matter of antagonistic interest, a conspiracy of silence among the tenants. In 1687 an informant wrote to the Bursar of St John's about one estate:

> I cannot learn what life is in it, I am told by some 'tis an old woman in Suffolke and by others that two old women have their lives in it. They possibly may be dead, and the thing conceal'd ...[14]

The Bursar was at a loss to obtain true information about matters in other manors. When he sought to secure the help of the incumbent of the College's living at Ipsden, asking him to enquire into matters at Northstoke (Oxon) in 1683, the vicar was thrown into a paroxysm of alarm. There would be 'suspition and great jealousies' if he was known to report to the College: his 'affections to the College' already made him suspect. As to one enquiry:

> This is a thing of so tender a nature that if there be given any shadow of suspicion I am unserviceable for ever, for it is the maxim of the country people to be very silent to these ... and it is in all virtue among them, to be vindificative [sic] where their Interest is affected ...

Even to set this down in writing made the poor gentleman sweat: 'I desire to hear that my letter cometh safely to your hand, I shall be in paine till I am assured thereof ...'[15]

A rich bishopric, like Winchester, was better equipped with a bureaucracy of stewards, woodwards, etc., to deal with such problems. St John's (and no doubt other colleges) got round the problem

---

[13] This was acknowledged by the Colleges' own defenders. Thus *Tables for Renewing, supra*, p. 55, agreed that leases 'of a considerable term of years', and reasonably renewable, were beneficial to both parties 'because Men of Letters and Bodies Corporate cannot so well manage their Estates as Laymen or a single Person may do, if they kept them in their own Hands, or let them out at Rack-Rent', especially where such properties were at a distance. In such circumstance a good tenant might be given favour much as if he were acting as the College's Steward: thus Mr John Baber was entered as tenant of the manor of Broomhall (at Sunninghill, Berks.) in 1719: he was long in possession, and when there was an extensive fall of timber in the manor in 1766 it was resolved that 'if the sale of the timber answers our expectations [we intend] to make him a present of fifty guineas for the care that has been taken of it'. The sale exceeded expectations and Baber's gift was increased to £100: St John's College archives, 'Old Dividend and Fine Book', p. 66; Conclusion Book, I, pp. 176, 178.

[14] Howard, *Finances of St. John's College*, pp. 71–2.

[15] Rev. T. Longland to Senior Bursar, 27 November 1683, St John's College calendar, drawer 86 (62).

in the eighteenth century by leasing whole manors to prosperous laymen. But in the seventeenth century the beneficial lease still involved non-economic mutualities, and even some paternal responsibilities. In 1610 Joan Lingard, a widow of over seventy, was petitioning the Master of St John's on a delicate matter. Her tenure (described as a copyhold) was by virtue of her widow's 'free bench' in the right of her first husband. But in the interval of twenty years since this husband's decease she had married twice more and had been left twice more a widow. Her second and third husbands continued the tenancy of the land, but in her widow's right. She had no issue by her first husband, and now wished to surrender her copyhold to her eldest son, by her second husband: her son had covenanted to reserve for her use a tenement 'together with other helpes towardes my maintenance during my life . . .'[16] Tenure is here being sought as descending through the widow's right: presumably this was contrary to the custom of the manor, and for this reason the permission of the Master and Fellows was solicited.

In the case of beneficial leases, renewal of tenure was not of right, but it appears to have been difficult to refuse. We still understand only imperfectly the tenacity and force of local custom. In a lease for three lives or 21 years surrenders must be made and fines paid for the renewal of years or lives with regularity. If the renewal was left over for more than seven years, the fine was raised in proportion. The balance between custom and courtesy here is illustrated by a letter to the College in 1630 from an old student of St John's, soliciting charity for a poor widow, his own kinswoman. She was the relict of a tenant whose lease was within four years of expiry, and she doubted whether the College would renew because of the tardy application. 'Peradventure', her kinsman wrote, 'you may thinke that hir husband and his son, both now with God, had noe purpose to be suitors to your Colledge in renewing theire lease in regard they detracted and let their lease weare out almost to the stumps.' But (he explained) her husband had had a lingering illness, had left debts, and six small children; while the son – a seventh child – had enjoyed only one year's tenure, during which time he had settled his father's debts, and then himself died, leaving a widow and three children in his turn. The widow so circumstanced

[16] Joan Lingard (a tenant at Staveley) to Master, *ibid.*, drawer 94 (25). The College held certain properties through gift or purchase in which regular copyhold (rather than beneficial leases) pertained.

could clearly not pay the high fine due at a point so close to the expiry of the lease. The charity of the Master and Fellows was invoked, in the name of 'the vowes and prayers of widdowes and fatherles children'.[17]

In theory beneficial leases could be allowed to run out, unrenewed, and the Church or collegiate owner could bring all back into its own hands, in order to lease the land out once again at its 'improved' or market value. This did happen on occasion, where only a few tenants were involved.[18] But it entailed an immediate loss of revenue – the existing lives and leases must be run through, and meanwhile there would be no revenue from fines.[19] This required an active, exploitive owner, or a rich one with several manors in hand. It also required an expansionist agriculture in which suitable new tenants, with capital on hand, were available. Moreover, where rights in usufruct extended over common lands – and this included open fields held in severalty but over which lammas grazing rights existed, etc. – the tenants, if they briefed a good lawyer, could prevent the manorial owner from entering into his land until the last lease had fallen in. For the 'inheritance' which we have here is that of communal use-rights, governed by the custom of the manor, and secured at law. When the College determined to regain possession of one manor in 1700, it was advised that this could not take place until the death of the last survivor – 'namely the lives then in being and the last widdowe . . .' Serjeant Wright of the Temple added: 'The Tenants must now spit on their hands and live as long as they can, and the estates will be good to them to the end of the last life and widdow's estate . . .'[20] Only then could the College accomplish its proposed rationalization, reletting the land at economic leases for 21 years.

[17] Robert Pain to Master, 26 October 1630, *ibid.*, drawer 94 (52). The tenant in question held land in Paxton Magna (Hunts.).

[18] George Davies, 3 July 1725, *ibid.*, drawer 109 (96), concerning a few tenants at Marfleet (Yorks.): 'I am of opinion it will be better for the College that they do not renew but take the estates, as they fall, into their own hands.'

[19] The College did not finally decide to end the system of beneficial leases until 1851. The Fellows endured a loss of revenue from fines in the 1850s, but benefited considerably from the improved income from economic rentals after the mid 1860s: 'Statement of the Senior Bursar at Audit for 1893', *ibid.*, drawer 100 (70).

[20] John Blackburne to Charles Head, 27 August 1700, *ibid.*, drawer 94 (284). This manor had come to the College as a gift from the Duchess of Somerset: Howard, *Finances of St. John's College*, pp. 98–9.

By the early eighteenth century we have the sense that there was a deepening (albeit submerged and confused) conflict as to the very nature of landed property, a widening gap between definitions at law and in local custom – and by custom I do not mean only what the custumal may say but the denser reality of social practice. In Berkshire and in Hampshire in the 1720s, conflict over turves, grazing, timber-rights and over the raids by deer upon the farmers' corn, contributed to episodes of armed disturbance.[21] But my point, in this comment, is only to emphasize that it is not helpful to discuss inheritance systems unless we keep always in mind what it is that is being inherited. If we refer vaguely to 'land' then at once anachronistic images spring to mind of the patrimonial farm, with its ancient olives or its well-drained pastures, laboriously-built sheepfolds or spreading oaks. But in many of the farming systems under consideration inheritance of tenure was not so much the passage of land from one generation to the next (although certain closes and tenements might so pass) as the inheritance of use-rights over land (sometimes inherited only as security upon debt), some of which rights might be held in severalty, much of which was subject to at least some communal and manorial control and regulation.

There is a distinction here in social psychology. The farmer, confronted with a dozen scattered strips in different lands, and with prescribed stints in the commons, did not (one supposes) feel fiercely that he *owned* this land, that it was *his*. What he inherited was a place within the hierarchy of use-rights; the right to send his beasts, with a follower, down the lane-sides, to tether his horse in the sykes or on the baulks, the right to unloose his stock for lammas grazing, or for the cottager the right to glean and to get away with some timber-foraging and casual grazing. All this made up into a delicate agrarian equilibrium. It depended not only upon the inherited right but also upon the inherited grid of customs and controls within which that right was exercised. This customary grid was as intrinsic to inheritance as the grid of banking and of the stock exchange is to the inheritance of money. Indeed one could say that the beneficiary inherited both his right *and* the grid within which it was effectual: hence he must inherit a certain kind of social or communal psychology of ownership: the property not of his family but of his-family-within-the-commune.

Thus alongside the 'Cartesian' logic of differing inheritance

---

[21] See my *Whigs and Hunters, passim.*

systems we must place the complementary logic of differing agrarian practices and tenures: and then assess the impact of the logic of the market, of capitalist agrarian practices. For what my scattered illustrations of the operation of some tenurial system shows, at the point of decomposition, is (1) the reification of use-right and its divorce from the actuality of use. An old woman whose death may be concealed is a property, albeit of uncertain value. Stints, abandoned messuages and tenements to which common rights are attached, the reversion of lives, may be bought and sold, independent of the user, just as dove-cots or pig-styes may be bought and sold for the burgage-rights attached to them. (2) The grid itself which validates the exercise of these rights is becoming increasingly insecure. The reification of the rights of some may mean in practice the limitation of the rights of the rest of the community. In extreme cases the manorial owner may be able to extinguish the grid without recourse to enclosure, although if his customary tenants know their law and have the stomach and purses to take recourse to it, the grid will survive as long as the last surviving customary tenant or his widow. As the grid becomes threatened, the small man (the copyholder or the freeholder with common rights appurtenant) must calculate his advantages. Enclosure may bring absolute freehold heritable rights, as well as the extinction of some petty customary claims over their land by the poor. But it may also threaten the equilibrium of crop and stock, in which the old grid carried many advantages. Some of these advantages were those sanctioned in practice in the village, although they could not be sustained at law.[22] (3) There is some evidence of the breaking-apart in the seventeenth and early eighteenth centuries of the agrarian inheritance system (conceived of as a body of rules enshrined in case-law) and the received customary traditions and practices of the village.

This breaking-apart lay along the lines of socio-economic cleavage, between the greater and the lesser rights of usage. Kerridge has identified the advance of capitalist process with greater security of tenure:

---

[22] Thus it was said that the signatories to a petition against the enclosure of the common fields at Hooknorton in 1773 were made up from 'the smaller' proprietors 'who have now an opportunity of committing trespasses on their neighbour's property with their sheep, which in so large a field cannot be altogether prevented': R. Bignall, 10 January 1773, Bodleian Library, MS Oxford. Archd. Papers, Berks. b.5.

To assert that capitalism throve on unjust expropriations is a monstrous and malicious slander. Security of property and tenure answered capitalism's first and most heartfelt need. Where insecurity reigned, it was because of the absence, not of the advent or presence of capitalism.[23]

No doubt, for tenures and rights of substance, the judgement is true. But to the degree that substantial usages were defined and secured, the insubstantial usages were disallowed. Kerridge (and many others) step bravely into a self-fulfilling argument, whose premises are entailed in its conclusions. Those usages which the law subsequently endorsed and secured as rights (such as heritable copyhold) are seen as genuine and lawful usages, those usages which the law subsequently disallowed are seen as pretended rights or illicit intrusions upon the rights of others. And yet it was the law itself which allowed one and disallowed the other; for it was the law which served as a superb instrument for enforcing the reification of right and for tearing down the remnants of the threadbare communal grid. At the outset of the seventeenth century the judgement in Gateward's Case both confirmed the customary rights of copyholders and disallowed those of vaguer categories — 'inhabitants', 'residents': if the latter were to be allowed their claims upon use-rights, then 'no improvements can be made in any wastes'.[24] But still in many areas indefinite rights of 'inhabitants' prevailed until demographic pressure or the realities of local power resulted in their extinguishment or their tighter regulation by by-law. In many forest areas — among them Windsor, the New Forest, the Forest of Dean — large and ill-defined rights were claimed throughout the eighteenth century, and they appear to have been effectively exercised.[25] How far this situation obtained depended upon factors

[23] Kerridge, *Agrarian Problems*, p. 93.

[24] 6 Co. Rep. 59/b. As Lord Eversley pointed out we should be careful not to confuse a legal decision of general significance with the general adoption of it in practice: 'so long . . . as a common remained open and uninclosed, the decision in Gateward's case did not practically affect the position of the inhabitants . . . (who) continued to exercise the customary user of turbary, estovers, or pasture'. Lord Eversley, *Commons, Forests and Footpaths* (London, revised edn, 1910), pp. 10–12.

[25] For a not exceptional example see the customs claimed in the manor of Warfield in Windsor Forest during a survey of 1735: all 'tenants and inhabitants' have common of pasture in all commons and wastes for all kinds of beasts 'as well without stint of number, as also without restraint of any season or time of year'. Rights were also claimed to dig loam and sand (and to cut heath, fern and furzes 'without any leave, lycence or molesta-

340   E. P. THOMPSON

peculiar to each region and each manor.[26] But where the appeal was made to law the decisions moved in one direction: that of reification and limitation.

Copyhold itself, as an alienable property with a cashable monetary equivalent, had been very widely secured by the sixteenth century, partly because many men of substantial property and interest had a stake in this kind of tenure themselves. During the eighteenth century it became of more evident advantage to such men to bring into their own hands messuages which would carry at enclosure, substantial common-right values. But as the indefinite rights of the poor were excluded, so what may be called the fringe-benefits of the communal grid were extinguished. In a Chancery decision of 1741 an indefinite claim by 'occupants' to enjoy the right of turbary was disallowed in the tradition of 'Gateward's Case': the claim was found to be 'a very great absurdity, for an occupant, who is no more than a tenant at will, can never have a right to take away the soil of the lord'.[27] Similar judgements extended over other fringe rights. In 1788 the claim of 'poor, necessitous and indigend householders' in Whaddon (Bucks.) to take dead wood in the local coppice was disallowed since 'there is no limitation . . . the description of poor householder is too vague and uncertain . . .'[28] The famous decision against gleaning in the same year did not of course extinguish (unless here and there) the *practice* of gleaning. What it did was to extinguish the claim of the villagers to glean *as of right*, even though that right may be seen clearly defined in dozens of early manorial by-laws.[29] Hence, at a stroke of the pen, a most ancient

tion'). Only the part of the claim inserted within brackets was objected to by the steward as an innovation on the old books of survey: Berkshire Rec. Off. D/EN M 73/1. For practice in the forest generally, see *Whigs and Hunters*, pp. 32, 239–40.

[26] In the poor soils of Windsor Forest (within the Blackheath Country) and of the New Forest the family farmer came into his own, 'largely in subsistence husbandry on land that working and gentlemen farmers considered unfit for their purposes': E. Kerridge, *The Farmers of Old England* (London, 1973), p. 81. In the case of the Forest of Dean the Free Miners were very fortunate that their ancient usages were *not* challenged at law in the eighteenth century since they would almost certainly have been disallowed in the spirit of Gateward's Case: see Lord Eversley, *op. cit.*, pp. 178–9.

[27] Dean and Chapter of Ely v. Warren, 2 Atk. 189–90.

[28] Selby v. Robinson, 2 T.R. 759.

[29] It is true that this right was controlled and regulated (like all other common rights) and often limited to particular categories of persons – the very young, the old, the decrepit, etc.: see W. O. Ault, *Open-Field Farming*

use-right was decreed to be uncashable at law – might one use such an ugly concept as *un*reified?

This law evolved from a Baconian and not a Cartesian mind. It is a law which resisted (as Blackstone proclaimed with proud chauvinism)[30] the influence of Justinian and of the revival of Roman law in general. Its precedents were piecemeal: it evolved with empirical caution. But behind this empirical evolution one may detect the no-less-Cartesian logic of capitalist evolution. Coke's decision in 'Gateward's Case' rested less upon legal than upon economic logic – 'no improvements can be made in any wastes'. The judges sought to reduce use-rights to an equivalent in things or in money, and hence to bring them within the universal currency of capitalist definitions of ownership. Property must be made palpable, loosed for the market from its uses and from its social situation, made capable of being hedged and fenced, of being owned quite independently of any grid of custom or of mutuality. As between substantial rights, and even as between the greater and the lesser of such rights, the law was impartial: it was tender of property of whatever degree. What it abhorred was an indefinite sociological praxis, a *coincidence* of several use-rights, unreified usages. And this English law, following upon the heels of the Pilgrim Fathers and of the John Company, attempted to reify and translate into terms of palpable property ownership the customs and usages of whole peoples which had inherited communal grids of a totally different character.

The consequences in these cases were far-reaching. The bearing upon the problem of inheritance in England was more subtle. Any system of impartible inheritance in an agrarian system which has ceased to expand must be subject to a delicate demographic

in *Medieval England* (London, 1972), pp. 29–32. Ault appears to take Blackstone to task for accepting gleaning as a right of 'the poor' by 'the common law and custom of England' (*Commentaries*, 1772, iii, p. 212). But it would not have disturbed Blackstone to know that there is no reference to such right in thirteenth-century by-laws, 'nor is there a single mention of the poor as gleaners'. Custom did not rest on suppositious origin but established itself in common law by four criteria: antiquity, continuance, certainty and reason – and 'customs are to be construed according to vulgar apprehension, because customs grow generally, and are bred and brought up amongst the Lay-gents': S.C. (S. Carter), *Lex Custumaria: or a Treatise of Copy-hold Estates* (London, 1701), pp. 27–9. By such criteria gleaning by the poor was of greater antiquity, and of equal continuity, certainty and rationality as most customary tenures.

[30] Blackstone, *op. cit.*, i, section 1.

equilibrium. The fringe-benefits of the grid are not things distinct from the transmitted tenurial rights. Some laxness in the definition of rights of grazing, gleaning, firing, etc., can help to support the sons who do not inherit tenures, stock and implements. With these benefits extinguished, the excess population may be reduced to a landless proletariat or ejected like lemmings from the community. One need not propose a simple typological model of a 'swapping' equilibrium, one son inheriting, one daughter married to a tenant or freeholder, half a son or daughter remaining to be provided for. It is rather that we have to take the total context together; the inheritance customs, the actuality of what was being inherited, the character of the economy, the manorial by-laws or field regulations, the poor law. If in the fifteenth and sixteenth centuries younger children sometimes inherited beasts or implements (but no land) we must assume that they expected access to land somehow. If (as I suppose) in the same centuries communal agrarian regulation became tighter, excluding those without land from certain unacknowledged but practised grazing rights, then to the same degree what the occupier inherited became better, what the younger child had left to him became worse. The yeoman is advantaged: it is less easy for his brother to make do as a husbandman or a craftsman with a few sheep and a cow on the common. What matters then becomes the inheritance of capital, for both land and stints on the common may still be rented.

In certain areas, such as forests, the fringe-benefits may be so large as to afford a livelihood of sorts for many younger brothers, and even immigrants. This will also be so in areas where a scanty agrarian income may be supplemented by developing domestic industries and crafts. Such areas, one might suppose, favoured practices of partible inheritance – practices which cannot be deduced from the registration of tenures in the court-roll. The successor who enters upon the tenure may be seen (from the evidence of the will) to be acting as trustee for the widow[31] or, as trustee for the children whose portions are to be divided 'share and share alike'.[32] Forms

[31] The form can be seen in the manor of Barrington-in-Thriplow: Benjamin Wedd is admitted (11 November 1756) according to the use of the will of his deceased father-in-law: he is charged by this will to pay an annuity of £60 to his mother-in-law: St John's College calendar, drawer 99 (214). Such practices were of course very widespread.

[32] The form may be seen in the will of William Cooke of East Hendred (Berks.), probat. 7 September 1728, who left two sons and two daughters.

may grow up whereby the lives in being[33] or reversionary[34] entered in the court-roll are fictitious. The actual practices of inheritance, as evidenced by wills, may be completely at odds with the recited customs of the manor; and even where custom specifically enforced the impartibility of a tenure, devices could be arranged to circumvent custom.[35]

In Windsor Forest in the early years of the eighteenth century there is a little evidence of such practices of partible inheritance.[36] Percy Hatch, a yeoman of Winkfield, with about 70 acres (mostly in freehold) sought in 1727 to benefit his four sons and a married daughter.[37]

In this will (p. 344) the oldest son is clearly advantaged, although the other sons receive some money in compensation. The second son, who is charged with his sister's dowry, is also advantaged, but as between the second, third and fourth there is clearly some notional sense of equality. Eleven acres of poor land might seem in-

After small monetary legacies, the residue of his estate was left to his brothers Thomas and Edmund Cooke, in trust to divide amongst all and every of his children 'share and share alike'. The lives of his brothers 'are in the copy of court roll by which I hold my copyhold', but the brothers are bound to surrender all rents and profits to the above uses, and to distribute it among the children 'share and share alike': Bodleian Library, MS Wills Berks. 20, p. 48.

[33] This form was especially used in copyholds for lives, as two or three lives in being, others in reversion: one or more of the lives in being were inserted as trustees for the actual tenants, as security that the tenure should pass on to his heirs: on occasion the actual tenant, who paid for the entry fines, was not even entered in the court roll: see R. B. Fisher, *op. cit.*, pp. 15–16.

[34] The form may be seen in the will of Timothy Lyford of Drayton (Berks.), probat. 5 December 1724: 'whereas my daughter Elizabeth Cowdrey is the first reversion named in my copyhold estate in Sutton Cortney my will is that the said copyhold estate be surrendered into the hands of the Lord of the manor pursuant to a certain obligation to me entered into for that purpose with intent that my daughter Jane the wife of John Chear may be admitted tenant thereof for her own life and such other lives as she can agree for': Bodleian Library, MS Wills Berks. 19, p. 239.

[35] As in Knaresborough, where 'it was possible . . . for a man with more than one son to make provision for the younger sons by transferring the title of part of his land to them during his lifetime, receiving back a life interest': *A History of Harrogate and Knaresborough*, ed. Bernard Jennings (Huddersfield, 1970), pp. 80, 178–9.

[36] When I say 'a little evidence' I mean that a little evidence has come to my hand while working on other matters. There may (or may not) be much evidence. The impressions offered in these pages are not intended as a substitute for the systematic research which I have not undertaken.

[37] Bodleian Library, MS Wills Berks. 19, pp. 338–9.

	House	Land	Furniture	Money
1st son	Messuage and Farmhouse, 'Sumertons'	27½ acres and 4 doles of land in common fields	Furnace Clothes-press Biggest spit Malt mill	–
2nd son	Messuage and Farmhouse, 'Berkshire House'	c. 14 acres	–	£30[a]
3rd son	–	11 acres	–	£20
4th son	–	11 acres	Is executor and has residue of estate	
Daughter	–	–	Best chest of drawers	[a]

[a] The daughter was married to a substantial farmer. The second son was charged to pay £60 to her husband. This presumably was her dowry, but it is not clear whether this debt was her settlement in part or in full.

adequate for a livelihood: but Winkfield, an extensive parish in the heart of the forest, enjoyed large grazing rights, for sheep as well as cattle,[38] substantial (if contested) rights of turbary, access to timber, as well as brick-kilns (perhaps this explains the furnace?) and a little forest industry. There were several branches of the Hatch family in the parish, the eldest of which 'time out of mind has had an handsome estate and good interest therein . . .'[39] We do not know the degree of kinship of Percy Hatch to this older branch: but some degree of kinship was likely to have added a supportive social context to the younger son's struggle for a livelihood – and we know

[38] Percy Hatch's daughter was married to William Lyford. This could have been the same William Lyford who was presented at the Windsor Forest Swanimote court in 1717 for staffherding sheep in the forest: P.R.O. L.R. 3.3 'Staffherding' (accompanying the sheep in the forest with a herdsman) was an offence since it frightened the deer and secured the best grazing for the sheep: left to their own unaided competition the deer enforced their own priorities.
[39] Reverend Will Waterson, Memorandum Book, I, the Ranelagh School, Bracknell, Berks.

from other evidence that Winkfield parishioners defended their community's rights with the greatest vigour.[40]

Much of this rests on inference. But it may add a little flesh to the bone of the conjecture that it was in such a context, where the grid of communal inheritance was strong and where fringe-rights were indefinite and extensive, that a yeoman could risk the practice of partible inheritance without condemning his children to poverty. Below a certain minimum further partition would be ridiculous: husbandmen (in the evidence of one local study) were unlikely to divide their land.[41] But in the normal course of succession portions would not only be divided but also, through marriage, death, legacies from childless kin, be thrown together: Percy Hatch evidently held two distinct farms, one of which ('Sumerton') he left intact to his oldest son, from the other of which ('Berkshire House') he took out portions of land for his third and fourth.

If we learn more about the regions where such 'egalitarian' practices were prevalent, these may throw light upon the relationship of inheritance customs to industrialization.[42] But in fielden, arable regions, in which little extension of land-use was possible, such 'share and share alike' practices would have led to economic suicide: tenure must pass as one parcel along with buildings, implements and stock. But this certainly faced the yeoman with a dilemma. Kiernan doubts whether a love of private property can be

---

[40] See *Whigs and Hunters*, Part I, *passim*: Winkfield was the epicentre of 'Blacking' in the forest in the 1720s.

[41] See J. A. Johnston, 'The Probate Inventories and Wills of a Worcestershire Parish, 1676–1775', *Midland History*, i, 1 (Spring 1971), pp. 20–33. The author finds that the husbandmen all 'showed an inclination to preserve their estates intact, all leaving their land to their eldest sons': they also 'favoured their male relations outside the immediate family'. No other social group showed such rigidity of custom, nor a stress on primogeniture: of 87 landowners, 36 willed their land intact to a single heir, the remaining 51 left their land to 122 new owners. The parish in question (Powick) is only two miles from Worcester: rich land with opportunities for dairy farming, fruit growing and some horse-breeding. Possibly this could be another kind of regimen in which partible inheritance was viable?

[42] Bernard Jennings informs me that in the very extensive manor of Wakefield practices of partible inheritance were continued analagous to those in Knaresborough (*supra*, note 35). His researches, with the cooperation of extra-mural classes, have demonstrated a coincidence between this practice and the density of looms in different districts of the West Riding: i.e. where the holding was too small to provide a livelihood this became an incentive for the development of domestic industry (spinning and weaving), in the first place as a supplementary income. One looks forward to the publication of these findings.

seen as a constant in 'human nature', and one may agree. But a desire to secure the expectations of one's children – to try to throw forward some grid which will support them – has at least had a long run in social history. It is here that Spufford's findings are important, for they seem to emphasize that the 'yeomen' were seeking to transmit down the generations not only 'land' (particular tenures) but also a social status to *all* their children. The nobility and gentry devised with care their own grid of transmission through entail and marriage settlement. Such a grid was not available to the yeoman. The merchants and professions might throw forward a grid of money. The small farmer could hope to do a little in this way himself, by bequeathing legacies as a charge upon his estate. In such cases, the moment of death was for the small man a moment of great familial financial risk. M. K. Ashby, examining the village of Bledington – a village with slight manorial presence and with a large number of freeholders – keeps a careful eye on the farmers' wills. She observes two points of change. In the early seventeenth century the wills of farmers and of widows indicate still 'a world of wide family connections and affections, a valuation of persons and also of objects, goods: charitable bequests are frequent'. But the movable property given away is in small amounts. 'After 1675 the family recognised is the immediate group of parents and children, charity is absent and money is prominent, and in larger amounts.' The second change is in accentuation of the first: by the early eighteenth century farmers 'are leaving their estates burdened by very large monetary legacies, to be paid by those who inherit the land . . . The pattern they adopt . . . is that of the owner of large estates in which, e.g. the head of the family provides for widow, daughter and younger sons out of the receipts of a landed estate.'[43] But the outpayments to be made by the heir sometimes appear as unrealistic. Mortgages must be taken up or debts incurred to meet the legacies. Possibly it is exactly in this inheritance practice that we may see the death-warrant of the yeomanry as a class? They were seeking to project forward a grid of legacies upon which the children who did not inherit land or its tenure could yet be maintained at yeoman status. In doing so they were withdrawing capital which could have been dunging their own land. Not all of this need leave the village: some would pass, by way of a daughter's portion,

[43] M. K. Ashby, *The Changing English Village: a History of Bledington* (Kineton, 1974), pp. 162–4, 194–5.

to another farm: some younger brothers might rent land and stints or settle to local crafts. But it would seem that the practice of laying legacies upon the heir (a practice with some analogies to the French 'recall') could equally have been a way of diverting capital from the countryside to the town.

The attempt to impose large portions – perhaps approaching to some notional 'share and share alike' – upon the heir led him not only into debt but into a different kind of debt from the neighbourhood borrowing often found in the traditional village. This neighbourhood petty indebtedness was itself a sort of 'swapping' which often had a social as well as economic dimension: loans were exchanged among kin, neighbours, sometimes as part of a reciprocity of services. The new mortgages carried the small man into a wider and more ruthless money market quite outside his own expertise. An alert manorial owner who wished to bring tenures back into his own hands could take advantage of the same situation by granting and foreclosing mortgages upon his own copyholds: by such means the St Johns of Dogmersfield managed in the years after the South Sea Bubble to lose a village and turn much of it into a deer-park.[44] In this case some of the tenants seem to have resorted to arson, to the shooting of cattle and the felling of trees. But so far as one can see they were victims not of forced dispossession but of 'fair' economic process, of good lawyers, and of the debt incurred by the Bubble.

The old communal grid had been eaten away by law and by money long before enclosure: eighteenth-century enclosure registered the end rather than the climax of that process. The tenures which we have been discussing can be seen also as roles, functions, access to use-rights, governed by communal rules and expectations as well as by customary law. They are part of one impartible bundle, a dense socio-economic nexus. The attempt to define these by law was in itself an abstraction from that nexus. For a practice to be offensive to the community or to the homage does not provide any compelling reason at law or in cash for the practice not to continue. But opinion can be more effective than we suppose: in some parts of Ireland in the eighteenth and early nineteenth centuries there was no reason at law why a landlord might not expel his tenants and lease more advantageously to new ones. The only trouble was that the steward might be shot and the new tenants'

44 See *Whigs and Hunters*, pp. 106–8.

cabins be burned down. In Hampshire in 1711 they were more polite. When Bishop Trelawny's assertive, rationalizing steward, Dr Heron, showed excessive zeal and rapacity in seizing herriots upon the death of a tenant, he was exposed by the bereaved son to public rebuke in front of his officers and strangers. This cost the steward no more than some loss of face; he should have taken it as a danger signal, an inhibition upon his action. When he failed to do so, the tenants and other episcopal officers closed against him and commenced an agitation which forced the bishop to replace his steward.[45]

Small victories like this, in defence of customary practice, were won here and there. But the campaign itself was always lost. (The bishop's next steward attained much the same ends, with a little more diplomacy and a little more care in favouring his subordinate officials.) For to the impartible bundle of communal practice capitalism introduces its own kind of partible inheritance. Uses are divorced from the user, properties from the exercise of functions. But once you break the bundle up into parts what becomes inherited is not a communal equilibrium but the properties of particular men and of particular social groups. Le Roy Ladurie speaks of the equal division by value of tenures as 'egalitarian'; and if we mean by this nothing more than equal division then the term need not be disputed. But he proposes to take the thought further: 'spreading progressively through the rural world this current of egalitarianism will . . . finally submerge all the hierarchies of ordered society'.[46] But we have here proposed that in some parts of England the egalitarian desire of the yeoman to advantage as far as possibly equally all of his children ended up, through a surfeit of mortgages, in submerging not the hierarchies of ordered societies but the yeomanry as a class. We should perhaps recall some lines of William Blake:

> Is this thy soft Family Love
> Thy cruel Patriarchal pride

[45] *Ibid.*, pp. 125–33, and 'Articles against Heron' and Heron's responses, Hants. Rec. Off. Heron's reply complains that 'at Waltham Court, without any Previous notice, the Son of the Widow was brought into the Room where wee dined (with some Clergymen & Strangers of Mr. Kerby's Acquaintance all unknown to mee) to Challenge mee publickly for this unjust Seizure'. This confrontation was engineered by Kerby, the Woodward, and Heron's rival.

[46] See above p. 50.

> Planting thy Family alone,
> Destroying all the World beside.

And Blake adds to this a suggestion of the same logic through which the yeomen fell:

> And he who make his law a curse
> By his own law shall surely die.

For it had been these same copyholders, anxious to maintain their status within the rural hierarchy, who had taken an active part in the previous two centuries in breaking the communal bundle apart, in drawing up more stringent by-laws which advantaged the land-holder and disadvantaged those without tenures, in limiting the fringe benefits of the grid, in setting use-rights to market.[47] In their anxiety as a social class to plant their own family alone they prepared the means of their own destruction.

Perhaps another characteristic of traditional tenurial society was lost. Free bench or widow's estate, as it pertained in many manors into the eighteenth century, did allow for a considerable feminine presence. Female tenure, either as free bench or in the woman's own right, does not of course prove that the agrarian and other attendant functions were always performed by the tenants: a subtenant could be put in, or the farm could be left under the control of male kin. But we would be making a hasty judgement if we assumed that most feminine tenures were only fictionally so. This was certainly not true at the top of society, which saw the formidable presence of such women as Sarah, duchess of Marlborough, or of Ruperta Howe, the ranger of Alice Holt Forest. And we must all have encountered evidence which suggests that women of the yeoman class acquitted themselves, at the head of farming households, with equal vigour. In the early eighteenth century a steward of St John's was engaged in a protracted and inconclusive negotiation with one infuriating tenant, whose evasions always left her in possession of all the points at issue: 'I had rather' (he wrote) 'have business with three men than one woman.'[48]

[47] I hope to substantiate these generalizations in 'Common Right and Enclosure', *Customs in Common* (forthcoming).

[48] St John's College, Cambridge, calendar, drawer 109 (16). But Mrs Allen who had outlived two husbands and had repudiated the debts of both – 'a very sharp self interested woman' – may be untypical and may offer evidence on Le Roy Ladurie's side of the question: since she turns out to have been a 'saucy Frenchwoman'; and 'an unaccountable Frenchwoman, and regards no body': *ibid.*, 109 (7), (13), (14).

The customary grid did allow for a female presence, although usually – but not necessarily – on condition of either widowhood or spinsterhood. There was an eye – and in the eighteenth century a continuing eye – upon the continuity of the familial tenure through the male line. Free bench was often conditional upon no remarriage, and also upon chaste living – a prohibition which arose less from Puritanism than from jealousy of the influence of new children, or of the waste to the estate which might be committed by the step-father. Where the widow did not lose her tenure upon remarriage there is sometimes a suggestion that the lord, his steward, or the homage had some kind of paternal responsibilities for overwatching the children's right. In 1635 a clergyman petitioned St John's on behalf of the children of William Haddlesen. In this case, the father had willed his lease to the children, who were not yet of age; and Haddlesen's widow 'hath married verry unluckely, so that if the Colledge stand not the children's friend to lett it to some in trust for their use (for the mother is not to be trusted) the children are like to be undunne . . .'[49] (One wonders whether it was cases of remarriage of this kind which would have been the particular occasion of rough music in England and charivari in France?)

Manors had different customs to make allowance for frailty or to deal with unusual circumstances. The 'jocular' customs of Enborne (Berks.) and of Kilmersdon (Somerset) – and probably of other places – were not as ridiculous as they may seem. In Enborne if the woman 'commits incontinency she forfeits her Widow's estate' –

[49] Reverend Richard Perrot to College, petitioning on behalf of a customary tenant at Marfleet (Yorks.), 2 February 1635, *ibid.*, drawer 94 (289). The Manor Court at Farnham also took unusual care to overwatch the interest of orphans. 'It is a principall poynt in the Court of this Mannor and to be remembered' that if a tenant left an orphan under age 'then the next in kind and farthiest from the Land shall have the tuition and Guardianship of such an heir untill he come to the age of 14 years', when he may chose his own tenant to farm. The guardian shall pay his ward's charges and education, and account to him for the rest. But if the appropriate person as guardian 'be insufficient by defect of Nature or otherwise', then the court, with the consent of the homage, could appoint a guardian. By 'next of kind and farthiest from the land' I understand the closest kin who is at the same time not in the direct line of customary inheritance: e.g. an uncle or aunt on the mother's side: Farnham Custom Roll, 1707, Dean and Chapter archives, Winchester Cathedral Library. Compare the custom at nearby Woking: 'If any copyholder die, his heir being within age, the custody of the body and the land of such heir shall be committed by the lord to the next of kindred of the heir to whom the land cannot descend, he being a fit person . . .': Watkins, *op. cit.*, ii, p. 559.

Yet, after this, if she comes into the next Court held for the
Manor, riding backward upon a Black Ram, with his Tail in her
hand, and says the Words following, the Steward is bound by the
Custom to re-admit her to her Free Bench:

> Here I am,
> Riding upon a Black Ram,
> Like a Whore as I am;
> And for my Crincum Crancum,
> Have lost my Bincum Bancum;
> And for my Tail's game
> Am brought to this Worldly Shame,

Therefore good Mr Steward let me have my Lands again.

At Kilmersdon the recitative required was more brief, and the
offender need only ride astride the ram:

> For mine Arse's Fault I take this Pain,
> Therefore, my Lord, give me my Land again.[50]

In other customs more rational controls or adjustments are established.[51]

One trouble with the customs of manors rehearsed between 1660
and 1800 is that we know rather little about the relation of custom
to practice. And this is, mainly, because we have not bothered to
find out. The Webbs noted in 1908 that there was no comprehensive
study of the Lord's Court in the period 1689–1835[52] and the position

[50] Josiah Beckwith's edition of Thomas Blount's *Fragmenta Antiquitatis;
or Antient Tenures of Land, and Jocular Customs of Some Manors* (York,
1784), pp. 265–6. A similar custom is claimed to have existed in Torr
(Devon).

[51] At Balsall (Warwks.) the customs presented in 1657 included the
provision: 'if any female heir, being in possession of any copyhold, for lack
of grace should happen to commit fornication or be begotten with child, she
was not to forfeit her estate, but she must come into the lord's court' and
pay a fine of five shillings: if a widow committed fornication or adultery
'she is to forfeit her estate for her life, until she agree with the lord by fine
to be restored': Watkins, *op. cit.*, ii, p. 576. It is doubtful whether such
customs were effective in the eighteenth century, unless in unusual circumstances: however, in 1809 Lord Ellenborough, C.J. upheld judgement for
the plaintiff, thus ousting from her tenure a widow (a tenant of Lord
Lonsdale in Westmorland) who had breached the custom of tenure during
'her chaste viduity' by having a child: but a witness could cite only one
other case in that manor in the previous sixty years (in 1753) and in that
case the widow had died before the case came to an issue: William Askew
v. Agnes Askew, 10 East. 520.

[52] S. & B. Webb, *The Manor and the Borough* (London, 1908), p. 11.

remains much the same today. (Recent advances in agrarian history have inevitably been addressed more to the improving and market-orientated sectors of the economy than to the customary.) In the case of customs of the manor governing inheritance, these came into force only when the tenant died intestate and without effecting a previous surrender: and it was usual to allow a death-bed surrender, in the presence of two customary tenants, bequeathing the tenure to an heir. Hence practice and recited customs of inheritance may long have parted company. But there is a further difficulty of a different kind. Customs formally presented at a survey (for example, upon the entry of a new lord) may have recited only a small portion of the uncodified but accepted customary practices of a manor. The uncodified portion could have remained in the custody of the memories of the steward and of the homage, with reference to the case-law built up in the court rolls. Only when we find a strong body of copyholders whose customs have become insecure in the face of an invasive or absent lord do we find an attempt to codify this case-law in all its dense social particularity.[53]

Probably the practice of widow's estate or free bench is least confused by these difficulties. Since the widow normally entered upon her free bench without any fine, this constituted a bonus of years to the existent tenure. Unless the husband had some distinct reason for making an alternative arrangement, he was likely to leave the free bench to run according to the custom of the manor: and even the briefest eighteenth-century recitals of customs normally take care to establish what the custom on this important point was. Thus custom here is some indication as to practice.

Perhaps custom within the manor may even have influenced practice outside the customary sector? The customs of Waltham St Lawrence (Berks.), rehearsed in 1735, afford to the widow full free bench during widowhood and chaste living. If she remarries or lives unchaste, she is to have one-third of the rental value of the

<hr/>

[53] An excellent example of this is to be found in the Farnham Customs of 1707. Here we have a strong body of customers prospering through hop-farming, claiming the security of socage tenure, but suffering from the insecurity of being a Church manor (the Bishop of Winchester). The homage recited its customs with unusual detail and precision because of continuing disputes with successive Bishops and their officers: 'every new Lord brings in a new procurator who for private gains Racketh the Custom and often-times breaketh it . . .' Mrs Elfrida Manning of the Farnham Museum Society has recently discovered an almost identical Farnham Custumal of the 1670s.

tenure – that is, a reversion to an earlier notion of dower.[54] But if she had had issue *before* marriage, then she had neither free bench nor moiety.[55] Waltham St Lawrence lies within the same hundred as Warfield, and it is interesting to find that a yeoman of Warfield, in 1721, willed eight acres of *freehold* to his widow for life, on condition that the timber was not to be wasted nor the land ploughed: if she broke these conditions 'my will is that she shall thenceforth have out of the same no more than her Dower or Thirds'.[56] At nearby Binfield in Windsor Forest in the same year another yeoman left all lands and tenements to his wife 'during her natural life if she keep her selfe a widow but if she should happen to be married again . . . then only to have and enjoy the Thirds thereof . . .'[57] For some forest farmers, custom and practice in free bench appear to have run a parallel course.

Customs varied between one region and the next and, within each region, from one manor to another. I can offer only an impression, based on limited research into two or three districts. It would seem that by the eighteenth-century free bench was one of the most secure and universal of customs, applicable both to copyholds of inheritance and tenures for lives; distinctions between customary and common law terms or between tenures of customary or demesne lands had generally lapsed, and free bench generally signified continuance in the whole tenure, not in a moiety of its profits. The customs collected in Watkins' *Treatise on Copyholds* (1825 edn)

---

[54] Dower in common law was defined as a moiety and the custom that the wife shall have the whole as free bench is contrary to the maxim of common law: but the custom of each manor remained good and overrode common law: S. Carter, *op. cit.*, p. 34. Thus a textbook of 1701. By the 1790s the terms free bench and dower were often being used indiscriminately, although they differed: 'Free bench is a widow's estate in such lands as the husband died seized of, and not of such lands as he was seized of during the coverture, whereas dower is the estate of the widow in all lands, the husband was seized of during the coverture': R. B. Fisher, *op. cit.*, p. 26, citing 2 Atk. 525.

[55] Survey and customs of Waltham St Lawrence, November 1735, Berks. Rec. Off. D/EN M 82/A/1.

[56] Will of Richard Simmons, probat. 21 April 1721, Bodleian Library, MS Wills Berks. 19, p. 100.

[57] Will of Thomas Punter, probat. 21 April 1721, *ibid.*, p. 97. But forest customs varied from parish to parish: in the neighbouring parish of Winkfield it seems that the widow could remarry and her husband enjoy her estate in her right during her life, subject to stringent provisions against waste: Rev. Will Waterson, Memorandum Book, pp. 362, 365 Ranelagh School, Bracknell, Berks.

offer no systematic sample, being such as came to the editor's hand or were sent in by correspondents. Custom is often reported in imprecise terms – 'the widow has her free bench', the manor 'gives no dower'. But for what the collection is worth it reports the status of widows in some sixty manors in terms which suggest that the customs were still operative or had at least survived into the eighteenth century.[58] Of these some forty show free bench, either for life or during widowhood; ten show no 'dower'; ten show dower of one-third moiety, and one of one-half. The manors with free bench are drawn from fifteen counties (with Worcestershire greatly over-represented). The manors with no 'dower' or moieties only are drawn from six counties: in these Norfolk is over-represented, while in Middlesex and Surrey it is probable that the custom of free bench was weak where the practice of the alternative form of security – the jointure or joint-tenancy of husband and wife – was strong.[59]

Where free bench was assured the main distinction between manors turned on the question of its continuance or discontinuance upon remarriage. At Mayfield (Sussex) the ancient distinction between bond-land and assert-land tenure survived: 'yard-land widow, to hold during widowhood. Assert-widow during life.'[60] At Littlecot (Wilts.) the widow has full widow's estate and may marry again without the loss of her tenure, but if she was a *second* wife she 'can have but her widowhood'.[61] At Stoke Prior (Worcs.) the widow enjoys 'the moiety' of the lands 'and to receive only the rent of the heir if they can agree' – any difference to be referred to the homage.[62] At Balsall (Warws.) free bench was granted to the widow if a first wife, but only one-third moiety of rents and profits if she was the second or third.[63] At Farnham, a manor with a strong homage, jealous of its privileges, the customs were rehearsed in 1707 with great vigour and detail and it is fair to assume that they were correspondent to practice and that we have in them some codification of the precedents that had come before the court. In these a surrender by the husband (even to the use of his will) bars

[58] I have subtracted from this 'sample' some customs which evidently dated back to the early years of the seventeenth century or before, but others may well have been obsolete.

[59] Watkins, *op. cit.*, ii, pp. 477–576. The North and the North Midlands are scarcely represented in this collection.

[60] *Ibid.*, ii, pp. 501–2.

[61] *Ibid.*, ii, p. 498.

[62] *Ibid.*, ii, pp. 552–3.

[63] *Ibid.*, ii, p. 575.

the wife's dower: such a provision was essential if the land was to be alienable. But the husband could, by surrender in the court or surrender to the use of his will, reserve his wife's life: that is, afford her free bench in precedence to the next reversion. If he were to surrender without making any such condition then his widow 'shall neither have tearmes of Life nor Widow's estate; but if he die without Surrender she shall have her Widow's estate if she live sole and Chastly'.[64] And, by an additional provision, 'if she comes to the next court after her husband's death and pays half a fine, she becomes tenant for life, and may marry again without forfeiting her estate'.[65]

These divergent customs record different solutions offered to adjust the same insoluble problems. On the one hand there is an attempt to afford security to the widow, and perhaps to her underage children. On the other hand if copyhold was to be truly alienable then no absolute security could be afforded. Moreover where tenure was expected to descend to the children, remarriage presented a threat to the line of inheritance. This also called for nice adjustments, sometimes recorded in the customs. Once again the Farnham customs of 1707 reveal a complex codification and sociological government. Where a tenant had a daughter by one wife, and a son and daughter by a second, the daughter by the second marriage had precedence over the daughter by the first, even if the son (her brother) had predeceased the tenant and never been admitted to the tenure ('yet shall his sister by his mother inheritt the land . . . as heire to her brother . . . notwithstanding her elder sister by the first woman . . .')[66] It is difficult to address Cartesian logic to this solution. It looks very much like a piece of case-law, decided by the court and then added to the custumal. What appears to be emphasized here is the transmission of the tenure with the least domestic friction: presumably the first daughter will already be likely to have left the farm, the second wife (now widowed) is likely to remain in residence with her daughter: she seems the most 'natural' heir.

In any case we are not looking at any sort of sexually egalitarian customs. No 'jocular' custom has yet come to light in which a fornicating old widower had to submit himself to the pain of riding

[64] Farnham Custom Roll, 1707., Winchester Cathedral Library.
[65] This last provision is cited by Watkins, *op. cit.*, i, p. 552 and indicates a slight modification and clarification over the 1707 Customs.
[66] Farnham Custom Roll, 1707, *loc. cit.*

into court on a goat. But we do have an accepted area of feminine presence, and this may have been an effective and creative one, and one felt, at any given time, palpably in the customary village.[67] Kerridge, who sometimes appears to hold a conspiratorial theory of tenure, in which the customary tenants are seen as constantly seeking for new ways to exploit their lords, has doubts as to the morality of the practice of free bench: it was 'open to abuse in a loose and disreputable manner, as when an aged and ailing customer took a young wife merely in order that she or a third party might enjoy the holding during her expected widowhood'.[68] No doubt on occasion this happened:[69] but as a general comment on the value or functions of free bench the judgement is flippant. It is even possible that habituation to this active feminine presence in areas of strong customary and yeoman occupancy served to modify sexual roles and inheritance customs more generally, even outside the customary sector.[70] Where I have compared the wills of Berkshire yeomen and tradesmen with the customs in Berkshire parishes in the 1720s and

[67] The effect of free bench in strengthening a feminine presence in the village in late medieval society is discussed by Rodney Hilton, *The English Peasantry in the Later Middle Ages* (London, 1975), ch. vi, esp. pp. 98–101. Many of his comments may remain apposite to districts in the eighteenth century which maintained traditions of yeoman customary occupancy: for an example of strong feminine tenure, see Matthew Imber, *The Case, or an Abstract of the Custom of the Manor of Mardon in the Parish of Hursley* (London, 1707): in this Hampshire manor, whose customs were borough English, more than 20 per cent (11 out of 52) of the copyholders were women.

[68] Kerridge, *op. cit.*, p. 83.

[69] By the custom of Berkeley (Glos.) 'marriage *in extremis* gives no free bench': Watkins, *op. cit.*, ii, p. 479.

[70] In the parish of Winkfield the Earl of Ranelagh founded a charity school for forty poor children. The Reverend Will Waterson, Rector of Winkfield, was also Master of the school for more than thirty years. He took in the daughters as well as the sons of the parish 'poor', but noted: 'Its much to be wish'd that the Girles were restrain'd from learning any thing that is not requisite in an ordinary servant, and that they were imploy'd in Spinning and makeing their own and the Boys cloths . . . Fine work . . . serves only to puff them up with pride and vanity, and to make them slight and overlook such places as they ought chiefly to be qualified for.' But Waterson, writing towards the end of his life, had perhaps become disillusioned and defensive in the face of accusations that the 'charity schools are nurseries of Rebellion, and disqualify poor children for such country business . . . as they are most wanted for'. For boys also (he noted) 'the plow must find them employment, or they'll do nothing': but he appears to have conscientiously afforded to the children of both sexes elementary instruction in literacy and numeracy: Waterson MS, Reading Ref. Lib. BOR/D: the passages cited were perhaps written in the early 1740s.

1730s I have noted no evidence in the former of any bias against female kin,[71] and, on occasion, a little bias the other way.[72] When in 1721 the Rev. Thomas Power, the curate of Easthampstead (Berks.) sought to persuade his recalcitrant wife to sign over some messuages to him by hanging her by a leg from the window and threatening to cut the rope, so far from meeting with the applause of the neighbourhood he was subjected by some local gallants to some very rough music and to a mock execution.[73] But this no doubt is another example of 'loose and disreputable' practice.

Freehold could of course also be transmitted to women: and it was so transmitted, to widows, to sisters, to daughters and to granddaughters. But if we accept that between 1660 and 1760 there was a severe decline in the numbers of yeomen, both free and copy, it may follow that there will also have been an equivalent decline in the effective female agrarian presence. Where lands came out of customary tenure, and were leased out again at will, they would be

[71] Among wills of yeomen and husbandmen in Berkshire at this time one frequently finds evidence of attention to the interests of female heirs. Thus Robert Dee of Winkfield, yeoman (probat. 10 April 1730), left two parcels of land, one of 16½ acres, the other of 2½ acres: the larger parcel was willed to his grandson, together with house and furniture, the smaller to his grand-daughter: but (in compensation) the grandson was to receive also £100, the grand-daughter £200. Among freeholders, tradesmen, etc., there is some evidence of egalitarian inheritance customs: thus Joseph Collier (probat. 12 July 1737), a Reading yeoman who owned some tenements and mills: all left to his brother in trust to sell and distribute 'share and share alike' among his six children (four daughters – all married – and two sons); Mary Maynard (probat. 20 May 1736) the widow of a Reading waggoner – a business which she had continued – the estate to be valued and to be distributed 'share and share alike' among six children (three of each sex) as each attained the age of 21: the two oldest children (one son, one daughter) to act as executors, but the daughter to lapse her function if she marries: Bodleian Library, MS Wills Berks. 20, p. 117; 21, p. 113, p. 72 verso.

[72] Thus the will of William Towsey, yeoman, of Letcombe Regis, probat. 22 August 1722, leaving to his daughter Ann Hawks £50 'to her own seperate use and disposicon wholy exempt from the Power or intermedling of her husband Thomas Hawks notwithstanding the Coverture between him and my said daughter': *ibid.*, 19, pp. 150–1.

[73] See *Whigs and Hunters*, pp. 71–2. If, as I suppose, Mrs Power was born Ann Ticknor, then she held more than 80 acres as well as barns, orchards, cottages, etc., in the forest, in jointure with her sister: the jointure explains why the land could not fall to the Reverend Power in consequence of his avaricious coverture. (Yeomen were perfectly capable of using the devices of jointures and of trusts to safeguard their daughters' rights.) It is reassuring to note that Mrs Power endured the hazards of her marriage and died 'without doing any Act to affect' her property: Abstract of Aaron Maynard's title to four closes in Wokingham, Berks. Rec. Off. D/ER E 12.

leased to men. A tenancy-at-will carried no widow's estate: at the most it would be allowed as a favour. Security of the customary grid was lost; and if the yeoman was only at a further point in his secular decline, the yeowoman had been served notice to quit.

As a final point I wish to return to the difference between the inheritance of a family, and inheritance of security, status, power, by a social group, caste, or class. The first depends generally upon the second. We have the particular inheritance practices of families, and the grid of law, custom, expectation, upon which these practices operate. And these grids differ greatly between social groups. What is happening is the devising of rules and practices by which particular social groups project forwards provisions and (as they hope) guarantees of security for their children. Cooper has examined the grid of the great. The moneyed class had a different grid, although it meshed in closely with that of the land. But the eighteenth century had also a third, complementary, grid for the propertied classes: that of interest, preferment to office, purchase of commissions, reversions to sinecures, placings within the Church and so on. In this grid of nepotism and interest, possession was not all: one must also supplement possession with continuing interest and the right kind of political connections. One must both have (or find for one's child) an office and maintain the influence to exploit that office to the full. The parent might attend to the first: his child must see to the second.

Throughout the eighteenth century the grid of interest and preferment remained as a bundle of that kind. Along this grid the lesser gentry sought to secure the future of their families. The papers of the great patrons show the incessant activity of petitioners on behalf of their kin, in the attempt to secure the whole structure of the Church and State as a kind of Trust for their own class. Middle-class reformers, rallying under the banner of the 'career open to talent', at the same time sought to secure the future status of their own children upon a grid of educational qualification and professional exclusiveness. Moreover this reminds us that a privileged group could – and still can – secure its own grid while trying to tear down the grid of another. In the twentieth century the see-saw of social-democratic and conservative politics has often turned on such rivalries. But in the eighteenth and nineteenth centuries similar contests were fought which will be overlooked if we only take into account post-mortem inheritance. Sabean appears, momentarily, to have allowed this oversight to enter when he cites the case of a poor village in the Sologne and concludes from its evidence that 'in the absence of property there is little tendency to develop extended kin ties'.[74] Of course if there is an absence of land and of movable property then neither of these can be transmitted through inheritance: nor are the poor in any position to 'arrange for good marriages'. So that Sabean's generalization may hold good for a poor peasant economy. But even for the landless rural labourer, and certainly for an urban proletariat, the critical point of familial transmission has not been *post mortem* but at the point of giving the children a 'start in life'. If we wish to examine inheritance and the family in the eighteenth century among urban craftsmen, we have to look, not at wills, but at apprenticeship regulations, apprenticeship premiums, and at trades in which a strong family tradition was preserved by offering a preference to sons or kin and by limiting apprentices.[75] Even among the rural poor (one suspects) the business of placing a son on a good farm, a daughter in service at the great house, occupied much effort and anxiety, and was part of the effort of transmitting to the next generation a 'respectable' status, on the right side of the poor law. And in the early nineteenth century, by clipping away at apprenticeship, by repealing the Statute of Artificers, the rulers of England were threatening the inheritance system of the skilled workmen; while in 1834, by striking at all out-relief, they threatened the only grid of ultimate security known to the poor.

Of course, no guarantee has ever secured to the individual family immunity from the accidents of mutability. Remarkable as are certain continuities among aristocracy and gentry, there are many more cases of the downward turn of fortune's wheel. As Raymond Williams has recently argued, the very literary values of landed estate and settlement are often those espoused by the newly-rich anxious to pretend to the values of settlement. Penshurst, the subject of Ben Jonson's classic country house poem, raised by 'no man's ruin, no man's grone', was in fact a manor which had lapsed by execution and attainder some fifty years before Jonson wrote.[76]

---

[74] Above p. 98.

[75] For a study of artisan occupational inheritance see William H. Sewell, Jr, 'Social Change and the Rise of Working-Class Politics in Nineteenth-Century Marseilles', *Past and Present*, 65, November 1974.

[76] Raymond Williams, *The Country and the City* (London, 1973), pp. 40–1.

For other poets the family and its fortune are taken as an illustration of mutability:

> And what if my descendants lose the flower
> Through natural declension of the soul,
> Through too much business with the passing hour,
> Through too much play, or marriage with a fool?
> May this laborious stair and this stark tower
> Become a roofless ruin that the owl
> May build in the cracked masonry and cry
> Her desolation to the desolate sky.

For Yeats no forethought could hold back the cyclical mutability of things:

> The Primum Mobile that fashioned us
> Has made the very owls in circles move . . .

Yeats underestimated certain continuities, and notably the remarkable longevity of certain corporate landowners – those wise old owls, Merton College and St John's College, Cambridge, have flown directly to us from the twelfth or thirteenth centuries. But common observation (or a brief consultation of any genealogical authority) confirms this thought: as Yorkshire people have it, from clogs to clogs in three generations. What this may conceal is that independent of the rise and fall of families, the inheritance-grids themselves have often proved to be extremely effective as a vehicle of another kind of corporate inheritance – the means by which a social group has extended its historical tenure of status and of privilege. We are busy with it still today, as accountants and lawyers devise new trusts, new hedges against inflation, setting up investment trusts with one leg upon each of the four corners of the capitalist world. But we should be on our guard. We commence by examining the inheritance systems of particular families: but, over time, family fortunes rise and fall; what is inherited is property itself, the claim on the resources of a future society; and the beneficiary may be, not any descendant of that particular family, but the historical descendant of the social class to which that family once belonged.

10. Private property in history

V. G. KIERNAN

> A critical knowledge of the evolution of the idea of
> property would embody, in some respects, the most
> remarkable portion of the mental history of mankind.
>
> L. H. Morgan, *Ancient Society* (1877), p. 6

History, which Hegel saw as an unfolding of ideas, has been much
more the unfolding of the institution of property. Material ownership once established could ramify and hypertrophy in extraordinary ways. In modern Europe individuals have claimed
possession of lakes and rivers, a pretension we are coming to think
no less grotesque than any seigneurial privileges of bygone days.
Someone or other at the present moment claims to 'own' Ben Nevis.
Modern nationalism displays this landowning mania in demo-
cratized form; imperialism expanded it into a delusion in the common man's mind that he 'owned' his country's colonies and their
resources. But the spirit of ownership once astir could percolate
into all sorts of corners and crevices. Public offices, or the reversion
of them, have often been private benefices, as in the old French
bureaucracy, or the – not so old – British army. In our busy competitive days 'time is money', and we 'spend' half an hour
grudgingly, unlike our careless ancestors; and the stronger our
possessiveness the more minutely time, like land, is measured, subdivided, recorded. Intellectual and artistic rights of property have
taken shape more slowly. Shakespeare and Handel thought little of
stealing or being stolen from, and copyright laws have been a very
late development.

Before their rebellion Americans talked, as Dr Johnson complained, of their right to 'Life, Liberty, and Property':[1] after it they
changed the prescription to 'Life, liberty, and the pursuit of
happiness'. Clearly the two notions were felt to be identical. Yet
about the same time in the Old World, with its longer and sourer
memories, the Spanish statesman Jovellanos was lamenting that
'fatal word property, hateful beyond all . . . an ill-omened, sinister

---

[1] 'Taxation no Tyranny', in *The Political Writings of Dr. Johnson*, ed.
J. P. Hardy (London, 1968), p. 112.

361

word, fountain and sole cause of so much evil'.[2] Through some of its spokesmen mankind has never ceased to think of private ownership as an incumbrance on human life, a shirt of Nessus. One English term for it is never used without the epithet attached to it in Tyndale's Bible-phrase, 'filthy lucre'. Another self-condemnatory name is 'pelf', which is related to *pilfer*, and meant at first plunder, before it came to stand for property indiscriminately:[3] the implication clearly is that 'property is theft'. Elizabethan poets indulged in endless tirades against Gold, and in general poetry, ancient and modern, has been faithful to its bardic origins, as the mouthpiece of collective wisdom, when it has condemned private ownership. Religion, which grew with it, has often done the same. 'O dear Southey!' the young Coleridge wrote to his friend in 1801, in the midst of war and industrial revolution, 'what incalculable Blessings, worthy of Thanksgiving in Heaven, do we not owe to our being and *having been Poor*! No man's Heart can wholly stand up against Property.'[4]

In humdrum times property has been taken for granted, like other established facts, in whatever local guise it may wear. Academic thinking has usually been apt to overlook it. 'Few thinkers in the social sciences have written works that are primarily devoted to the elucidation of the institution of property.'[5] For some time now sociology seems to have considered the whole subject as threadbare, used up. Psychology grew up too much in the atmosphere of private-property relations to be often conscious of them. When Freud turned his thoughts to *Civilization and its Discontents* he scarcely thought it necessary to refer to them. In more ordinary minds property has come under question at times of change and social dislocation, like those of Coleridge's youth, when its burdensomeness, its distorting of humanity, are felt acutely. Both the English revolution[6] and the French brought misgivings about it

[2] *Obras escogidas* (Madrid, 1945) i, p. lxii.
[3] This and later derivations are taken from *The Oxford Dictionary of English Etymology*, ed. C. T. Onions (1966).
[4] Letter of 1 Aug. 1801, in *Collected Letters of Samuel Taylor Coleridge*, ed. E. L. Griggs (Oxford, 1956), ii, pp. 749–50.
[5] *Encyclopaedia of Social Sciences*, introd. to 'Property'. One can turn over a surprising number of recent works by historians and others, where some discussion of the subject might be expected, without finding any.
[6] See C. B. MacPherson, *The Political Theory of Possessive Individualism. Hobbes to Locke* (Oxford, 1962), part iii, 'The Levellers: Franchise and Freedom'.

into the open. During the voyage to Egypt in 1798, when Bonaparte in his pose as intellectual was holding debates on all kinds of themes, a three-day discussion of property was inspired by Rousseau's theories about inequality. General Caffarelli maintained that property was only 'usurpation and theft', and produced an elaborate blueprint for its abolition.[7] In the later nineteenth century, with knowledge about non-European peoples widening, and with the socialist challenge making itself heard, there was much dispute about the status of property in primitive society. Engels and Lafargue sought to prove that it arose out of social evolution, and Marx was vastly impressed by Morgan's independent treatment of the same thesis; their opponents preferred to think of property as *natural*, of a possessive instinct inseparable from man as human being. In the bewildered Britain of the interwar years this controversy flared up afresh.[8]

A good part of what a 'primitive' deems his property would scarcely seem to a modern man to enter into that category; though the converse would be equally true. Three classes of property have usefully been distinguished: natural (land or livestock), man-made, and 'incorporeal', including personal names or magic charms.[9] Perry, the diffusionist, pointed out that most food-gatherers do not try to store up reserves, but live from hand to mouth, and that in all later stages ownership seems to be 'influenced by other motives than that of the mere desire to possess'. He was sensibly rejecting the notion of 'an Instinct of Acquisition', and the tendency to go on multiplying innate instincts, each with its converse, like pugnacity and peacefulness.[10] (Early physicists multiplied hypotheses like gravity and levity with the same prodigality.) Malinowski judged it foolish for anthropologists to be drawn into argument about whether primitive human nature is communistic or individualistic, though he at once proceeded to show himself a simple-minded anticommunist by arguing that collective use of tribal land is only like use of the streets of New York in common by competing business-

[7] J. C. Herold, *Bonaparte in Egypt* (London, 1962), p. 53.

[8] This point was brought out by D. McCrone in an instructive seminar paper at Edinburgh University in 1974: 'Property – a concept revisited'. The psychological study by E. Beaglehole, 1931, is summarized in his article on 'Property' in the *Encyclopaedia of Social Sciences*. To 1943 belongs R. Gonnard, *La propriété dans la doctrine et dans l'histoire* (Paris).

[9] R. Bunzel, cited in J. Wach, *Sociology of Religion* (1931; English edn, London, 1947), p. 211.

[10] W. J. Perry, *The Primordial Ocean* (London, 1935), pp. 87–9.

men.[11] His own picture of his Trobriand islanders shows them toiling very much as though in the grip of a Calvinist work-ethic, but growing yams more for the satisfaction of demonstrating their skill than for any utilitarian advantage.[12] There is something more like a Puritan acquisitive spirit in Manus society as depicted by Margaret Mead, where commercial enterprise is keen.[13] It may be explainable by the fact that the Manus are not a self-sufficient community, but live by trading their fish for the agricultural products of other tribes, so that commercialism is in a manner thrust on them. A commodity changing hands on debatable terms may well stimulate the sense of *meum* and *tuum* more than one that is always ours.

Strict respect for *mine* and *thine* is one of the few lessons drilled into Manus children.[14] Believers in the naturalness of property have found an inborn desire for it in infants, as well as in primitives, and certainly acquisitive habits are often precocious. Tom Sawyer reduced the other boys of his village to bankruptcy by taking toll of their toys and valuables in return for letting them paint his fence. But whether any of this impulse is implanted at birth remains questionable. It is a familiar observation that men grow more eager to accumulate as they grow older, and youth's confident sense of inheriting the earth fades. Property is a consolation for the senescence of the physical self, making up for the decay of eye and ear and muscle and conferring artificial strength. Byron observed this in himself, and Shelley in his villain:

> I must use
> Close husbandry, or gold, the old man's sword,
> Falls from my withered hand.[15]

Much of the history of property can be sought for in the fossil record of language. The word itself is from the Latin *proprius*, probably derived from *pro privo*, private or personal, which gave

[11] B. Malinowski, *Sex, Culture, and Myth* (London, 1963), pp. 185–6.
[12] *Ibid.*, p. 184.
[13] Margaret Mead, *Growing up in New Guinea* (1930; Penguin edn, 1954), pp. 66ff.
[14] *Ibid.*, p. 161. Cf. Jessie Bernard, *Marriage and Family among Negroes* (Englewood Cliffs, N.J., 1966), p. 140: 'The set of norms which constitute the institutions of private property are very early inculcated into children in Western societies' – and this forms a dividing line in the U.S.A. between white and Negro.
[15] *The Cenci*, Act i, Sc. i.

thirteenth-century English its word 'proper'. This evolved towards its modern self-complacent meaning – whatever is *ours* must be *right* – and the idea of 'propriety'; also towards the word 'property', meaning ownership, usually private, and from the fifteenth century, but more generally from the seventeenth, things owned. 'Wealth' is related to 'well', and in the thirteenth century meant both riches and welfare. About the same time the plural *goods* came into circulation, a parallel to *bona, biens,* and a Norse equivalent: the 'goodness' of things consists in their belonging to men. On the other hand an Elizabethan 'miser' might be either an avaricious person, or as in Latin a pitiful wretch. It is good to possess, but not to possess too many goods, or too selfishly.

Apart from names of things, we may hope for light on property relations from the grammatical forms which serve to express them in different language groups. Both the Latin and the Germanic are uncompromisingly direct. 'I have a book' – though there are many ambiguities about a verb which also enables us to say that we have a cough, or a fear, or children, besides its service as an auxiliary. Greek has a verb with similarly meandering functions. Latin has *tenere* and *possidere* as well as *habere*; in addition it has the construction used by Horace in talking of his Alban wine, 'There is to me a cask.' Such an idiom may seem appropriate to an article only temporarily possessed. But when we find languages with no other way of indicating possession than this, where the thing owned is subject instead of object and has as it were an autonomous status, it may suggest a looser, less highly individualized sense of possession; such a relationship as really can be recognized in early societies, especially in respect of land.

Oblique grammatical constructions are the commonest even within the Indo-European family, both west and east of the Latin–Germanic area. A Gaelic speaker 'has' nothing but *feelings*: when he owns a thing, that thing 'is to him'; and he has no noun signifying ownership.[16] Irish has no 'have' verb, but says: 'There is a book at me.' Welsh has such a verb, as well as a term for ownership, but its flavour is literary, and the common phrase is: 'There is a book with me.' Russian reserves its 'have' verb chiefly for abstractions, and prefers 'There is to me –' for concrete objects. There is no verb of possession at all in Hindi, or in its cousin Panjabi, still a rustic

[16] I owe this to J. Maclean, and part of the following information to other colleagues at Edinburgh University.

vernacular as Hindi was until not long ago. Here the usage is: 'There is a book near me' (more literally: 'Near me a book is'). Sanscrit, a highly polished literary medium, had a possessive verb, but was already drifting away from its use. When we turn to other linguistic groups, straightforward 'having' again seems more the exception than the rule. It is absent from the Dravidian languages of southern India. In Arabic 'There is no verb "have", the idea is expressed by a preposition.'[17] Turkish, another speech of nomads, is again indirect: 'A book-of-mine is.' It may not be simple co-incidence that in China, where private property early came to include land, the verb *yu* expresses possession, whether of property or of other things, whereas Japan, where a feudal order with its indeterminacies of landholding persisted for ages longer, adhered to a periphrasis.

To a Roman *dominium* meant either authority or ownership, and its root-word, akin to the English 'tame', meant 'to subdue'. Spain's feudal nobles were called *ricoshombres*, before becoming officially *los grandes*, unofficially often *los poderosos*, the power-ful: the word 'rich', with cognates in many Latin, Celtic, Germanic languages, meant royal, splendid, dominant, before it came by its modern meaning. We still talk of a 'rich wine', or a 'rich joke'. Possession confers power, but itself has very often been derived from power. Property has emerged in fact by two routes – from below, out of production, and from above, by force. The first has been a humble, plebeian process; the glorious way to ownership has been extorting wealth from others, by means of taxes, feudal dues, robbery, or even by others being transformed into property, through enslavement. War and wealth, Mars and Ploutos, have stood close together. War was the main purveyor of slaves; booty such as an Assyrian monarch or a sultan of Delhi boasted of carry-ing off enriched ministers and commanders. A 'will to power' may be one of the strongest, earliest ingredients in the complex sensation of ownership; it may represent a gradual individuation of the energy of humanity's collective struggle against nature.

When a man turned a bit of stone into a tool he was exercising power over it. But dominion over other living creatures must always have held a subtler fascination, even if primitive men did not draw

[17] A. S. Tritton, *Teach Yourself Arabic* (London, 1949), p. 35. ' "The man has a book" can be said in three ways with shades of meaning. . . .'

as hard and fast a line as ours between animate and inanimate; over beings not perpetual like stone or vast and impersonal like the earth. In the Garden of Eden, God left it to Adam to choose names for all the other creatures,[18] and to confer a name is to impose a subordination. Adam's descendants began by hunting and killing them, and went on to breed them for milking or eating; a significantly new feeling would enter when they learned to *enslave* dog, ass, horse, ox, and compel them to labour for their masters. In particular the horse, which almost elevated man into a member of a new species, might well become the object of a peculiarly strong blend of mastery, attachment, possessiveness. Two things a man should never lend to anyone else, according to an old Boer saying, are his horse and his wife.

Reduction of animals to servitude can easily be supposed to have led on to that of fellow-men, the earliest example of conquest recoiling on the conquerors, and this would intensify the 'instinct' of property and domination still further. Authority over either animals or slaves must have reacted on men's attitude to their women and children, and inclined them to think of these two as chattels. *Domus* is another word related to *dominium*. In the Commandments wife and maidservant, ox and ass, stand side by side in the catalogue of man's assets. In the Jewish code, the Mishnah, betrothal came under the head of *acquisition*, and regulations about how to acquire a bride were followed by those about slaves, cattle, or other belongings. 'Romanticists may resent the immediate switch from marriage to slavery, but in rabbinic law the two institutions had much in common – legally speaking.'[19] Another link between sexual and other possessiveness shows itself in the very widespread adoption of cowrie-shells, by virtue of their sexually suggestive appearance, as currency. 'Cupidity' meant at first the concupiscence stirred up by the god Cupid, and then came to mean greed of gain. How close were women and property in men's minds may be gleaned from Rob Roy's aphorism: 'women and gear are at the bottom of a' the mischief in this warld.'[20] It is an old saying in northern India that the chief causes of strife among men are *zar, zan, zamin* – gold, women, land.

[18] Gen. ii, 19. Adam was created to 'have dominion' over all creatures (i, 28).

[19] E. J. Lipman, *The Mishnah. Oral Teachings of Judaism* (New York, 1970), pp. 190, 192n.

[20] *Rob Roy*, ch. 35.

As some men grew to be richer than others they collected women, who were also means by which they could amass further riches. 'The more pigs a man has', we read of the Dani tribe in New Guinea, 'the more cowrie shells he can get. The more shells he possesses, the more sweet potato gardens can be cultivated; the more sweet potatoes, the more pigs he can feed, the more cowrie shells, the more wives. . . .'[21] Here is primitive accumulation in the most literal sense. Being herself a possession, woman could not easily be an owner. In Homeric times 'it is highly doubtful that a woman could in any proper sense be said to own slaves or the other basic forms of wealth'.[22] Yet in some societies a slave has been able to earn money for himself, even to own another slave, as in an aboriginal hill district of China where 'every gradation of ownership and part-ownership of slaves' existed, and a slave might buy a half-share in his own wife.[23] Women often had rights over certain kinds of goods, chiefly domestic. How these limited rights slowly and painfully expanded, in Rome for example,[24] makes up a large chapter of human history.

Prehistoric man's belongings were often buried with him, and so have been those of various modern primitives, such as the Cheyenne Indians.[25] A man's indispensable tools, weapons, ornaments, were thought of as more intimately and indelibly his 'own' than any material property known to us. He had probably made most of them for himself, they were part and parcel of his existence, for his fellows they must have been a large part of what stamped him as a person. It was by a very false analogy that in later days, when chiefs and lords arose, valuable possessions not of their own making, and their attendants and women, came to be buried with them, and much wealth lost to the community. Such transposings of elemental associations into different and more complex contexts must account for a great deal of the growth of human culture, in which the

[21] R. T. Hitt, *Cannibal Valley* (1962; London edn, 1969), p. 117.

[22] M. I. Finley, 'Marriage, Sale, and Gift in the Homeric World', in *The Jurist* (Washington, D.C.), xii (1954), p. 23. This and several other articles and books were brought to my notice by R. J. Hopper.

[23] A. Winnington, *The Slaves of the Cool Mountains* (London, 1959; Berlin edn, 1962), p. 46.

[24] See Simone de Beauvoir, *Nature of the Second Sex* (trans. H. M. Parshley, London, 1961), part II, ch. iii.

[25] One possession of a Cheyenne which might be buried with him was his horse.

irrational has had, oftener than not, the upper hand. Even in such madness, nevertheless, some method is still to be looked for. These acts of destruction, as marks of respect to the dead, served also to emphasize the respect due to their living successors, and to the sanctity of all that belonged to them.

In Virgil's catalogue of crimes and their infernal punishments, his most numerous class of miscreants are those who gathered riches without giving any share to their folk.[26] In some tribal societies all movables not indissolubly linked with the individual were expected to be shared, by those who had them, with all in need: food above all, and any superfluities, creature comforts like the blankets and bottles that trade with the white man brought to the red. This freedom from dog-in-the-manger habits contributed to eighteenth-century Europe's fantasy of the noble savage, unspoiled by the snares of the acquisitive society. If a novel turn of events like trade with the white man brought wealth beyond the ability of a group to consume, as it did to the Kwakiutl people of the Northwest coast of America early in this century, it might seem the best solution to get rid of it. The *potlatch* ceremony, where tribesmen vied in exchanging costly gifts, or displayed greatness of soul by destroying them,[27] may be viewed as a community's last attempt to prevent wealth from subverting its unity. All tribal societies have had to look for some such safeguard, usually of a more sensible kind, against this danger and the inequalities giving rise to it. 'The leveling mechanism may take the form of forced loans to relatives or coresidents', or of a feast given to them by anyone who has a windfall.[28] At a more sophisticated level something very like this went on in Greek towns down to the second century A.D., proof of how much of the old clan philosophy still lurked in their civic spirit. 'Rich men spent their means, generation after generation, until they were bankrupt, in providing meals and amusements for the poorer citizens, or in building baths and foundling-hospitals for the benefit of their cities.'[29]

Land as a form of property has always had unique features.

---

[26] *Aeneid*, Book vi, lines 610–11.
[27] See C. D. Forde, *Habitat, Economy and Society*, 2nd edn (London, 1937), ch. vi.
[28] M. Nash, 'Economic Anthropology', in *Encyclopaedia of Social Sciences*.
[29] E. Barker, *Greek Political Theory. Plato and his Predecessors*, 2nd edn (London, 1925), p. 22.

Agriculture was bound to be the starting-point of a transformation not only of the productive process but of ownership-attitudes, towards land and through it indirectly to everything else. Before cultivation began to set one man against another it set one clan against another. Among some tribes of New Guinea, that museum of prehistory, clan strife seems to have been frequent and bloody, and its economic motive, desire for land to settle on, as naked as any in civilized Europe.[30] But while the collective sense of possession was thus sharpened, it also began to be undermined, because most of the working of the land could be carried on most readily by the individual family. Plots of ground would be assigned by the community to households, though what was given was not the land itself but the right to use it. Something like this semi-communal system, or clan ownership with family occupancy, has been found among many simple agriculturalists of recent times; among the Indians of Chile, for instance,[31] and of South America generally. Much of it survived in Europe, into the nineteenth century, in the village with its ring of common land open to all for gathering of food or wood or for pasture, and its family holdings often made up of scattered strips, sometimes as in Russia still periodically re-shuffled.

It was the coming of full private ownership of land, nearly always accompanied by more or less extreme inequalities, that marked the grand revolutionary breach in the old fraternity. Ownership of large-scale holdings was often accelerated by the process of conquest. In Britain the Romans found a 'broad distinction' between big landowners and their tenants or smallholders. 'Celtic story and legend indicate that the relationship must have been one of great variety.'[32] In Greece an 'aristocratic system of ownership' was a legacy from Homeric times. 'The problem of land ownership was an acute one in all the states of Greece, and was settled, or not settled, in various distressing and violent ways.'[33] In general, in the ancient world exclusive possession of land had to make its way

[30] Illustrations of this can be found in the 'Oral History No. 1' paper of the History Dept, University of Papua New Guinea, Dec. 1972, e.g. p. 13.

[31] See G. M. McBride, *Chile: Land and Society* (New York, 1936), pp. 66–7, 248, 308–9, 362. For evidences of former collective ownership of land in the world generally see E. Mandel, *Marxist Economic Theory* (trans. B. Pearce, London, 1962–8), pp. 33–6.

[32] I. A. Richmond, *Roman Britain* (London, 1955), p. 126.

[33] H. Michell, *The Economics of Ancient Greece* (Cambridge, 1957), p. 40,

against a persistent feeling that it was somehow wrong, a nostalgia for older days romanticized in dim memory into the myth of a golden age of communism. This idyllic time was always one of peace, as well as plenty: the myth looked back beyond even the harmony of collective clan property, or magnified this into a harmony of all mankind, older than agriculture itself. Josephus preserved an old tradition of Abel as harmless shepherd, Cain – the cultivator – as avaricious seeker of wealth.[34] In Genesis IV the Lord accepts Abel's offerings from his flock, and in enigmatic terms rejects those of Cain from his crops; it is, apparently, this that moves the latter to murder his brother. Our latter-day poetic pastorals with their guileless shepherd swains must have been coloured by a similar notion that landlords and farmers, bent on owning land instead of being content simply to make use of it, are a different and more sordid race.

Both emergence of private ownership and encroachment of larger properties on smaller would be greatly assisted by the advent of money, in the sense of some universal equivalent. This could not come about at a single bound. Men's early possessions fell into distinct categories, subject to alternative species of 'ownership', and not all of them were mutually exchangeable.[35] Currency that a canoe can be bought with may not be legal tender when it comes to requiring a wife. Before any form of money could be acceptable against all commodities, and replace man as the measure of all things, many old barriers of custom had to be broken down. Formerly 'possession of property usually involved the performance of some religious rites',[36] and items changed hands by way of gift, to the accompaniment of formal ceremonial. Once fully established, money brushed all this aside. There was moreover no limit to men's thirst for it, as there was to their real need of any tangible asset. Piling it up would help to form the habit of piling up other kinds of wealth too. It quickly got itself detested as an evil thing, as if malignantly alive. Horace praises a good man for holding aloof from 'money that draws to itself all things'.[37]

We speak of our 'selves', as we do of our clothes. Everyman's *I* –

[34] M. Beer, *A History of British Socialism*, i (London, 1929), p. 4.
[35] See M. Godelier, *Rationality and Irrationality in Economics* (trans. B. Pearce, London, 1972), pp. 297ff.
[36] F. R. Cowell, *Cicero and the Roman Republic* (London, 1948), p. 142.
[37] *Odes*, Book iv, no. 9.

that entity which seems to fade or crumble when inspected too closely, like seaweed removed from water – is or seems to him his basic, inexpugnable possession, his own in a way that must have coloured all his other sensations of ownership. It involves all the same a hazy duality, an inmost essence and a sentinel standing guard over it against the outer world. We humorously complain of total destitution or unfreedom by saying that 'We can't call our soul our own.' Odysseus believed in doing a good turn when he could to his own 'dear heart', Horace recommends his reader to bestow his goods on cheering up his own 'dear spirit' instead of leaving them to a gaping heir.[38] Everyman has always had a *ghost*, born it may be when he himself first became human by learning to make and use implements, part of himself yet distinct from him – an *alter ego*, a second self – and capable of outliving him, along with the utensils buried with his corpse. But this ghost was a frail, piping, shadowy creature, dependent for continued existence on the memory and the offerings of the living, of the clan of which it was one strand. Its evolution into a true *soul* accompanied the blossoming and ramifying of private ownership, which lent it vitality.

Parallel with this progress was that of early 'natural' religion, or animism, through paganism with its semi-human gods, towards religions in the modern sense, deliberately founded to embody a specific ideology. At each stage before this it lent a sanction to unfolding property rights. All these began as forms of divine right. Taboo, in the Pacific, was an effective mode of protecting them by laying their disturbers under a curse; a curse invoked at first, we may surmise, by the clan, then by chiefs who clothed themselves in its authority, and finally by commoners who aped them in trading on the universal fear of ghosts and of the unseen. But as individual property and individualism spread on earth, gods had to emerge in heaven with more marked personality and with prescribed functions and duties towards human beings under their patronage. Gods of wealth arose, in Greece, India, China. Riches could begin to be regarded as a mark of divine favour, as by Abraham and his multi-plying flocks and descendants and his watchful Jehovah; and this could be an effective way to free private property of its ill repute and bad conscience. It has been argued that the European concept of 'God' formed itself on that of proprietorship: that *deus* and *divitiae* (riches) have a common root, and that God is the grand

[38] *Ibid.*, no. 7.

proprietor of the universe.[39] It has even been urged as a proof of God's existence that the universe *must* have an *owner*[40] – so alien to us has become the thought of anything not owned, of even a nebula or comet not subject to the lawyers' doctrine of *nulle terre sans seigneur*.

On land, always in a class of its own, the guardianship of religion lay heavily. 'In many parts of Europe early literature describes how land boundaries were first drawn with a plough, a rite whose sacred meaning was often emphasized by special ceremonies.'[41] Under the Inca sway removal of boundary marks was a heinous crime, and commoners never ventured to cross the limits of the lands reserved for noble and priest 'without repeating ritual prayers for this special purpose'.[42] Boundaries were at first those of the clan territory, including probably those guarded by images of the Roman god Terminus, a faceless, featureless deity appropriate to a time when private holdings and personalized gods were still in their nonage. But in Mesopotamia already in the Kassite era (about the seventeenth century B.C.) it was customary to record royal grants of land to individuals on steles, along with maledictions against any who might tamper with them, and these records were deposited in the temples.[43]

With Jehovah and his prophets we are on the threshold of the era of founded religions, each in its own way a response to the fact of mankind's widening divisions, each compelled to stand on both sides, those of old social order and new, poor men and rich. They undertook to sanctify private property afresh, but imposed conditions on it in return which upheld in some sort the old faith in collective right and obligation. To claim any exclusive possession was to put oneself at a distance from one's fellows, an act calling for amends and purgation. In Islam the *bait ul-'am* or common treasury marked a transition to another species of social insurance; in addition, all property was laid under a special tax (*zakat*) for the benefit of the needy. Land, the source of all wealth, could not lightly be consigned to private selfishness. Hebrew prophets

[39] Article by A. Chiappelli, 1931, summarized in Antonio Gramsci, *Passato e Presente* (Rome, 1971), p. 195. Gramsci himself was convinced that the Russian words *Bog* (God) and *bogatii* (rich) must be related.

[40] Cited by Chiappelli, *loc. cit.*

[41] E. Hyams, *Soil and Civilization* (London, 1952), p. 143.

[42] J. A. Mason, *The Ancient Civilizations of Peru* (London, 1957), p. 177.

[43] G. Roux, *Ancient Iraq* (1964; Penguin edn, 1966), pp. 224–5.

denounced the laying of house to house and field to field that private ownership, once introduced, was always liable to lead to. Their words echoed down the ages. At the English farm-labourers' conference in May 1974, when a motion in favour of land national-ization was being passed, one supporter appealed to the Biblical statement that heaven and earth were made by God.[44]

Christianity began with a strong bias against private property of every kind.[45] It took over from secular philosophy a commonly held idea that the fall of man and the rise of private property came together. War and *amor habendi*, 'love of having', were the twin plagues that ended the Saturnian golden age of Italy.[46] Saint Francis' patroness, the Lady Poverty, dwelt in paradise with man while he was still naked, carefree, unafraid, but withdrew when she saw him clothing himself in the skins of dead animals, 'giving himself up to multiplied labours by which he might become rich'.[47] But only in heaven could Christianity succeed in carrying out a revolution, the abolition of private property which its zealots pined for here below. In its thinking the individual soul, after its age-old mysterious growth, stood out at last as something independent and immortal, quintessence of all the multifarious elements woven together to make up 'I'; woven from some of the same strands as the Roman law which made private property so absolute and unconditional. Christianity sublimated the whole sense of ownership, along with the personal identity that dawned and grew with it, into this soul which alone left one world for another. In the classical other-world spirits of departed heroes were provided with horses, chariots, phantom replicas of all that once delighted them on earth. The Christian soul was purified in heaven from all taint of ownership, its base material cradle (and, significantly, from the kindred bane of sex). It has scarcely occurred even to the Toriest theologian to enquire whether each new arrival will be assigned his own personal harp. Buddhism had taken a long step further on the same road towards annihilation of *own-ness* by abolishing personality, identity, the soul itself, altogether. It sought perhaps in Nirvana a return to

---

[44] B.B.C. report, 11 May 1974. A good deal of 'old-fashioned idealism' showed itself in this debate, it struck the reporter.

[45] See e.g. Karl Kautsky, *Foundations of Christianity*, 13th edn (1908; English edn, 1925), Part iv, ch. i.

[46] *Aeneid*, Book viii, line 327.

[47] *Sacrum Commercium. The Converse of Francis and his Sons with Holy Poverty* (London edn, 1904), pp. 11, 13.

the undifferentiated or latent consciousness of a human species before human beings were born.

In material possessions Buddhism recognized the dead weight that hindered 'I' from reaching liberation from 'me'. Early texts abound in laments over backsliding brethren seduced by the temptations of gain.[48] Jainism, contemporary with Buddhism, likewise began with prohibitions against wealth-seeking, but these, in a busy mercantile community, were speedily relaxed. 'The celebration of Divali, one of the great feasts of Jainism, is originally a Hindu festival in honour of Lakshmi, goddess of wealth.'[49] As for Christendom, no part of the reception of Aristotle into medieval thought, under the auspices above all of Aquinas, can have been more pregnant than the reinforcement it brought to property by helping to lay the ghost of the old Christian antipathy to it.

What was retained in Jain morality, from the original austere outlook, was a regard for 'scrupulous honesty' in business. It was akin to the 'well-grounded basis for commercial ethics' that can be ascribed to post-Exilic Judaism;[50] likewise to the mercantile principles of Puritans and Quakers, heirs to the old ascetic Christian tradition. Such ethical restraints place limits on haste of acquisition, or indiscriminate gain; they are the counterpart of a chivalrous code of honour, and represent the residue left behind by an old religious aversion to property. They stand for acceptance of property only on condition of its being honestly come by. These scruples have proved highly favourable to success; so that condemnation of property has undergone a change, like so many other things in history, into its opposite.

Roman law moved away in course of time from recognition of male heirs only, members of the patrilineal *gens*, and arrived at a form destined to influence all later concepts of property in Europe. Its 'absolutist' character must have owed much to the climate of conquest and slave-holding that it grew in, the rolling juggernaut of Roman imperialism. Yet this, after all, it shared with a great part of Asia. On another side its spirit was political. The city-state concentrated the inarticulate consciousness of a tribe into an intense

[48] See e.g. Mrs Rhys Davids, *Psalms of the Early Buddhists* (London, 1909), Part ii, pp. 141, 333–4.
[49] Wach, *op. cit.*, p. 264.
[50] *Ibid.*

civic spirit; this included a profound recognition of authority, not, however, of the 'Oriental' type, for the State equally recognized the rights, even against itself, of the freeborn citizen, or, in practice, of the propertied citizen. State and individual thus formed two poles of the same complex. In this setting, property – 'the mainspring as well as the foundation' of political society, as Morgan wrote[51] – could be a defence of the individual, now for good or ill detached from old fraternal ties and placed in a more artificial society, capable of crushing him. Europe ever since has been able to look quite genuinely on private property as a necessary protection of the individual and his rights, and of the unfolding of individuality itself – even if the majority have often been excluded from it, more completely at times than most Asiatics.

With the growth of a secular legal system, having precise property rights for its chief basis, came professional lawyers, and with them, to a great extent, politics, as a regular contest of parties under regular rules. Without lawyers a fundamental ingredient in European history would have been lacking, as it was lacking in nearly all Asian history. 'How can a country exist without lawyers?'[52] was a natural question for an English lawyer to ask a Persian visitor. They have spread over other continents along with the rest of European civilization. With the coming of law-courts those keen traffickers the Manus, always at odds over debts and bargains, have become fervently litigious.[53]

Medieval-feudal concepts of landownership brought back, with Christian blessing, something of a collective quality, making land the object not of a single undivided right but of a network of rights, and entitling all from prince to ploughman, if very unequally, to a share. By one of the antinomies that property has so often given birth to, this widening of benefits had for corollary the practice among the upper classes of primogeniture. This has been a great rarity in the world; so has monogamy, likewise (except for the involuntary monogamy of the poor) mostly confined to Europe. Primogeniture was attached to lordship, it embodied a political concept displacing 'natural' usage. It had some of the inequity of

[51] Morgan, *op. cit.*, p. 224. For a reassessment of Morgan's ideas see E. Terray, *Marxism and 'Primitive' Societies* (trans. M. Klopper, New York, 1972), pp. 9ff., 'Morgan and Contemporary Anthropology'.

[52] J. Morier, *The Adventures of Hajji Baba of Ispahan in England* (1828), ch. xxxviii.

[53] Mead, *op. cit.*, p. 227.

the Christian doctrine of election; by turning younger sons on the world to seek their fortunes it could often stimulate society, help to keep it from stagnation, at the cost of untold bitterness within the family. Envy and rancour of disinherited younger sons and brothers, so pervasive in Elizabethan drama, must have hung over all feudal Europe like a miasma.

After outliving its time of social utility, primogeniture had a long further career in the many variant forms of modern entail, of which the Spanish *mayorazgo* may be deemed the most remarkable. An entailed estate had a close resemblance on one side to land among a people like the Siane of New Guinea, for whom it was one of the 'sacred inalienable goods', together with magic flutes and rituals, which were 'the property at once of living people, their dead ancestors, and their descendants yet to be born'.[54] But entail debarred all these owners except one long narrow ribbon, the successive generations of a single lineage from father to eldest son. Renaissance Europe was obsessed with fear of death, a new dread of extinction competing with the medieval dread of judgement. An estate destined to belong perpetually to a man's descendants was a way of circumventing fate, or blunting consciousness of it, like the fame that Shakespeare and Milton longed for. To achieve this the family had to be reduced from a clan to an abstraction – a name, a title, a coat of arms. Clearly also there could be no untrammelled possession for the heir himself, who was only the occupant, one of a long line each following the other in turn. Land has always somehow baffled the individual's efforts to engross it, to make it altogether his own. British landowners, a critic wrote a century ago, still viewed primogeniture 'almost as a fundamental law of nature', whereas no other civilized peoples 'tolerate the dominion of a bygone generation over the greater part of the national soil, under settlements and entails designed to limit the ownership and control the action of living owners'.[55]

In modern Europe vast legal and political energy has been expended on the task of demarcating feudal from capitalist forms of property, and weeding out the older while preserving the newer. Entails, resting on feudal conceptions fortified by others of more

[54] Godelier, *op. cit.*, p. 270.
[55] G. C. Brodrick, 'The Law and Custom of Primogeniture', in J. W. Probyn (ed.), *Systems of Land Tenure in Various Countries* (revised edn, London, (?) 1881), pp. 105, 140.

unconditional temper, were only one of many amalgams between the two species. In the decay of the feudal order the revival of Roman law had a marked bearing on notions of property, over things and men, as well as of political sovereignty. Luther deified the State; he likewise elevated property-right into a bond as mystic as a Pacific taboo when he asserted that a captured Christian slave must submit to a Turkish master as his rightful lord.[56] In the ethics of capitalism theft – except as practised by capitalists, under due form of law – would be the sin against the Holy Ghost. Aquinas had authorized men in desperate want to steal; the Victorian moralist continued Luther's metaphysical extremism in her fable of the virtuous mouse which would rather die of hunger than steal a householder's corn. When the great famine was descending on it Ireland was called on to play the virtuous mouse and go on exporting food, to pay rents. 'Men had elevated landlord property and capitalist political economy to a fetish to be worshipped, and upon the altar of that fetish Ireland perished.'[57]

A better way of thinking was already visible, but it was making its way very unevenly. As early as 1851 a revenue commissioner far away in Bombay could lay it down, as 'generally admitted, both by philosophers and practical statesmen, that private property with its rights and privileges, has no other basis for its existence than the general welfare of the community', and must be modified when community interests required it.[58] He was of course dealing with Indian property, malleable in the British ruler's hand. So far as Europe was concerned he was far too sanguine; the fact that 'the rights of property rest upon the goodwill of society' is one that modern reformers have had laboriously to reassert.[59]

As a humble counterpart to the entailed estate we find the peasant smallholding, likewise jealously kept in the family, at the expense often of much toil and hardship. Peasant proprietorship has not by any means always been the direct successor, the heir apparent, of

[56] I am grateful to Professor the Rev. A. C. Cheyne of Edinburgh University for this reference to Luther's teaching (1541) on war with the Turks.

[57] James Connolly, *Labour in Irish History* (1910; Dublin edn, 1973), p. 107.

[58] Cited in A. J. Roberts, *Education and Society in the Bombay Presidency, 1840 to 58* (Ph.D. Thesis, University of London, 1974), p. 347.

[59] L. T. Hobhouse, *Morals in Evolution*, 7th edn (1906; reprint, London, 1951), p. 336.

the clan. The Roman peasantry, as individual owners of holdings of standard size, were to a great extent a creation of the Roman State and its seizures of neighbouring territory. Shortage of land, as in old Italy, has always morbidly deepened the cultivator's attachment to his plot; its essence is possession of something that others can be kept out of. Where there is no crowding, ownership is more casual. In the Cayman Islands it is only now that a land register is being prepared, and boundaries are often hard to fix, because though most inhabitants have had land and passed it on from father to son they did not bother about legal titles to it.[60]

In Europe in recent times many governments have little by little been understanding how useful an insurance of social stability peasant proprietorship can be; how content the rustic with a few acres to call his own will be to spend his life and strength on them. France required a revolution to teach it this lesson thoroughly; elsewhere the State often led the way in promoting break-up of big estates into smallholdings. The change 'afforded to the major part of the population the sweets of property, and respectable comfortable existence'.[61] There was besides, after the thunderclaps of 1789 and 1848, a strong 'defeudalizing' tendency in Italy, Portugal, Greece, and elsewhere towards division of properties among children, in place of primogeniture.[62] Alarm at the class strife engendered in Britain by industrialism swelled the call, very loud a century ago – as again today – for landlords to be got rid of. Alfred Russell Wallace wrote of the land monopoly as 'the terrible disease under which the social organism in our country is labouring';[63] another writer pointed to it as a 'grave political danger', and contrasted Britain with France 'where the millions of the peasant proprietors constitute the one great barrier against Communism'.[64] At the fag-end of tsarist rule, Stolypin tried to give it a broader foundation by patronizing the better-off Russian peasants. Nazi demagogy made a parade of 'peasant estates' entailed on docile farmers and their eldest sons. But peasant proprietorship in modern

[60] I owe this information to a letter from Mrs Margaret Cavers, in Grand Cayman, 15 Dec. 1973.
[61] H. Passy, *On Large and Small Farms* (1844; English edn, London 1848), pp. 19–20.
[62] Brodrick, *loc. cit.*, pp. 134–5.
[63] A. R. Wallace, *Land Nationalisation. Its Necessity and its Aims*, 2nd edn (London, 1882), pp. 191–2.
[64] Brodrick, *loc. cit.*, pp. 146–7.

Europe has been increasingly an anachronism. Politically retro-
grade, it is often trapped in financial entanglements; through these
it may even verge on the opposite condition, the negative or *minus*
ownership of the Asian peasant who inherits a scrap of land and a
load of debt which he can never shake off. It ends as an appropriate
theme for caricature. 'There have always been Starkadders at Cold
Comfort farm. . . .'

In an early manuscript Marx looked to cooperative agriculture
to foster a healthier relationship between men and land than any
'silly mysticism of property'.[65] His ancestry was a peculiar dis-
qualification for comprehending the mystic marriage of cultivator
and farm, and he and nearly all his associates and followers were
townsmen. About the Protean impulse or pseudo-instinct of possession in general socialists never did enough thinking: they treated it
as delusion, superstition, much as missionaries and colonial officials viewed African witchcraft, a vestige of the past to be summarily
banished. Comte felt able to write of communism in a politely
sceptical style. 'In France, at all events, where property is so easy
to acquire and is consequently so generally enjoyed, the doctrine
cannot lead to much practical harm.'[66] Catholicism, offering itself
as a bulwark against socialism, took up the idea and helped to
extend it to other kinds of property besides farmland; Leo XIII's
Rerum Novarum of 1891 recommended the widest diffusion of
property and the spirit of ownership among the masses. England
with its capitalist agriculture could not return to peasant proprietorship, but there and elsewhere a house of his own for the worker
could supply an industrial equivalent of the small farm. Engels
wrote a set of articles in 1872 condemning this and the Proudhonist
illusions it blended with, as a bogus solution to working-class
problems.[67] A century later capitalism has been able to throw in a
car with the house, and is pinning great hopes on what it calls
'property-owning democracy'.

On the plane both of production and of appropriation there may be
very long-lasting survivals from the original loose collectivism of
the clan, bifurcated now into classes. On the first level, reduction of

[65] 'Rent of Land', in *Economic and Philosophic Manuscripts of 1844*
(Moscow, 1961), p. 64.
[66] A. Comte, *Positivism* (English edn, London, 1910), p. 180.
[67] Engels, *The Housing Question* (English edn, London, 1936).

the mass to a simple collection of individuals has proceeded haltingly in Europe until very modern times, held back by slave labour and manorial serfdom as well as by cooperative tradition. On the second level, appropriation of the surplus by members of dominant classes individually can more definitely be said to have characterized Europe, first in the context of the Mediterranean city-state, then, less distinctly, in that of medieval feudalism: the two forms perhaps combining in the end, by a complex process of fusion, into modern capitalism. Collective appropriation was more habitual over much of western and middle Asia, though with many fluctuations, from the earliest to very late times. Nothing so firmly attaches Russia to European instead of Asian history than the fact that its nobility created for State service settled down in the long run, like their congeners further west, as private landowners.

This contrast underlies an inclination of Europe to look down on Asia, from their first acquaintance, as barbarous, in spite of all its pomp and show, because it allegedly had no respect either for the rights of private property, or for the liberties of the individual. These two concepts have been interwoven, and modern Europeans have often felt 'free' because their property was sacrosanct even when they had no voice in government, except the negative voice represented by 'the power of the purse'. It may be that a latter-day traveller like Bernier[68] (who influenced Marx's thinking on the subject) exaggerated the insecurity of property in Asia in order to flatter the self-esteem of Europeans, especially of his fellow-citizens under the tyranny of Louis XIV. Bernier's remote precursors were the Greek authors, steeped in Mediterranean city-state tradition, of the Hellenistic epoch, when Macedonian conquests brought East and West suddenly into closer contact than ever before. 'In the eyes of the Greeks an oriental king was the owner of his kingdom; his subjects were his slaves, and all that they possessed was in the ultimate analysis his property.'[69]

Eastern despotism was best exemplified by the Persian empire; absence of private ownership, above all of land, was most convincingly reported of Egypt. Here the small local collectivities of prehistory seem to have been absorbed into the large collective of a

[68] François Bernier, *Travels in the Mogul Empire* (trans. I. Brock, London, 1826; original 1670).
[69] A. H. M. Jones, 'Egypt and Rome', in S. R. K. Glanville (ed.), *The Legacy of Egypt* (Oxford, 1942), p. 292.

'State-socialism', practising centralized economic regulation. A 'hydraulic theory' of the State, implausible for later times, may be applicable to some regions of Asia in antiquity; water-control formed the economic basis of Egyptian centralism, which may have lasted so long because by comparison with Mesopotamia it was a simple matter, chiefly of the State taking advantage of the natural supply provided by the annual overflow of the Nile. All land seems to have been regarded as belonging to the Pharaohs. To the Greek mind this might appear very reprehensible, but Alexander's successors had no intention of abolishing it, whether here or in his other realms: they were quite ready to take over the system, as later European conquerors have often been. In Ptolemaic times 'the Crown claimed ownership over the whole surface of Egypt', and apart from grants to temples, or to royal servants for their own lifetime, the soil was 'rack-rented in small farms to the peasants', and all agriculture directed by an administration 'incredible in its complexity'.[70] Romans, unlike Greeks, were not settling down in Afro-Asia, but building an empire with its centre in Europe. Land-purchase in the provinces was among their favourite investments, and in Egypt they favoured private ownership and established an elaborate land-register to facilitate this.[71]

Hellenistic preconceptions about the East and its dearth of property rights may have coloured Greek commentaries on India too. Megasthenes, who served as envoy at the court of Chandra-gupta Maurya, faithfully reflected the Greek or 'European' outlook in his assumption that it was 'but fair and reasonable to institute laws which bind all equally, but allow property to be unequally distributed'. According to his account, all land in India belonged to the king.[72] The Mauryan empire of the fourth and third centuries B.C. had for heartland a section of the Ganges valley, broader than the Nile's but hemmed in on each side by jungle as Egypt was by desert. Here too a State could take advantage of a vast flow of water. Megasthenes describes most of the land as being irrigated, and makes it clear that irrigation was organized by the govern-

---

[70] Ibid., pp. 291–2.
[71] E. Seidl, 'Law', in Glanville (ed.), op. cit., p. 215.
[72] Megasthenes, Fragment i, in J. W. McCrindle, Ancient India as described by Megasthenes and Arrian (London, 1877). For a sceptical comment on the assertion of all land belonging to the ruler, see Romila Thapar, Aśoka and the Decline of the Mauryas (London, 1961), p. 63.

ment.[73] On this basis the State seems to have attempted something like the bureaucratic regulation that Egypt, within its narrow confines, was able to maintain for far longer. There was an 'unprecedented expansion of the economic activities of the State', directed primarily towards the financing of a vast military effort.[74] As in all such cases it was taking over the omnicompetence of the old collective, but vesting it in an élite drifting further and further apart from the commonalty.

A first version of the *Arthashastra*, that encyclopaedic treatise on administration, may have been compiled in the days of the empire, which its author Kautilya may have served.[75] It claims many natural resources as royal monopolies; mines may be leased out to contractors, but all traders are regarded as profiteers, to be kept under strict supervision.[76] With the crumbling of the empire much of this broke down, along with centralized control of irrigation. Initiative in water-control passed to the districts, and 'once the tendency began it was bound to undermine the influence of the central power in the countryside'.[77]

Some far earlier chapters in the history of property can be traced in Mesopotamia. In the Sumerian south a type of city-state led the way, more theocratic or monarchical than the Mediterranean, a sort of middle term between 'Europe' and 'Asia'. A tenacious municipal tradition continued, as within the Roman empire, long after the city-states were absorbed into larger polities; it might well be an effective incubator of both property and law. Sumerian towns were scattered over an alluvial plain requiring water-control, both drainage and irrigation, to make it habitable. The work seems to have been organized mainly by temples, in partnership with local rulers who represented local gods. Continuous large-scale labour was needed to maintain it; even then success was always precarious. Hence the growth of 'a largely state-controlled society' where 'private enterprise was restricted and hazardous'.[78] Each city's god

---

[73] Megasthenes, *loc. cit.*
[74] R. S. Sharma, *Light on Early Indian Society and Economy* (Bombay, 1968), p. 65.
[75] A. L. Basham, *The Wonder that was India* (London, 1954), p. 79.
[76] *Kautilya's Arthaśastra*, trans. R. Shamasastry, 6th edn (Mysore, 1960), pp, 86–9, 232ff.
[77] Sharma, *op. cit.*, p. 74.
[78] Roux, *op. cit.*, p. 160.

'not only protected but *owned* the state'.[79] In other words the primitive community's ownership of its territory had passed to the élite grouped round temple and monarchy; in course of time it could be transferred to individuals. A good many of the roads mankind has travelled have made detours like this through a heavenly fourth dimension.

It is open to conjecture that in the longer run (and Mesopotamia, unlike the Inca empire and its irrigation works, had a very long run) the fact of the soil being man-made might have a de-sacralizing influence on it, and encourage, at least among the higher classes, a utilitarian attitude favourable to private ownership. If so, this may supply one reason why modern rationality found its first home in Holland. But the sense of personal ownership could extend more readily to house, furniture, and other valuables, than to land. Mesopotamia appears always to have been a country of eager traders: it required many things from outside, to be obtained by commerce – as with the Manus trading their fish for grain – or by conquest. Urban life and trade could foster private property, which might eventually include land.

Many Sumerian documents point to a 'growing importance of private property and private business'.[80] From a quite early date there are records of extensive tracts of land, made up of numbers of smallholdings thrown together, being secured by individuals, usually members of the royal family or high functionaries.[81] Somewhat like a joint family deciding to partition its assets, the élite was turning from collective to individual appropriation of the surplus. Inequalities were doubtless at work within its own ranks, and the more successful or ambitious wanted to strike out on their own. This would be furthered by the shift from temple to secular authority that was going on; religion, as a conservative force, maintained collectivist habits within the dominant group as well as holding society as a whole together. There was land-buying by 'small agricultural producers' as well,[82] but the small man on his own would always be very much at the mercy of an unstable environment. We hear of the poor 'engulfed in debt to the point of selling their children as slaves', so that they often preferred employ-

[79] R. M. Adams, *The Evolution of Urban Society. Early Mesopotamia and Prehispanic Mexico* (London, 1966), p. 122.
[80] Roux, *op. cit.*, p. 158.
[81] Adams, *op. cit.*, p. 106.
[82] *Ibid.*, p. 65.

ment as labourers to independence.[83] Usury has often worked powerfully to emancipate the common man from any property or occupancy rights he may have come by. Under the laws of Hammurabi the debtor could be taken as a slave. Debt, the obverse of ownership, has been one of the great powers of history; in England only a hundred years ago it could cost a man his liberty, and in many regions of modern Asia it has done so in another way, by reducing myriads to slavery.[84] The alternative facing men has been to own or be owned.

Law follows in the wake of property, and marks its arrival at a more self-conscious stage. Local custom was no longer adequate when diverse provinces came under a single rule, as in the Babylonian kingdom where the 'code' – or rather the corpus of royal edicts – of Hammurabi was drawn up in the eighteenth century B.C. By this date land had come to be a commodity, like any other, transferable by sale, loan, lease, or gift. Property was divided among sons, with rights reserved to the widow. Fiefs conferred in return for military or other services were numerous; such grants, often becoming hereditary, have been a chief means of land in many countries passing from State possession into private hands. All ownership was protected by draconic sanctions, including liberal resort to capital punishment. It has been a notable feature of penal law that treason against sovereign or nation, and violation of private property, have been treated as about equally wicked. Having arisen by usurpation, like kingship, property was compelled to defend itself vindictively, and like kingship to pretend to all the right of the original community, as if any injury to it was an injury to all.

Property institutions and laws radiated outwards from Mesopotamia to the borderlands. Most of the records surviving from early Elam, at the southern corner of what is now western Iran, bear on civil law, and practically all of these nearly five hundred texts are concerned with the law of property.[85] There was a god of justice, Mahhunte. 'His special domain, however, was trade; he fixed the rate of interest, standardized weights and did business in commercial

---

[83] Roux, *op. cit.*, p. 159.
[84] See B. Lasker, *Human Bondage in Southeast Asia* (Chapel Hill, N.C., 1950).
[85] W. Hinz, 'Persia c. 1800–1550 B.C.', in revised *Cambridge Ancient History*, ii (1964), ch. vii, p. 18.

partnership with human businessmen as a large-scale capitalist.'[86] This betokens temple management of trading ventures. But among laymen by the sixteenth century B.C. a 'patriarchal' mode of inheritance by children was supplanting a 'fratriarchal' practice under which 'brothers held their fortunes in common'.[87] The earlier principle preserved a vestige of clan collectivism, reduced to the scale of the family. By this time 'communal husbandry . . . was already in full process of disintegrating'.[88] Royal and ecclesiastical lands were left as shrinking survivals of collective possession, like Crown and Church estates in medieval Europe, though possession in reality by privileged groups, only nominally by or on behalf of the community.

Among the Hittites, whose imperial age stretched from about 1500 to 1200 B.C., another legal code developed, under the influence it must be supposed of Mesopotamian example. Two tablets of laws from their capital Boghazköy in Anatolia comprise about two hundred clauses,[89] of which 132, not counting those relating to arson, relate to property. Bigger landholdings (if not minor ones too) seem not to have been unconditionally owned, but to come into the category of military fief common in this whole region of warring states. 'Land-ownership among the Hittites was bound up with a complicated system of feudal dues and services.'[90] Hittite and Persian and much other later history was to exhibit a series of conflicts and fluctuations between large fief and small family homestead.[91] By and large, the coming and going of huge amorphous empires, lacking Mesopotamia's firm roots in local institutions, was to make for forms of military-feudal centralism rather than permanent naturalization of either larger or smaller units of privately owned land.

In Palestine, on the western fringes of the Mesopotamian world, the Hebrew settlement was a 'people's imperialism', in contrast with the expansion of the big sprawling empires, and likelier to lead on to individualistic patterns of life. It was a tenet common to Hebrews and Arabs, and probably to other nomadic peoples, not

[86] *Ibid.*, p. 24.
[87] *Ibid.*, pp. 29–30.
[88] *Ibid.*, p. 32.
[89] O. R. Gurney, *The Hittites* (London, 1952), pp. 89–90.
[90] *Ibid.*, p. 82.
[91] *Ibid.*, pp. 81, 101–2; R. Ghirshman, *Iran* (English edn, London, 1954), pp. 85–6, 239, 285.

tied to any defined territory, that 'The earth is God's', not man's. When they settled down this could be translated into attachment of pieces of ground inalienably to cultivating families. With the occupation of Canaan 'fixed tenure of landed property became a natural institution', and each tribe, clan, and household was allotted its share.[92] But conquest, and expropriation or enslavement of the Canaanites, would generate undemocratic tendencies, leading to a growth of the landed estate from below, through the operation of economic forces, instead of from above by State grant. There must have been difficulties for a migratory people trying to adapt itself to cultivation, in a novel environment, and the devil was soon taking the hindmost. Family shares ceased to be inalienable, and fields, or fields and slaves, 'were deemed the primary fund for the payment of debts'.[93] Wars, always one of the worst plagues of a peasantry, helped to bring on that other scourge, indebtedness: commercial activity furnished loan-capital and whetted greed. The story of Jacob, that pious swindler, cheating his brother out of his inheritance,[94] graphically symbolizes the break-up of the old fraternity, and the fierceness of the *auri sacra fames*. It presents the same antithesis of farmer and herdsman or hunter as the tale of Cain and Abel; but by now the Lord is on the side of the kulak.

In such a society, democratic at the outset but now bitterly disputing the spoils of conquest, preoccupation with law and legal definition of property rights was to be expected. The Mishnah, or collection of oral precepts finally codified in the second century A.D., began with and was chiefly devoted to these matters, pursuing them into minute detail. Rights of gleaning in harvested fields were reserved to the poor,[95] a remnant of collective ownership which survived until yesterday in Europe. But fellow-Hebrews as well as Canaanites could fall into bondage, though they could be held only for six years.[96] Sons, not as a rule daughters, inherited: as in early Rome, property had to be kept within the clan, however this as a real unit might be fading: as so often, the family remained faithful to an order of things which belonged to the past. A double share went to the eldest son; this unusual approach to primogeniture may

[92] *Jewish Encyclopaedia*, 'Agrarian Laws'.
[93] *Ibid.*, 'Real Estate'.
[94] Gen. 25.
[95] Lipman, *op. cit.*, pp. 44–6.
[96] *Ibid.*, p. 192.

have originated from the need for a strong tribal headship, but in the changed conditions would hasten accumulation of wealth.

Learned commentators in later Indian times differed over the ultimate ownership of the soil, but 'the majority of thinkers on the subject favoured the doctrine of royal ownership'.[97] This may have been academic theory more than practically relevant, like most political philosophy in Europe as well as Asia; but it provided a conveniently vague cover for the fact that rights in the soil were multiple. Village lands were always in some sort in the collective custody of the cultivators, to the exclusion of low-caste artisans or menials, even though farming was carried on in severalty. Still, from the collapse of the top-heavy Mauryan empire private ownership was enlarging its scope, and the big man encroaching on the small. At first when land was coming to be subject to transfer between individuals, there was some attempt to prevent tax-paying cultivators from selling or mortgaging their fields except to others of their own class,[98] so that no loss of revenue would result. But mortgaging seems to have spread more widely,[99] and must often have been, as in other countries, the smallholder's highway to ruin.

From above also, from late Gupta times (earlier sixth century A.D.), new strata were being interposed between State and villager. In this species of feudalizing process it seems that the pacemaker was not the military fief, as in some Asian regions or in medieval Europe, but the granting of lands to temples.[100] Such grants were perpetual, and enjoyed a stability – like similar alienations in the Muslim world – not rivalled by any form of lay property. But there was also the practice, increasing after the Mauryan period, of State employees being remunerated by having conferred on them the right to collect the land revenue from a certain area. It was to prove a very persistent Indian institution. In principle only the revenue, not the land itself, was affected, but the weaker a central power grew the more tenuous this distinction became: as tenuous as that between tax and feudal rent, both of them extortions of tribute from the ploughman by *force majeure*.

Parallel with the evolution of property went that of civil law, and

[97] Basham, *op. cit.*, p. 110.
[98] This rule is laid down by Kautilya, pp. 194–5.
[99] Sharma, *op. cit.*, p. 135.
[100] *Ibid.*, p. 74; cf. p. 83.

a slow drift, within the Brahminical tradition, away from the religious and ethical standpoint of the early treatises towards a more secular tone. After Manu (probably second or third century A.D.) 'the works of his successors approach more and more closely to purely legal textbooks'.[101] There was no authority so rigid as a Quran to shackle them. Initially 'there was as yet no hard and fast law of inheritance': women might own property, for we hear of them bestowing gifts on Buddhist mendicants.[102] As a rule, however, women had no right to inherit, beyond their dowries; sons shared equally, or with no more than a trifling weightage in favour of the eldest.[103] Katyayana assigned equal rights to father and sons in ancestral property, though the father could dispose of whatever he acquired himself; if it was agreed to partition a joint property all sons had equal shares, with one quarter reserved for unmarried daughters.[104] Restrictions on individual use of belongings, whether land or movables, were far-reaching. According to the leading school of jurists, medieval codifiers of far earlier custom, a head of a house was 'little more than a trustee and manager on behalf of the family, without the right to give property away so as to impoverish dependents'.[105] Growth of large holdings was counteracted, moreover, by a tendency to divide them at his death. Joint-family possession was an echo of clan collectivism; equal sharing, of antique equality or democracy. In either form the family was, once more, a stronghold of conservatism, preserving something of ancient ways while the world around it altered.

Subdivision does not – as the example of China shows – prevent the landed estate from attaining a prominent position. New units may emerge as fast as others crumble. At several points in Indian history hereditary landlordism may have been ready to assert itself, only to be broken in on by fresh irruptions from the north. India's successive invasions or infiltrations, from Aryan to Turk and Afghan, were by men of pastoral, nomadic background, and after the Aryans they were coming as scattered war-bands, or groups of adventurers, not as migrant peoples. They were less likely to settle as landowners than to set up centralized methods of control and

---

[101] Basham, *op. cit.*, pp. 112–13.
[102] I. B. Horner, *Women under Primitive Buddhism* (London, 1930), p. 54.
[103] Basham, *op. cit.*, p. 158; cf. Kautilya, Book iii, ch. vi, 'Inheritance'.
[104] U. N. Ghoshal, in R. C. Majumdar (ed.), *History and Culture of the Indian People*, iii, *The Classical Age* (Bombay, 1954), p. 361.
[105] Basham, *op. cit.*, p. 156.

appropriation. What we find developing in late medieval and modern times, under a Muslim sway based on garrison towns, is the peculiar Rajput blend of land-occupancy, lordship, and clan unity, though the clan was far removed from original equality within its own ranks. It or its leading groups would secure a licence to collect land revenue over a given area, paying over to the government as much of it as the government was strong enough to insist on. It thus occupied a territory without actually claiming to own it. 'Proprietary rights – or more correctly, managerial rights over land – were more fragmented than political and kinship alliances.'[106] In the decay of an empire or kingdom the clan might achieve something like sovereignty; once this happened, its chief could be expected to enjoy a more dominant position over his followers, and equal sharing among his sons would give way to primogeniture. As in feudal Europe this was an essentially political institution. 'Primogenitural succession and proprietary impartibility are important diagnostics of the rise of the raja.'[107]

Much evidence can be marshalled to suggest a prevalent insecurity of property in old India, under Hindu and Muslim rule alike.[108] At any rate the British on their arrival encountered an extraordinary medley of coexisting rights over land, resting on 'occupancy, enjoyment and use, rather than on possession', by 'families, brotherhoods, clans and tribes' rather than individuals.[109] Marx and Engels were among many observers who were intrigued by the apparent absence of true private ownership in India and other (chiefly Muslim) parts of Asia known to them, and they built large speculations on it. Britain as ruling power sometimes laid claim, by right of succession, to universal ownership of the soil, as the Hellenistic monarchies in Asia did. The practical effect of its measures was to create full landed estates for the first time, and to expose both them and peasant holdings to the full rigour of the market. British India offers a striking instance of the havoc that can be wreaked by imposition of an alien concept and law of property. But it was only one of many regions where Western imperialism – from the English conquest of Ireland – disrupted traditional semi-

[106] R. G. Fox, *Kin, Clan, Raja and Rule* (Univ. of California, 1971), p. 49.
[107] *Ibid.*, p. 81.
[108] See e.g. L. Dumont, *Homo Hierarchicus. The Caste System and its Implications* (1966; English edn, London, 1972), p. 359.
[109] P. Hardy, *The Muslims of British India* (Cambridge, 1972), p. 42.

collective forms and transferred ownership abruptly to individuals, native or foreign.

Islam sprang from an archaic tribal society, and its conceptions, of property in particular, only partially extricated themselves from it. In the patrilineal Arab tribe inheritance went to male agnates alone, so that no property could go out of the community, which was thus recognized as in some degree the owner of all that its members owned. Muhammad provided no blueprint for a new State, but he laid down rules for the family and its belongings, always of far more interest to the common man than the question of how he is to be governed. He broadened considerably the narrow Semitic framework. Jehovah had been the god of one people, Allah was to be a universal deity, and his laws required a more cosmopolitan cast, like those of the Rome which had aspired to universal empire. Muhammad was opening the way to a wider society when he included other relatives, six of them female, as heirs; though the old order was being modified, not abolished, since a son's share was double that of a daughter.[110] Among sons there was equality, and it was protected by the rule that while one-third of the property might go by bequest – a concession to individual as distinct from family ownership – it could not go to any of the natural heirs.

One Arab custom that Islam could not shake, but carried abroad with it instead, was that of patrilineal marriage between cousins. This was 'a pattern of immense durability, which already existed in Sumerian times'.[111] It persists to this day, an evasion in effect of the broadening tendency of Quranic law: its chief rationale has been to keep property within the family, and so preserve in miniature the self-sufficiency of the old clan. Cousin marriage must have deepened the parochialism, too habitual in Muslim societies, the narrowness of real horizons that has underlain the visionary world-horizons of the faith.

Older customs of sharing within the primitive community were transmuted, or diluted, into an Islamic doctrine of trusteeship, of the owner of property being its custodian on behalf of all in need, beginning but not ending with his own dependants. This must have served to stimulate works of charity and public benefactions; in our

---

[110] For detail see N. J. Coulson, *A History of Islamic Law* (Edinburgh, 1964), pp. 15ff.
[111] Adams, *op. cit.*, pp. 81–2.

time it has been refurbished by Muslim revivalists like Muhammad Iqbal in India as an answer to socialism. In the *Siyasat-Nama* – the treatise on statecraft composed in the late eleventh century by a minister of the Seljuk kingdom – we have a pious fable about Haroun al-Rashid and his consort Zubeida being reproached by some worthy, needy citizens for spending all their revenue on their own luxuries, instead of devoting most of it to their subjects' weal. Admonished by a dream of judgement-day, the royal pair repent, throw open their treasury, and bestow their wealth on the deserving.[112]

Arabs, and then Turks, were not occupying territory in order to settle down and cultivate it, like the Hebrews in Palestine: they were military aristocracies ruling far-flung provinces, and to share in the proceeds of centralized rule came more naturally to them than to carve out private estates. It was by abuse of official position, by governmental extortion, that wealth was obtainable. Nizam al-Mulk, author of the *Siyasat-Nama*, was an advocate of just, humane, paternal administration. Another of his parables may be taken as more true to historical realities, even if luridly over-painted. A provincial commander was found to have amassed about two million gold dinars, 600,000 dinars' worth of jewels, 30,000 horses, more than two thousand slaves, and lands, mills, and much else. On this discovery his sovereign, the legendary Nushirwan the Just, ordered the miscreant to be flayed, and his skin stuffed with straw and hung up as a warning to other malefactors.[113] In any such conditions wealth was bound to have a disreputable flavour; frequently, as in this case, it was cut short by confiscation; in India and most of the Muslim lands it could not win respectability by being invested in land. In any society the general feeling about property will be coloured by the reputation attaching to large-scale fortunes, those which stand out like Sinbad the Sailor's and stir the resentment of the poor Hinbads. Military societies have often left commercial and financial activity to ethnic groups excluded from the mainstream of life; of this the Ottoman empire is the most striking example, Minorities like the Greeks or Armenians there, the Copts in Egypt, or exiles like the metics in Athens or the Jews in Europe, have been rendered more odious by their pursuits, and

---

[112] *The Book of Government or Rules for Kings . . . of Nizam al-Mulk*, trans. H. Darke (London, 1960), pp. 144–7.
[113] *Ibid.*, pp. 39–40.

their unpopularity has deepened the disrepute connected with all money-grubbing.

If a man did happen to be rich, his right course was to give his money away. In a feudal society – and the more so the closer it is to a tribal background – the grand virtue is giving, not, as in capitalist society, saving. Sadi's *Gulistan*, that compendium of folk wisdom and conventional morality, dismisses the ambitious plans of the rich merchant with his forty attendants and hundred and fifty camels, as a futile waste of life,[114] and pays repeated tribute to the fabulous Hatim Tay, personification of overflowing bounty. But in a thirteenth-century Persian satire on society in the guise of animal-tales, any such notions are treated as utopian. Only in days of yore were there good men who bestowed largesse out of means honestly come by: today anything given has first been stolen – 'smoke only rises from men's kitchens after they have set on fire the grain-stocks of a hundred Musulmans'.[115]

Turks who on the steppes counted their prosperity by their flocks, in India piled up wealth – far more for display than for use – in other but less productive forms of livestock: horses, elephants, household slaves, harems. The contrast between East and West comes out in the fact that while these orientals multiplied troops of women and jealously shut them up, but treated land as a mere utility, in Europe a rich man equally wanted access to women, but only for casual use: it was his land, his park, that he built a wall round. Lack of the anchorage of guaranteed landownership must have tended towards a general instability of property rights. It may be also that in any conquest-state, where property and plunder are apt to be twins, possession will lack moral legitimacy and security. Mughal rulers were entitled to take over all that their nobles left at death, and Burton reports the same of the robber-state of Dahomey,[116] even if in neither case was the claim always exercised. In Roman Italy, gorged with the loot of the provinces, property whether real or movable was often highly unsafe: peasants were turned off their farms to make room for veterans, proscriptions and confiscations were for long endemic. In the Muslim world there has been a besetting and fundamental contradiction between the

---

[114] Sadi's *Gulistan*, trans. J. Ross (London, n.d.), pp. 181–2.
[115] *The Tales of Marzuban*, trans. R. Levy (London, 1959), p. 84.
[116] Sir Richard Burton, *A Mission to Gelele, King of Dahomey* (London edn, 1966), pp. 213, etc.

ideal of the upright, self-respecting individual, with his own soul
and his own undivided responsibility for its fate, and the reality of
political degradation, the rule of the sword; and the dearth of any
true civic tradition cannot be separated from an uncertain condition
of individual ownership.

Early in Chinese history congeries of feudal-bureaucratic principalities, resting to some appreciable extent on water-control, were
absorbed into a loose pacific federation, equally distant from the
theocratic centralism of Egypt or the military centralism of Islam.
On land tenures in feudal times, or on any 'traditional communal
rights' of the peasantry, the ancient histories are silent.[117] We are
free to suppose that fiefs resembling those of medieval Europe
gradually changed into private estates, their service obligations
shaken off; and that such an evolution underlay a political transformation so complete that it might almost be called – after a phase
of imperial dictatorship – a withering away of the State.

As in Mesopotamia at a certain stage, land became a commodity
to be bought and sold. Its ownership indeed always remained in
some ways nebulous. 'The land all belonged to the Emperor, and
was leased out to the farmers,' in the words of a modern authority.
'As a rule it was leased by a clan. . .'[118] Although a land-tax was
always due to the government, the clan, vigorous to the latest days
of the old China, was a more tangible obstacle to full private right.
Down to the end it was expected that house or land should be
offered for sale first to kinsmen.[119] Inheritance followed familiar
lines. Property was divided equally among sons, to the exclusion,
except for their dowries, of daughters, who did not belong to the
clan. With this incomplete enfranchisement, by comparison with
Europe, of individual from clan went the absence of any true code
of civil law, as distinct from custom, and any class of lawyers. In
the body of edicts of the last two dynasties 'such laws as related to
inheritance, mortgages, the transfer of property, and the like, are
found scattered through the various sections of the criminal law'.[120]

In his political philosophy Mencius was quite close to the

---

[117] W. Watson, *China before the Han Dynasty* (London, 1961), p. 114.
[118] V. Purcell, *The Boxer Uprising. A Background Study* (Cambridge,
1963), p. 39.
[119] J. H. Gray, *China* (London, 1873), ii, p. 109.
[120] G. N. Steiger, *China and the Occident. The Origin and Development
of the Boxer Movement* (Yale, 1927), p. 6.

Siyasat-Nama, and to the norm of feudal-bureaucratic thinking. His ideal was a paternalistic welfare-state of benevolent rulers and conscientious officials guiding and protecting a grateful people. His heaviest censures were directed against magnates who wallowed in luxury while the poor went hungry.[121] Already China exhibited, full-blown, each of the opposite impulses that were to wrestle all through its history, the 'intense acquisitiveness', 'unscrupulous competitiveness', which impressed Weber so deeply,[122] and the revulsion against them. As elsewhere men became *conscious* of private ownership, as a new, incalculable force invading their lives, when it gave rise to glaring inequalities, riches piling up at one end of a social scale, destitution at the other. Chuang Tzu told a story of a man plunged into poverty, and unable to comprehend why.[123] Many sufferers must have felt as he did that a mysterious fate held them in its grip.

This sage endeavoured, as moralists everywhere have done, to persuade men that wealth and self-indulgence are a curse, not a blessing: a rich man 'carries a heavy load up the slope of a hill'.[124] He extolled a good man who, rejecting office or patronage, lived in ascetic penury.[125] A cult of poverty haunted many Chinese thinkers and poets; it was an expression of solidarity with the poor, a lingering of an old spirit of brotherhood. The theme of the hermit poet, renouncing the burdens of office, family, possessions, was a recurrent one, a Chinese equivalent of the religious asceticism of Christendom and like it inspired by the spectacle of mass suffering. Tu Fu went beyond it in his dream of a vast mansion offering shelter to all,[126] which comes close to a vision of the socialism of days to come.

Literati of commoner stamp surveyed their world through different eyes. They and their world are both graphically portrayed in the eighteenth-century novel *The Scholars*,[127] which depicts the

---

[121] W. A. C. H. Dobson, *Mencius* (London, 1963), pp. 28–9; cf. pp. 48, 178.

[122] Max Weber, *The Religion of China*, trans. H. H. Gerth (New York, 1951), p. 63.

[123] *The Complete Works of Chuang Tzu*, trans. B. Watson (New York, 1968), p. 91.

[124] *Ibid.*, pp. 336–7.

[125] *Ibid.*, pp. 316–17.

[126] Trans. by Rewi Alley, *The People Speak Out* (Peking, 1954), pp. 7–8.

[127] Wu Ching-tzu, *The Scholars*, trans. G. and H.-Y. Yang (Peking, 1957).

life of officials and aspirants to office. Its atmosphere is an intensely mercenary one; clearly, only in polite pretence were learning, culture, virtue, the supreme concern of the Celestial empire and its managers. As in Asia at large, the sources of wealth were tainted; it flowed most abundantly from bureaucratic graft or extortion in partnership with merchant capital. Mandarins on retirement came home to their native districts and bought land; merchants were anxious to do the same, because with land they bought their way, as in Europe, into gentility.[128]

Government seems to have disliked large estates. They might be troublesome either politically or, by causing discontent among impoverished peasants, socially. Chinese conservatism might claim to have anticipated Europe in seeing the advantages of peasant proprietorship. At various times measures were taken, or envisaged, to fortify it. What must have done more however to check the rise of big estates was the absence of primogeniture[129] – although a family might hold on jointly to its patrimony, instead of dividing it, in order to keep up its local importance. But the 'precarious nature of landownership' of which Weber spoke owed much also to what he termed a 'naïve peasant Bolshevism'.[130] 'I hate the unequal distribution of wealth,' was the watchword of Wang Hsai-po, leader of a rising in Szechwan in 993.[131] The secret societies which honeycombed the population down the ages had communistic features, like Anabaptism in Europe. There were strong collectivist elements in the great Taiping rebellion in the mid nineteenth century, and its agrarian programme, very imperfectly carried out though it may have been, might be called a reassertion of old, never-forgotten rights vested in the community. More fully developed than in most parts of Asia, private landownership subjected China to ever-recurring convulsions, by provoking a stronger reaction than anywhere else in Asia. As an ultimate consequence China became the first communist nation of the continent.

Writing in the sceptical interwar years, Wedgwood rejected the conservative dogma that 'great inequality of wealth is conducive

[128] See the interesting discussion by L. Dermigny, *La Chine et l'Occident. Le commerce à Canton au xviiie siècle 1789–1833* (Paris, 1964), Conclusion, ch. iii.
[129] R. H. Tawney, *Land and Labour in China* (London, 1932), pp. 32ff.
[130] Weber, *op. cit.*, pp. 79–80, 94.
[131] Purcell, *op. cit.*, p. 143.

to the achievement of the highest degree of productivity'.[132] If
private property and the social fission accompanying it were necessary to push human progress along the road it has followed –
whether or not another road might have been found can only be
speculation – they have done it at best bunglingly, with prodigal
waste and destruction. How much was thrown away, as Gordon
Childe said, of what men early in the reign of Property learned to
produce: treasures were buried in tombs, 'gallons of beer were
brewed daily to invigorate a Sumerian idol'.[133] In our time, about as
rationally, millions are poured out daily on arms to placate the
War-god. In between, fitful progress has been interspersed among
millennia of stagnation punctuated by war and its, for most of
mankind, senseless violence.

In the same interwar time of doubt R. H. Tawney pointed to the
'bewildering rapidity' with which the nature of property had been
altering, while conventional theory had failed to advance beyond
declamation on the sanctity of property in the spirit of the late
eighteenth century.[134] Stocks and shares, like money when it first
came in but far more sweepingly, have rendered ownership mutable
and anonymous: most of it consists now of holdings in corporations
the owner knows no more about than the nomad about the corner
of the wilderness where he crops a patch of herbage today and is
gone tomorrow. At the same time the family, in which to perpetuate
themselves men have toiled for wealth, has been growing almost as
unfamiliar. They can no longer count on their descendants to be
replicas, reincarnations, of themselves; even physically, if biological
engineering has its way, their great-grandchildren may look like
offspring of an alien race.

In old India a man who arrived at the threshold of age would
often hand over his earthly goods to his heirs, and retire into medita-
tion. Today it may seem high time for Property to follow this
example, and abdicate. At the end of his great book Morgan was
already, nearly a hundred years ago, calling it 'an unmanageable
power', baffling to its human creator. It was time, he declared, to
proclaim that 'The interests of society are paramount to individual

---

[132] J. Wedgwood, *The Economics of Inheritance* (1929; Penguin edn,
1939), p. 61.
[133] V. Gordon Childe, *The Prehistory of European Society* (London,
1958), p. 83.
[134] R. H. Tawney, *The Acquisitive Society* (1921; new edn, London,
1937), p. 60.

interests', which left to themselves would destroy society, and for mankind to return, on a higher level, to the communal life in which it was cradled.[135] Mankind has paid dearly since he wrote for facing this task so sluggishly.

[135] Morgan, *op. cit.*, pp. 561–2. Engels quoted this passage at the end of his study, based on Morgan, *The Origin of the Family, Private Property and the State* (1884).

Glossary

ad voluntatem domini: tenure at the will of the lord.

alimenta, alimento: provision for younger sons, or unmarried daughters.

allod: an estate not subject to a feudal superior.

allodial rights: rights of absolute ownership in an estate, without acknowledgement to a superior.

appanage: grants of lands and fiefs to younger sons of magnates; those by French kings were in tail male and carried extensive rights of jurisdiction.

bookland (O.E. bócland): land and rights granted by charter, under the sovereign's orders, to a private owner, devisable by will; suits about it could only be heard by the king and witan (the supreme council of England in Anglo-Saxon times).

borough English: form of tenure in some parts of England under which all lands and tenements fell to the youngest son.

cartulary: a register, book of charters, evidences of title of a monastery, or similar foundation, or lay family.

censo: a rent charge secured upon land or other property, usually to pay the interest and/or capital of a loan.

champion (country): a landscape or region of unenclosed arable fields worked in common.

charivari: French equivalent of the English 'rough music', i.e. noisy popular rituals expressive of mockery or hostility towards individuals, occasioned by second marriages or by offences against community norms.

charter, cartae: a formal written document accompanying and lending additional authority to an unusual transfer which might otherwise be challenged.

co-parcener: a co-heir or co-heiress; one who shares equally with others in an estate inherited from a common ancestor.

copyhold: customary tenure by copy, i.e. by transcript from a manorial court-roll; land held by copy.

court baron: a court, not of record, held in every manor to redress nuisances; lawyers later distinguished two courts baron, one for freeholders and one for copyholders.

court leet: a court of record held in a manor before the lord or his steward; deriving from the crown by prescription, or charter, it tried minor offences and presented graver ones.

courtesy: in English law, a husband's right to an estate for his life in all lands after his wife's death of which she was seised in fee simple or tail during their coverture provided they had issue born alive.

coverture: condition of a woman under her husband's protection.

custumal: a compilation of customary laws of a manor, or other unit.

devolution: the descent of property by due succession; lapse of an unexercised right to its ultimate owner.

devise, devising: gift of property by last will and testament, in later English law it was applied only to real property.

domainal (or dominial) rights: rights over demesne or heritable property, or rights to dispose of property.

dower: within the European context has two meanings (1) That which a free man gives to his wife at the church door at the time of his marriage. (The Common Law usage); (2) That which is given with a woman to her husband, which is commonly called a *maritagium* or *marriage portion*. (Roman Law Usage.) The Common Law usage is the older and more correct interpretation, but in most continental countries the widow received back the equivalent of her marriage portion with supplements, so that the portion itself often came to be called a dowry, *dot, dos, dote*. In the paper by Cooper dower and dowry are always used in the first sense.

emphyteusis: a grant of lands for a term or in perpetuity in return for a rent, giving the grantee a secure title.

enfeoff, see feoff.

enfeoffment to uses, *see* use.

engross: to write in legal form; to add holdings together.

entail, *see* tail.

escheat: (n.) property falling or lapsing to a feudal lord (or to the state) in the absence of an heir or by forfeiture; (vb.) to fall to the lord or to the state on the owner's death intestate.

Falcidian quarter, *see* Trebellianian.

fee simple: an estate of inheritance, held without limitation to a particular class of heirs; unconditional inheritance.

fee tail: inherited estate held with such a limitation; an entailed estate which, on failure of heirs, reverts to the donor.

feoff: (vb.) to grant possession of a fief or property in land.

feoffment: (n.) originally the gift of a fief, comes to signify the grant of any free inheritance in fee.

fideicommissiary, *fideicommisum, fedecommesso* (Ital.): a conditional grant, or legacy in Roman law, e.g. a man might leave land to his son, requiring him to leave it intact to his eldest son under the same conditions. In French law such devices were known as fideicommissary substitutions.

fine: In the King's Court: a fictitious suit employed as a means of conveying property or barring an entail. In the manor Courts: a customary payment, of certain or uncertain amount, made to the lord upon (a) admission to a property or renewal of the tenure, (b) upon the death of the lord, or (c) on application for a licence to do something which the custom of the manor in question does not otherwise allow.

fratellanza (Ital.): holding of property in common by brothers, usually involving a joint household.

free bench: a widow's right, by custom of the manor, to continue in possession of the whole or a portion of her husband's lands during her own life.

frèrèche (Fr.): household of brothers, living together and holding and working their patrimony in common.

gavelkind: a form of tenure, prevalent in Kent, under which lands descended from a father to all his sons or, failing sons, to all his daughters in equal proportions.

half-blood: (n. and adj.) relation between those who have only one parent in common.

houseful: all persons inhabiting the same set of premises (Laslett).

household (stem): in which a single married son remains with his parents (though unmarried siblings may also be present).

in bondagio: in villeinage; servile tenure.

in chief: a tenure in chief is one held immediately from the Lord Paramount usually the crown.

in personam: personal actions, for personal rights, remedies against the person, as against specific things.

in rem: actions against things or property, also suits to obtain judgement on personal status, e.g. divorce, bastardy.

jointure: property settled on a husband and wife for their lives in survivorship on their marriage, or subsequently, in lieu of the wife's rights to dower.

juro (Sp.): (n.) perpetual annuity, secured on some form of revenue, bought by paying a capital sum.

kindred: here understood as a descent group, i.e. a body of kinsmen united by common ancestry.

laboureur (Fr.): relatively prosperous peasant proprietor, or tenant farmer, approximately the equivalent of an English yeoman; a 'tillage-farmer' in pre-revolutionary France.

legitim, legitima portio: in Roman law, the right of children, or other kin in their absence, to provision from a deceased parent's or relative's estate (usually in a fixed proportion), unless they have already received equivalent provision. *See* portion, child's.

maritagium (*see also* dower): in Roman usage, a marriage portion; in English law of the twelfth and thirteenth centuries land given as a marriage portion with a woman.

mayorazgo: an unbarrable entail of land or other property, commonly in primogeniture, but other modes of descent might be stipulated.

merced (Sp.): (n.) grant, favour, or privilege, usually from the crown.

messuage: a dwelling-house with its outbuildings and the lands appropriated to the household.

métayer: a sharecropper; one who pays a fixed proportion of the crop of their holding to the owner rather than a money rent.

mortmain: grants in, or lands in, grants to or held by religious corporations, especially monasteries.

portion, child's, or child's part: similar to legitim in the disposition of chattels in English customary law, notably in the custom of London.

portion, marriage: the sum contracted to be paid at marriage on behalf of the wife by her kin. *See* dower.

préciput (Fr.): (n.) property, taken out of property held or inherited in common before partition by law, custom, or agreement, by one having a right, e.g. an eldest son.

recopilación (Sp.): a digest of laws.

recovery: (common) recovery is a method of transferring entailed estate by a legal fiction. *See also* fine.

remainder: if a man grants land to X and, if X died without heirs of his body, to Y, then Y is in remainder, or is substituted.

representation: if in determining descent of property at a father's death, the son of an already deceased elder son, is preferred to his uncle, a younger son, then representation takes place.

retrait lignagier: rights of kin to buy back land alienated by a member of the lineage, or to be preferred as purchasors before non-kinsmen.

roture (Fr.): in the broadest sense 'the commonalty', non-nobles.

seigneurial: (adj.) pertaining to feudal lordship, manorial rights.

seisin: (n.) (freehold) possession; the act of taking such possession; such an estate or possession.

socage: (n.) feudal tenure of land involving payment of rent and/or service, fixed and determinate in quantity.

Stammgut (Ger.): (n.) estate held jointly by a family.

stem family: *see* household (stem).

strict settlement: English settlement of land to the father for life and after his death to his first and other sons or children in tail, with trustees to preserve the contingent remainders; the eldest son, taking for life and younger children being provided for by portions charged on the land.

substitutions *see* fideicommissary.

swidden: (n.) shifting cultivation, or slash and burn farming, in which fields are cleared, farmed for one or more years, then allowed to return to brush.

tail, entail: a settlement of property on a designated series of possessors so that it cannot be bequeathed or alienated, without barring or breaking the entail.

tail, general: an entail which did not exclude females.

tail male: an entail which excluded females.

tanistry: (n.) the system of succession by a previously elected member of the family (from *tanist*, a Celtic chief's heir elect).

tenement: a holding, by any tenure; a kind of permanent property, such as lands, rents, a peerage, held of a superior; the property so held.

Trebellianian quarter: The Falcidian quarter was the reservation of a quarter of a man's estate to his heir, or heirs, whatever the amount of his legacies. The Trebellianian quarter applied the same reservation to property subject to *fideicommissum*. In late Roman and medieval law the Falcidian quarter was in common usage assimilated to the legitim *ab intestat*. In France the addition of the quarters to the legitim was allowed in the lands of written law, but not in those of customary law. In the former it was possible for a universal heir in some circumstances to add the quarters to his legitim. But testators could forbid the taking of the quarters, though not that of the Trebellianian in Franche Comté in the seventeenth century.

unigeniture: the fact of being an only child; succession of property to a single (or only) child.

use: a device in English law separating the legal title to land from its beneficial enjoyment. A man enfeoffed others (feoffees to uses) with his land who then held it to his use, while he had the profits and could instruct the feoffees to devise the land according to his last will or in his lifetime.

vellon (Sp.): (n.) copper, or copper and silver alloy, used for debased coins.

villein: (n. and adj.) a feudal serf; a tenant holding by bond services.

villeinage: (n.) tenure of lands by bond service.

virgate: (n.) an early English land measure, varying greatly in extent but generally averaging some thirty acres.

yardland: an early English land measure, *see* virgate.

Index

An asterisk indicates a full bibliographical reference to an author's work.

405

Smyth*, J., 211, 309
Smeeton Westerby, 130, 139
Sneyd*, C. A., 185
sons, 2, 7, 8, 10, 23–4, 27, 31, 41, 44,
    53–4, 97, 122, 125–6, 131, 136,
    142, 153, 169, 171–2, 176, 182–3,
    185–90, 192, 195, 199, 212–16,
    218–20, 225–7, 232, 238–41, 243,
    255, 261, 268–9, 272, 303, 344,
    377
sons-in-law, 8, 10, 23, 31, 44, 122,
    125–6, 131, 153
sources, 6
  account rolls, 134
  censuses, 85, 29
  church consistory court, 101
  church manuals, 144
  correspondence, 330, 201
  court rolls, 101, 113, 118
  Curia Regis rolls, 120
  deeds, 77, 211
  extents, 31
  fire-insurance register, 93
  legal records, 113
  listings, 85, 94–5
  parish council, 101
  parish register, 101, 123, 138–41,
    175
  probate, 101, 113, 138, 148–9, 163
  rentals, 137–8
  settlements, 200, 306–12, 328
  statutes, 280
  surveys, 73, 83, 156, 158, 133
  tax lists, 85, 93, 123, 132
  tithing list, 123
  wills, 15, 45, 62, 63, 118, 120–1,
    123, 139, 141–2, 145–6, 149,
    156–8, 163–6, 169–76, 189–90,
    200, 203, 208, 210, 259, 306–
    12, 313–28, 342–3, 346, 356,
    357
socage land, *see* tenures
Sologne, 98, 359
Somerville*, R., 308
'*souches*' (Fr.), 264
soujourners, 6, 174, *see* retirement
South America, 370
Spain, 5, 89, 177–8, 181, 190, 233–52

Spence*, R. T., 210
Spedding*, J., 203
Spufford*, M., 144, 153, 157–8
Squibb*, G. D.,
Stafford, 148
Stamp*, D., 154
Stammgüter (Ger.), 198, 234, 403
Starkey*, Thomas, 183–5, 202
state, attitude of, 24, 77, 178–80, 183,
    187, 195, 197, 212, 250–1, 267–8,
    297
Steiger*, G. N., 394
Stenton*, D. M., 15
Stoke Prior (Worcs.), 354
Stone*, L., 153, 202, 212
Stonton Wyville (Leics.), 130
Storch*, D., 77
substitutions, 270, 276, 403; *see also*
    entails
subtenants, 156, 137–8
supervisors of tenements, 138
surnames, 122–4, 130–2
surveys, 73, 83, 133, 156, 158
Sweden, 294
Switzerland, 44–5

tail general, 199–201, 204, 207–8,
    224, 303, 403
Tamassia*, N., 285
tanistry, 403
Taunton, 121
Tawney*, R. H., 396, 397
tax lists, 84, 94–5
Taylor*, A. J., 120
Taylor*, S., 188
Taylor*, W. B., 296
Temple*, Sir William, 223
tenures, 2–3, 26–7, 30–1, 71–3, 81–2,
    92–3, 118–19, 131–4, 142, 163,
    172, 174, 194, 228, 297, 328–32,
    340, 355, 370–1, 399
Terray*, E., 376
territory, 115–16
testators, 15, 20, 104, 141, 159, 161–
    4, 166–9, 171, 173, 280
Thapar*, R., 382
Thirsk*, J., 14, 153, 187, 225
Thomas*, D., 289